PACIFIC BASIN BOOKS

Editor: Kaori O'Connor

OTHER BOOKS IN THIS SERIES

The Gakiyami Kuruma.

TALES OF THE SAMURAI

BY JAMES S. DE BENNEVILLE

Introduction by Trevor Leggett

KPI

LONDON AND NEW YORK

DEDICATED

TO MY SONS

George, Marion, Daniel, Peter

IS THIS TALE OF OLD NIPPON

First published in 1915

This edition published in 1986 by KPI Limited
11 New Fetter Lane, London EC4P 4EE

Distributed by
Routledge & Kegan Paul, Associated Book Publishers (UK) Ltd.
11 New Fetter Lane, London EC4P 4EE

Methuen Inc., Routledge & Kegan Paul
29 West 35th Street
New York, NY 10001, USA

Printed in Great Britain by St Edmundsbury Press Ltd,
Bury St Edmunds, Suffolk

ISBN 0 7103 0233 9

PREFACE.

The story of Oguri Hangwan Sukeshige and Terute-hime is one of those attractive legends based on fact, containing so many essential features of the enduring moral view of a people as to give it a continued life from generation to generation down the centuries. Hence every feature of the tale is familiar, from childhood to age, to the Japanese, to whom such stories are an important method of learning the history of the land and the deeds of famous fore-bears. The announcement of their representation, whether on the boards of the theatre, on the screen of the moving picture, or by the appearance of the *kōdanshi* (lecturer) before his table, always arouses the audience to a subdued but excited applause. The great favourite unquestionably is the " Chūshingura " or Story of the Forty-seven Valiants. But others have their share in inspiring this pleasurable anticipation. That of the " Oguri Hangwan Ichidaiki," or Biography of the Councillor Oguri, holds an honoured place. As scene after scene of the adventurous life of Sukeshige, or as the unfortunate and faithful Terute makes her entrance, the less controlled of the audience accentuate their applause in audible manner. They give open expression of feeling at what touches an essential chord of their nature. How close these tales stand to the Japanese moral man has been dealt with elsewhere. What was said in the preface to the life of Benkei need not be repeated here. It has the same application.

Something, however, is to be said as to the *kōdan* or dialogue-lecture (story). This Japanese word applies to the historical romance, with an essential difference from such as understood in the West. There the historical romance, it is true, depicts some

historic scene or even character.   But it is the period not the person
which carries the accent in the painting.   The main characters as a
rule are fictitious; or if historical are so vague in outline that they
can be treated as fictitious.   Such are Hereward the Wake and
Robin Hood, in which fiction and legend overwhelm historical fact.
Kings and ministers stalk through the novel to cut the Gordian
knot of the crisis by benevolence or malice.   But such a character is
a *deus in machina*.   The reader is glad to get rid of it.   It always
detracts; never is an advantage to the freedom of the tale.   The
noble Richard Coeur de Lion of "Ivanhoe" is a little out of place,
and the reader feels it.   D'Artagnan and the three musketeers,
their actions, carry through the story of Dumas.   Kings and Court,
the masterly sketches of the two cardinals, are but outlined.   History
is very properly made a serving wench.   The contrary is the case
with the Japanese.   True history is treated as romance, even in
this twentieth century and by the Mombushō, or Department of
Education.   It has always been the case with the *kōdan* writers.
All the characters are historic, the events themselves are historic or
believed to be so, and are merely embroidered by the fancy of the
lecturer, who, however, is supposed to cling as close as he can to
fact.   He does so, takes on good faith the statements of his predecessors, adds his own adornment to the tale, and here his mission
ends.

Such romance has wide range.   In the stories which surround
the lives of Yoshitsune and Benkei, of Kusunoki Masashige, of Katō
Kiyomasa, it is dangerously close to genuine history.   As to the two
first named, the original romance-chronicles of the "Gempei Seisuiki" and the "Heike Monogatari" can hardly be distinguished from
the more formal "Adzuma Kagami," except in the advantage of
their style.   All three are written within close range of the period
described.   A writer does not dare to embroider too extravagantly
a period close to his own generation, the events of which are familiar
to living men.   At the other end of the scale is a *kōdan* such as this
of Oguri Hangwan.   How slender is the historical basis can be seen
by some of the translated pamphlets appended to this volume.   In
another sense the tale is advantaged.   Originally it was told in the

puppet-shows, the *karakuri* ; again, to the accompaniment of music by story tellers. These *saimon-katari* were not reduced to literary form. The puppet player had nothing but his memory to prompt him in his tale. But as with many things Japanese the story at an early date took on rigid form. Then the *kōdanshi* (lecturers), after moulding it by some generations of lecturing in the traditional form, put it in book form. This has been the fate of this kind of literature. It is the belief of the writer that the *kōdan* has a very genuine value. Its dialogue form takes hold of the reader. It has been sadly neglected in the description of the life habits and thought of this curious people. One has only to enter a book-store and cast his eye on the space given to these tales on the book-shelves. This is a very practical and commercial measurement of the importance of the *kōdan* to the Japanese reading public.

As to the story of Oguri Hangwan, it can be said that the *kōdan* writers have a tolerably good case against tradition as handed down by the temple scribes at Fujisawa. The " Dai Nihon Jimmei Jisho " says that the original tradition, as found in the " Sukeshige Den " and the " Chōshō-In Engi " confuses the lives of Mitsushige and Sukeshige in wondrous fashion, distorting and mixing the events of both. But these facts stand out—Mitsushige did rebel against Prince Mochiuji in Ōei 29th year (1422 A.D.). The prince besieged and stormed Oguri castle the following year (1423). Now in the Eikyō Nengo, the date varying from the 6th to the 10th year (1434-1438), it was Sukeshige who secured from the Bakufu the restoration of the Oguri House. This renders decidedly apocryphal the story of the escape of Mitsushige to Mikawa, and *his* subsequent restoration to his honours and fiefs in Hitachi province. The identification of Sukeshige with Sōtan the painter is also disputed. Sōtan figures as Oguri Kojirō Sukeshige, and the identity of name is strong enough ground to make him pass current, not only in the story of the *kōdan* writers, but with many as good history. Moreover, this feature of the tale is more sentimental than useful, whether it be good history or not. Attention can be called to the wide spread geography of the tradition. It is found at Oguri in Hitachi province, at the Yūgyōji of Fujisawa in Sagami, and at the Tōkwōji

The Grave of the Hangwan at Oguri-Niihari.

of Yunomine in Kii no Kuni (Kii province). It does not seem to enjoy much popularity with the *gidayu* writers—of the tales recited by *geisha* to the *samisen* accompaniment. At least it only figures once (in the Gidaiyū Hyakuban) in the collections secured. Inquiry at the Imperial Library in Tōkyō, made for me, failed to disclose the presence of either of the *yashi* (authorities) cited by the Dai Nihon Jimmei Jisho, viz: the "Sukeshige Den," the "Chōshō-In Engi." The idea of having a transcript made had to be abandoned. The Oguri Gwai-den, an illustrated *kōdan* in eighteen volumes, published in the first decade of the last century, turns up occasionally in the old book stores.

Best gathered at the source something is to be said as to such information. Oguri village in Hitachi is reached from Niihari station on the Mito-Oyama cross line.* Two miles, through a beautiful country in which the dry farming (*hatake*) shares equally with the sea of rice field, brings one to Niihari village. The village is one of those oases of shade found planted in the open plain. At a large farm house on the western side are found some interesting relics connected with the Hangwan. The house itself occupies the site of a temple to Tenjin-Sama, destroyed long since by fire. Unfortunately the helmet of Mitsushige was then lost. The bridle bit of his horse, his *kaimyō* (mortuary tablet), a *chikara-ishi* or stone bearing the deep impress of his thumb as a test of strength, and the *mamori-honzon* or metal image of Hachiman the war-god which he always carried with him, are preserved. The image of the tutelary deity is a figure two and a half inches in height, and is kept in a *butsudan*, or little cabinet, a foot high. Just to the west of the house, in the thick underbrush, is pointed out the grave of Mitsushige, an imposing stone nearly twenty feet in heighth. Close by are ten graves, and two later ones of the Tempō period (1830-1843). Near at hand is a very modern burial, with elaborate memorial stone. To the east of the farm house, about 300 yards, in the open *hatake* are the remnants of the castle mound. Though but ten feet high at the most elevated part

---

* Niihari (Tsukuba), a mere hamlet, is mentioned in the 8th century Nihongi I. 207 as to Yamato-Takeru.

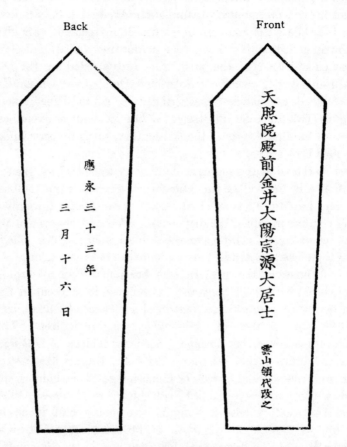

Back   Front

This tablet is shown at Niihari-Oguri as the *kaimyō* of Oguri, lord of the castle which fell in Oei 30th year (1423). It reads: *Tenshō-In-Den Zen Kanai Daiyō Sōgen Daikōji. Unzen Ryōdai kore wo aratamu.* On the back— Oei 33th year 3rd month 16th day (23 April 1426). The *Tenshō-In-Den* is the posthumous name of the deceased (*daikōji*) formerly known as *Kanai Daiyō Sōgen*; the posthumous name being given by the priest *Unzen Ryōdai*. The *ji* reverse *kore wo aratamu.*

they are well marked. The castle stood in the open plain, a mile from the foot hills of the ranges of lower Hitachi. There is no river in the immediate proximity. At an equal distance to the west (say 300 yards) is the shaded village of Oguri. Though not very germane to the subject, a detour of half a mile to the east, brings one to a *muku* tree (aphananthe aspera) standing on a mound on the hillside amid *hatake*. Two flat stones lean against the tree, and these are said to mark the grave of Heishi (Taira) no Masakado, who here fought his last battle and was killed by Tawara Tōda. A few feet distant is a *suzuri-ishi*, ink stone. Sunk down several feet in the ground this huge base, with its socket at least a foot wide, evidently supported a large pillar. Such is the tale this neighbourhood affords. It does not support the Fujisawa tradition—naturally.†

The present story has strictly followed the *kōdan* writers. Indeed it was a temptation to make the trial of marrying together the often bright dialogue. This could readily be done with the *kōdan* of Takarai and Matsubayashi. They follow closely the same lines. Any little bit of archaeological lore (the history of the bow) usually belongs to Matsubayashi. Takarai is more jovial in method, though on this point there is not much to choose. The two *kōdan* unite very well. That of Momogawa would not enter so well into the composition. His effort is " to get back to the original tale ;" that is the tale current at Fujisawa but fathered on Sukeshige. The result is a wide departure, even if an interesting story result. More-

---

† Multiplicity of "tombs" need disturb no one. On the site of the castle at Numazu in Suruga is a Rokudai-matsu, which marks the place of execution of the son of Taira Koremori and the protegé of Mongaku Shōnin. A magnificent *keyaki* (zelkowa acuminata) at Dzushi marks the " tomb " of Rokudai, who was executed at the Tagoe bridge close by. The tree is in plain sight and a bare two hundred feet from the main road leading from the station to the sea beach. Hence it is entirely unknown and unvisited by the average local resident and tourist, Philistines of the deepest dye in such matters. But it is well worth a visit—for a sight of the tree. " Tomb " in fact often means monument. At the great cemetery of Kōyasan a single hair or a bone represents the body buried elsewhere; sometimes not even so much of the cadaver. Twenty-five Osaka *geisha* have their graves prepared in full completeness near the Saint's (Kōbō Daishi) expected resurrection, but the little ladies, I believe, are still very much alive.

over, in style his dialogue at times is almost narrative, and he is fond of introducing the ways of humble folk of later days which contrasts with the characters stalking through this fifteenth century tale. To weld together a connected romance of Ashikaga times there was much historical matter to be introduced, and some semi-historical from the Go-Taiheiki. This chronicle is to be handled with great caution, as its editor points out in his preface. As far as history is concerned the *kōdan* writers and the chronicle have been put aside, and the best judgment of past and present followed in describing the period. There were a number of leaflets and pamphlets of the temples, local histories and guide-books, to be consulted. Taking the *kōdan* of Matsubayashi and Takarai as a single volume, in total there were nearly 800 pages of material to condense in one consecutive historical romance. It seemed better to re-write the story from beginning to end. Instead of padding out material at hand, the problem was one of condensation without omission from the ample sources of the native writers. To them all due acknowledgment is made. It is the Japanese tale which is re-told. This is for western ears ; not the product of the imagination of the scribe who acts as medium in this transference. If the reader is inclined to find too much blood spilled in the recital, reference is readily made to the histories and the chronicles of these Ashikaga times. The *kōdan* does not sin by excess. When Hōjō Takatoki fell, and cut his belly open in the cave at the Kasaigayatsu, 877 of his followers at the same time did likewise on the hill-side. As the eye sweeps the line of hills girding Kamakura from West to East it passes over the most blood-stained ground in Nippon ; and that is saying a good deal.

In these days of rehabilitation of past reputations one man is not to be forgotten. Among the devoted adherents of the Bakufu Government of the Tokugawa figured Oguri Kōzuke no Suke, once known as Mataichi Bungo no Kami. He is described as one of the few financial experts the country then possessed. In the early days of foreign intercourse Oguri went to America and Europe to study financial problems, and questions of military and naval training. He was not long in ascertaining that at the existing ratio of gold to silver Nippon was rapidly being drained of the more precious metal.

This was one contribution to his country's service. A second contribution was his work as military commissioner. To him was due the plan for the establishment of the navy yard at Yokosuka, the model for the others established later. Oguri fell from favour in most honest fashion. He had no belief in purity of motive as the inspiration of the men of Satsuma and Chōshū, and still less in their ability. They wanted office and the spoils of office. When they secured these *desiderata* they would issue paper money and drive the country into financial ruin. A few years of such government would turn the tide in favour of the Tokugawa. Hence he was strongly opposed to any waiving of the clan's rights. To Prince Keiki he presented an earnest remonstrance; he advocated war. When the prince started to leave the room he held on to his skirt. The harsher his treatment, the greater his persistency. Then Prince Keiki dismissed him from his service. Oguri went forth to raise an armed force in Jōshū. This was dispersed, and Oguri was executed as a rebel in the intercalary fourth month of the first year of Meiji (28 April 1868). According to his lights he had acted the part of an honest, if obstinate, man. The founder of the great naval arsenal of Yokosuka his memory remains to be formally rehabilitated, as has been the case with Saigo Takamori, Etō Shimpei, and other leaders of a lost cause. To be sure he was but a hatamoto— of 10000 koku. More important to this preface, he is said to have claimed lineal descent from the hero of our story.

Ōmarudani, 30 June, 1914.

CONTENTS.

PART I.

THE HOUSES OF OGURI AND SATAKE.

PART II.

THE ADVENTURES OF SUKESHIGE AND TERUTE.

PART III.

THE MISADVENTURES OF TERUTE AND SUKESHIGE.

PART IV.

THE VENDETTA ACCOMPLISHED.

The pronunciation of the Japanese vowels and consonants follows closely the Italian ; in diphthongs and triphthongs each vowel is given full value.

a=a as in father, e=a as in mate, i=e as in meet, o=o as in soap, u=oo as in fool.

g is always hard. In the Tōkyō district it has the sound ng.

ch has full value, as in church. It is *not* k ; c is only found as ch ; i.e. cha, chi, cho, chu.

The vowels also have long (continued) sounds, marked by the accent—.

At times a vowel is elided, or rather but faintly touched by the voice. Thus Sukeshigé is pronounced Skeshigé ; Sukénaga=Skénaga ; Kuranosuké=Kuranoské. *Bu* and *mu* at the end of a word lose the vowel sound—Shikibu=Shikib.

Kami used in connection with a man means " lord." Wakasa no Kami=Lord of Wakasa Province.

LIST OF ILLUSTRATIONS.

MAPS.

[The illustrations are by Mr. Kaneko Sanji (Hōzui)
of Yokohama.]

INTRODUCTION

The story of *Oguri Hangwan* here translated from Japanese originals is an example of what came to be called Kōdan or Public Lecture; they were at the top or educational end of the scale of traditional public entertainment, the lower end being the mainly humorous Rakugo stories. Kōdan is traditionally said to have originated in public lectures and readings from histories, arranged by great lords from the fourteenth century on, to educate themselves and their courts. However that may be, by the beginning of the seventeenth century the genre was firmly established; by the eighteenth century, straight reading had developed into fairly free narratives, though still based on the original texts, and given before the general public in auditoriums large and small. Their popularity steadily increased, till at the end of the nineteenth century there were some fifty in Tōkyō alone.

The earliest and most popular text was *Taiheiki*, or Chronicle of the Great Peace, something of a misnomer as it deals mainly with war, ending up with the Mongol attempted invasions of Japan in the thirteenth century. It was highly esteemed for literary style, which included also extended passages in verse, and the Kōdan narrator was expected to speak in cultivated, erudite diction. He sat behind a desk like a teacher, with a book stand and a fan to mark the rhythm of his bombastic periods. A Rakugo story-teller too has a fan, but as a stage prop; it becomes a brush, a sword, a pair of chopsticks, or when opened, a headdress or an umbrella or a dish. The Kōdan master never permitted himself any such vulgarities, so unbecoming to his status.

His repertoire however gradually came to crumble a little at the edges, extending to personal histories such as the present one, though still mainly concerned with heroic exploits, family vendettas, and the like. After foreign literature became available in the second half of the nineteenth century, Kōdan narrators would even give their versions of works like Hugo's *Les Misérables*. The Kōdan versions of even the best-known Japanese classics could differ considerably; the translator of the present story explains that he has made use of several of them. In 1915 he would still have been able to hear it narrated by different speakers, and probably also to read a number of their published scripts.

In the heyday of Kōdan at the end of the nineteenth century, a master like Enchō was a well-known national figure. His recitals were taken down in shorthand, to appear in serial form in newspapers and magazines, and then in book form. One of them sold out 120,000 copies very quickly. From such books developed the popular Japanese literature of today.

Stories such as this well-known narrative about *Oguri Hangwan* still purported to be historical; they include a number of supernatural events and visions, but such appear also in the histories on which they claim to be based. Discernment of a pattern in sinister portents was an important function of historians; they sought precedents in order to discover what effective religious and other measures had been taken in the past to at least mitigate impending calamities.

The great sufferings of the loyal wife Teruté, carting the disease-ridden body of her husband in a long pilgrimage to seek a cure, is an illustration of the almost superhuman strength of character which Japanese tradition attributes to a devoted wife.

The sufferings of the virtuous pair are explained on familiar Buddhist lines as the result of sins committed in previous births. The almost mechanical process of purification by austerity, and subsequent transfer of the merit thus earned, is a familiar theme in Japan even today. No one would find incredible a report in the media of how a devout believer vowed to polish a long corridor in the shrine for fifty mornings in mid–winter, on the knees the whole time, in order to transfer the merit to a desperately ill spouse. The skin of the knees cracks in the cold, and bleeds profusely in the first week or so, but the vow is completed; in the cases reported, it nearly always has had the desired effect.

Trevor Leggett

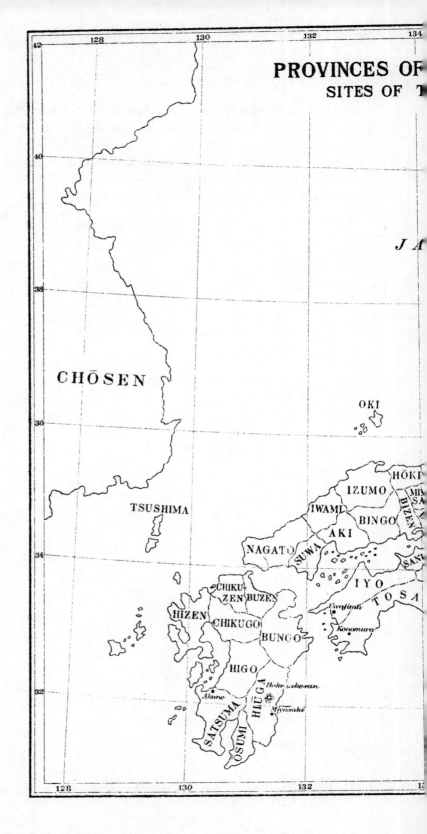

PROVINCES OF

SITES OF T

J A

CHŌSEN

OKI

HŌKI

IZUMO

MIN
SA

IWAMI

BIZEN

BINGO

AKI

TSUSHIMA

NAGATO

SUWA

SAN

IYO

TOSA

CHIKU-
ZEN BUZEN

Uwajima

HIZEN

CHIKUGO

Konomura

BUNGO

HIGO

Hokezakesan

Akune

HIŪGA

SATSUMA

Miyasaki

OSUMI

AEVAL NIPPON

RI LEGEND

YEZO

42

140

142

136 138 140

40

DEWA

MUTSU

SEA

SADO

38

NOTO

ECHIGO

ETCHŪ

Kawaji

Nikkō

SHIMO-

TSUKE

HITA-

CHI

KŌTSUKE

KAGA

Daichji

ECHIZEN

HIDA

SHINANO

Hirai

Yuki

Oguri

Ota

36

MUSASHI

Tsukuba

SHIMOSA

GO

WAKASA

MINO

Hiraoka

KAI

Hatashi

Kōtozashi

Edo

Tarui

Aohaka

Yaguchi

Ebina

KAZUSA

OMI

Biwa-ko

OWARI

TŌTOMI

SURUGA

SAGAMI

Kamakura

AWA

AMBA

Ōtsu

Kyōto

MIKAWA

Yahagi

Fuchu

IZU

Mishima

Minawa

ETTSU

Maisaka

Ōshima

KAWACHI

YAMATO

ISE

Hamana-ko

KII

Hongū

Shingū

Yunomine

Nachi

34

PACIFIC OCEAN

32

136 138 140

PART I

THE HOUSES OF OGURI AND SATAKE.

" Though worshipped, these unequalled Ones, alike
" By gods and men, unlike them all they heed
" Neither a gift nor worship. They accept
" It not, neither refuse it. Through the ages
" All Buddhas were so, so will ever be "—*Sariputta.*
Questions and Puzzles of Milinda the King (Rhys. Davids.)

CHAPTER I.

THE KWANNONDŌ OF SASAMEGAYATSU.

Much like the shape of a clam shell is the site of Kamakura town, as it lies hemmed in by sea and hills. From Inamuragasaki on the West the slope of the curve rises gradually to the hinge of the shell at the Hachiman shrine of Tsurugaoka. The shorter side of the triangle descends at a sharp obtuse angle to the sea at Iijima, which marks the bounds of Zaimokuza and the district on the East. The valley therefore is of varying width, and has its widest extent in the avenue of pines leading from the Hachiman shrine to the sea, the Wakamiyaōji. Disregarding the short section of the Zaimokuza beach, that of Yuigahama is so little concave as to give likeness to the comparison. The valley is completely surrounded on two sides by precipitous and irregularly notched hills. Indeed there is no way out of it except by some deep cut roads (*kiridōshi*) over them. The modern means of access, the railway, has to burrow its way into the town through a tunnel, and out again to the South by the same means. The natural strength of the place is so evident, especially under the mediaeval conditions of warfare, that it is not surprising that Taira Hirotsune recommended it to Yoritomo as his capital. The sea offered every means of escape ; and the land every means of defence.

From the two land edges of the shell there run back into the surrounding hills short and steep valleys, their basins levelled and terraced by ages of cultivation. The surrounding hills are well wooded. From West to East the most important are—Kuwagayatsu and the long valley behind the left shoulder of the Daibutsu, the Sasamegayatsu, the Sasukegayatsu, the Ogigayatsu, the Okuragayatsu (large and important), the Kasaigayatsu, the Hikigayatsu. As said, the

Hachiman shrine. originally at Zaimokuza near the sea, then transferred by Yoritomo to the hill—the Tsurugaoka—lies at the hinge of the shell. Close by, to the East, Yoritomo built his *yashiki* (mansion), closely surrounded by the Hatakeyama, Hōjō, Wada, and others of his greater vassals. Around these *yashiki* sprang up a great city of shop-keepers to cater to the necessary and agreeable. The present Komachi and Ōmachi were at the centre of this hive, which in the days of the Hōjō is said to have contained nearly a million people. At the foot of the hills the whole valley was filled from Hase Kwannon to the Kōmyōji. The villages of Saka no Shita, Yuigasato and Zaimokuza covered the sea with their many sails. Impartially planted among their houses were the *yashiki* of the great nobles ; the hill sides were for temples. The prosperity of the town received a blow when Ashikaga Takauji changed his coat, adopted the cause of Go-Daigo Tennō then engaged in the over-throw of the Hōjō Shikken (Regents), and gave opportunity to Nitta Yoshisada to take the town by surprise and storm. The first move of Yoshisada was to fire the city as he burst into it, and a good part of Kamakura was burnt to the ground. It rose slowly from its ashes, for the early years of the Kamakura Kwanryō (viceroys) were not peaceful. These officials, really Shōgun of the North, barely subordinate to the Shōgun of Kyōto, were of the younger branch of Takauji's stock. With the Southern court established at Yoshino, Takauji['realized that it was impossible for him to adopt the plan of Yoritomo, and sever Court and Shōgunate so completely as the latter had done. The great fighting of the next half century was to centre around Kyōto. He established his second son Motouji at Kamakura as Kwanryō ; and although the life of this latter was mainly spent in camp, and although Takauji himself had at times to come to the North to give his personal attention to military affairs, the Kwantō* was fairly pacified during the life time of these two men ; that is, as far as peace could reign during this period. When Ujimitsu, son of Motouji, died in Oei 5th year 11th month (9th

---

* The eight provinces—Izu, Sagami, Musashi, Shimotsuke, Kotsuke, Hitachi, Shimosa, Awa. The lord of Dewa and Oshū also took the title, and usually acted with Kamakura.

Dec. to 8th Jan. 1398-99), the Kwantō had long been free from anything but spasmodic rebellion, and could and did give aid to Kyōto. The Kwantō Kwanryō by this time were so powerful that they cast covetous eyes on the Shōgunate at Kyōto. Uesugi Noriharu, the *Shitsuji* (Premier), unable to turn his master Ujimitsu from this design, remonstrated by the drastic method of committing suicide. Ujimitsu had drawn back. His son Mitsukane succeeded him, a powerful prince at the head of the strongest and most united fighting force in Nippon, and with very much the same disposition to take his cousin's place as suzerain.

The Ashikaga, on their establishment in Kamakura, had not retained the centre of the old Bakufu at Ōkura. They had moved up the valley to a site close by the Jōmyōji, where it begins to contract before rising to the steep and difficult Asahinakiridoshi, a pass on the road to Kanazawa. Here was their *yashiki*, and the valley occupied by their more immediate vassals. Close by, toward the town centre, was the *yashiki* of the Inukake Uesugi. The aging Tomomune had been the Shitsuji of Mitsukane. According to the rule of alternation the Yamanouchi—Ogigayatsu branch now held the office in the person of Norisada. Tomomune's son, Ujinori, was marked out as his successor. Descended from Fujiwara Yoshikado these Uesugi were related on the mother's side to the House of Takauji. *Kuge*, that is a noble affiliated with the Imperial Court, Shigefusa had left Kyōto, assumed the name of Uesugi from a fief held in Tango province and with it the responsibilities and duties of a *buke* (military vassal), and drifted to the Kwantō. His daughter married the grandfather of Takauji ; hence the intimate connection with this Ashikaga House. The Uesugi were good guessers as to politics. Most opportunely they abandoned the failing fortunes of the Hōjō clan in its last days.

Very different therefore was the appearance of the valleys now covered with crops of rice, wheat, barley, millet. In these days of five hundred years ago theground was occupied by the houses of labourers and shop-keepers ; by the *yashiki* of the fighting nobles occupying vast stretches of ground, with quarters for many score of fighting men. The pleasure quarters of Komachi and Kaizōji—Ogigayatsu, with

the inns, cook-shops, and brothels catered to the desires of a great
city. In passing along the streets at frequent intervals was seen
a gateway opening into the grounds of some great temple monastery.
Kamakura was not only the scene of spasmodic carnal warfare, but
of an unceasing spiritual strife. Particularly fierce was the struggle
between the Zen and Nichiren sects ; although also it was Nichiren
against the field. The modern town has retained what features it
could. The names of Zaimokuza, Komachi, Ōmachi, Wakamiya-
Ōji, Yuigahama, Saka no Shita, Hase, are as old as Kamakura itself.
But the seaside village is nothing but the faded ghost of a vanished
and great city.

It was in the palace of Ōkuragayatsu—the Kuboyashiki—that
Oei 15th year 9th month (20 Sept.—20 Oct. 1408 A.D.) Prince Mitsukane was holding an assembly for the making of poems and the telling
of tales. The apartment was long rather than wide. At the top
was a dais ascended by several steps. On this was seated Mitsukane,
occupying a small stand not unlike a camp stool. Squatted around
him was a number of the palace waiting ladies, watchful of every
movement made, and in readiness to anticipate every wish of their
lord. Below the dais, at the front, were scattered some fifteen or
twenty of the greater nobles. At the back of the apartment, at
some distance, was a promiscuous group of the samurai, such as had
rank and right of entrance to the presence of the suzerain. With
the exception of the prince, all present squatted on the *tatami*, using
cushions. The assemblage this night to inquire as to their lord's
health was a large one. It seemed rather bored, as did Mitsukane
himself. Old Tomomune was finishing his interminable series of
tales of the wars of ages before. He had told of the portents which
foretold the end of the wicked Taira Kiyomori. The prince, then
in the full tide of power, the balance wheel removed by the death
of his son Shigemori, had moved the capital from Kyōto to Fuku-
hara (Kōbe), the emperor passing from one prison to another.
The change had been accompanied by the most evil portents. His
couch drenched by rain leaking through the roof, the emperor was
on the move all night and could not sleep. Though in drier quarters neither could Kiyomori. Armies of men noisily tramped the

The Vision of Kiyomori Kō.

roof of the palace at night. Tremendous was the uproar. Yet when the guard made its way above not a sign of a living soul was to be seen. Then the favourite horse of the prince nested a brood of mice in his flowing tail, and the attendants ran more risk from his hoofs than from the pest itself in dislodging them. Again, one night as Kiyomori was preparing to go to bed, all were amazed and thunderstruck as the *fusuma* (screens) opened wide and a lady glided into the room. She had long black hair, blackened teeth, face of ghastly pallour, and floated rather than paced the *tatami*. Glaring fiercely at the prince she slowly wafted toward him. Petticoats never scared Kiyomori; nor much of anything else, for it is the hostile animus of chronicle and *kōdan* which has grafted cowardice on him. He glared fiercely in return, and as the lady came near sprang forward as if to seize her. Thereupon the spectre disappeared. A mocking evil wail rang through the apartment, chilling the hearts of the witnesses to the scene. Then the *fusuma* were seen slowly to close as of themselves.

It was with such experience that on a late fall night Kiyomori prepared to retire to his couch. His head was buzzing with *saké*, and he was little inclined to slumber. In such condition small companionship was to be found in his night's bed-fellow. She was sober and sleepy. He was drunk and excited. He looked into the next chamber. The *samurai* on guard, overcome by sleep, was in the land of Nod. No company was to be had there. Kiyomori frowned. He wanted distraction, if not discipline. But this imperious wilful man had a softer side—toward youth. He left the boy to his slumbers. Then from the garden came a sound—*goto-goto-goto*. Here at least was excitement. Thieves or conspirators? Kiyomori grasped his pillow sword (*makura-gatana*). Making his way to the *amado* (wooden shutters) he let fall the bar and gently pushed back a panel. The moon was shining brightly. Every detail without was clear as if outlined in sunlight. At first he saw nothing. Then he noticed a skull hopping and rolling along the ground. Then others appeared; then still more. From the stone lanterns (*ishidoro*), from jars (*tsubo*), from the trees, from the artificial lake (*ike*), from the ground itself they sprang forth in num·

bers too great to count. Forming in long lines, these met to pile into heaps. They moved as if human and alive. Then the skulls began to fight fiercely with each other. They clasped and bit each other. Their jaws and teeth clashed and creaked hideously. Forming huge piles they fell apart, only again to give battle. It was horrible to witness this sanguinary fierceness in this bloodless contest of malicious evil will. Kiyomori felt as if he was witnessing one of the interminable contests in the hell of fighting ((*shurado*). "Spring and flowers, the beauty of life belong to earth. The place of these was beneath its surface, out of sight of the living." So had said the men of old. Nyūdō Dono would drive them thither. Great was his courage. As he grasped his sword the skulls formed into one vast overwhelming pile. This towered some fourteen or fifteen *jō* (140 or 150 feet) and appeared to form one great shaven-pated priestly visage. From its orbits the spectre glared with concentrated hellish hate on Kiyomori. Nyūdō Dono bared his sword and stamped the *roka* (verandah) fiercely. He prepared to leap down to the garden and the combat. Lo! All vanished. The cold moon of autumn shone on the frost covered ground. The gentle lapping of the sea waves sounded close by. The garden was a scene of ineffable peace. Kiyomori rubbed his eyes and looked again. Nothing! He shivered. Aroused by his shouting and stamping his attendants came flocking to him. The prince was escorted back to his apartment. Physicians and diviners were summoned. Men took the affair gravely and shook their heads. The common people murmured to each other. As for Kiyomori, he had taken cold and spent some days in bed as the result of his nightly vision.

Such was the tale of Tomomune. Many were the Ahs! Kowa! Iza! Polite sucking in of the breath, and well aped wonderment. But they had heard Tomomune tell the story before, and he was none too short in the telling. Who would be the next? Eyes brightened and attention was aroused as Mitsukane called on Isshiki Akihide as next in order to entertain the company. A member of the powerful family whose centre was at Kyōto, related to the Seiwa Genji, Akihide was rapidly advancing to the post of confidence in his lord's favour. Men hated and feared him.

Isshiki knew no scruples in the means used to gain favour. Men had risen by valour, by wisdom, by time-serving. Valour and wisdom he lacked. Moreover these means were too slow and painful to secure promotion. His elder brother Naokane held the important post of Provost of Kamakura town. Himself he proposed to study the character and weak points of his lord. They were nearly of an age, the two men ; and the experience of Isshiki among men was of course much the greater. This made him more dangerous. He was the channel of his lord's more intimate connection with the outside world. Mitsukane trusted him. On this occasion he prostrated himself in obeisance. At a sign from his lord he squatted again near the dais. On his face was a smile, hard to interpret whether as cynically sly, or cynically deprecating. The aged uprightness of Tomomune was in secret a mark for his shafts of ridicule. He fathomed no particular greatness in either Tomomune or his son Ujinori. His House was as great as that of the Uesugi. If the latter were in the road so much the worse for them ; and the spoil was great. He began by complimenting his predecessor and senior. Ancient tales were beyond his ken and experience. He was one who lived in the present. To serve his lord his whole-hearted allegiance was devoted to that present. To the past he had no obligations. These words were meant to sink into Mitsukane, to call to mind the protest of Noriharu. Was not the whole Uesugi House tainted by an ill-timed fealty to Kyōto? Isshiki began: " All know what is meant by a Jashin (Snake Divinity), and the " Jashin belong to all places and periods. Now it is conceded that " among men are found descendants of these Jashin.* The distin- " guishing mark is scales on the back, so that the authenticity of the " fact is beyond question, and doubtless there are men present who

---

* The superstition is well known. Momogawa cites the descendants of Hori Kyutarō (pp. 222-3). His second son was a *Jashin*. At first the crest (mon) was a snake's eye. In time this was altered to *kuginuki* (pincers). Sayemon-no Jō Hidemasa, and Katō Kiyomasa carried the crest of the snake's eye ; as did many of the retainers of the Taikō Hideyoshi who was more likely to hunt out such men than otherwise. This descent is also attributed to Ogata Saburō Koreyoshi, he who drove the Taira out of Kyūshū when they sought refuge at Dazaifu.

"know such. It is respectfully hoped therefore that our lord will
"deign not to regard this tale as a mere fairy story.

"In the province of Echigo is a pass (*tōge*) known as the
"Oritōge, and the reason for its being so named is as follows. In
"days not long since, to be remembered by our grand-fathers, there
"lived near the village at the foot of the pass a hunter by the name
"of Yosaku. This man made neither accident nor pleasure of his
"hunting, but for him it was a means of gaining his livelihood. His
"success was great, owing to his skill with bow and spear. Hares
"seemed fairly obsessed with the desire to walk into his traps. The
"wild boar fell an easy victim to his skilled eye; and Yosaku did
"not hesitate to attack with the spear and alone in the forest the
"fierce bear. Even badgers and foxes shared in what seemed to
"be a grudge against the living. Great was the slaughter he per-
"formed in nearly two score years of hunting, and the *karma* of
"these deeds of blood surely was distateful to the gods, as the
"sequel shows.

"Yosaku was a widower. He had a daughter named Ori, a
"pretty mountain girl of eighteen years She kept her father's
"house, and during his sometimes prolonged absences spent much of
"the time in the village, where she was regarded as the child of the
"place—and as a spoiled child. Her father let her have her own
"wilful way, and his reputation for success, and her beauty, made
"the daughter the object of matrimonial diplomacy to both parents
"and suitors. Now one day Yosaku received an order from the *nanu-*
"*shi* (bailiff) of the village, Kinsa by name, for such game, great
"and small, as he could secure. The lord was soon expected on his
"return from guard duty at Kyōto, and the fief was making great
"preparation for a feast of welcome on his arrival. Yosaku received
"the commission with great glee, made preparation for an absence
"of several days from home, and equipped himself for most unusual
"havoc among the beast kind, feathered and four-legged. Before
"he left he strictly charged Ori to see that the house was well
"barred, particularly at night—'or indeed it would be good for you
"to spend the night at some house in the village. At any rate it
"will be necessary to go there for some dainties for yourself. Above

"all do not touch the *misozuke* (pickles) in the cup-board (*todana*).
"This *misozuke* is good for men; but for women to eat of it is
"fatal. Be sure not to touch the *misozuke*.' With this parting
"warning, spoken from the door, and without further explanation
"in his haste, Yosaku set off at a rapid pace up the mountain and
"soon disappeared from sight.

"Yosaku had breakfasted; Ori had not—as yet. Her first
"thought was that her father was very unreasonable. He was so
"generous to her that she never dreamed of charging him with
"being stingy; but then all men dearly love food, and in all like-
"lihood he was a gobbler. Being a man he never considered that
"in the days of his absence the *misozuke* would surely mould and
"spoil. Not only would it be no offence, but a positive beneficent
"deed to eat the *misozuke*. More than a mile lay between herself
"and the village, and Yosaku had cleared the larder of everything
"in his preparation for a longer absence than usual. To confine
"herself to *daikon* (radish) and boiled barley without savouring seemed
"ridiculous when this nice mess was within a few inches of her
"nose. Anyhow there was no harm in looking at it. Besides,
"she ought to see that it was really what he said it was. Opening
"the closet she found enough, not only for one but an ample feast
"for two persons. It smelt very nice. What a shame! She would
"take a taste to make sure it showed no signs of spoiling. This she
"did; and smacked her lips. How nice! Then she took another
"taste. There was so much of the mess that her father would
"never miss it or care if she took a little. Enough for two she
"would surely leave half. *Pekori, pekori*, Ori gobbled and gobbled
"until not an atom of the delicious mess remained in the huge bowl.
"Then she sat down to think. What explanation could she give
"for not leaving even a little bit for such a kind father. To uneasi-
"ness of conscience was added uneasiness of body. An intolerable
"and increasing thirst seized her. She seemed to have swallowed
"fire instead of food. She made hot water and drank cup after cup.
"She made infusion of roasted wheat and poured down into her
"throat bowl after bowl. Neither thirst nor fire was quenched.
"Her body swelled and swelled as if with the liquid she imbibed.

" Pressed by necessity she left the house.*   Once in the open air the
" roofs of the village houses far below inspired her with the idea of
" seeking company if not aid in her sufferings. The distance was not
" so very great, but with her now unwieldy body it took hours for
" Ori to waddle and roll down the mountain path. Not far from
" the trail lay a mountain tarn (Ōnuma), half pool, half marsh, with
" black and muddy depths. In fact the villagers had a tradition
" that it had no bottom. Ori could no longer contain the thirst that
" consumed her. That the pool was bottomless seemed a very
" modest capacity to her desires. She turned aside from the path,
" and clumsily sank down by the water's edge. Supporting her-
" self on her two hands she lowered herself to drink. The distance
" was too great. In her efforts she lost balance. Her now huge
" body hesitated and trembled on the brink. Then with a mighty
" splash it fell into the depths of the pool and disappeared from
" sight.

" Yosaku had great success in hunting. The animal kingdom
" came to the call of his earnest wishes. Many deer, several boar,
" scores of partridge; nay, at the end of the fifth day of absence
" he succeeded in grappling with a huge brown bear. Escaping
" with an ugly claw in the fore-arm he laid low the mighty beast. He
" cached the game until aid could be secured from the village. As
" his last acquisition was close by this was easily secured, and with
" it the commendation and large reward of the gratified Kinsa. In
" pure merriment and sureness of hand he transfixed a fox almost
" on the threshold of his house. Approaching the door he gave a
" great shout of triumph to attract the attention of Ori. He found
" everything wide open, but no sign of Ori. He shouted again.
" Knowing that she had not been to the village for several days he
" then thought she had gone to draw water at the spring. He deter-
" mined meanwhile to get things ready for the meal. The first thing

---

* Shikiri ni nodo ga kawaku kara hajime wa yu wo nomi cha wo nomi-
mashita ga, sore kara mizu wo nomu nambai mo nambai mo nambai mo nomi-
mashita ga hara ga kō hi no yō ni natte ite tachimachi no aida ni shōben ni
demasuru no ga nettō no yō ni natte kudaru, naonao ʃnodo ga kawaite tamari-
masenu kara ōnuma ga gozaimasuru. . . . . etc., etc. Momogawa p. 169.

The Biwa-hoshi at the Jizōdō.

" to mind was the misozuke. The closet was empty, and for the
" first time he saw that the bowl on the table was the one which
" had contained the savoury mess. He laid his hand on the board.
" It left its mark in the dust of several days blown in from the
" clearing. The unfortunate man sank to the floor. Everything
" was now clear to him. Ori had eaten the misozuke which was
" made of *uwabami* (a huge poisonous serpent). To men of his
" cult this was harmless ; and it inspired and gave success in hunting
" efforts. To women it was fatal. At the thought he sprang up and
" rushed forth calling the name of Ori in hapless effort to find some
" trace of her. Chance led his steps to the side of the pool. Here
" on the bank were her *geta* (wooden clogs), the marks of her hands
" as she leaned to drink. Koriya ! Not even the consolation of
" uncertainty was left. Never again would he see Ori. In their
" transmigrations through the eternity of ages his beloved child was
" lost to him forever. Severely had the gods punished his thought-
" less disregard for life. Why had he not been content to dig the
" rice field and *hatake* (dry crops) in company with the other
" peasants ? The work was monotonous, and left one almost too
" weary to wash off the accumulated filth of the day. He had
" preferred the forest, and now paid for his worldly desires. Yosaku
" was not a poor man. Forsaking the world he secured the seal
" and stamp of a *shugenja* (wandering friar.) For the rest of his
" life he passed from province to province, praying at every shrine
" for a happier rebirth both for himself and for his daughter Ori.

" Years passed. At evening a *biwa-hoshi* (minstrel priest)
" was struggling up the pass which led into Echigo. His progress
" was slow for he was blind. Fortunately his burden was light and
" his ·necessities were small. ' To the blind there is neither day
" nor night ' says the scribe. Nay ! It is all night. The *biwa-*
" *hoshi* had reached the Jizō temple just below the top of the pass
" on his descent. Experience told him that night was close
" at hand. At least he would rest for a while. This he did, touch-
" ing from time to time the strings of his *biwa* (lute), and chanting
" scraps of the Heike Monogatari, telling of the battles and loves
" of the heroes still remembered. Then to his nostrils came ' a breeze

" smelling of fresh gore, presage of spectral visitation.   But the blind
" are brave.'   The priest cared little for spectres and much for
" guidance on his road.   The gentle voice of a woman was heard at
" his side.   ' Night approaches and a helping hand is needed.   At-
" tracted by the sweet strains of the biwa I have come to offer
" shelter with me this night.'   But the priest in the man refused.
" ' Nay, honoured lady, I, a priest, must find a priestly home.   If
" a village is too distant I will rest for the night at this Jizōdō.   But
" it is said that one is close at hand at the foot of the pass.'   For a
" time the woman's voice was silent.   Then in harsher tone—' I
" wish you well.   Your music has soothed my feelings.   Do not
" stop at the village below.   Go further.   Why conceal the fact ?
" I am Ori, daughter of the hunter Yosaku.   The villagers have
" failed in their offerings to my shrine.   This night they will be
" overwhelmed in a torrent of mud.   Seek shelter elsewhere.'

" Again the smell of blood passed across the nostrils of the
" biwa-hoshi.   The rustle of a woman's garments swept by.   Stum-
" bling and falling the priest made his way as best he could to the
" village at the foot of the pass.   Here his urgent entreaties secured
" a guide to the house of the nanushi, worthy descendant of the
" worthy Kinsa.   Surrounded by a crowd of wondering villagers
" he told his fearful tale to the nanushi.   ' This night you are to be
" levelled with the mud, and your names likewise.'   Kinsa shook
" his head.   He knew the tale of Ori, daughter of Yosaku.   ' Our
" fathers suffered in their day, and in late years the shrine erected
" to Ori on the site of Yosaku's house has been shamefully neglected.
" Without doubt Ori is now the nushi (sprite or demon) of the
" swampy pool, and will bring it down on our heads over night.
" There is but one thing to do.   Collect all the iron, old and new,
" that is to be found.   This is to be cast into the pool.   The rustier
" the better, for the nushi will take the rust for blood.'   Forth,-
" with the villagers in haste gathered all the old kitchen knives,
" choppers, adzes, hammers, chains, fire-tongs, pots, everything of
" rusted iron that they could find, and of unrusted in the hope that
" it would rust.   A mighty heap it all made at the side of the pool.
" On the order of the nanushi in it went at the reputed spot where

" Ori had lost her life. Then, with the feeling that the danger had been "averted the long procession took its way back to the village. There was " a strife as to who should give shelter to the *biwa-hoshi* that night, " but it was a mournful hospitality. Hardly was the village reached " when he was seized with the most atrocious pains. His tongue " was swollen with thirst until it blocked the throat, preventing all " relief. His body was bloated into a shapeless mass. Then he died. " The grateful villagers did not forget his service to them. He " became a *kami* (god), and a shrine was erected at the entrance to " the village. Here he is figured with biwa, staff, and *geta* (clogs). " As for the pass, henceforth it was called the Oritōge. Such the tale " of this Akihide, recited at his lord's command."

What would have been the verdict of lord and vassals as to the tale of Isshiki Akihide remains uncertain. As Mitsukane Kō opened his mouth to speak the *shōji* (sliding screens) were blown apart by a violent gust of wind, and a dazzling glare filled the whole apartment. Men rose on one knee. Only the prince displayed no agitation. To conceal his fright Isshiki took the cue. " It is no longer the turn " of Akihide to claim his lord's benevolent attention. However, " with the suzerain's permission, it is to be said that here is room " for youthful vigour in the service of their lord. For weeks this " bright light has wandered at night over Kamakura town. " Disease has been wide-spread, and the rains of the present month " have been such that the farmers have become *sendō* (boatmen). " The cause of this unhappiness is not difficult to trace, for it has " been reported that the light issues forth from the Sasamegayatsu " at this late hour of the night. May his lordship deign to com- " mand that one of the enterprising and younger samurai take horse " at once and catch the spectre at work......Don't embarrass our " honoured lord in making a choice......What! No one moves! " Nay, no wonder these feeble visions of the under-world show front " when the young and strong show so little courage." Isshiki thus spoke in derision with little idea of finding a candidate to ride out into the storm and darkness, and with much idea of showing zeal in his lord's affairs. Then a voice was heard in the extreme rear of the hall. " The mansion of the lord Isshiki is close by Sasamega-

"yatsu. If these visions have been so prolonged it is strange
" that his lordship's retainers have not examined into the matter
" long since. He who speaks is a mere youth ; but rain, wind,
" darkness hurt no one. Will his lordship deign to grant a token
" and the honour to do him service. Unworthy and impertinent is
" the request." Mitsukane bent forward to scrutinize the depths of
the hall. " Naruhodo! It is Yūki Shichirō Ujitomo, thus pre-
" pared to face the demon. The token you shall have, to leave as
" evidence of the mission accomplished. Give him this folding fan
" (ogi). And now, to await the report." The prince rose to close
the audience for the night.

He had hardly left the hall when Ujitomo was on his way.
The distance to the Sasamegayatsu was short. Down the Ōkura
valley he gallopped, past the long lines of yashiki and temple walls,
then of shops. What is now a smiling rural scene of hatake and
rice field, in those days harboured two thousand houses. Not
far from the goal stood the great mansion of Isshiki. Awaiting the
return of its lord the building still showed many lights, and the
guard, safely housed, watched the burning torches which marked the
entrance gate. As Ujitomo turned up toward the Sasamegayatsu all
semblance of a path was lost. The hills rose steeply around him,
thickly clothed with pine and cedars. Within the narrow entrance
the valley opened into two wider bays. For a moment Ujitomo
hesitated. Deciding to leave these to later examination he rode up
the narrowing slope. The storm had ceased; the clouds in ragged
masses scurried through the sky, the moon shone fitfully through
them lighting up the wet tufts of the suzuki grass which reached
nearly to his horse's belly. The place was most ragged and unkempt,
thinly sprinkled with pines. The horse stumbled and climbed over
the fallen tree trunks with no little trouble, but Ujitomo talked and
encouraged, and aided by the fitful light of moon and lantern he
soon reached his journey's end. Here he halted and looked around
on every side. Not a sign of anything was to be seen except the
almost impenetrable grove of cedar trees at the valley head. Into
its darkness he thrust his horse. Ah! In a little clearing stood a
shrine. Ujitomo leaped down and tied his horse to a tree. Then

he approached the shrine. It was very dilapidated, but the carvings carried around the outside showed that at one time it had had some pretensions to importance. Entering he found an image of the Thousand Handed Kwannon on the Butsudan. Before this he placed his lord's token. Then he worshipped. Evidently no spectre haunted the interior. Nor was aught found without. Going to the edge of the grove he looked down the valley. A strip of silver sea lighted by the moon was visible in the distance over the Kamakura plain. Ujitomo again turned toward the shrine, clapped his hands and prayed. "If any supernatural influence causes the " present manifestations, may it be granted to this Ujitomo to see "and make report to his lord. Namu Amida Butsu! Namu " Amida Butsu!"

Still nothing; not a shadow of the doubtful appeared. Ujitomo shrugged his shoulders in something like wrath and turned to untie his horse. As he did so he saw full before his eyes, standing before the little shrine of Fudō in the shadow of the temple, an aged man. He was leaning on a staff of *akaza*, wood much prized by the old. He fingered a rosary of quartz-crystal beads. To all appearance he was oblivious to the presence of any stranger. Ujitomo leaned forward and glared. His hand on his sword hilt he began to approach the aged man, ready to spring on him. A thought held him. How ridiculous if he should seize some old pilgrim come to say his prayers before the shrine of Kwannon. The old man seemed to divine his presence and his thoughts. He turned to him "with a face as smiling and tranquil as that of (Ujitomo's) father."—Said he—" You too, young samurai are an "early worshipper at Kwannon's shrine. Surely you mean her no "evil. Being a youth you have some mission here besides worship." The voice was reassuring, human and musical. Then ever watchful for any supernatural manifestation, with sword loose in the scabbard and ready for instant action, Ujitomo told his tale and mission ; how he had been sent to clear up the doubts of his lord as to the monster said to issue forth from the Sasamegayatsu, to the fright and consternation of Kamakura town. " Venerable Sir, with " age and experience perchance you live hereabouts and are well ac-

" quainted with the place. Deign to grant any information on
" which report can be made to his lordship."

The old man laughed. " The portents are due to the issuance
" of Kwannon. The history of the temple is easily called to mind
" for the name of Yoshioki is famous in the land. Nitta Yoshioki,
" in his youth known as Tokuju-maru, was the second son of the
" famous Taishō Yoshisada. He was the child by a concubine, a
" woman of humble origin, and his father had small consideration
" or thought of the seed fallen by the wayside, passing him over
" for his younger son Yoshimune. But as the boy grew to young
" manhood he showed himself the worthy son of his sire, and proved
" to be the terror of the Kamakura Kwanryō and his Shitsuji.
" When Minamoto Akiiye was sent into the Kwantō by Go Daigo
" Tennō, commissioned as Chinjufu Shōgun, the youthful Yoshioki
" forthwith set about a practical display of his own consideration in
" the country, and was soon ready to join him with thirty thousand
" men. Akiiye, however, did not await this important succour,
" and defeated he was compelled to withdraw from Kamakura.
" Yoshioki, however, became as the right hand of the brother
" Akinobu. In Shohei 7th year (1352) he joined himself to his
" brother Yoshimune and his cousin Yoshiharu (Wakiya). This
" triumvirate of the younger Nitta for the succeeding years kept the
" Kwantō in a blaze. Battle after battle was fought against Takauji,
" who lead his army in person and often without success. On one
" occasion three hundred of his men had surrounded Yoshioki and
" Yoshiharu, and felt secure of their game. On this occasion
" Yoshiharu is said to have killed a hundred men, and the twain
" escaped to join Yoshimune. Then the Miura and Ishidō raised an
" army of many thousands. Yoshioki forthwith joined it. Many
" battles followed. Takauji fled defeated, and Yoshioki burst over the
" Kobukuro-zaka to seize Kamakura (1353). But the discontent
" with Takauji in the Kwantō was not lasting. The army of the
" South court soon melted away, and Yoshioki again found himself
" a partisan chief and the particular thorn in the side of the
" Ashikaga party of the Kwantō.

" Yoshioki had one defect—youth. The Shitsuji, Hatakeyama

" Nyūdō Dōsei, unsuccessful with his legions, now determined to play
" on this quality of his antagonist and his known fondness for
" woman. Thus he was to be encompassed by treachery. There
" was a man named Takezawa Ukyō no Suke Nagahira, with a
" fief in this upper Musashino, and who had served Yoshioki in
" a minor capacity. This man was easily bribed to worm himself
" into the confidence of Yoshioki, to grasp any occasion to take him
" at a disadvantage. The prospects at first were not bright.
" Yoshioki was induced to leave Echigo in order to start a move-
" ment in Kotsuke and Musashi. But he was suspicious of Dōsei's
" movements, and carefully kept himself from any but well tried
" associates. On appeal from Takezawa, Dōsei secured from Kyōto a
" very beautiful girl and sent her to him. Passing her off as his
" daughter Takezawa saw to it that Yoshioki had a glimpse
" of her. Of age sixteen years, lady-in-waiting, (tsubone) of a
" princely house, she was the flame to the stubble. Yoshioki fell
" violently in love and sought the intimacy of Takezawa. The victim
" well in the trap it was determined to close it with a *saké* feast at
" which *shirabyoshi* (dancing girls) and music were prominent
" features. This was Embun 9th month 13th day (5-6 October, 1359).
" The girl, however, succeeded in sending Yoshioki a letter in which
" she told him of an evil dream and begged him not to come. His
" retainer Ida Masatada, who suspected Nagahira, also protested.
" Under plea of illness Yoshioki failed to keep his appointment.
" Takezawa was in a great rage. Suspecting that the girl had be-
" trayed him he promptly struck off her head and buried her in his
" garden. Now Yoshioki had much love and mere suspicions.
" Again he began to pester Takezawa with complaints of his
" daughter's coldness.

    " Takezawa was in great straits. Answering that the girl was
" very ill and had been sent away to Kyōto, he sought time to consult
" Dōsei. Edo Tōtōmi no Kami Takashige was brought into the
" affair. He was suffering from rage aroused by a raid of Yoshioki
" on his fief at the head of the bay. He advised playing on the
" ambition of Yoshioki. ' Promise him the head of Kunikiyo Dono.'
" Dōsei shivered until matters were explained. It was not so

" difficult. A bold attempt to secure Dōsei's head would appeal to
" Suke-Dono. Fore-warned Hatakeyama was tolerably safe. Take-
" zawa began his cozening appeals. Yoshioki was a great influence
" in the land. Thousands were ready to rise at his call. Ashikaga
" Motouji was bitterly hated. Deign to make a bold stroke. Yoshi-
" oki could live in secret in Kamakura. Two or three thousand
" men introduced into the place would make him master of it and at
" the head of great army. With the heads of Motouji Dono and his
" Shitsuji Dōsei in hand there was no reason why the Nitta should
" not replace the Ashikaga in Kyōto itself. Was not a Kwantō *bushi*
" worth a hundred westerners ? Yoshioki swallowed the attractive
" bait. The 10th month 10th day (2 November 1359) he set out
" for Kamakura with twelve of his retainers. Takezawa followed,
" really to complete the ambush at the Yaguchi ferry.* When
" the boat reached mid-stream of the Rokugogawa the boatmen un-
" ceremoniously sprang into the water and swam vigorously toward
" shore. The soldiery of the Edo, father and son, lying prostrate in the
" bamboo thicket now rose and discharged volleys of arrows as thick as
" the summer rain. The same tribute came from the traitor Takezawa
" and his company. In a burst of wrath Yoshioki shouted. " Surely
" this act of treachery is unmatched in Nippon. For seven births as
" enemy shall Yoshioki harass you. ' With this curse and evil
" intent he seated himself, plunged his dagger deep into his left side
" and drew it to the right. Twisting the weapon he made the double
" cut upward. Thus he died. Ida Masatada, plunging the dagger
" twice into his own throat, severed head from body. Serata
" Uma no Suke and Ōshima Suwa no Kami thrust their swords
" down their throats. Leaping into the river thus they died,
" Yurabyō Kuranosuke and his brother Shinzaemon, standing on the
" gunnel of the boat mutually killed each other. Doi Saburō Sae-
" mon, Mimaseguchi Rokurō, Ichikawa Gorō, stripping naked, with
" long swords held in their mouths, swam to shore to land in the
" midst of the three hundred men of the Edo. Here the casualty

---

* A short distance up-stream from Kawasaki on the left bank of the river,
in Egara district. The Dai Nihonshi strictly follows the Taiheiki. Cf IV
362-365 : Taiheiki 976-986) (Hakubunkwan).

" list of the foe mounted to five killed and thirteen wounded before
" these mother-naked men were despatched. Takezawa and Taka-
" shige carried the heads to Prince Motouji, camped at Irumagawa.
" Here Takezawa remained to enjoy his good fortune."*

" Edo Tōtōmi no Kami, with his son Shimotsuke no Kami,
" took himself homeward to hunt out the remnants of Yoshioki's
" faction. On reaching Yaguchi ferry he learned that disaster had
" overtaken the boatmen. Pushing out after a drunken spree
" the boat had capsized in a sudden squall. All were drowned.
" Takeshige drew back from the crossing. This was plainly the
" work of the evil and angry spirits of the men treacherously done
" to death. Riding far up stream he crossed, and in blackness of
" mind and fright fled homeward. Reaching the foothills a black
" and heavy cloud descended on the party. At the thunder of
" hoofs Takashige turned. Close behind rode Yoshioki. His armour
" was of flames; from under the golden dragon of his helmet his
" face glared hideously. Riding a dappled chestnut horse and
" brandishing a bow he passed close by on the left of the frightened
" lord of Edo. A moment later Takashige fell to the ground. Placed
" in a litter with great difficulty he was conveyed home, for his body
" was as if turned to stone. In seven days he died. Then Dōsei
" had palpable proof that Yoshioki had become an evil demon. He
" dreamed that a black cloud overhung the camp at Iruma. Drums
" beat. Yoshioki and his ten men, in the guise of demons dragged a
" fire chariot into the midst. All was ablaze. Dōsei woke to the
" beating of real drums. Lightning had descended on the farmers'
" houses of the village, which was in flames. Then ghostly
" lights were reported from Yaguchi. Kamakura also suffered.
" The people were beset by supernatural influences. Bright lights
" flashed in the sky. Violent gales and rain destroyed the houses.
" Famine was added; pestilence ensued. Singing, groans, shouts as
" of battle were heard in the sky by day. In the kitchens people
" heard the voices of the dead, and the food was tainted. Prince
" Motouji became very gloomy. The land tax was remitted, for
" there were no crops. The death penalty was rarely enforced, for

---

* Twenty miles west of Tōkyō on the Kawagoe line.

" men feared death less than life. Everything was in confusion and
" prayers at shrines and temples were without avail.

" Then it was decided to consult the Yūgyō Shōnin (Bishop).
" Not long since at Fujisawa had been established ;the Tōtakusan
" Shōkwōji ; its founder Donkai Shōnin. Tōshū Shōrin, the then
" bishop, at once attributed all these events to the evil spirits of
" Yoshioki and his ten retainers. With due exorcisms he laid the
" ghosts. On this spot was built a temple to Kwannon. At
" Yaguchi ferry a shrine was set up, known as the Nitta Daimyōsha.
" The uneasy spirits were repressed for all future time. These are
" not to be suspected. The history of the place has naught to do
" with present sights and sounds. The prosperous times of Ujimitsu
" have passed. The days of Prince Mitsukane again are troubled.
" Hence the Kwannon Bosatsu is ill at ease, and flies abroad at night.
" Be easy of mind, for if evil counsellors be dismissed, and the people
" be tranquillized, all will be well again."*

The old man ceased. Ujitomo eyed him with awe and in-
tentness. Was he really human ? " Respectful are the thanks
" this Ujitomo has to offer. There are men possessed of wonderful
" power in this life. Some can even rise unsupported in the air
" (Tsuriki=Iddhi). Venerable Sir, will you not tell the fortune of
" Ujitomo ? He has to make report to his lord." Thus he spoke

---

* The shrine of the Nitta Daimyōsha (under Government superintendance)
is still in existence. It is easily reached by a ride or walk of something more than
two miles across the flat from Kamata station. For a Shintō shrine the decoration is elaborate. The saddle, sword, and helmet of Yoshioki, together with
other relics are shown. Devotees of the War God are conspicuous. A huge
bow is one of the offerings ; ditto swords, halberds, bows and arrows. Just
behind the shrine is the mound on which is the grave of Yoshioki. This is
fenced and the public are not admitted. The mound is covered by trees and a
tangle of underbrush, the straight bamboo being an unusual feature. In ancient
times the bed of the Rokugogawa, now at some distance, passed close to the
mound. Its outlines are still easily made out. The river was very wide at this
point, and the actual scene of the ambush and killing of Yoshioki and his
retainers is two hundred yards " up-stream," marked by two huge pine trees.
Here was the old Yaguchi Watashi (ferry). There is also a minor shrine to the
retainers. The isolation of Yoshioki's grave is probably connected with his
very bad reputation as a ghost. He is not to be angered by intrusion. Ikegami
is a mile and a half distant over a good road.

to test the aged sire. The reply was earnest. " Iza ! Of these
" matters say nothing to your lord. Surely he will be advised to
" give order for the destruction of the shrine. Disbelieving the
" apparition of Kwannon he will think that it has become a mere
" haven for the evil spirits of Yoshioki and his *rōtō*. Great mis-
" fortunes will occur in the land. For yourself—great shall be your
" fortune, noble your end."

The old man's figure became larger and larger before the
astonished eyes of Yūki Shichirō. The kindly look changed to an
evil leer. Then the apparition faded away like smoke, dispersed by
the strong breeze blowing up valley from the sea. Ujitomo
was left standing, his bared sword in hand and his hair on end
wildly waving in the violent gust of wind. Aiya ! Ujitomo turned
again to the Kwannondō and knelt in prayer—for fortune in
war for his lord, and for counsel as to what report to make. In the
full dawn slowly he rode down the valley, and crossing the waking
town passed up the Ōkuragayatsu to the palace. Here his arrival
was earnestly awaited. Prince Mitsukane had passed a bad night ;
and so had Isshiki Akihide, who was so earnest to have first news
as to what really took place in the Sasamegayatsu that he had remained at the palace. He was the first to greet Ujitomo as he entered.
The only thing the latter had determined upon was to seek counsel
before making report to his lord. To violate the shrine of Kwannon would be an evil influence in the life of any one even remotely
connected with such sacrilege. So much he told to Isshiki, who fell
into a great rage. Learning that he had been warned by the
apparition to say nothing beyond the warning to dismiss evil councillors he fell on Ujitomo forthwith with a storm of abuse. "The
"first duty of a samurai is to his lord, no matter what the
" consequences be to himself. As matter of fact you are a mere
" coward, even thus young in life. You have not been near the
" Sasamegayatsu, but have been warmly hidden under the *futon*
" (quilts) at the Sasuke *yashiki* of Norimoto. Now you appear with
" this excuse for not making report. But the case is clear. The shrine
"of Kwannon in the valley is ineffective and no longer confines the
"evil ghosts of Nitta Yoshioki and his *rōtō*. It is to be destroyed.

"Without a home at the least they will seek other refuge than
"Kamakura, and our lord will no longer be disturbed." Ujitomo,
though but seventeen years old, was not one tamely to take such
insult. "Shut up Akihide (*damare orō Akihide*). You are very
"wrong in your conclusions, for Yoshioki and his retainers have
"nothing to do with this matter. As for cowardice, it is known that
"no one is better supplied with the quality than yourself. If his
"lord so orders this Ujitomo is ready at once to cut open his belly.
"Isshiki Dono would seek refuge in a shaven pate (*nyūdō*=turn
"priest); a worn out samurai and good for nothing but to slander
"better men than himself." Then the eyes of Isshiki stood out of
"his head with rage. "Rebuke an inexperienced ill-trained cub and
"he is sure to snap. Your courage shall soon be put to the test.
"Your belly will be found to have greater craving for a peasant's
"fare than for cold steel." Ujitomo fumed and would have drawn
his sword, if by-standers had not seized him. Protests were raised
against the quarrel. Said one old samurai—"Why shout so
"loudly at the very entrance of our lord's chamber? What drug
"have you fellows swallowed with your spittle?—Said another,
"Carry this unseemly disturbance elsewhere. The open air will
"cool the tongue of Isshiki, and youth will never attack the feeble."
But this good council was rendered useless by the appearance of
the prince. Said Mitsukane, "Cease your strife. As *kerai* of
"your prince you have no cause for quarrel. Ujitomo forthwith is
"to make report." The youth then told the whole course of his
adventures to his lord, together with the urgent command of the
apparition that the Kwannondō be left unharmed. With benevolent commendation Mitsukane Kō dismissed him, and then he took
himself to the council chamber.

Now Isshiki Akihide was a member of the council, and here
the tale of Ujitomo easily was discredited. Plainly the Kwannondō
was a mere harbourage for Yoshioki and his band of evil spirits. It
was easy to decide on destroying the shrine, but the question was—
who would undertake the task? Although performed on the orders
of the suzerain yet the act had a taint of sacrilege about it. Excuses
were sure to be offered, and the example of one would be contagious

with others. The Shitsuji Norisada was summoned in conference.
Norisada was non-plussed. At first he respectfully pointed out the
nature of the deed to his lord, but the mind of Mitsukane was
obstinate.   " It is true that our revered ancestor Motouji Kō estab-
" lished the shrine in order to secure peace to the land. Far from
" doing so its effect is much otherwise, and he himself would be the
" first to destroy his work. It is not the advice of Norisada that is
" sought on this occasion. In council its destruction has been decid-
" ed on, and the matter is transferred to the Shitsuji for execution."
Norisada was the last man in Nippon to oppose his lord even in
behalf of Kwannon. He plead his infirmities as excuse for not
acting in person.   " But," said he, " the men are at hand fit to carry
" out the mission thoroughly and in due form. Satake Atsumitsu
" is of Seiwa Genji, stock, being descended from Shinra Saburō
" Yoshimitsu. His fief is at Ōta in Hitachi,* and he is neighbour of
" the Yūki. The other man needed is found in Mago Gorō Mitsu-
" shige, lord of Oguri in Hitachi. He is in the eighth generation from
" Hitachi Daijō Kunika of the House of Katsubara Shinnō. These
" two can safely be entrusted with your lordship's order. The
" command shall be sent to them at once to be in attendance."
Said Prince Mitsukane—" be it so."

A summons to personal attendance on the Kwanryō was
not so common to either lord as to make them easy in mind. The
land was at peace, and the danger to be welcomed was likely to
find its substitute in some mission of unpleasant nature. Atsumitsu and Mitsushige were close neighbours in Hitachi, and equally
close in friendship—as fish to water is the expression of the Nipponese. The two men prostrated themselves before the prince and
heard with respect and growing astonishment the mission entrusted
to them. To answer in unison was disrespectful, so they spoke in
turn, urging on their lord the prejudice of the popular spirit, its
firm trust in the efficacy of the shrine, and the sacrilege of the deed
they were asked to perform. Mitsukane Kō became very angry.
" Hold your tongues ! You were not summoned for conference but

---

* A short distance south of Iwase Station on the Mito-Oyama line. It is
in the foot hills of the range joining Tsukubasan with the Hitachi hills.

The destruction of the Kwannondō.

" to carry out the command the prince deigns to give you. Instead
" you show yourself to be cowards. The Shitsuji Norisada recom-
" mended you for this important task, but he can find others, before
" your disloyal conduct infects your companions."* He made a
move as if to dismiss them. The two men forthwith prostrated
themselves in fear. " We can only beg the forbearance of our
" lord. We spoke, not in protest, but merely expressing the common
" foolish opinion. As for service, we are mere vassals of our lord,
" and ready to obey any command he gives." Mitsukane, already
warned by the unwillingness of Norisada, was only too glad to find
no greater opposition. Charged with the mission and the commendation of their lord the two men left the palace.

As they went forth said Satake—" Provision must be made for
" the image of Kwannon. Its destruction would surely bring
" disaster on our Houses."—Replied Oguri, "True : in this matter
" nothing is to be disregarded to mitigate the offence. It is best to
" bear it to the *yashiki* at Inamuragasaki. It is nearer than that
" of Satake Dono at Koshigoe. The later disposition is easy." To
this Satake agreed. Workmen were gathered, and attended by a
number of their *rōtō* the two lords made their way up the Sasamegayatsu. The shrine was soon reached, the image of Kwannon was
removed. The stone monument to the Nitta, lord and retainers
eleven men, was next to be cast down and broken, but its foundations went deep. At last it was removed. Beneath it was found a
slab engraved with sixteen characters : Satake read :

將 常　　維 法
絕 陸　　四 室
佛 二　　十 寓
緣 兒　　年 居

---

* Often the directness of the English pronoun can express rudeness or
harshness of Japanese speech, even when honorifics merely disguise the speaker's
intent. The *kōdan*, however, makes no pretence to consistency throughout.

  " The' Sovereign lady's dwelling ;
  " For forty years it stands.
  " Two Sons of Hitachi,
  " Their lives to end in Buddha's Way."

  " Oguri Dono, just forty years have passed since the Yūgyō
" Shōnin tranquillized the Spirits of Yoshioki and his retainers.
" How clearly he has foreseen our mission, for we ' men of Hitachi '
" are indicated. The performance of this deed was not to be escap-
" ed in this existence."—Replied Oguri, " True indeed ! To our
" misfortune we set free the evil spirits of Yoshioki and his *rōtō*.
" Our lord cannot be disobeyed, and the Butsudō is to be destroyed.
" May the Buddhas and Kami secure him from all harm, and
" grant him and his success in war." Clapping their hands the
two men faced the temple and prayed.

  Then the workmen were urged on to their task. With great
difficulty the edges of the huge mass were set free and the stone
raised to the surface of the ground. Beneath it was a deep hole.
As Oguri and Satake made ready to leap down a heavy rumbling
was heard within. Then a thick smoke poured forth enveloping
and choking all near by. The Heavens became black, as the eleven
spirits rushed forth on their mission of evil. Then the smoke disappeared. Half dazed the Oguri and Satake, lords and retainers,
rose from the ground. There was nothing left to do except to set
fire to the temple. Soon it was a blazing mass, and the stones only
of its foundation remained to mark the site. Even these were rooted
out and cast haphazard into the valley below the terrace. Then
taking the graven slab of stone they made their way to make report
to their lord Mitsukane. His object secured the prince bestowed
great praise upon them, and marked them for his favour. Henceforth great was to be the prosperity of the Houses of Satake and
Oguri. With due ceremony the statue of Kwannon was later conveyed by the lords of Oguri and Satake to the ancient Sugimoto
temple, where already the goddess was installed—the Ōkura
Kwannon.

CHAPTER II.

THE FLOWER-VIEWING AT THE MANSION OF SATAKE.

Oguri Mitsushige had reached the age of forty years as yet child-less. The worthy daimyō was neither so busy with affairs, or so indif-ferent to posterity as to let this state of affairs pass without effort material and mental. Every old trot and gossip within a radius of miles was called into council, to propose at least a remedy and to pocket fee and feed. Then as a last resort Mitsushige took to prayer. The kindly favour of Kwannon, the Lady Merciful, especially was invoked. Mitsushige, attended and unattended, visited the local shrines, from the Hase Kwannon on the West to the Nagoe Kwannon on the East. Both the Kwannondō of Sasamegayatsu, and the imposing shrine of the Sugimotoji benefitted by his enthusiasm and suppli-cation. Whatever other methods he used, in the third year of Oei (1396) he was granted the favour of a boy. This wonderful child, a very jewel, from his earliest years to this twentieth century has been endowed with all the graces of mind and body that imagi-nation can conceive. He was learned, yet not an ass; his memory was prodigious, and a scroll once perused was as engraved on his brain, twice perused he could preach a sermon thereon, three times perused he could write a better one than the original. Kojirō Suke-shige was also carefully trained in all the technicalities of the service of a *bushi* (knight). In fact nothing was left undone to make him valuable to himself and others, in war and in council.

In the 16 year of Oei (1409) the town of Kamakura was poured into its streets. Men and women stood before the houses. The children gathered silently close to their parents. All scuttled or crouched as the long lines of priest and samurai wended their way to the temples. Beating of drums, the boom of bells, the tinkling of

the *suzu* (hand bells), the chant of the clerics, were the only sounds
to be heard ; if indeed any sound could have been heard above the
din thus made. The lord of Kamakura, Mitsukane Kō, was desperately ill. The Shitsuji Norisada had summoned doctors and
learned priests from all over the land, but some maleficent influence
baffled their efforts. The beating of drums, the chants of the priests
now rose to a huge uproar. On this occasion, however, it was to
propitiate the spirit of the prince, prematurely deceased. He was
given the name of Shōkō-In-Den. Out of sight out of mind. Men
turned to the youthful successor Tendai-maru, who now became the
Kwanryō in the room of his father, under the name and title of
Sahyoye no Kami Mochiuji Kō.

Norisada's first task was to provide for the household of the
young prince at the Ōkura palace. In doing so he summoned
Mago Gorō Mitsushige. " Your son Kojirō is now of an age pro-
" perly to enter the palace in the service of page. Mochiuji Ason is to
" be surrounded with the‎ best of influences for his reign as prince.
" The name of Kojirō is spread abroad, as of a youth accomplished
" in mind and body, of serious habit and seemly disposition. It has
" been decided therefore to issue a summons in order that he may
" enter on his service at the palace. It is to be obeyed forthwith."
Mitsushige could not find terms to express his thanks. Even his
wife Hatsuse would rejoice in the loss of their son to such profit to
his career. " Long may be the reign of the suzerain, honoured
" and feared. It is but object of wonder that one so insignificant as
" this Mitsushige should be so favoured by his Lord in the first
" place, and by heaven in the second place. Good fortune attains
" even to the foolish. Mitsushige finds words too weak to express
" gratitude." Forthwith he waddled forth in his long court robes ; to
be carried home to Inamuragasaki ; and to tell the good news to wife
and son.

A lucky day was chosen, and thus did Kojirō Sukeshige enter on
his long struggle with his lord. Of the same age, possessed of most
lovable qualities Sukeshige enjoyed high favour from the start. If
Mochiuji wanted a companion on his temple visitations, his hunting,
his landscape viewing, his sports at foot-ball and military exercises,

Sukeshige was sure to be the one summoned, profiting far more than the prince by the careful tuition to which the latter was subjected in his presence. Thus the months and days passed in the palace service. Princes are capricious and hence very observant of the little niceties of life. Mochiuji was not long in noticing a distraught and melancholy condition in his attendant. Indeed Sukeshige sometimes seemed to have indulged in the impertinence of tears, whereas the mere presence of the suzerain should shed a happiness on the mortals favoured with admission. Walking in the garden one day Mochiuji Kō found him more forced and random than usual in his answers. " Koriya ! Sukeshige, your complexion is " a mirror of this green turf. Are you ill? Assuredly there is some- " thing the matter." Sukeshige answered—" Nay, my lord, Suke- " shige is not ill ; but some days since it has been learned that my " mother is desperately sick. Foolish and disloyal as it is Sukeshige " cannot free his mind of the thought. Deign, honoured lord, to " accept this apology for deserved reproof." Said Mochiuji—" Iya ! " Iya ! It is a very important matter (for me to have cheerful " faces around me). Ill and reduced to her couch no wonder you " are anxious. Go home at once and nurse her, to the relief of your " mind (and mine)." Thus freed of his service Sukeshige could but weep tears of gratitude at this peremptory dismissal. " The " depth of Sukeshige's thanks for his lord's favour is greater than " ever. The command is obeyed forthwith ; and Sukeshige, with " fear and respect, asks leave of absence until such presence of mind " is recovered as again to be allowed in his lord's presence." In obeisance he prostrated himself. Mochiuji Kō promptly turned his back on him and forgot him Sukeshige, more or less in disgrace and happy, took his way to the *yashiki* at Inamuragasaki, to report the kindness of his lord, not his curt dismissal.

Joyfully did Hatsuse receive her handsome and filial son. But Sukeshige's mission did not lie with her. Joy rarely kills ; neither does it cure. The oppression of the little woman's breathing grew worse and worse. Finally, with the cold of winter, she no longer breathed at all, and took her way forthwith out of this life. On the hillside of the Fujisawa Yūgyōji her grave found place, well

kept with flowers and sticks of incense, and the favoured resort of
the favoured child. In fact Sukeshige carried his grief to such
limits that Mitsushige was alarmed, and felt called on to
remonstrate. In place of a son and a samurai, to carry on his line
and fiefs, he seemed more likely to have fathered another priest for
the temple's service. Hence he made his son his constant companion, took little excursions into the country round about, and
whenever he had a mission in Hitachi Oguri in his company went
Sukeshige. Thus close together grew father and son, the older and
younger forming one habit of mind, and the younger becoming older
than his years in the process. But Mitsushige was always looking
to the lighter side, to the relief of the boy's gloom. He hailed the
spring with joy as it approached. The *yashiki* of the Oguri was
at Inamuragasaki, at the important entrance into Kamakura by the
Gokurakuji *kiridoshi* (Temple of Paradise covered way.) Further
on other *yashiki* were posted—of the Yūki, Utsunomiya, Nasuno,
the Kwantō nobles who looked to the defence of the town at that
quarter just as the Uesugi guarded Yamanouchi and Ogigayatsu.
Farthest removed, and near Koshigoe Mampukuji was the *yashiki*
of Satake Atsumitsu. Now here was a famous flowering peony
cherry tree (botan-zakura), which in the middle of April showed
a magnificent and beautiful display. Besides, there was other
attraction in the fine and unusual *asagi-zakura* (with cream yellow
blossoms).* Mitsushige determined on a visit to the Satake.
Horses were brought, and Oei 18 year 3 month 22 day (15 April
1411) father and son set out on their ride along the Shichirigahama.

Their welcome was as warm as the truly brotherly feeling between Mitsushige and Atsumitsu. A banquet of fish·and *saké* (rice
wine) was served, and the little daughter of Atsumitsu, Terute by
name, was the one to pour the wine for the honoured guests. In
the 7 year of Oei (1400) the same belated favour of a child had been
granted to Atsumitsu. In this case a girl was born, a very jewel
of attraction. Her long black hair, delicate oval face, lofty eye-

---

* Some specimens of this beautiful tree are found at the Jōsenji of the
Taya no Ana near Ōfuna. They bloom about the middle of April.

brows, and high forehead displayed a coming intelligence and beauty which later generations have liked to compare to the famous Sotohori no Iratsume.   Says the ancient tome†—"the Oto-"hime's countenance was of surpassing and peerless beauty.   Her "brilliant colour shone through her raiment so that the men of that "time gave her the designation of Sotohori Iratsume."   At this time Terute was a little girl, obedient, quick, light-handed, all eyes for the pleasure and comfort of the guests of the House.   The tales turned to war and archery, and the brother-in-law of Atsumitsu, one Yokoyama Tarō Yasuhide, bragged long and manfully of his powers.   Yokoyama Tarō formerly had held a fief in the Tōshima district of Musashi, under the late Kwanryō Ujimitsu Kō.   For some unsavoury offence he had been deprived of his fief, and lacking courage to cut his belly open he had taken refuge with Atsumitsu, who treated his boastfulness with tolerant contempt and supported him for his wife's sake.   Tarō had a most unsatisfactory reputation, apart from his record.   He is described as "arrogant, avaricious, dull, a boor, a fool, and a scoundrel without pity or sympathy."   His position he did not feel.   As was the custom of the Nipponese of his day Yokoyama was in full touch with his former retainers; robbers and thieves, riff-raff of the very worst kind.   Although he was thirty odd years of age he had eyes on the budding beauty and very positive dowry of his niece.   The visit of the Oguri gave him no pleasure, but he was careful to make his dis-like felt rather than manifest.   In the midst of this talk of war and the bow a heron flew down to the side of the garden pool (*ike*), and deliberately fishing out a fat carp sent it down its capacious gullet.   Atsumitsu watched the robber with anger.   Said he—"Who "will avenge me on this infamous thief?"

Tarō at once was on his feet.   He was always ready "to shove forward his elbow at every opportunity."   He seized the occasion to be insolent.   "At last there is an object of interest come to the "feast.   As for this rascal Tarō shall make short work of him." He went to the rack and picked out a bow and arrow.   Advancing to the *rōka* (verandah) he posed and took careful aim at the bird

† Nihongi (Aston) I 318; Kojiki (Chamberlain.) 293.

The Archery of Sukeshige.

which stood beneath the flowering tree.   Tarō was as Tametomo
prepared for the famous shot from Ōshima.   An uproar of merriment from Atsumitsu followed the twang of the bow-string.   The
arrow severed the twigs of the tree, and the heron flew off unharmed amid a shower of blossoms.   Atsumitsu made not slightest
effort to hide his glee at this glaring failure.   " Why, deign
" to look !   Even the bird recognizes a bad archer.   It returns
" to its former post and fishing."   Then as Yokoyama Tarō with
contracted brow, black looks, and face aflame strung a second
arrow—" Iya !   You have had your chance.   There will be
" no greater success with the second than with the first arrow.   You
" are nothing of a shot under any conditions, and love the wine
" cup far too much to make a successful archer after indulgence.
" Let Kojirō take the bow.   His reputation is wide spread."   As the
astonished Sukeshige made a deprecatory gesture of denial Atsumitsu
turned to Mitsushige.   Continued he—" The samurai of Kamakura
" know your son as the strongest and best bowman of his years in
" the Kwantō.   Don't allow him to be backward.   Deign to add your
command to the request of Atsumitsu."   Mitsushige was anything
but pleased at this contest in archery.   He saw that Tarō was very
angry, and did not like to make even such an insignificant enemy
for Sukeshige.   However the repuest of Atsumitsu was direct and he
could not refuse.   " To shoot the bird after a banquet requires more
" than skill.   However let Kojirō do his best.   Fortune at least
" may favour him and accomplish the vengeance of Atsumitsu
" Dono."

So Sukeshige arose and approached the glowering Tarō.
" Respectful thanks to Yasuhide Dono, for permitting the oppor-
" tunity to obey the command of Satake Dono.   Deign to favour
" this Sukeshige with the loan of the bow ; but it is to be feared that
" the bird is destined to longer life since fortune refused to favour
" your lordship."   Scowling Yokoyama handed him the weapon
and stalked off to his cushion in angry dignity.   Sukeshige advanced
to the *rōka*.   The heron was again at its post, watching the fish
gliding through the water.   It was the last opportunity.   The hiss-
ing arrow severed the extended neck of the bird.   The greedy head

and bill fell into the water, the body flapped aimlessly along the ground for a few yards then toppled over. Sukeshige slowly returned, replaced the bow, and again took his seat on the cushion. Terute raised her lowered face for a moment. Mitsushige looked down, cudgelling his brains as how to turn the attention of Atsumitsu to some other subject. Tarō was choking with rage; and Kojirō was as one who has returned from his daily archery practice at the dogs. Atsumitsu broke the silence—" To expect Tarō to be " successful in such a long and difficult shot never occurred to mind. " But that even Kojirō should succeed hardly seemed possible. " Truly Mitsushige Dono the skill of your son is not over-praised. " The bird, almost indistinguishable amid the blossoms has been " brought down at a distance of twenty jō (200 feet). Kojirō, such " steadiness of vision and power of arm at your age frightens one. " What will you be as full grown knight; a rival of Chinzei " Tametomo himself. The Kamakura world must know of this " feat. Atsumitsu will publish it abroad. Great as the future of " Sukeshige is destined to be, it should have still wider field." Mitsushige thought of nothing but tempering the manifest wrath of Yokoyama. " Fortune has favoured Kojirō, and has frowned on " Tarō Dono. Indeed after a banquet of *saké* much milder feats " than this are too likely to miscarry." Said Sukeshige—" If Tarō " Dono had not been blinded by the blossoms the arrow without " doubt would have reached the bird. Accident has favoured my " humble effort."

Tarō seized the ball on the rebound. " Aiya! It is well re- " cognized that success in these matters is ' as an arrow in the dark " night reaching its mark—or a dog's success in catching fleas,' " he added insolently. Sukeshige was in a great rage, but his father's composure calmed hot blood. He said nothing. Atsumitsu was prepared to rebuke Tarō, when the latter continued. " But after all " there is more to the bow than mere use. In this perhaps Kojirō " Dono is a master hand, and he can tell us something of its history. " A banquet should always offer more than mere pleasure and the ac- " cidents of Fortune......What! You know nothing of the bow, but " to twang it? You are as silent as your teacher evidently has been;

" and silence is the sign of ignorance. But this Tarō can inform you,
" for it is the early lesson of every well-disciplined samurai.   To
" know one's weapon with familiarity is the best evidence of know-
" ing how to use it.   Know then that the bow was first used by
" Shōkō of Morokoshi (China) who lived in the time of the later
" Han.   From that land it was introduced into the divine Nippon
" by Yamato-Takeru no Mikoto, and used by him in subjugating
" the barbarians who then possessed this very land where we reside.
" The bow then had thirteen joints known as *Jūsan no buttai* or
" thirteen holy objects.   Now you are fully informed, and hence
" can add knowledge of your weapon to the gifts of accident."

On hearing this ass bray Sukeshige could no longer contain
himself. He forgot his father, he forgot Atsumitsu ready to
interfere, he forgot even Terute. Atsumitsu scented a dressing
down for Tarō and held his tongue. Sukeshige gravely turned to
face Yokoyama. " The indebtedness of my humble self to the erudi-
" tion of Tarō Dono passes measurement.   Deign to receive reveren-
" tial thanks.   But in what books can these matters be learned ?"—
" Not in books, but in age and experience, in a good teacher, are to
" be found the sources of such knowledge ; and to all appearance
" you have had none of these advantages." Thus was the rude and
" complacent reply of Tarō.   Said Sukeshige calmly—" Great is the
" erudition of Tarō Dono—and most misdirected.   Learn that the
" bow dates from the time of Fukuji of Morokoshi, of the period of
" the earlier Han.   It is mentioned in the 'Taihaku Inkyū' and
" the ' Hogishiki.'   In those early days it had no cord, but the
" arrow was used to bend the wood.   Later, in its perfection, it
" possessed six parts—the pliable wood, horn, sinew, glue, cord,
" and lacquer.   In the ' Shinrei ' three lengths are given.   The best
" was of six *shaku* six *sun* (6 feet 7$\frac{1}{5}$ inches) ; a medium length of
" six *shaku* three *sun* (6 feet 3$\frac{3}{5}$ inches) ; an inferior length of six
" *shaku* (6 feet) as the lowest standard.   As for our land, the
" ' Nihongi Jindai ' first mentions it in connection with Amaterasu
" Oho-no-Kami (the sun-goddess), who confronts her brother Susa-
" no-oho-no-Mikoto, brandishing bow and arrows.   Yamato-takeru-
" no-Mikoto was far from being the first to use it.   As for the thir-

" teen jointed bow being the oldest in use this was by no means the
" case. The thickness of bamboo used was irregular and few bows
" were good. As for its use, says the ' Reki Shōji '—' let him who
" takes aim assure in every way his conduct, if he would attain a
" happy issue. Let his inward disposition be upright, just as out-
" wardly he holds his body upright '—a maxim to be remembered
" by all samurai."

The face of Atsumitsu displayed undiluted pleasure. Mago
Gorō looked down frowning. Tarō jumped up in a rage ; " Hatsu !"
" —Said Atsumitsu coldly ; " The rebuke you drew on yourself, in
" displaying not only crass ignorance of the use, but ignorance of the
" history of the bow known to any samurai who has had occasion to
" show not only skill but affection for this weapon of the manly art.
" You were rude, and have been put in the wrong "—" But
" equally so with Kojirō," put in Mitsushige, turning in open dis-
" content to his son. " You are too young to offer to correct one so
" much older than yourself "—" Deign to let the matter rest on the
" part of all," interposed Atsumitsu. " There are other means of
" entertainment. Terute here shall touch the *koto*, and may her
" music turn our thoughts to calmer topics." Then Terute left the
" room, to return in a few moments with a maid carrying the beloved
" instrument. Rarely did the child touch the chords, bringing forth
" music to ravish her hearers to the skies. Indeed this marvellous
" nicety and skill of touch, whether on the strings of the *koto* intradi-
tion, or in the beautiful brush work of the nun Chōshō-In in fact, has
been handed down to later generations. As she played the men
watched and listened in rapt attention—" the refulgence of her
" person passed through her garments." Then Atsumitsu made a
sign to the servants to withdraw.

Turning to Mago Gorō Mitsushige gravely spoke the lord of
" the Satake House. " Oguri Dono there is a request to make "—
" Satake Dono is to this Mitsushige as fish to water. Deign to
" express the command. As far as it lies in his power Mitsushige
" adds performance to promise." Atsumitsu laughed gleefully.
" Then the favour to be asked is already granted. Atsumitsu is no
" longer young. This child will be left without protection or con-

" nection to guard her interests. Deign to accept her as the wife
" of your son Kojirō Dono. Terute is yet a child, but these matters
" already are to be considered and the contract closed. Thus will
" the minds of her parents be at ease." Answered Mitsushige—
" What Satake Dono puts as a request properly should come from
" Mitsushige, so much is it desired. The honour granted to the
" Oguri House is matter of congratulation and most earnest thanks.
" Deign that the contract be at once concluded "—" But Kojirō
" Dono ; what of him ? " said Atsumitsu turning to the boy. Said
Mitsushige—" What his thought may be is matter of indifference.
" He will obey his father, although his face already answers for him,
" and no wonder at the prospect of possessing such a jewel."

Said 'Atsumitsu—" Terute has heard what has been said.
What are her thoughts—of pleasure ? "—" Hai ! " said Terute—
" And your answer ? " said Atsumitsu—" Hai ! " replied Terute—
" Your answer Terute ? It is known you are not deaf."—" The
" honoured command is heard and obeyed," said the child, prostrating
herself before her lord and father. Atsumitsu and Mago Gorō with
cheerful countenances faced each other and made salutation. The
affair was settled, the agreement made. Yokoyama Tarō unwilling,
and O-Shimo wife of Atsumitsu joyful, witnessed the contract. The
first lucky day was appointed for the exchange of gifts and the
formal espousal. Then the Oguri took their leave. Mago Gorō
Mitsushige was silent as they rode back along the shore. At the
Yuki-ai bridge he stopped a moment. " An obstinate and wilful
" man—this Nichiren escaped man's vengeance only by Heaven's
" aid." This was all he said, and more to the air than to Sukeshige. At night he came to his son's apartment. " Kojirō, to a
" samurai greater control is necessary than has been shown to-day.
" Because Tarō Dono displayed rudeness is no reason that Suke-
" shige should match it. You are too young to set up as a teacher
" of older men. By reference to flowers the awkwardness of Tarō
" was well condoned. The argument as to the bow was wholly out
" of place. Would you lecture to Satake Dono and your father ? "
—Sukeshige bowed low : " With fear and respect the honoured
" rebuke is received "—Said Mitsushige ; " A samurai has many

"perils to face; a belly ache the contingent circumstance of all
"affairs. See to it that no unnecessary hatreds are acquired to add
"to embarrassments always pressing. As for the events of the day
"they are most important. Your life is determined for the future
"and the important connection with the Satake House secured.
"Never forget the obligation to Satake Dono in choosing this Suke-
"shige for the husband of Terute. And now to consider the matter
"of the espousal gifts." These were selected in long consultation
with the *karō* (chief retainer). Many rolls of valued silks, utensils of
lacquer for feast, ornament, and ceremony, were in due state carried
to the Satake mansion on the propitious day. In return a *shitataré*
(mantle) of damask of blue ground on which was embroidered
foaming waves and plover (*tatsunami* and *chidori*), a magnificent
sword and suit of armour sewn with light green thread, a fine charger
with saddle glittering with gold braid, came to the mansion at
Inamuragasaki. Sukeshige and Terute, thus betrothed, became
formally husband and wife.

CHAPTER III.

THE VENGEANCE OF KWANNON.

Yokoyama Tarō was spurred to revenge by a double incentive. He hated Satake Atsumitsu with all the concentrated dislike of a dependant; and the alliance with the Oguri had overthrown his own most cherished plans. He was by no means helpless, however, as to finding means to satisfy his grudge. He could turn to Isshiki Shikibu Akihide. Between the Isshiki and the Houses of Satake and Oguri there existed an intense dislike. The latter were strong adherents of the Uesugi House, the influence of which the Isshiki were endeavouring to sap in the mind of the youthful prince. Whatever Yokoyama Tarō did, he was sure to find support in Akihide. His intercourse with this man was frequent and secret; no difficult matter, as there was mutual avoidance of any contact, as far as possible, between these jarring nobles. The *rōtō* were enjoined not to seek quarrels; best secured, as the *karō* thought, by the least contact. Oguri and Satake were so strong in Hitachi province, so strong in the support of each other, that backed by the influential Yūki clan, and with the Uesugi (Norizane) in Oyama, they could disregard the politics of Kamakura. Hence the course of Yokoyama was to watch his opportunity; nor did he have to feed his hatred for many months.

Spring passed into summer. The episode at the viewing of the cherry flowers had passed from memory. Certainly from that of Yokoyama Tarō, who showed himself more subdued, less boastful, and more genial than one would have thought possible of this sneering boorish fellow. Even to the Oguri, whose visits at Koshigoe were frequent, he acted as one joined by a blood alliance.

To Atsumitsu he became as his right hand.   In those days, as now, frequent were the visits paid to the shrine of Benten at Enoshima. Child as she was Terute firmly refused to enter the cavern in company with Sukeshige, it being current superstition that unhappiness is sure to ensue in the relations between husband and wife, if they present themselves in company before the capricious goddess.   But accident will sometimes bring about what the most obstinate and careful prevision seeks to prevent.

On a mid-day in the heat of the seventh month (August), straying along the Shichirigahama (beach) the child had found a fisherman's boat pulled up on the sand.   It was filled with the nets neatly piled, and all was ready for the launching as soon as the tide and the hour for fishing came.   For a :time Terute played around the abandoned craft.   Then overcome by the heat of the sun she clambered into the boat, and lying down on the soft nets, with her own long hair as pillow in short order she went to sleep.   Whether by accident, or carelessness, the boat had no moorings, and the fisherman did not appear to look after his craft.   Gently rose the tide, and as gently it floated the boat off into the bosom of the great ocean.   The rising wind and strong currents around the Enoshima shore rapidly carried it out to sea.   Terute slept soundly, and it was only a heavy peal of thunder that woke her, to find herself in the rocking craft under the blackened sky, and on a sea whipped into foam by the sudden squall.   In her childish terror she crouched at the bottom of the boat, protecting herself as best she could against the pelting shower by the straw rain-coats of the fishermen which lay in the bottom of the boat.   Then with her hand on the metal image of Kwannon which had hung around her neck since birth, she prayed earnestly to the goddess to protect her in this danger to her life, until in a violent plunge of the craft she struck her head violently against the gunnel and sank down unconscious.

Now whether the prayers were effective or not aid certainly was much closer to hand than she thought.   It happened that this day Sukeshige had paid a visit to the cliffs of the island.   The sudden storm arising he had taken refuge in the cavern of the

Sukeshige rescues Terute.

goddess Benten, and protected from the rain stood at the entrance
looking seaward at the foaming water. Riding on the tops of the
billows a boat suddenly came in sight, drifting straight toward the
steep cliffs and perilous reefs which line the island on the seaward
side. Moreover the occupant of the boat was evidently helpless
and unskilful, for the craft was at the mercy of the waves, without
guidance or resource, even if such was possible. Sukeshige took
another look. It was a woman or child. His eye fell on the
tranquil water within the cave, on the channel leading seaward.
Without further thought, casting off his upper clothing, in he
plunged and swam vigorously seaward toward the drifting boat
now rapidly coming to the shore. Throwing himself in its course
Sukeshige awaited its approach. A vigorous hand laid on the
gunwale, a favourable swing of the boat, and the next moment he
had boarded it. Hardly glancing at the slip of a girl prostrate in the
bottom of the boat he threw out the oar and prepared to guide the
craft into the channel leading into Benten's cavern. The cliffs were
impossible, to attempt to turn and seek sea room in this whirlpool
of waters would have left himself and his charge struggling in the
waves. The one chance was to catch the swirl which would send
them into the narrow passage to safety.

Terute slowly came back to consciousness, to find herself lying
at the foot of the shrine of the dreaded goddess Benten with Sukeshige leaning over her. She felt sick in mind and body, so shaken
that it could well have been Benten herself, and not the sea, which
had so roughly treated her. But Sukeshige lifted her up, consoled
her with the bright spirits of youth, pointing out the now brightly
shining sun at the cavern's month, lighting up the tumbled sea
beyond. As for the Goddess, had she not brought Sukeshige to her
assistance, given her the shelter of the holy place? Then he picked
her up and carried her along the rocks high above the tossing
waves, up the side of the lofty cliff, until aid could be found in the
fishermen's village and news sent to the Satake *yashiki* of the little
lady's mishap. Terute was the hope of a great House. In short
order the *karō* himself, Mito no Kosuke, with litter and attendants was at hand. Prostrating himself before the young lord

of Oguri the *karō* spoke his reverential thanks, congratulations on
the happy chance of his lordship's presence, and of the union of the
two Houses of Satake and Oguri in the loyal devotion of their
retainers. Then the procession took its way across the sandy strip
of ground :which at low tide converts island to peninsula. The
goddess Benten was completely forgotten. Not so the fisherman,
rendered careless by his cups of *saké*. Hunted out by the *karō's*
emissaries terrible would :have been the fate of man and family.
The rescue of the *himegimi* (her little ladyship) and the tears of Terute mitigated the punishment and left him and his with life. But for
long generations no boats remained unmoored on the Koshigoe shore.

A bare month later the Satake House again tempted fate upon
the water. Yokoyama Tarō continually was urging Atsumitsu to
go fishing, and the worthy knight as steadily refused as a good
Buddhist, on the ground of his growing disinclination to take the
life of animals : Man not being an animal according to good samurai ethics. This time Tarō found two good arguments. "Iza!
" Fish are not animals. They are plants, as is well known to the
" Sutra (Scripture). Besides," he went on quickly, "man must live,
" and to have strength the rice needs the savour of more than weeds
"and roots. To catch fish does not imply eating them. How
" else will they attain Nirvana, or at least chance of a better birth in
"a future existence ? Have mercy on them and the rest of your
" household. Any fish caught by Atsumitsu Dono can be allowed
" to go free. On this Tarō be all the sin and profit of the expedi-
" tion. The Katasegawa is now reported to be swarming with trout
" (*ayu*), and in its lower reaches the young mullet (*ina*) can be
" netted for the mere casting. Make up your mind to just one day
" of sport." Now Atsumitsu had no faith in Tarō as theologian.
Neither fish as animal, nor the animal of a householder, can attain
supreme enlightenment as such. But he knew that if there was
any occupation of the idle kind, requiring more squatting than lively
stir, Tarō was likely to be an expert therein. Besides, in his day he
had been a very fish himself. Inclination carried the day. Tarō
was given the order to have all in readiness for the sport on the
next morning.

It was the eighth month 15th day (17th September). O-Shimo, the wife of Satake, would have raised some objection, for at this time of the year the weather is treacherous. The men laughed at her fears. With' a single retainer to do the dirty work, an aging man of fifty odd years named Dosuke, and with Tarō at the oar they pushed off from the Koshigoe beach. Taking advantage of the tide they found water to carry them across the sand strip between Enoshima and Katase. Entering the river Tarō rowed steadily up its winding course far above the groves of Fujisawa Yūgyōji. Then they halted and drifted very slowly down stream, fishing and netting as they went. The Katasegawa is a beautiful stream, bordered by pine woods and cedar groves more thick and continuous then than now. It varies in width from a bare thirty feet to ten times this distance at its dangerous mouth. The river has a reputation for dark and treacherous depths far up its course, and the sea so close at hand backs up its waters, so that in conjunction with squalls sweeping down from the neighbouring hills difficult and uncertain currents are created. But there are more dangerous things than currents. The sun was declining, the sport had been bad, the *saké* had been consumed mostly by Atsumitsu, and the worthy *daimyō* was ready for home. Tarō, with an eye to the rising breeze, plead for time. " One more cast over yonder in the shadow of the trees. The spot " looks likely. Our empty hands and efforts will be derided." He directed the boat to the deep pool. Dosuke in the bow had sunk into slumber. Atsumitsu and Tarō were at the stern. The former prepared to make one deep and mighty cast of the net. Far over he leaned to plunge it far down within the water. As he did so Tarō strained thighs and oar until they cracked with the effort. The boat made a sudden tilt, and into the water went Satake Atsumitsu head first. This was no serious matter for he swam like a fish. As he rose to the surface and struck out for the boat Yokoyama Tarō lifted the heavy oar and struck him a hard blow over the head. " Atsu ! " This was all Atsumitsu said. Yokoyama quickly dropped the oar, and seizing the net involved the infortunate and stunned man in its toils. Then with the oar he pressed him down under the water. His struggles soon ceased. Yokoyama turned to meet

Yokoyama Tarō kills Atsumitsu.

the astonished and frightened eyes of Dosuke. "Ah! Yokoyama
"Dono! This is a wicked act to do. What now will become of the
"Satake House, his lordship perished in this manner and none to
"guard it! A bad and wicked act; thus to slay one's lord. Life
"cannot be restored, and what is more valued than life?"—"True
"enough," grumbled Yokoyama. "Dosuke's life answers for his
"silence. Fool! Prepare to receive a sword cut." Drawing his
weapon he sprang toward the man. Dosuke did not wait to be cut
down. He tumbled over the bow into the water. Yokoyama
looked over, under, around the boat. No sign of the man appeared.
Uncertain in which direction he had disappeared he hesitated before plunging after him. The sun had set, and in the darkness
of the wood it was not easy to make out so small an object
as a man's head. However Yokoyama was certain he had not risen
to the surface unobserved. Dosuke was a blunderer, in water as on
land. For that reason he had selected him to attend the day's
sport. The minutes passed with no sign of the man. Growled
Yokoyama—"He is no fish. Tarō is sure of that. The stiff and
"clumsy fellow has been held down by the reeds. Doubtless he
"stands below, eyes wide open, hands tightly grasping what has
"killed him. Good riddance to a bad witness. Now for Satake
"Dono, ex-lord of Ōta!" He pulled the dead man's body to the
surface and extricated it from the net. Then rowing down stream
to the mouth of the river he came to land. With a sigh he looked
himself over. Then pushing the boat he waded back into the
stream until his garments and person were thoroughly soaked.
Turning the craft over he gave it a shove seaward. Returning
to shore he threw Atsumitsu over his shoulders and proceeded to
the Satake *yashiki*.

It was late, and with the exception of the guard at the gate
and a single light at the entrance of the inner apartments all was
in darkness. At the approach of a man's heavy step the guard challenged. "Open!" replied Yokoyama "Let me pass unobserved.
"His lordship has taken too much *saké* and this Tarō has carried
"him home."—"Kowa! The *okugata* (lady wife) is very anxious.
"With reverence salutation is made. Great will be the joy at this

" auspicious return of Tarō Dono." Yokoyama first made his way
to the apartment of Atsumitsu ; leaving the body there he sought out
his sister. O-Shimo gazed at his dripping garments and gloomy
face with growing terror. " It is very late ; but surely nothing has
" happened. Why so wet Tarō? And Atsumitsu Dono?"—
Yokoyama made sign to her to let him speak. " Alas! Sister
" you must have courage. Remember that you are the wife of a
" samurai, prepared always to entertain bad tidings. An accident of
" fearful import has taken place. At the entrance of the river the
" tide did not serve. Attempting to pass the bore at the mouth the
" boat was upset. Atsumitsu had taken much *saké* and never rose
" to the surface. Dosuke was drowned. Although this Tarō made
" every effort it was only after some hours that he could secure the
" body of our lord. See! Here he lies." Thus ' with eight hundred lies in his mouth ' he lead her to the apartment of Atsumitsu
and pushed back the *shōji.* O-Shimo was as turned to stone. The
full import of the disaster, in connection with her grief for the loss
of her husband fell upon her. How meet the situation? Squatting
on the floor Yokoyama shed water like a duck and copious tears.
In the midst of this scene appeared Terute. A glance and she was
beside the body of her father, her beloved companion. Weeping
she called upon him, breathed into the silent lips, clasped him to
the warmth of her young body. Protests and prayers from O-
Shimo made her turn toward her elders. Yokoyama Tarō had
abandoned tears for action. " This Tarō has been most unfortu-
" nate. To perish thus ignobly, strangled by the waters of this filthy
" stream, is the result of some deed performed in a previous exis-
" tence. That Atsumitsu should thus meet his end is no fault of mine.
" But Yasuhide is a samurai. It is fit occasion to cut belly. Now
—" forthwith—at once ! " With rising crescendo and great deliberation he seated himself upright and opened his garments. With
greater deliberation he drew his dagger and carefully examined its
edge. With greatest deliberation he heaved a slow and mighty sigh
and prepared for action. Of course these well directed efforts at-
tained their object. The frightened O-Shimo seized one arm. The
tearful Terute threw herself on the other. Both wept and plead

strenuously with the implacable Tarō to hold his hand. If he killed
himself the House of Satake had nowhere to turn for aid, no blood
relation to press for the restoration to the House of its honours forfeited by the ignoble death of Atsumitsu. For their sake he must
condescend to forego his noble intention. Such pleadings carried
conviction. Yokoyama ' as if ill from his own hardships leaned over
the spit-jar to conceal his growing laughter.'

Then he asked for dry garments. To O-Shimo he said—
" Keep this matter strictly secret from all until arrangements can
" be made to support the House. Tarō will consult Yūki Ujitomo
" at once. He is young, but the *karō* will advise support. The
" Oguri are to be relied on. Thus will Uesugi Norizane be brought in.
" The fiefs will be retained in the Satake House. If the news of such
" a plum fallen to the ground gets abroad there will be demand at
" once for forfeiture. The prince has many in his train to favour.
" Terute is a girl and mere child. Be careful to say nothing.
" Show no grief or sign of loss." With this he left the *yashiki*,
but not to seek Yūki Dono. At dawn he entered the mansion of
Isshiki Akihide at Sasamegayatsu. He even seemed to be expected·
Ushered at once into the private room of Akihide the two men sat
down opposite each other. Akihide eyed Yokoyama in open admiration, even with a little fear. " Ideya! Tarō Dono is not only
" fertile in wicked plans, but bold in the execution. Thus to drown
" Atsumitsu is a master stroke "—" And how did your lordship learn
" of it," replied Yokoyama, somewhat nettled at Akihide's acumen
or early information. Said Akihide shortly—" You should have
" finished with the old fellow. He swims like a fish and soon got
" to shore. Fortunately he fell into the hands of some of my *kerai*,
" and they brought him here after securing his story. There you are
" safe, but if the tale gets out it is sure to reach the ear of Prince
" Mochiuji, and Tarō will end badly." He eyed Yokoyama sharply.
Replied the latter gravely—" Your lordship and this Tarō have
" too much to gain by this affair. The fiefs of Satake are forfeited
" through the ignoble and disloyal nature of his end. With this
" information first to hand and his favour with the prince their
" guard will certainly be given to Akihide Dono. As for this Tarō,

" your lordship can find no more devoted vassal than myself, one
" more fit for use. Secure to me the wardship of my niece Terute.
" When your lordship chooses to secure the restoration of the Satake
" House who can [better be charged with your interests than my
" humble self." Replied Isshiki—"What a treacherous fellow you are
" Tarō. You have an eye not only to property but to the premature.
" The matter has been thought out very completely. Accept the
" congratulations of Akihide over the happy issue of your venture,
" past and future. On such a basis agreed between us Tarō Dono
" can regard himself as secure. Now for the Kwanryō and an au-
" dience." Isshiki made ready to urge his claims on Prince Mochiuji
without delay. Yokoyama Tarō left the *yashiki*, and with due
slowness made his way to the distant Yūki mansion, to make report
as a matter of form to Yūki Ujitomo, that is to his *karō*.*

The news of the death of Satake Atsumitsu created a sensation.
The fief was a large one at Ōta in Hitachi, and the struggle over it
was certain to be fierce owing to the manner of its lord's death.
Yūki Ujitomo was new to his position. He sought the support of
the older and more experienced Oguri Mitsushige. Thus valuable
time was lost. They were forestalled. On petition being made it
was found that the fief had been put in the guard of Isshiki Akihide,
and Terute in the ward of Yokoyama Tarō. The only resource was
the Shitsuji Norisada. Wearied and ill he heard the plea of Ujitomo
with great gravity and some irritation at the inexperience of his
petitioner and the craft of Isshiki. " How has the fellow obtained
" such early news of this event? Fortune itself seems to favour his
" slanderous tongue by granting him a fox's ears. But that is a
" matter for Ujinori.† " Then he made reply to Yūki Dono. " As
" already adjudicated the matter is difficult. However it can be
" presented to the suzerain in council. This is all Norisada can offer."
Ujitomo bowed to the *tatami* (mats) in gratitude, and Norisada

---

* The *karō*, or chief retainer, was a most august person. He was the prime
minister of the daimyō, in fiefs of which the administration was almost absolute
in its powers, especially in the Ashikaga period of a weak central government.

† Norisada died in the 11th month (December) of Ōei 18th year. Uesugi
Ujinori of the Inukake branch became Shitsuji in his place.

called for his *norimon* (litter) to go to the Ōkura palace.   As Prince
Mochiuji took his seat at the council he turned to the Shitsuji for
direction.   "The business of the day; has the Shitsuji matter for
"attention?"   With obeisance answered Norisada—"There are
"some details connected with the Satake affair which might incline
"the August Presence to give favourable ear and receive the reveren-
"tial thanks of the survivors of the family of the late Satake Atsumi-
"tsu. His long and devoted service to the suzerain's father and grand-
"father are well known, and the favour he enjoyed but recently
"from the revered ancestor Mitsukane Kō, in the destruction of the
"maleficent Kwannondō of Sasamegayatsu is fresh to mind.   As
"there is an heir the opportunity offers for the suzerain to show bene-
"volence, and if it seems good to permit the restoration of the House
"and revocation of the decree of deprivation of honours and fiefs
"(*kai-eki*) Such is the petition to the suzerain, humbly presented
"by the Houses of Yūki and Oguri."

Then Isshiki came forward.   He glowered so fiercely that the
prince had to call him to himself by a genial and encouraging look.
Said Isshiki—"The Shitsuji does not put the matter correctly.
"There is no male heir to Satake Hitachi no Suke Atsumitsu.
"There is a girl, a mere child, Terute. Atsumitsu lost his life seeking
"his own pleasure and forgetful of his lord's service. His end was
"an ignoble lack of breath in the foul waters of the Katasegawa.
"The suzerain has already given decision most justly, and the
"decree should stand. These fiefs are in his lordship's distribution,
"dependent only on his favour. Other interests have no claim in
"the suzerain's decision."   Giving Isshiki full view of his posteriors
Norisada at once spoke to press his strongest point—"But the
"suzerain has been misinformed as to this Yokoyama Tarō, chosen
"as guardian of the girl Terute. The wardship is a mere blind.
"He has the girl herself in view. He is a thoroughly bad man, and
"was deprived of his fief by the revered ancestor Prince Ujimitsu,
"maintaining as he did a place half brothel and half den of thieves
"to the terror of his neighbourhood and the danger of travellers.
"His lack of courage to behave as a samurai, or to shave his head, is
"the only reason he is still in life. Such a man is notably unfit to

" have in ward the heiress of the Satake House." Isshiki was ready
" of tongue—" A well known political case! Tarō Yasuhide had
" enemies. Why, for years he has lived in the house of Atsumitsu,
" protected by him ; and Prince Mitsukane, father of our revered
" lord, knew and condoned his offence. Doubtless he intended the
" early restoration to favour and service of so able a man."

Mochiuji Ason, the Kwanryō, was puzzled. He looked from
Norisada to Akihide, and from Akihide to Norisada. He turned
to his council. These supported Norisada to a man, endorsing the
character given of Yokoyama Tarō. Isshiki sneered—" The talk
" and advice would be different in the absence of the Shitsuji. You
" are all afraid of the Uesugi. However it is a bad thing to revoke an
" adjudication made on so well determined precedent as in the
" case of the forfeiture of these fiefs. The disposition of the matter
" lies in the hands of the suzerain alone. None can interfere
" with his sovereign will, and he has already decided. Be
" silent." He spoke in loud and angry tones. Norisada rebuked him—" An humble and reverential attitude and conduct
" in the Presence, this only is befitting. It is the place of Aki-
" hide to prostrate himself and hear the decision of the Prince.
" Else plead indisposition and leave the council." But
Isshiki was not likely to leave. He saw by the expression of
Mochiuji that his last plea had gone home. " The matter has
" been adjudicated and cannot be re-opened. When the girl Terute
" is of age the question of a husband will be an issue. Until then
" matters are to remain as they are. Thanks, reverential though
" they be and pleasant to receive, can be valued too highly.
" Precedent is to be observed." Taking the sting out of his words
with a pleasing smile cast toward the Shitsuji, Mochiuji rose in
signal of dismissal and left the council chamber. Norisada gave
account of the sitting to the anxious Yūki Ujitomo. The affair
was difficult. It had been adjudicated and nothing could be done
until Terute was of nubile age and left the protection of her
guardian. Here the contract with the Oguri would avail. Meanwhile they must wait. Yūki Ujitomo was a youth well endowed
with patience.

Not so was it with others. Isshiki Akihide had at once told his brother Sakyū no Tayū Naokane to take possession of the Satake *yashiki*, and this had been done long since. O-Shimo and Terute, in the charge of a retainer of Yokoyama had set out for Musashi, to a fief held by the favour of Akihide. They were stripped of all the great possessions and consequence of the Satake House. Yokoyama had hastened the departure. His intentions and hostility to the Oguri were made manifest. Terute timidly raised the question with her mother as to the espousal with Sukeshige and the necessity of consulting the Oguri; but when her mother addressed Tarō on the subject great was his wrath. "Terute is the "only representative of the House of Atsumitsu; as is Kojirō "Sukeshige of the Oguri. He can only enter this House as *muko* "(adopted son as husband of the daughter) ; otherwise Terute would "leave the House, unfilial conduct and the unpardonable sin. The "subject henceforth is to be dropped, and her feelings to be directed "elsewhere." As said Yokoyama Tarō was a most indifferent theologian, but his tongue was glib and his power now was great. O-Shimo was much less difficult to convince than Terute. After-all Tarō Yasuhide was her brother. But Terute kept silence, and Yokoyama could gain no sign of consent from her of broken troth. The very day of his interview with Isshiki he sent the two women from Kamakura. With the support behind him he felt sure of the issue of events in his favour at the court of the Kwanryō.

The Oguri had sent at once to bring mother and daughter to the Inamuragasaki *yashiki*, but they were baffled by the tergiver-sations and cynical hostility of Yokoyama now in full charge. The early transfer of the *yashiki* to the charge of Naokane gave notice that the women were no longer in residence. Inquiry showed that Yūki Ujitomo knew no more as to their whereabouts than the Oguri themselves. Meanwhile one day there came in haste to the Satake mansion a samurai of the fighting country stock. At the entrance he was halted by the guard. Said he—"The dreadful fate "of my lord Satake Atsumitsu is known. The house is extinguished "and the fiefs forfeited. But this visit is made to the Okugata (lady "wife), and the lady Terute. Deign to grant admittance to

" them." Said the guard—" With such matters we have nothing
" to do. We are merely on guard at the *yashiki*. None can be
" given entrance." And as the samurai persisted—" What a fellow !
" He seems to have no ears. Isshiki Dono! Here is a filthy
" rascal asking whether he can enter or not"—" Neither," was the
blunt reply of Naokane. " If he is obstinate, arrest him." Taking
this for an order, and the obstinacy being evident, the guard
rushed out on all sides to seize Mito no Kosuke, the *karō* of the
Satake House just come in great haste from the fief in Hitachi.
Kosuke laughed. " Ah! Fox-samurai! You shall soon be
minus your tails." As they made at him to knock him down
with the staves, he gathered the points in a bundle and sent the
holders sprawling on the ground. " Their bodies were as flying
birds " as he seized first one fellow and then another coming to
attack him. Swords were drawn and there was a rush toward
him. But Kosuke too had drawn his weapon. Three men lay
dead on the ground, and others wounded withdrew in haste.
Seizing a heavy bar near-by Kosuke rushed at the closed gate (*mon*).
At the third blow it gave way and he burst in. An arrow grazed
his hair and killed a crow seated in solemn meditation on the roof.
" Fit game for such carrion," jeered Kosuke. He ran from room
to room. The private apartments were empty. Every sign of the
women or of woman was removed. Evidence of feasting and riot
was ample. Pained at heart and angry Kosuke again sought the
entrance (*genkuan*). The *yakunin* were gathering. It was
merely throwing away his life to remain. With a last look he
turned away and made his exit from the rear. Well on his way
over the hill to Fukazawa and the road to Fujisawa he came
suddenly on his younger brother Koshirō. " Ah! Kosuke; and
" her ladyship ? "—" Gone," was the reply of Kosuke. " But this
" is no time to cut belly or act rashly." Said Koshirō—" The
" Oguri Dono also are in search of them."—Said Kosuke—" The
" same task lies before this Kosuke and Koshirō. Living in
" disguise among the common people the place of their seques-
" tration will soon be found. Yokoyama Tarō and Isshiki Akihide
" in all likelihood are at the bottom of this affair. This ascertained

" they are to be put to death." Thus agreed the brothers left Kamakura for the North ; to conceal themselves at Kanzasa-mura, their object in life to find the whereabouts of the *himegimi*, the Lady Terute.

CHAPTER IV.

The Valiants of Oguri.

The Tanabe brothers; Mito no Kotarō; the Gotō brothers.

It was the twenty first year of Ōei (1414) and Kojirō Suke-shige was fast approaching his nineteenth year. Matters had changed somewhat for him. A decent time from the death of Hatsuse having elapsed, Mitsushige took to his bed one of the attendant maids at the *yashiki*, a woman named Fujinami the daughter of a fisherman of Miura district. In earlier days she had acted as nurse to Kojirō. She was thirty-five years old, possessed few good looks, and habit rather than other qualification was her recommendation to the old Daimyō. At all events, by one expiring effort, from the flanks of this mare he was presented with a son, and as usual the infant became the chosen object of affection of his aging father. Fujinami had every intention of securing the succession of the Oguri House to Manchō at the cost of Sukeshige. At this time "fair" means only were present to her thoughts. Her first object was to re-move Sukeshige from Kamakura into the accidents of strife. Fortune favoured her. Early in the government of Mochiuji Kō, Uesugi Ujinori of the Inukake branch of the powerful family had been made Shitsuji (premier). He had been a favourite of Prince Mitsu-kane, who had sent him to the North to aid in suppressing the re-bellion of Masamune against the Ōshū Kwanryō, Ashikaga Mitsunao. Ujinori had been soundly thrashed, and Mitsukane had to send a second army to extricate him. Luck this time was with Ujinori, and numbers were against Masamune. The latter was defeated and slain. Ujinori returned with the halo of victory, and carefully nursed it by attempting nothing else. Norisada died in Ōei 18th year 11th month (November-December 1411) and was succeeded by Ujinori the son of Tomomune, who shaved his head (Nyūdō) and became priest and Shitsuji much at the same time under the name of Zenshū. The Inukake Uesugi thus alternated with the other branch of the House, and such was Ujinori's favour that they seemed firmly seated at the expense of their western cousins. This was not taking in account the uncertain temper of Ujinori. He had been Shitsuji for a few years when news came from the family centre in Hitachi province which raised his wrath and obstinacy. A retainer of the House named Koshibata Rokurō Nobuchika had offended the governor (*kokushi*). Report was made to Kamakura and the fief was confiscated. Ujinori received news of the transaction by way of Hitachi. He hastened to the palace and expostulated with Mochiuji, much as if the prince had been premier and Nyūdō the prince. Mochiuji rapidly lost all liking for his former guide, philosopher, and friend. He now sought to get rid of him. The underground contest became more and more bitter between them. As yet the Uesugi family as a whole backed their representative in view of the growing power and favour of the Isshiki lords. It was a question, however, how long the prince would stand the acid temper of the premier and his constant remonstrances. The Yamanouchi-Ogigayatsu branch was not willing to sacrifice family interests to the obvious bad temper of the Inukake Nyūdō. Hence it was willing to profit by his fall when this event occurred. Meanwhile Nyūdō Zenshū, and in Kyōto the Dainagon Minamoto Yoshitsugu, brother of the Shōgun Yoshimochi, were in unison weaving the meshes of a vast plot which was now almost matured. The Oguri of Hitachi were closely connected with the Inukake Uesugi. Mitsushige disliked the affair intensely, but in any struggle, other things being equal he was vassal of the Inukake House. When matters therefore had to be looked into in Hitachi, pleading his age and inactivity he sent his son Sukeshige to act as Hangwan-dai (vice-Hangwan*) in

---

* The office of Hangwan properly speaking is judicial. In ancient times this high official directly represented the lord acting in his judicial function. But, as with the lord, his powers also were executive—as in Europe of the

his stead.   Ostensibly the mission was to suppress the robber bands
said to be roaming the province ; really it was to ensure the prompt
answer of the Oguri retainers at the call of their lord.

Sukeshige therefore set out for Hitachi, accompanied by the *karō*
of the House, the able and acute Tanabe Heitayū and his two
sons, Heirokurō Nagahide and Heihachirō Nagatame.   Of these two
young men, the first of the Valiants, more is to be said later. Simply
noting the fact, Sukeshige can be accompanied across the Musashi
plain into Shimosa, along the banks of the Sakuragawa (Tsukubaga-
wa) as he skirted the slopes of the famous mountain, until he reached
his native town and castle of Oguri at the foot of the hills of western
Hitachi in what is now Makabe-gori (district or parish).   It was
while his preparations were being made to attack the robber bands
that the following tale reached his ears.

When the Satake House had been extinguished and its retainers scattered, Mito no Kosuke the *karō*, unwilling to give up the
search for his lady as long as he had life and any means to prose-
cute it, had retired to Hirai in Shimotsuke province (now in Shi-
tsuga district on the Naganogawa, not far from Tochigi).   Here he
was not too far from the fief of his lord in Hitachi, and yet too far
to come under the watchful eyes and ears of the Isshiki retainers
established on the fief, with due attention to any attempts of the
rōnin of the extinguished House.   With him lived his son Kotarō
no Tamehisa, and his two nephews Gotō Hyōsuke Suketaka and
Daihachirō Takatsugu.   Kotarō was but twenty years old ; Daihachirō was twenty-two years old ; and Hyōsuke, who later became
the *karō* of Oguri Sukeshige, was already twenty six years old.   All
three young men were noted for soldierly accomplishments, especially
on the racetrack and in the fencing school.   Kamakura under
Ujimitsu and Mitsukane had offered less opportunity for active
service in the field.   Kosuke lived as a *gōshi* farmer (gentleman
farmer), and the three young men passed as his sons.

Middle Ages, whether king or baron. To-day the Executive dominates and
interferes with the Judiciary in Japan ; but the office of Hangwan is confined to
the law-court. The *kokushi* was an imperial officer, the *shugo* the military
governor. At this date the powers of the *kokushi* were nearly extinguished.

One morning it was determined to go hunting. The foothills of Shimotsuke were close at hand, and the three were soon deep in the forest. The very demon of ill luck, however, pursued them. The day wore on, the game usually so plentiful seemed to have notice of their coming. Not a sign of living creature could be detected. It was already three o'clock and darkness came early in the late fall days. Mito no Kotarō was the first to make a reasonable proposal. " We are going back empty handed and will be well derided. Let " us at least cover as much ground as possible. Deign to go straight " forward up the valley. This Kotarō going westward will girdle " the hill. Thus perhaps luck will fall to one of us, or we may drive the game into each other's track." The idea was adopted. With respectful salutation they parted, the Gotō brothers going up the valley. Mito no Kotarō turned to scramble up the hill and come down into the neighbouring valley to the West. The scrambling up went famously. The downward course threatened disaster. Stepping on a bed of dried leaves, scattered brushwood, and general forest rubbish of stones, moss, sticks, calculated to deceive the sight, Kotarō found himself precipitated into a deep hole. Sitting up somewhat stunned by the fall he looked upward into a track of light far above him. Emerging from the mass of rubbish and stones which had accompanied him in his fall he tried to get some idea of his surroundings. Stretch as far as he was able with his bow he could not reach the roof of the cavern. Things had come to a pretty pass ! Obviously the way out was not the way in, unless he had wings. He was in the midst of a wild forest to which the villagers rarely resorted except for game. Rescue in that way was unlikely. He had no prospect of other company than his own. This would get tiresome. Alas ! He would become the *nushi* (demon) of the place, devoid of any worshippers but the hares and bears, and these already knew him to avoid him. Truly fortune might have distinguished him a little better. Hundreds of years hence perhaps a later generation would find his whitened bones and rusted sword, and make the Ō-Ana-Sama an object of reverence and worship in a huge temple. But long since his unfortunate ghost would be worn thread-bare through lack of sustenance. What light was there to illuminate such a gloomy outlook?

Then it was impressed on him that what light there was, shining before his eyes, was not above him but in front of him. He looked up. Yes, there were two sources of illumination, the place of his descent, and a luminous point at some distance before his eyes. Was it supernatural? Kotarō loosened his sword in the scabbard and groped his way toward the place where this second light appeared. The cave widened. Then came the sound of running water. A few moments brought him to the entrance of the cave, below which flowed a mountain stream. Truly he was fortunate. Doubless this was the valley of his pilgrimage for game. Should he go up or down? He was thirsty and bent down to drink. Watsu! He drew back. The waters of the little stream were flowing red. Thought Kotarō, " Someone is washing women's " skirts up-stream. The dye is poor and runs out. Assuredly a " village will be found above where guidance as to the road can be " obtained." With a spring from the mouth of the cave he cleared the little stream and directed his steps up its course. Soon he came upon a woman crouched by the side of the brook. Vigorously she was pounding and rubbing garments which seemed to be soaked in a red dye. Zabu, zabu, zabu she scrubbed away. " Kowa! " thought Kotarō; " what a pretty girl! Who would suspect that " such a beauty was hidden away in a mountain valley! Miyako " itself could claim such a prize—Nesan! (Elder sister). Fallen " in a cave thus awkwardly the way on the mountain has been lost. " Doubtless there is a village above, where direction and refreshment " can be found." The woman looked up with a start. Fear at the sight of a man, and pity for the handsome fellow appeared in her face. She answered—" Alas! I too am a stranger here. " Gladly would direction be given ...... " Kotarō, who was sharply eyeing the garments she was washing, abruptly interrupted her. Said he—" Nesan, what is that you are washing? "—" Blood ; by " no means continue your course up the stream. Above is the den " of the infamous thief Chikuma Tarō. He and his band levy " tribute far and wide on the neighbouring villages, plundering the

" farmers and carrying off the girls.   The more likely and compliant
" are sold, to be taken by kidnappers to the Nakasendō towns and
" even to the capital.   Those who are not compliant to the wishes
" of the thieves have their breasts cut off as punishment.   Such a
" woman has just suffered in this way.   She was proud and
·' rebellious, and the chief, as example to the rest of us, delivered
" her over to the band to suffer.   It is her garments that are being
" washed.   Her flesh will be cooked for the wine banquet which
" is their nightly riot.   Doubtless, honoured sir, you are some
" young farmer of the neighbourhood.   My father, a gōshi-
" samurai of Shimotsuke, was summoned with his men to attend
" his lord at Oyama.   In his absence the thieves raided the village
" and carried me off with other women.   Deign to make your
" way hence to safety.   Your torture will be sport at their foul
" feasting.   By no means go further."

Kotarō eyed her with pity.   She was now weeping.   " Nesan,
" take heart.   It is neither farmer nor skulker who speaks.   You
" and your companions shall see home again.   Do but say where
" these thieves harbour.   Chikuma soon shall have his own ransom
" to pay."   He pointed with his bow vaguely up-stream, half in
menace, half in inquiry.   The woman understood.   Joyfully she
seized his sleeve and prostrated herself.   " Above will be found a
" log bridge and a road once good.   This is a mere blind, the
" remnants of a stronghold of the wars of Nitta Taishō.   The
" thieves have left it as it is, to misguide those seeking honest
" quarters.   Keep to the bank of the stream.   Soon a stone gate
" (sekimon) is reached.   This is the outer guard.   May the kami
" (gods) protect you and grant success.   But deign to reconsider the
" enterprise."   Kotarō gently released the sleeve she still clung to
as if to turn him from the venture.   " Don't be afraid.   Act as
" usual in your duties and give the thieves no cause of suspicion."

Leaving her he followed the directions.   Turning into the
footpath at the bridge he entered the forest and began to climb the
trail which ran over and up the cliffs bordering the brook.   Soon
he came to a kind of clearing.   In this was a stone wall and gate.
Kotarō began to bawl at the top of his lungs—" Heh !   Yai !

" Aiya ! With fear and reverence deign to grant a stranger lost
" on the mountain a night's lodging. Hungry and tired it is not
" possible to go further, nor to feed on the drugs gathered." At
this last a rough fellow appeared at the gate. " Drugs ! Are you
" a doctor, and did the devil himself (*onisama*) bring you here?
" This is neither hospice nor hotel*. But since you have got here
" you are reasonably sure to stay ...... Buta San, go and notify
" Chikuma Dono that a doctor is at hand. Perhaps a cure can be
" found for his arrow wound. As for you, Sir Leech, cool your
" heels and your liver for a time." The wait was not for long.
Chikuma Tarō, wounded in his recent raid into the plains, was only
too glad to hear the name of doctor. He ordered that the medical
man and his impedimenta be at once brought before him. " Cure
" first and payment afterward," was his grim thought. " However,
" after all the fraternity needs a leech as well as leman."

With some astonishment he scrutinized Kotarō as he was
introduced. Such a medical equipment Chikuma had never seen,
but he remembered that his experience was small. His treatment for the ills of life had been *saké*, and more *saké*, stolen
at that. What a bandage and a drunken bout would not
cure he regarded as hopeless. Nothing but his fright and pain
now reconciled him to other treatment. He would much have
preferred the doctor's head as such, to its operation on himself. Meanwhile the inspection had been mutual. When introduced into the dimly lighted hall Kotarō saw a huge unwieldy
body seated on a pile of cushions arranged on a sort of dais. From
a shock of hair like to that of the demon-queller Shōki shone two
fierce brightly gleaming eyes. The drunken low-browed hairy
fellow swayed from side to side. " Naruhodo ! Does a leech carry
a bow ? " growled Chikuma, savagely eyeing the youth. Kotarō
laughed. " That is for rabbits, not for drugs. The honoured teacher
" requires not only plants, to be gathered in the mountain recesses,
" but a savoury stew to strengthen his aging body, to be gathered
" in the warrens."—" And the *mukahagi* (greaves) ? They savour

---

* *Yado* or *yashiki*. The latter, by the way, has something of the sense of
the old French " hotel."

" more of war than of weeds "—Calmly answered Kotarō ; " If
" my humble self were a samurai. See ! They hang quite loosely.
" Often in the mountain excursions wolves are met, and poisonous
" snakes. These are to protect the legs against their fangs."

Chikuma grunted. He was suspicious, but a fierce twinge in
the swollen arm turned the current of his thoughts. " There is a
" slight wound here in the arm, a matter of no moment. Doubtless
" it can be cured without difficulty. If so the reward will be such
" that the leech will never need to go abroad for drugs again. So
" deign to be at ease. Apply the drugs and gain the reward."
Said Kotarō—" To do that it is first necessary to examine the
" wound. Umu ! Is that to be called slight ! The arm is swollen
" to twice its size. This blackness indicates rotting flesh. This does
" not hurt you ? " He poked an arrow point into the darkness.
Chikuma made no movement. Then he touched lightly the swollen
red mass surrounding the black. Chikuma howled. He made a
half-sign for the supposed doctor's annihilation. Fright at the
unsightly mass of corruption held his hand. Kotarō to all appearance had eyes for nothing but the wound. "This must be treated
" at once ; a little pain to be sure ; not too much. Then a dress-
" ing according to a hereditary formula, and a short time will see
" the wound healed. Release from all pain is promised, and that
" very soon."—" And this Tarō shall have the formula ? " said
the eager thief—" The formula you certainly shall have," was the
very grave reply.

" There must be a number of women in a grand place like this.
" They are the proper attendants. Let these fellows give room,
" and have the women bring saké, plenty of linen, and a sharpened
" bamboo stick." At a sign from Chikuma the thieves filled the
lower end of the hall. Women came bringing the required articles.
Soft linen, stolen from the Kyōto traders ; hot water in beautiful
brass bowls stolen from the rich gōshi in the neighbourhood ; saké
stolen from the villagers. Only the spring water had an honest
source. Kotarō first examined his patient. In good truth this
gangrened mass needed prompt removal. Grasping the wrist he
felt the pulse. *Dab, dab, dab, dabu, dab, dabu, dab*—" It is good

" that accident led me here. The fever is in a very bad way. The
" tongue? Red, pale red! If white you were a dying man;
" if black the fever would finish you.* Be patient. Only a
" little pain, and then........." Kotarō grasped the pointed bamboo
stick and thrust it deep into the wound. He twisted and tore and
cut. Chikuma roared and howled, and the minor thieves roared and
bawled in chorus. "Fushi!" mumbled Chikuma. "What pain!
" A thousand arrow wounds are to be preferred to such treatment.
" Ah! It hurts! It hurts! Sir leech the reward shall be still
" greater than intended. Every pleasure shall be offered (my
" company). No new device (of torment) shall be omitted.
" Aiya!"—"Don't wriggle," was the only comment of Kotarō.
" This treatment is that handed down by the famous Sōtō of Sō
" no Kuni (China). But tradition says that by such Shin no Jofuku
" escaped all injury for many decades, to die of extreme old age in
" this happy Nippon. There! The bandage?" He drew this tight
over the raw and bloody mass, exerting his full strength. Chikuma
sighed—not with pleasure. "This Tarō finds nothing in the
remedy," he groaned. "The pain is much greater than ever
before"—"That is because the other arm is in sympathy with the
" wounded arm. It still transmits its pulsations. Let that be
" bandaged too and the pain will disappear." Obediently Chikuma
Tarō held out his left hand. Kotarō wrapped the sound arm with
the same mechanical care and completeness as the other. He held
the two ends of the bandages. A quick jerk and the giant's arms
were tightly bound behind his back. At last Chikuma Tarō saw
light. "Ah! What a rascal of a doctor. Tarō is a prisoner."—
" Truly so," quoth Kotarō. "Where to put the rascal? Ah!
" The pillar." He dragged Chikuma to the post close by, and
bound him tightly thereto with his *obi* (girdle). The thieves and
Chikuma joined in an uproar. Kotarō drew the sword of Chikuma
and stood by the helpless chief. "Now minor thieves; if any raise
" a hand the chief loses his life. Obey orders and he shall be re-
" leased. Meanwhile the women are to bring *saké* and fish—
" no other flesh." He shuddered a little at the idea of the horrible

---

* For these medical details Takarai is relied on. Cf. the *kōdan*.

feast doubtless already in preparation. Then he neatly piled the cushions beside the helpless Chikuma, where he could watch chief and followers. The women served him as if he were Chikuma himself. *Gaburi, gaburi,* he gobbled. Thus he is to be left to this occupation.

Meanwhile it is time to turn to the fortune of the brothers. For some time they climbed and descended, clambered, and rolled through the unkempt forest. Not a sign of game was to be seen. Truly they were unlucky. There was nothing to do but to turn homeward. As they were about to do so the cry of a deer was heard. Eagerly they looked in the direction, but nothing was to be seen. Again— *kii, kii,* came the sound ; yet nothing in sight. Said Daihachirō— " One would think it came from the trees, but deer are not birds." Cautiously they advanced. Then the cry came almost over their heads. Looking up, to their astonishment a huge serpent was seen* coiled on the massive bough of a *hebi matsu.* It had grasped the deer by the hind legs, and the half-swallowed and dying animal was uttering the feeble cries in this strange process of digestion. The huge knots of the tree, simulating the serpent's coils, made it too seem as if alive. Hyōsuke strung an arrow. Zip—the shaft went straight into the left eye of the snake. A second arrow pierced its gullet and came out at the back. Slowly the monster uncoiled. Letting drop the deer it began to descend the trunk of the tree, and then advanced glaring furiously on the two brothers who stood their ground valourously. Said Hyōsuke—" Daihachirō, have the sword in readiness." He strung a third shaft. Taking careful aim he let fly. Straight the arrow went to the right eye of the huge serpent. A moment later its severed head lay on the ground. Daihachirō kicked the still writhing body. " A famous shot brother. What a " laugh on Kotarō. Doubtless he has obtained nothing and has " gone home. See ! It is already night. Let us take the deer and " the head. Why abandon such trophies ? " Said Hyōsuke— " Yes, we can expect no other fortune now ; but we are more likely " to spend the night in the forest than reach Hirai. Torches grow

---

* Tales of such huge serpents are common. *One* haunts the hills around Kamakura, "seen" from time to time. It is known (1914) as the *hebi-nushi ;* and haunts the Kōgane-iwaya more particularly. There is a fine *ryūtō no matsu* (*hebi matsu*) on the hill-top to the left of the Kwōmyōji ; and a good view.

The Adventure of the Gotō Brothers.

" on trees, but not ready lighted. However some hunter's hut will
" harbour us for the night."

Forthwith the snake's head was thrust into the hunter's bag
they carried. Shouldering the deer the two young men took their
way down the nearest valley. As they stumbled along a light was
seen among the trees. Soon they came to a stone gate. No one
was on guard, but on entering many men were seen in a dimly
lighted hall reverentially prostrate (o-jigi) before one who seemed to
be their chief. He was being served with wine and food by a
number of beautiful women, who seemed both anxious and ready to
please. In the smoke of torches and the dim light his features
could not be made out, but it was plain that he was young. A man
was tied to a post near-by. Doubtless this was some captive or recalcitrant awaiting punishment from the chief of the band. Said
Hyōsuke—" A suspicious place! Plainly it is a den of thieves.
" But we will ask lodging, and before morning add this fellow's head
" to the one we already possess." Approaching boldly he claimed
shelter from the row of men nearest to the verandah (rōka). " We
" have been overtaken by darkness in the forest. Deign to grant
" shelter for the night and receive reverential thanks." Far from
showing the spirit and impudence their numbers and calling war-
ranted, the thieves were thoroughly cowed. The sight of
this addition to their enemy's forces paralysed them. One
man had their chief captive and a hostage. These two also were
evidently samurai. The thieves were more inclined to run away
and let them do as they pleased. But Chikuma was the giant and
tower of strength of the band. Without him they were without a
head. Bowing in reverence they besought the new guests to enter.
Kotarō detected the unusual stir at the end of the hall. He was
quick to recognize the new-comers. " Ah! Strangers "; he bellowed.
" Lodging? That shall you have. Thieves are notoriously gene-
" rous—with other people's goods. Enter forthwith. Your enter-
" tainment shall be generous and your business despatched early in
" the morning. Bring more torches!" Hyōsuke was in a great
rage. " Filthy scoundrel! To brag thus of his infamous call-
" ing! His intentions toward us are as plain as his words. Draw

" your sword Daihachirō. When his followers appear with the
" torches they will find the feast in other hands, bound for other
" stomachs." Silently the brothers stole through the dim light,
keeping the rough pillars between them and the man on the dais,
ready to rush on the chief of this infamous band of thieves, the
luxury of whose fare more and more attracted them with nearer
approach. But Kotarō had kept his eyes on them. As they came
quite near he used the natural tones of his voice. " Koriya ! Sure-
" ly it is Hyōsuke and Daihachirō. And who is it, honoured Sirs,
" to be cut down by your weapons ? Welcome ! My humble self
" is in position to offer *saké* and a banquet of fish of most excellent
" service. Deign to be careful to avoid other flesh. It is tainted.
" But the fish is good and fresh." Hyōsuke gasped and Daihachirō
gaped. Both let drop the points of their swords. " Kotarō !
" Turned thief ! "—" Not exactly," replied Kotarō. " Here is the
" genuine thief, and chief of this band ; Chikuma Tarō. But to the
" banquet." The thieves had now returned with fresh torches. The
women merrily served fish and wine. Hyōsuke and Daihachirō
thus unexpectedly broke their fast and rejoiced at such an adventure. Snake and deer ? This was small game compared to the
catch of Kotarō. Warm were their congratulations.

Then Kotarō spoke. " It is time to leave. The promise is to
" be carried out. Guides are to be furnished to the waterfall which
" is a *ri* (2½ miles) from Hirai-mura. Tarō goes in company as hostage.
" The women are to be set free. These are our words." Humbly the
thieves made obeisance, and set out to show by their torches the way
down the valley. With the captive Chikuma in their midst, and
the women in attendance, the three samurai prepared to follow.
" These fellows will always have a place of refuge if things
be left as they are," grumbled Hyōsuke. The little pig eyes
of Chikuma glittered with rage as the women collected straw,
screens, and oil. Fire was set to the mass and the buildings
were soon wrapped in flames. Then down the valley, brightly illuminated, all set forth. At the waterfall Kotarō gravely
faced the band. " Your lives are spared. The release of your chief
was promised." The thieves fell on their faces. " With fear and

reverence ; accept respectful thanks."—Continued Kotarō : " The
" same release and reward that Chikuma so generously promised
" the leech. You shall have the body ; we want his head." His
sword flashed and the hairy relic rolled on the ground, eyes glaring
and lips still twitching the muttered shout of anguished protest.
The thieves made no stand, but fled in all directions.

Kicking the body into the pool at the foot of the fall Kotarō
and the Gotō brothers proceeded with the women to the village.
Here Kosuke was still on the watch. At the hail from without the
wicket was opened. The young men approached and prostrated
themselves in reverence before their father. Kosuke looked from
them to the women. " And the game ? " said he. Daihachirō
came forward—" Alas ! There is but this to contribute." He
laid down the carcass of the deer before the *rōka*. " No mean find,"
quoth Kosuke. Then Hyōsuke advanced and presented the hunting
bag. Shaking out the snake's head the eyes of Kosuke grew large.
" Truly a monster ! The arrow wounds show the skill of Hyōsuke.
" And Kotarō—is this his game ? A fair tribute ! " He waved his
hand toward the group of pretty girls prostrate in obeisance. Replied Kotarō—" In part, revered Sir. These women are at your
" honoured order and disposal. This is the other part of the same
" prize." He handed Kosuke his game bag. On opening it, out
rolled the hairy head of Chikuma Tarō. Kosuke was startled. " A
" head, even when expected, always brings surprise. Kotarō has
" acted well. Now for the tale." This was soon told. The parents
of the women were notified. With gifts these were returned to
their homes. Deep were the reverences, earnest the thanks, at this
unexpected recovery from the clutches of the wicked Chikuma.
The tale was thus spread wide through the country-side. It came to
the ears of Sukeshige, who was not long in learning the true status of
Kosuke. " Kerai of the Satake House are now kerai of Oguri.
" Let them be summoned at once by letter." Great was the joy of
Kosuke Tamekuni at the prospect opened to his sons. For himself
and Koshirō there was a mission in life, and Sukeshige willingly
accepted the excuse and apology. Dispensation was granted from
attendance in view of this more important object.

CHAPTER V.

The Valiants of Oguri.

The Kataoka Brothers; Ikeno Shōji; the Kazama Brothers.

Two more recruits were early added to the Valiants of Oguri. Soon after Kotarō and the Gotō brothers had become retainers of Sukeshige he determined on a personal inspection of the immediate surroundings of the castle. For this purpose he set forth one day accompanied by the *karō* Tanabe Heitayū and his train. The old man's eyes showed calm satisfaction as his young lord expressed his commendation at the neat and flourishing condition of field and farm house. Little indication was there here of disorder, or bandits, or other form of neglect. Sukeshige dismounted, and the horses being left with the attendants, the company started to walk across the narrow paths which separated the rice fields. The crop now was rapidly being garnered. The farmers with mattock, spade, and sickle were earnest in the fields; with the former to repair the embankments which surround every little plot, with the latter to harvest what remained of the ripened crop. The days were short and busy. There was no time to return to the village for food. The mats which served as rain coats were spread on the ground, and the frugal meal taken in company. Walking along a shoulder high embankment which carried a wider road Sukeshige heard voices. The scene attracted him, and as he halted those behind necessarily did the same. Two young men, farmers and almost boys for the oldest was not more than eighteen years, were taking their meal together. They were evidently brothers, and in friendly contest over a precedence the older insisted on yielding and the

younger refused to take. " Says Kōshi (Confucius), ' the younger
" brother shall serve the elder, who to him is as his father.' Surely
" brother you would not have me violate the fundamental precept
" of the sage "—" The Sage speaks wisely brother," replied the elder ;
" but the sage also says that the elder shall cherish the younger, guard
" and protect him, and that the younger shall obey him. You have
" been ill recently and need nourishing food. Deign first to satisfy
" your appetite to the full, as the more necessitous "—" Nay brother,
" I am fully recovered. Such kindness is to be expected of this good
" brother, but duty requires that he be given precedence "—" Nay
" brother......... "

Said Sukeshige to Heita ; " who can these youths be, with the
" precepts of the sage thus on their lips. By their garb they
" are farmers ; by their manners, courtesy, and information far
" otherwise. Heita, cause inquiry to be made." So Tanabe
going apart had one of the farmers summoned. The man
prostrated himself as dust before the powerful *karō* of his lord.
Said Tanabe—" Who are these two youths labouring at the em-
" bankment. Speak quickly and tell all you know for the information
" of his lordship "—Said the farmer ; " With fear and respect the
" answer is given. These are the sons of one Kataoka Kadayū who
" came to the village twenty years ago. Kadayū was a man of
" learning, although he took up the life of an ordinary farmer.
" Also he taught the children writing, and such numbers as their
" daily life required. He was the village *sensei* (teacher and
" pundit). To none was he more severe than to his own children ;
" and wife and child shared impartially in his rebuke. Politeness
" most perfect, consideration for others, 'and absolute truth were his
" requirements. As he said, ' children learn lying and deceit from
" their parents. Unless taught by their elders they would know
" nothing of either.' Such was his own conscientious and exact
" virtue. When the boys were budding into youth a pestilence
" reached the village. Both Kadayū and his wife perished. The
" village has adopted the two young men. Soon plots of land will
" be allotted to them and they will be regularly enrolled. Mean-
" while every farmer is glad to be teacher and father in the farmer's

"task, so highly are they esteemed. The elder is eighteen years
"old and his name is Katarō Harunori. The younger is sixteen
"years old and his name is Kajirō Harutaka." Such was the
report that Tanabe carried back to his lord. Said Sukeshige—
"Summon them hither."

The two youths this summoned showed respect but no fear.
Prostrating themselves before the lord they awaited his questions
with silent self-restraint. In no way did they act as clownish
peasants. Said Sukeshige—"It is reported that you are the sons of
"Kataoka Kadayū who came here some years ago with his wife. In
"the army of his highness Prince Minamoto Akinobu was Kataoka
"Nobuharu, the right hand man and devoted *kerai* of his lordship in
"many secret missions. Evidently you have not been brought up
"as farmers or people of low class. Tell me of your stock and
"fortunes." Replied Harunori—"With fear and respect humbly
"the command is heard. It is true that we are not properly
"farmers; but the family fortunes have been extinguished by the
"decline and fall of the South Court. With the final defeat of the
"sons of Nitta Taishō (Yoshisada) our father Harumitsu lost all hope.
"He was the son of Nobuharu, especially detested by the Ashikaga
"faction in Kamakura. Feeling that no fortune was to be antici-
"pated for the Southern party, and fearing that his connection with
"the lost cause would be fatal to him he fled North and settled in this
"village under the name of Kadayu. Gradually his name of Kata-
"oka was again assumed. To us he left his spotless fame and his
"sword together with that of our grandfather. Being farmers the
"name of Kataoka becomes superfluous. We are known simply
"as Katarō and Kajirō. Such is the report made to our lord with
"due reverence." Said Sukeshige—"To such as you the farmer's
"life is not suitable. Henceforth you are to be enrolled among the
"retainers as samurai. With this command be sure to report to
"the castle." Thus did the Kataoka *kyōdai* (brothers), Katarō
"and Kajirō, become the retainers of Oguri Sukeshige.

The Hangwan's preparations for the accomplishment of his task
were soon finished in such vigorous hands. The general commission issued by Prince Mochiuji for Hitachi and Shimosa and the

suppression of thieves in these provinces was to be carried into effect. In one of his raids on these gentry Sukeshige swept the country some twenty *ri* (50 miles) to the South. The provincial levies had departed, and with his more immediate train in the guise of wandering samurai headed by the bailiff Ikeno Shōhei the Hangwan was slowly returning, making a wide circle through Shimosa in the direction of the lagoon of Kasumigaura which cuts deep into lower Hitachi. Skirting the southern edge of Tsukubasan the castle would be but a day's long ride from the lagoon. In this stage they had reached the banks of the Fujishirogawa. Ordinarily a peaceful stream the river was now swollen by the rain of late summer, and was pouring a muddy and tumultuous flood bank-full to the sea. But a single boat was to be seen, and the *sendō* were somewhat doubtful as to making the passage. Sukeshige, however, entered the craft and his train followed. Waiting travellers crowded in. The boatmen with a vigorous push shot the craft out from the shore. Just then a loud shout was heard and a man came running up in haste. Although the boat was now some thirty feet out into the stream he made a vigorous leap. Landing in the craft thus tumultuously it swayed from side to side. *Zaburi*, the water poured in. Standing by the gunwale was a tall *yamabushi* (hedge priest). He was a fearful looking fellow " of a size to " make children weep." He carried his *kongō* cane and *horagai* (conch), and had a most wicked face. Not budging an inch, the swaying of the boat and the tossing waves of the river gave him something of a ducking. Scowling and grasping his cane he turned on the presumptuous youth. The unconscious object of his wrath had calmly sought out a place near the *sendō*, disregarding the black looks sent him by priest and layman. The *yamabushi* was not slow in displaying his resentment. "Kora! Rude fel- " low! Some *kozō* (errand boy) with no thought of any but him- " self. Do you make no apology for thus ducking my robe in the " filthy stream? Truly you are too much of a dullard to see beyond " your own nose and belly. But even a fool can undergo punish- " ment." As the youth made no sign of hearing this polite objurga- tion—"Son of a she-mule! Your sconce shall be broken for your

"own enlightenment and my satisfaction. *Yatsu* (filthy scoundrel) !"
He raised his iron cane as if to strike. The youth turned on him.
His face wore a scowl fearful as that of the demon-quelling Shōki,
so hideous and full of fearful wrath was it. The *yamabushi* started
back in terror and surprise. As he did so he tripped over the cane and
went head first into the boiling flood, sending the cane in a graceful
curve through the air. For a moment a hand tossed up helplessly
from the waves. Then the priest disappeared from sight, carried
down by the swift waters.

Not a word was spoken aloud, although the whispers ran from
one to the other of the plebeians crowded in the bow. "A fearful
fellow ; to kill a human being with a glance ! " Thus spoke one.
" He is hardly human. The *yamabushi* lost his life most carelessly.
" One should reckon before starting a quarrel," said another. Thus
they commented and counselled one another, some trembling and
not daring to look in the direction of the youth through fear, or
toward the samurai through respect and fear. Their eyes fastened
on their feet they were as men already entered on the Stony River
of Souls. The youth who had caused all the disturbance showed no
sign of noticing the incident. " Sendō San, is skill to row the craft
"forgotten ? Come ! Here is aid." Seizing an oar he thrust it
into the stream. A moment and the boat was flying through the
water. The *sendō* added their own vigorous efforts and the passage
was soon accomplished. In haste, without thanks or looking back,
the travellers escaped as from the claws of a tiger. The youth
stalked off toward the village with rapid strides. Sukeshige halted
his train near the ferry. " Shōhei, a remarkable fellow ! Such
" display of power and strength is rarely found in a man. A huge
" fellow too ; find out who he is ? " Shōhei called the *sendō*—
" Sendō, who is the youth to show such display of vigour with the
"*yamabushi*. Answer with truth for we mean well to him."
Said the *sendō*—" This can easily be done. He lives close by. His
" name is Koyata, and he is nineteen years old. He is noted for his
" physical strength and filial affection for the mother with whom he
" lives. For months thieves have raided the country side. The
"farmers, not daring to leave their villages even by day, have

" suffered from famine and been robbed of property and girls. If
" it was not for Koyata none would be left alive, for he makes it his
" mission to hunt these fellows down and none dare to face him.
" Indeed he is said to be a Jashin, and there are those who claim to
" be able to prove it. But he cannot be everywhere. As it is he is
" the only hope of the village. Here at least the people feel
" tolerably safe from harm"—" Act as guide to his dwelling. You
" shall fare well in the result." Under the guidance of the *sendō*
the samurai and their lord took their way toward the house of
Koyata.

This was on higher ground safe from the floods of the river.
A thatched cottage shadowed by a huge catalpa tree (*hisagi*) was
protected by a thick hedge of thorn bush (*ibara*). Dismissing
the *sendō* with ample drink money Shōhei advanced to the door.
On calling an aging woman came forth. At the sight of the samurai
in their deep straw hats, their broken and torn *waraji*, and their
big swords, she was taken with distrust and fright. " With fear
" and respect: if aught has gone wrong deign to be merciful."
Answered Shōhei—" Nay, no harm is intended to you or your son ;
" much the contrary. This is the house of Koyata San is it not ? "
Still finessing the old woman replied—" It is the house of Koyata,
" but unfortunately he is away, and there is little likelihood of his
" early return. Could not my insignificant self report to him the
" order to be transmitted ? " Said Shōhei smiling—" That is easily
" done. Koyata San has just displayed such vigour and ability as to
" attract the attention of our lord who stands close by. It is his in-
" tention, if everything is suitable, to desire him as *kerai*. Mean-
" while he will doubtless appear shortly from the village, and we will
" wait." Somewhat reassured said the oldwoman—"Deign to enter
" the humble dwelling. It is uncleanly and indifferent for one so
" great as your lord, but at least it is a shelter from the burning sun."
Thus did the lord of Oguri deign to enter the lowly house of Koyata.
The old woman's description was hardly accurate. " The place
" shone with cleanliness. *Teyari* and *bokken* (short spears—wooden
" swords) hung on the walls together with pots and pans which
" shone like mirrors." Sukeshige fingered over an open scroll lying

on a *zen* (table). With a suggestive smile he pointed it out to
Shōhei. It was a Chinese work on military tactics. Meanwhile
the old woman served hot infusion of parched wheat. In answer
to Shōhei she disclaimed any control over her son's feelings. " But
" he has a great desire to serve the young lord of Oguri whose reputa-
" tion is so widespread. Hence, be it said with fear and reverence,
" it is to be anticipated that he will seek to be excused from the
" command of your honoured lord "—" Nay," said Shōhei laugh-
" ing, " answer is already made ; for it is my lord here who is also
" lord of Oguri, so the bargain is fairly made by the lips of his
" honoured dame."

As he spoke the sound of steps was heard outside. Koyata's
voice called to his mother. As she went out—" Mother, there were
" some samurai at the ferry crossing of the Fujishirogawa. Instead of
" continuing their journey they lingered. Fearing trouble I went on
" to the village to throw them off the track. Have strangers ap-
" peared hereabouts ? " Replied the mother—" Son, prayers to
" Buddha and the *kami* have been answered. Within is the young
" lord of Oguri, with the command to join him as *kerai*. Truly
" conspicuous has been your good fortune in being received in the
" train of so great a lord." With joy Koyata hastened to present
himself before Sukeshige. Prostrated at a distance, his nose to the
ground, he made obeisance. " For this poor shelter to receive
" such an honour is beyond hope and propriety. May his lord-
" ship deign to disregard such poor surroundings as are fit for
" the humble Koyata, for his name for wisdom and valour is only
" equalled by his benevolence." Quoth Sukeshige—" Koriya ! The
" dwelling has little to do with the man it shelters. 'Tis said that
" Mofun of Sō (China) tore off the horns from wild and raging
" bulls ; but he performed no such feat as to kill a huge man with a
" single glance. With the courage of Chōshi you are said to unite
" the counsel of Kōmei. Hence the desire to summon you as *kerai*."
Koyata was fairly sweating with fear, respect, and joy. But he
answered—" with reverential thanks the order of my lord is received ;
" but what would become of the mother? Other support she has
" none. Thus humbly Koyata is compelled to ask leave of absence.

" When the time comes ' as horse and dog ' will he serve his lord."
But the mother interrupted—"A filial son you have always been.
" Now comes this honoured and desired command of your lord. Do
" not hesitate. As it is your duty to obey as son receive forthwith
" the mother's order to become *kerai* of the lord of Oguri. Living
" in the village safety is secured and your mind can be at ease." Said
Koyata—" The command must be obeyed. The petition for
" absence is withdrawn."

The *saké* was brought and poured. The ceremony of initiation
was completed. Koyata became the *kerai* of Oguri Sukeshige. His
lord presented him with a gold ornamented sword, for which he
prostrated himself in respectful thanks. " Watsu! If my lord's
" visit had been foreseen this Koyata would have carried him hither
" on his own shoulders " ; and his huge frame promised that the
performance could be carried out. Then the mother was well
supplied for her needs and recommended to the *nanushi* of the
place. Now the name of Koyata smacked too much of hut and rice
field, and was not suited to the new condition of *kerai*. It happened that Ikeno Shōhei was childless. Gladly therefore did he adopt
Koyata in his lord's presence. Named Shōji he took the character
Shō (庄) of his adopting father ; and given the name Sukenaga he
was granted the character Suke (助) from the name of his lord.
Great was the joy of this strongest and mightiest of the Oguri Ten
Valiants. Of these Gotō Hyōsuke was the oldest and ablest. It was
to him that fell the duties of *karō* of Oguri Sukeshige in the many
subsequent adventures.

When all was ready again to start on the return to Oguri
town Sukenaga prostrated himself before his lord. Said Sukeshige ;
" Speak, what is the petition ? " Said Shōji—" Near by on Mount
" Tsukuba is a notorious den of thieves. Under the leadership of
" their chiefs, the Kazama brothers, this band have made them-
" selves masters of the district south of the mountain. They plunder
" and levy taxes on the farmers at will. Both men are notable for
" their great strength and daring, true devils issued from Shuradō
" (Hell of fighting). Shōji would make humble petition that our
" lord gives consideration to these rascals on his return." Said

Sukeshige—" The suggestion is good ; which is to be expected from
" a man so bold and resourceful. Besides, it is not fair to deprive the
" district of its champion without freeing it from its incubus. For such
" fellows the present company is sufficient. Tsukubasan is our goal.
" Sukenaga shall act as guide." Ikeno Shōji roared with joy and
slapped his knee. " His lordship's plan is wise. The fewer in
" number, the less suspicious will these fellows be. Deign my lord
" to adopt the guise of rice traders. In such form no news will get
" abroad of the mission to the mountain "—" Strong and clear-
" headed," said Sukeshige. The suggestion was at once adopted.
Over silken garments was donned the coarse cloth of trader's attire
secured in the village. Thus did Sukeshige and the rōtō, seventeen men in all, set forth for the mountain. Now Mount
Tsukuba is a jumbled mass of two main peaks and many summits
with intricate vallies between its folds. It rises from the flat country,
and its numerous ridges extend from Tsukuba proper on the South
to the Amabikiyama on the North. Ashiosan and Kabasan are two
notable peaks intervening ; both holy likewise. Of considerable
height, nearly 3000 feet, it is a conspicuous object in the Shimosa-
Musashi plain, and is a fit watch tower for any posted on its flanks,
overlooking a wide range of country cut up in every direction by
the many streams flowing from its own flanks and the mountains of
Shimotsuke and Northern Hitachi. Tsukuba as a holy mountain is
dedicated to the physical founders of Nippon itself as well as of its
sons, for the generations of Izanagi and Izanami were fearfully and
wonderfully performed. Hence the shrines on its summit from time
immemorial have been objects of solicitous worship, and the phallic
cult long held sway on the mountain. With pilgrims or their per-
formances the lords of the hill interfered not at all. It was a
clientele mainly of the lower class and from the neighbouring villages. Through fear or favour it was more likely to aid than hinder
their operations.

On the right bank of the Sakuragawa (also called Tsukuba-
gawa), not far from the hamlet of Kunimatsu, was the inn of one
Shikaroku. The place itself was a ferry for travellers, and connected
the districts lying along the two sides of the river. This gave

some excuse for such a pretentious establishment in this isolated spot; but the real business of its *teishu* (landlord) was that of go-between for the band of thieves on the mountain, and to sell and forward the plunder and women captured to Kamakura and even to Kyōto. As the band of Sukeshige tramped up to his inn this fat rascal rubbed his hands with pleasure. High was the pile of luggage his *kozō* (help) piled up on the *rōka.* Talkative and noisy were the would-be 'guests. Smiling was the landlord as at once he showed them to an apartment fronting on the inner garden of his house. Infusion of parched wheat (*mugi*) was placed before them. Prostrate Shikaroku awaited the order. This was liberal as befitted a successful tour; *saké* and fish, whatever delicacies his place offered. Shikaroku made his obeisance and excuses, then withdrew, pleased that one of the party, a very big fellow, came recommended by an old gossip well known to him, a pimp from Mito town. "Young and foolish is the leader. Traders, these are "easy prey for our noble chiefs on the mountain. And the quills of "gold dust! Now to get them all as drunk as possible." The *saké* was heated, the bath announced. As the company gathered again they found the feast awaiting them. The wine was poured again, and yet again, by the women in attendance. Part of Shikaroku's stock awaiting shipment, these were beauties culled from the neigh-bouring districts. Under the severe eye of their owner they were by no means unkind and unbending. When the feast had made a fair start Shikaroku, more and more satisfied and feeling that the time was ripe, withdrew to write a letter. Then he called his *bantō* (clerk). "These fellows are now getting quite drunk. The girls "have them fast. Denkichi, you are to carry this letter in haste to "the Kazama chiefs on the mountain. In itself it is an introduc-"tion on this first trip. If questioned by the guard say that Shika-"roku has received a company of traders, seventeen in number, "who are now feasting carelessly at the inn. From the wealth "openly displayed they are big birds, not sparrows, and they are "entirely without suspicion. Great will be the booty for the chiefs, "and easy the task of securing it "—" With reverence the command "is heard and understood." With this reply the shock-headed

Denkichi disappeared in the direction of the river. Here taking boat he started to row up stream a short distance, intending to land and make his way up the mountain.

The only dissatisfied man at the feast was Ikeno Shōji Sukenaga. " Too much feasting and entertainment, wine and *tabo*, here for the matter in hand to go well." Quietly he disappeared. Meanwhile Denkichi was well on his way up-stream. There seemed to be a sort of rustling below in the boat. Ku, *ku*, ku, ku, ku— but it was not the sound of the water. He peered below*, to see the pile of matting rise. Then appeared two huge hands which grasped his throat as in a vise. He tried to struggle, but his hands vaguely waved in the air, while his eyes bulged horribly from the sockets. Then he died. Shōji was not long in rifling the corpse and securing the letter. Casting the body overboard into the stream he took the oar and pushed vigorously toward the landing. Springing to shore he plunged into the mountain trail, brought close by a projecting spur to the river, and began to climb the slope. A mile (13 or 14 *cho*) brought him face to face with a patrol. Challenged he explained his errand. These were mere " key and rope " men, charged with examining any who approached the mountain, and making prisoners of any suspicious or unwary profitable stranger poaching on the mountain precincts. They carried *nagamaki* (long hilted swords) and showed some signs of discipline. The letter from Shikaroku was a ready passport through the guard, and they directed him to go another mile where his mission could be more directly examined. Here he found a stone gate guarding the approach to the robber stronghold. A guard of a dozen men was on watch. The challenge here was equally sharp, and the examination still more strict. " The letter is from Shikaroku without doubt, but " you are not known on the mountain." Replied Shōji—" Iza ! " This Denkichi is new to the place. Younger brother to

---

* The Japanese oarsman stands behind and above in his boat. He shoves with his sweep ; does not pull except in backing water to change the course or turn. The boats are heavy, deep, and flat-bottomed ; even river craft. *Tabo*—a woman's method of dressing the hair. Used as in our expression—wine, woman, and song : i.e.=woman.

" Shikaroku I have been living at Horage.   The old *bantō* En-
" shichi is no longer fit for anything, and has returned to his
" home in Tamba Kumashichi with the last lot of women
" sent to Kyōto.   As he was not to return my elder brother
" has summoned me to replace him."—" Horage is close enough ; "
put in one of the guard.   Said another—" It is true that Shikaroku
" has a younger brother living there.   And these merchants ? "—
" To all appearance they are easy game," replied Denkichi.
" They are getting thoroughly drunk, the women have them well
" in hand and they have eyes for nothing else.   The chief is young
" and inexperienced, not older than this Denkichi.   Great is the show
" of gold dust, and many the packages left in the *teishu's* charge."
" —For *kyaku* you shall have ' *kwaku* ' (ducks for ducats).   The
" chief has a supply for the *teishu*, with wings and without wings.
" But their delivery can wait. Meanwhile notice is to be sent within.
" Deign to rest here for the moment."

The wait was not for long.   The scent of the game was too
good.   Kazama Hachirō read the letter.   Forthwith he sought out
his brother Jirō.   " Great news from Shikaroku's place, brother.
" He lodges well-feathered game, traders returning lined with goods
" and fat pockets.   Few in numbers they are easy prey.   He is as
" anxious for his commission as any Kamakura shop-keeper ; old
" swindler ! "   Jirō was thoughtful.   " The Hangwan of Oguri is
" abroad.   Be careful.   He is young in years, but the corres-
" pondents of Shikaroku in Kamakura give him a great reputation
" for valour and sagacity.   It is quite likely that some trick is being
" played on us.   It is long since traders of such quality have dared
" to invade the territory of the mountain.   Indeed the field is
" growing so poor that a move to fairer quarters seems advisable "
—" There is no danger, brother," replied Hachirō.   " With fear
" and respect : deign to allow this Hachirō to undertake such a
" small venture.   Even if it were the Hangwan himself the number
" of his company is too small to offer resistance.   Surely these men
" are mere traders, for he would never come accompanied by so
" few to a place like this.   Oguri is not so far distant that the name
" of Kazama is unknown.   Pray give permission."   With grudging

consent Hachirō was allowed to manage this affair as he thought best. The *toritsugi* (name porter) soon appeared at the gateway. "It is decided to go. The leader is; Hachigashira (chief Hachi-rō*)."* Blurted out Shōji ;—" Yatsugashira ? (Filthy Scoundrel "Chief.)"—" No, you fool ; the Hachigashira, Chief Kazama Ha-"chirō himself. You are summoned within. Keep a civil tongue "and your head." Brought before the chief the messenger saw a big fellow with his long black stiff hair gathered into a mass sticking out at an angle behind his massive head. He was a most formidable looking fellow. Abruptly—"This is Horage Denkichi, "from the inn of Shikaroku ? " Replied Shōji :—" Great is the "respect and fear. Horage is the village of birth ; Denkichi my "humble name. Hence comes the nickname Horage Denkichi "— "Of small moment," growled Kazama. "You are big enough to "require a whole village to yourself ; as big as this Hachirō. "Better work can be found than that of *banto* in an inn. There "you will merely grow fat, and finally be compelled to take to "wrestling."—" Reverentially heard and understood : thanks are "offered," replied Denkichi. "And my master ? "—" Tell him his "message will be answered by Hachirō in person, and within two "hours. The night gets on apace." With this reply Denkichi was conducted through the various guards. Fairly good was the discipline, fairly strict the watch and ward, as was noted by a pair of very good eyes. These thieves had no ordinary men in command, young though they were.

So Kazama Hachirō armed himself for the venture, He carried a long *nagamaki,* and wore helmet and a belly-guard which was ablaze with decorated silk. *kogusoku* (mail lacking the trunk of the body) protected his huge legs. With thirty men, in garb as varied as the army of Falstaff, he set out down the mountain, to take boat with his followers to the inn. Meanwhile here the feasting had gone on without intermission. The women exerted every charm and complaisance ; the men met them more than half-way. Ikeno Shōji quietly entered and took his place. Sukeshige was hardly visible through the garments of his fair company. Shōji frowned. Then yawning he said abruptly—" where is the *teishu* ?

" Call him here for company. With only ourselves this is getting
" monotonous. Let him tell us tales of the mountain and country-
" side to wile away the time." Shikaroku was nothing loath.
Anything to command attention until Denkichi returned with the
band of the Kazama. So the *teishu* squatted respectfully at the end
of the apartment and began his entertainment. The inn staff of
men and servant girls gathered without to listen. Shikaroku had
spent many years on the mountain and attended many of the
orgiastic *matsuri* (festivals). His tales if broad did not lack wit, of
confusion of couples and ghostly visitations on the holy hill. Shōji
rose as if to absent himself for a moment. He passed behind Shikaroku. The next moment the *teishu's* head rolled on the floor. The
Oguri *rōtō* were on their feet in an instant and at and out of the *shōji*.
" *Are-yo!   Are-yo!* " The women crouched and cried shrilly.
Said Sukeshige—" This is the judgment of Heaven on Shikaroku for
" long years of wickedness. Don't be afraid. No one will injure
" you. Shōji, these are mere girls and unable to do us harm." Said
Shōji—" As women they are born cats, without feeling and
" treacherous. Your lordship is merciful ; but their claws are to be
" pared, and it is best to shut them up safely during what follows,
" for their own sakes and ours.......there is such a place here-
" abouts? " He turned glumly toward the women. They answered together—" The *kura* (store-house) is large and can hold all.
" Deign to spare our lives. We make no resistance." In tears they
prostrated themselves in turn before the fearful man and his more
merciful lord. With the serving men and women they were
taken to the store-house and safely locked inside. Then Shōji made
his report to his lord as to the visit to the mountain fort. Said
Sukeshige—" In a short time the thieves will be at hand. Now
" to carry out the plan." The *rōtō* set energetically to work.

Kazama Hachirō and his band landed and approached the inn.
It was the tenth month (November) and raining. All was
quiet as a graveyard. Said Hachirō—" The wine of Shikaroku has
" done its work. Let one of you go and inspect. Then come
" back and make report." The man found nothing. Of Shikaroku and the men and women of the place there was not a sign.

All was dark and the inn tight closed. Said Hachirō—" It is but " the hour of the pig (9 to 11 P.M.). Shikaroku surely expected us. " Perchance his messenger has delayed, and we have outstripped " him. All-forward ! " With a rush the thieves began to break and tear off the wooden panels (*amado*). Entrance was soon effected and they swarmed over the *rōka*. As they did so a terrific racket ensued. They had stumbled into a *naruko** stretched across the entrance. This in itself was enough to create confusion, but pressing on each other they found themselves involved in a maze of ropes stretched in every direction, and were tumbled hither and thither. The *rōtō* of Oguri were on them at once cutting and slashing in the apartments now blazing with the torches which Sukeshige calmly lighted and put in place. In a trice Kazama Hachirō had lost half his band of thirty men. The rest fled in disorder, Kazama guarding the retreat as best he could. At the river they jumped into the boats pell-mell, and with small regard for their chief made off up-stream. As they progressed a short distance from the shore the planks began to yawn and the craft fell apart leaving them to struggle in the water. The pursuing *rōtō* of Oguri made short work of them thus helpless. Only two or three escaped to Tsukuba-san, to carry the tale of defeat to the waiting Jirō.

Meanwhile Kazama Hachirō was left to face the huge samurai whom it was easy to recognize as the quondam Denkichi. " Ah, " you rascal ! This is as things should be. Here is Ikeno Shōji " Sukenaga, *rōtō* of Kojirō Hangwan Sukeshige. Your presence is re-" quired by our lord. To him you shall go, to have cut off that shock " of hair, and the head with it. Submit at once, you filthy fellow. " Such as you are not the ones to make resistance to the lord's order." Said Kazama Hachirō—" No stranger pays a second visit to the "mountain, but this time the privilege is yours, and you come " invited. For your boy lord this Hachirō cares that ! " He snapped two fingers in derision, and gnashed his teeth with rage. His halberd whirled viciously in effort to cut down his opponent.

---

* Short pieces of bamboo strung together and the ends fastened on a board. A rope to pull forms the rattle. Used to 'scare birds, or to give notice of ap-proach at a ferry.

Ikeno Shōji binds Kazama Hachirō.

Shōji was too active. Avoiding the weapon he sprang to close quarters and grappled with Hachirō. Mighty was the struggle between the two big men. Tight clasped over and over they rolled, first one on top and then the other. An ornamental boulder in the garden stopped this performance. Unluckily Shōji was underneath at the time. But Kazama Hachirō was in the position of Sanada Yoichi, nor did he have any Bunzō within call.* His dagger which had fallen lay within reach of his hand behind him. He stretched out to grasp it. In a moment he went backward through the air. This time it was Shōji who was on top. Quickly the arms of Hachirō were bound behind his back, and his victor took breath. With some respect Shōji viewed his quondam antagonist. " But it is for " my lord to judge you. Come along ! " Unceremoniously dragging his prisoner, much like a bag of rice, he hauled him into the pre∙ sence of Sukeshige.

The Hangwan greeted his big retainer with pleasure. "Great is " your strength Sukenaga; and clever the plan devised. Truly mighty " in mind and body. And this is Kazama Hachirō? Release him from " his bonds." Confused and wondering the robber chief prostrated himself before the lord. Said Sukeshige —" Your looks and actions " show that thieving is no part of your nature. How a man like you, " so young and promising should engage in this unsavoury occupation, " despised and hated of all honest men, is difficult to understand. " However, it is no part of the mission of this Sukeshige to press "brave men too hard. Reform your path, engage in some fair " means of living, and pardon is secured. Nay ! To Prince Mo- " chiuji your names shall be recommended, doubtless to your ad- " vantage. What say you? " Said Kazama Hachirō —" Such " benevolence thus displayed is unheard of. Not since the days of " Shun of Sō (China) has such kindness to the wicked been vouch- " safed. Gratitude too deep for words, fear too great for expression, " holds this Hachirō. Allow me to go hence, to make report to my " brother Jirō, to convert him to the true life, both to humbly petition " that your lordship will admit the brothers to his service in the "lowliest capacity." Shōji promptly stepped forward in protest.

* Gempei Seisuiki p. 533-4. Cf. "Saitō Musashi-bō Benkei," II p. 29.

" May your lordship deign to do nothing of the kind, but turn a
" deaf ear to the honied words of this rascal. Do not let loose a
" tiger in a bamboo forest of a thousand *ri* (great extent). This
" fellow has not the least intention of doing anything but consulting
" his brother Jirō as to vengeance. His strength this Shōji can
" answer for. His wickedness and insincerity are patent. He is a
" dangerous fellow. May your lordship be pleased to order
" me to strike off his head." But Sukeshige made a friendly
sign to be silent, and to Kazama gave sign of dismissal. Amazed
the robber bowed to the ground and staggering left the inn to take
the road to Mount Tsukuba. When he had gone said Sukeshige—
" Mercy is first to be used ; the sword last of all. Such is the samu-
" rai code. Warned by his brother of this fair offer, Jirō may re-
" pent of his wicked course. In such case much is gained. Besides,
" they will be no more successful in a second than in the first
" attempt. Sukeshige has chosen the battle ground. To storm the
" mountain fort means certain loss of life. This is to be avoided if
" possible. Let us await results. Meanwhile be prepared for any
" further attempt." The *rōtō* heard and applauded ; none more so
than Ikeno Shōji Sukenaga. More fighting ? It was meat and
drink to this hungry man.

Kazama Hachirō did not have to complete his journey to the
mountain fort of Tsukuba. Hardly had he left the bank of the river
when he met Jirō riding at the head of eighty men to vengeance.
Jirō greatly rejoiced, and was amazed at the sight of his brother yet
in life. " Ah, fortunate meeting ! Now this Oguri Sukeshige shall
" be taught a lesson ; thus to come in deceitful guise against the Kaza-
" ma brothers ! He shall visit the mountain fort of Tsukuba, but as
" captive ; and his fate shall be such that the carpet knights of Ka-
" makura shall tremble at any order to attack us. The horse of
" Hachirō Dono ! Now mount brother, and all go forward." But
Hachirō made obeisance to his elder brother. " For one moment
" consider ! To the Hangwan this Hachirō owes life. It is as if one
" was born again. Besides, his words sank deep into Hachirō. Why
" lead this wicked and riotous existence when better is offered ? Con-
" sider brother ; decide to reform, to make petition to be received as

" *kerai* of Oguri Dono. Then indeed will life offer a task to us who
" are yet young—the service of samurai to their lord." Jirō laughed
at him and raged. " Hachirō you have been limed by the sweet
" words of Sukeshige who merely seeks to entrap us. With both
" brothers in his net very different would be his song. Our moun-
" tain fort destroyed the brothers Kazama would be led to Oguri
" town, to please the multitude as they crucified and sliced our
" bodies in public for their enjoyment. In arms alone is Oguri
" Sukeshige to be met. Then he shall suffer the fate reserved for
" us, be victim of his own lure, and amusement for our company......
" What ! You still hesitate ! Nay, brother you have turned coward.
" Take horse then and return to the mountain. Crouch under the
" quilts until your warmth and courage are restored. Drink *saké*
" until the blood not only flows once more in your veins, but even
" before your eyes." Contemptuously he spurred forward his horse.
Hachirō was left white with passion. " This Hachirō is a dead
" man already. Why not truly take the journey to Meido (Hades)?
" The elder brother must be obeyed ; so once more to attack the
" Hangwan and receive his judgment and punishment." He followed rapidly in the train of his brother, who once more smiled
and encouraged the gloomy Hachirō as when they were mere
children together.

Crossing the river the band approached the inn of the late
Shikaroku. This time things were very different. The place was a
blaze of light ; but again there was no sign of life to be seen.
Warned by his brother's fate Jirō looked on this with misgiving.
" The Hangwan will not play the same trick twice. What can be
" his design ? Have they in fright deserted the place and fled
" toward Oguri ? They will soon be overtaken." Said a follower—
" With fear and respect, report is to be made." Said Jirō—" What
" is it ?"—" Over yonder on the hillock is kindled a small fire.
" Doubtless it is a signal of some kind "—" Suspicious, of that there
" is no question. Divide at the hillock and go round the two sides.
" Thus the foe will not take us in the rear." At Jirō's order this
was done, but nothing as yet appeared. Then suddenly at the foot
of the hillock appeared the figure of a *bushi* on horseback. Shouted

Sukeshige—" What kind of answer, Jirō, is this to my command!
" Favoured with a pardon you attempt once more to force yourself
" into my presence, and be subject of punishment instead of mercy.
" Surrender at once, and make petition for the pardon offered your
" brother Hachirō." But to this mild command Jirō bellowed
back—" Ah! You met my brother with treachery and honied
" words, not arms and face to face. Now it shall be made evident
" that the Kazama brothers are equal to any samurai whelped in
" Kamakura town." Whirling his halberd like a windmill he rushed at the lord Sukeshige. Parrying the blow, with one stroke
Sukeshige severed the shaft of the halberd. Jirō rode a finely-trained
war-horse. Sukeshige a mere colt found in the stables of Shikaroku ;
but such was his skill that the animal and his rider acted as a unit.
Misgivings began to enter the mind of the confident Jirō. Dropping the useless shaft the bandit chief drew his sword. Up and
down, right and left, mighty were the strokes. Sukeshige kept the
enemy busy, laughing and jeering as he parried the desperate blows.
Suddenly the feet went from under Jirō's horse. Shōji had approached with a stout birch sapling some twelve feet in length torn
from the ground. Handling this as if it had been a mere walking
staff he brought horse and man to the ground at a blow. In a
trice the bandit chief was trussed up like a captive swine.

Kazama Hachirō hearing the noise of the fighting rode in haste
around the corner of the hillock just in time to witness the discomfiture of his brother and to be confronted by the victorious Shōji.
The latter roared with joy. " Again you come to the feast uninvited.
" Rascal! This time surely there shall be no escape through any
" favour of our lord."—Kazama Hachirō boiled with rage at the
sight of his brother prostrate and bound with ropes. With a
shout he rushed to the rescue. But Shōji stepped aside. Again the
mighty staff came in action. With broken knees the unfortunate
animal pitched headlong to the ground. Kazama Hachirō landed at
some distance, stunned and helpless under the pressing weight of
the active Shōji. As the *bushi* trussed him up Hachirō was in a
great rage. " Coward! Why make prisoners? Cut off our heads
" to take to your lord. Show some kindness "—" Thieves are thus

" treated," was the brief response of Shōji to the plea. Meanwhile, amazed and frightened, the minor thieves witnessed the treatment of their chiefs. "Great is the strength of the brothers; but this "man is a very demon. The chiefs are now prisoners. They are " not our parents. It is our duty to run away, not to rescue them. " Let us escape." They fled, but only to fall under the blows of the Oguri *rōtō* led by Shōhei, or to surrender as prisoners. Thus some thirty five were taken. The rest were killed or escaped to hide themselves in other districts. Shōji pulled his captives to their feet, and with a fist clenched at the nape of the neck of each he pushed them into the presence of Sukeshige seated in judgment. With hardened fists he stood behind them, ready to dash out the brains of either at a blow, but Sukeshige again ordered them to be unbound. Said he to the prostrate Jirō—"To your brother nothing " is to be said. He is the younger, under your command, and " doubtless has made his report. What have you to say? Do you " accept these terms, make reformation, and abandon your vile pur- " suit, so unsuited to men like you?" Said Jirō, his forehead on his outstretched hands—"Great, almost unbelievable, is the benevolence " and charity of our lord. First hear our story. We are brothers, " natives of Maruyama in Musashi province. When mere " children the village was attacked by Tsukuba Jirō, a famous " robber. Peasant and property were raided and plundered. Our " father, a *gōshi-samurai*, offered resistance to the band. He and his " wife were cruelly put to death. Brought before Jirō the band " made petition that our lives be spared. Having decided to allow " us to live the robber carried us off to the Tsukuba mountain fort. " There we entered as pages in his service. Thus years passed. " From boys of eleven and ten years we reached the ages of fifteen " and fourteen years. The time of vengeance had arrived. As Tsu- " kuba Jirō slept off one of his drunken bouts we killed him and cut " off his head. Attempting flight we were captured by the band " before we left the mountain precincts. Brought back for judgment " the choice was offered; death or to take the place of the slain chief. " Habit had made the life familiar. Its excitement and danger were " congenial to both. The offer was accepted, and thus the Kazama

" brothers became chiefs of the Tsukuba band of thieves.* The
" mountain fort has been our home since that time. Now
" we are twenty and eighteen years of age. Apology is made for
" daring to disturb the rest of your lordship. Deign to accept these
" our words. Grant the hope of entrance to service even in the
" lowest capacity, or the favour of the command to cut belly as
" punishment for the displeasure incurred."

Sukeshige laughed with joy. " As to service that is accepted.
" In life you are more useful to your lord. Let the *saké* cup be
" brought to bind the ceremony of lord and retainer. No severe
" probation will be enforced." Then Kazama Jirō addressed the
robbers—" You have witnessed what has taken place. By the
" order of our honoured lord such as are suitable for his service, *rōnin*
" not thieves by nature and of good repute, will be permitted to
" enlist." Selected by Jirō and Hachirō these men were presented
to Sukeshige. The rest were dismissed with a present, and warned not to be found engaged in their old occupation. Then Sukeshige crossed the river and ascended the mountain. The fort was
set on fire, and every convenience that could harbour or protect
any future band was destroyed. Then all set forth for Ogur
castle. The province was in complete peace, the door of the
peasant was left unfastened, and boy and maid wandered the hillside in security. Thus did the Kataoka brothers, Ikeno Shōji, and
the Kazama brothers Jirō Masaoki and Hachirō Masakuni become
kerai of Oguri, to the credit and reknown of their lord Sukeshige.

---

* Kazama town to-day is found North of the mountain, on the branch railway between Mito and Oyama ; an important place. Granite is largely quarried,
and the coal district of Ibaraki lies just north.

CHAPTER VI.

THE UPRISING OF UESUGI ZENSHŪ.

The stay of Sukeshige in Hitachi was soon brought to a close. Late in the ninth month of Ōei 23rd year (October 1416) the order was received from his father to march the Oguri levies up to Kamakura in support of Uesugi Zenshū, equally well known as the Inukake Nyūdō, from the place of his residence and his shaven pate as priest. The course of these events is necessary to the thread of the story, and morever the particular details are but scantily treated in modern histories. At all events, the crisis was grave enough to start off Sukeshige and his Ten Valiants, the young chief riding in their midst with some seventeen hundred samurai to represent the House of Oguri.

The bad temper of the Inukake Nyūdō had at last brought affairs to a head. Early in Ōei 23rd year (1416) in a polite but peppery audience with his prince the premier was turned out in more than one sense. Dismissed from office this was made more bitter to him by the selection of Uesugi Norimoto of the Yamanouchi House as Shitsuji.* With his able son Norizane the government was conducted in the lordly Uesugi way, giving full rein to the extravagance and capriciousness of Prince Mochiuji, and paying far too little attention to the doings of Zenshū. This latter retired to his mansion in the beautiful Inukake valley near by the Ōkura palace (the Kubōyashiki), and did more than merely suck his paws. Though they thoroughly understood each other Nyūdō Zenshū now

* With Mitsukane, in imitation of the Kyōto Shōgun, the Kwantō Kwanryō began to call themselves *Kubō*; the Shitsuji took the title of Kwanryō. Kyōto never recognized this change of title; and historians of the day and of modern times have followed the example. The Shōgun himself usurped this properly Imperial title. He is often called the Japanese Ō (king).

paid a formal visit to Prince Mitsutaka at the Midō palace. Mitsutaka was the brother of Mitsukane, and hence uncle to Mochiuji. Moreover he had an adopted son Mochinaka, younger
brother of Mochiuji and as yet a mere boy; which did not
exempt him from all the excitement and exigencies of the politics
of Nippon. Introduced into the presence of the Prince, Zenshū
prostrated himself and with tears said—"When small offences are
" magnified, and injury sought where none exists, then matters are
" taking a bad course. It has been the offense of Nyūdō to be com-
" pelled to reprove his lord. The obedient child is no sycophant,
" the loyal vassal no flatterer. The suzerain has not received the
" reproof; instead he has visited Nyūdō with his anger. It is not
" long since that this very Norimoto imperilled the prestige of our
" lord's House, and yet now he governs the land as Shitsuji, and his
" son Norizane waits the succession against all precedent. The gate
" of confinement is opened, and he conducts the rule of the flying
" dragon. But the world changes fast. Affairs press. Deign to
" give ear to the plan which will rectify this matter and save the
" House in its peril from the hands of this lecherous and drunken
" prince." Salt were the tears of Zenshū and bitter was his wrath,
as with smoothly modulated voice and smiling grief he made
petition to Prince Mitsutaka.

This latter was not hard to persuade that the house was in danger
and his son was the one to save it—under his direction. *More Ja-
ponico*, the more the Inukake Nyūdō smiled and the softer his voice,
the madder he knew he was, fit instrument to his ambitions. He
sought time to consider, but Nyūdō showed the advantage of quick
rebellion. "Besides," he hinted, " the means are close at hand, the
" prince unsuspecting. One rapid blow and his person is in your
" honoured hands. The Shōgun when informed will accept the
" accomplished fact and give consent. Thus the House founded by
" the ancestor Prince Takauji will shine in all its glory. Besides,
" the Kwantō can match Kyōto man for man twice over." In this
he was right. The ambition of the Kwantō Kwanryō was founded
on the unity of the Kwantō interests. Kyōto was distracted by the
rapid making and unmaking of emperors; and *buke* (military Houses)

and *kuge* (court nobles) were badly divided on these issues. Plots of rebellion put in action were of constant occurrence.

When Nyūdō told the prince that the means to act were at hand he spoke with knowledge. From the Kwantō an army of samurai had been marching on Kamakura and were now close at hand. The Chiba, Nitta, Shibukawa, Takeda, Ogasawara, Kamō Sōga, Doi, Nasu, Utsunomiya, Nikaidō, Sasaki, Kidō, headed the army of 113000 men in which marched the Oguri contingent. Of the faithful few were the Yūki clan, but cut off by the unexpected movement they could neither move a foot or send the news to Kamakura. Hence at the beginning of the 10th month (end of October) this vast force quietly took possession of all the entrances to the city. The men stood under arms. Even the horses seemed to share in the secrecy and silence, mumbling rather than champing their bits. Mitsutaka and Mochinaka, from the palace of the Shin-Midō provided for the great host. Ujinori left the Inukake *yashiki* to take command.

Kamakura learned what was going forward as the great force began to move. Great was the fright and consternation as Doi, Tsuchiya, and the Chiba left the Gokurakuji to pass into the Saka no Shita and Hase quarters. On the other side the Hitachi and Shimosa contingents lay at Kanazawa, and held the Asahinakiridōshi, waiting the appearance of the western levies. The Takeda and Nitta advanced on Yamanouchi. Mochiuji, totally unsuspecting, was lying in a drunken slumber. Then came in haste to the nuptial chamber Kidō Shōgen Mochisuye. *Do, do, do, do,* he hammered on the outside. Roused by the summons Prince Mochiuji refused to believe the news. The Inukake Nyūdō was known to be ill. His son, Chūmu no Taisuke, was as morose as his father and as much of a hermit. Mochisuye wept with fright and pain. Alas ! His lord was acting very foolishly. The enemy was close at hand, the whole Kwantō was in arms behind Zenshū. Through his lord's carelessness the fortunes of his House would be destroyed. The whole of Kamakura plain was covered by the foe. He must escape before the palace was attacked, for no defence could be made in such cramped quarters.

Convinced at last Mochiuji hastily seized such clothing as would best disguise his condition. Mochisuye was in waiting with thirty men and horses. At the Jū-ni-shō they crossed the little stream before the palace and dashed up the mountain paths over the hill to the Myōhōji and Nagoedōshi.* Reaching the village of Kotsubo a fisherman's boat was seized, and hasty oars pressed to the Yuigahama beach. To join the Shitsuji at his Sasuke mansion, the one chance was to penetrate the enemy's rear where unsuspected they would escape notice in the motley army crowding through the narrow lanes of Yuigasato. It was a good plan and successful. Norimoto has been as unsuspicious as Mochiuji himself. Norizane had been feasting at a *saké* banquet. There rode up to interrupt this Uesugi Shuri no Tayū. "The Inukake Nyūdō with the whole Kwantō "behind him is attacking the Kubōyashiki. Unless some means be "sought to oppose him all is lost." After all this was a family affair. As Norizane buckled on his armour the poem of Tōda Kōgen came to mind :

"Firm stands the dragon amid the world ;
"Unmoved his face, though great hills shake."

The news now came that the enemy had reached the sea front. Clouds of smoke and fire rose from the burning shops and houses. What was taking place at the *gosho* (palace)? Norizane clasped his *iwaobi* (girdle over the armour) and called for his horse. His first duty was to rescue his lord at the cost of his life. In all directions the flags of the enemy could be seen. Fortunately they thought more of pillage than of fighting. As he prepared to start out his lord saved him the trouble by riding into the enclosure of the Sasuke *yashiki* with his train. Marching on the Ōkura palace the enemy had reached the Wakamiya-ōji, leaving their rear free to passage. Hence his easy escape.

Norizane had nearly 7000 men. Mochiuji himself had picked up on his short course five hundred scattered and wandering ad-

---

* The Ju-ni-shō shrine represents the twelve Kumano foundations. It is just beyond the Kwōzokuji, founded by Ippen Shōnin. Kwōzokuji possesses an Amida by Unkei. The Shionama-Jizō in the *tsuchido* before the gate has a history. Nagoedōshi—Hōjō Tokimasa lived here.

herents. The dispositions were rapidly made. At the entrance to the valley stakes were planted and ropes stretched. The front toward the sea was defended by Norizane and Izumo no Kami with 2000 men. Satake Uma no Suke with 800 men guarded the maze of narrow lanes on the Sasame—Hase side, and Yūki Sōdai with 1000 men watched the side of the Yakushido to the East. Uesugi Bitchū no Kami Tōnaka with 800 men guarded the approach to the Muryōdō. The danger point of the Kokushōji was defended by Miura with nearly 2400 men on the Kishōzaka front.* Danjō no Shōhitsu with 800 men pushed out into the Ogigayatsu to put up a defensive battle. In the rear were but few men to guard the steep hills, obstacles to approach and easy of defence. Arranged in *kwakuyoku* (crane's wings) the attack was awaited. The 10th month 3rd day (23rd October) was an unlucky day. On the 4th day (24th October) the war shout was raised at the Rokuhon-matsu (Six Pines). So hard were the besieged pressed that the force was drawn in from Ogigayatsu. Backed by his vast army the Inu-kake Nyūdō breathed war and bloodshed. Decidedly he saw red in this opportunity to square accounts with his quondam master. Fresh men could be continually thrown forward, whereas worn out in continued single combats many of the besieged were slain. Yet with his own men Uesugi Bitchū no Kami drove back the much superior force of the two Nikaidō, Owari no Kami and Yamashiro no Kami.

The battle was lost. Too weary to stand, too intent to plan, so engaged as to "swallow their spittle," effective resistance was no longer possible. The hope had been a change of heart in the attacking force thus brought into open warfare with their lord and into more intimate relations with the real merits of Nyūdō's pretensions. Of this change there was no sign. Mochiuji was heartily disliked as extravagant, grasping, wasting the resources of the provinces on an idle luxury. Until the Shōgun spoke the Kwantō was behind

---

* The site of the Muryōdō is in the little valley just north of the palace (go-yōtei), running under and to the West of Genjiyama. The location of the Kokushōji is not specified by Ōmori further than at Sasukegayatsu. Probably close to the big cliff, at the eastern entrance.

Ujinori to a man. Norimoto mounted his horse and rode the lines to take in the aspect of affairs. His report was unfavourable. Mochiuji at once wanted to cut belly. "Since all is lost let the " preparations be made forthwith. Delay is not permissible." But Norimoto remonstrated. " There are still a thousand men fit for " action, ample to cover retreat. Affairs may yet prosper. The " Kyōto Shōgun will never condone rebellion against the House. " Prince Yoshitsugu is undoubtedly involved in this affair, and it is " a blow at the Shōgun himself. It would be foolish to act so " prematurely when the common soldier displays the bravery of a " leader of men." Then his son Norizane reported to him that the enemy had made the mistake of pressing *en masse* to the Kubō- yashiki. The hills in the rear and the sea road at the Gokurakuji were open. Leaving Norizane to fight defensively at the Sasuke mansion, Norimoto conducted the prince up the winding valley. Hands were clapped at the Inari shrine ; then climbing the hill in the rear the company descended the long valley at the left shoulder of the Daibutsu and crossed the hill opposite to the Gokurakuji. The road taken still exists, a bad one to-day and probably no better then. As the sun declined they left the temple and leper hospital and took the sea road to Katase. Wives and children had been abandoned in the burning city, and sad were the hearts as they fled looking backward, stumbling in the gloom. Some inkling of the movement was at last gained. Nitta hastened over the hills and through the old pass to Koshigoe once used by his famed relative Yoshisada. Doi and Tsuchiya streamed back through the Goku- rakuji-kiridoshi with their forces.   With barely a hundred men Ima- gawa Shuri no Suke and the two Isshiki, Uma no Kami and Hyō- bu no Taisuke, threw themselves across the narrow road, bandying epithets and exchanging arrows with the foe. The only coward in the family was Akihide. In the dark night and strong position at Koshigoe a thousand men were as a hundred. The foe were halted.

Thus their lord succeeded in reaching the Fujisawa post-town. Here Norimoto left him, to ride off to Echigo for assistance. Deprived of this mainspring Mochiuji made his way painfully to

The Fujisawa Hangwan.

Odawara, listening for a pursuit which was not made. At Odawara the people were indifferent, even hostile, more ready to attack than give aid. Again the prince talked of cutting belly. This time it was the Bettō of the Hakone Gongen* shrine who came to his aid with fifty men. He pointed out that the enemy would not dare to engage in the mountain trails. Themselves, they knew the roads by night as by day. Thus was Prince Mochiuji brought to the Nagoya temple in Izu. After a rest of three days it was dared to raise the white flag (Minamoto standard) at Kohage. Mochiuji had been lost to sight; his whereabouts were unknown. But the Kanō of Izu were adherents of Ujinori.† At the news of the presence of Mochiuji, now at the Kokushōji, a large force gathered to attack him. He had been joined by Norizane, but only had two hundred men. Under the leadership of Kidō Shōgen Mochisuye these rode forth to make such front as they could against five times their number. Again the position became desperate. Within the temple itself the monks were surly in the presence of the prince; deservedly so for the shrine and seven halls were soon in flames. Afraid of being seized Mochiuji and Norizane fled up the forest covered hill in the rear of the temple. The end seemed to be reached, and even Norizane was disposed to counsel *seppuku*. But again the priestly garb was seen. The Hakone Bettō in company with his fighting monks threw themselves eagerly into the fray. The hasty levies of the foe, many mere villagers, hesitated, then dispersed in flight. Said the Bettō—"Deign to witness the effect of the suzerain's "presence when support is offered him. By no means are the fortunes "of the House lost. Condecend to accept the escort here provided as "far as Bō no Ōmori. As this is in Suruga your lordship is sure of "the hearty support of the Imagawa, father and son, Nyūdō Ryōshun "and Kazusa no Suke Noritada." The Bettō was right. The Imagawa soon appeared at Bō no Ōmori. Numbers now began to flock to the standard of the prince.

---

* Superintendant of the Hakone shrines. The gift of office was a plum of the Court (Imperial or Shōgunal).

† Kanō Masanobu the famous painter was of this family and contemporary with these events. Nagoya is not far from Daiba.

From this time the affairs of the Inukake Nyūdō went badly. His success was all on the surface and prepared his fall. The Shōgun Yoshimochi was a weak, dissipated, suspicious man, given to temporizing and cruel in his fright. His first idea was that his brother Yoshitsugu was engaged in this uprising of Ujinori, and the culpability was soon proved. Matters were settled by seizing the prince, cutting his hair (making him priest), and shutting him up in the Shōkokuji of Kyōto. The Kwantō plainly was in great confusion. The loyalty of the vassal to his lord was grievously shaken. Although he suspected the feelings and ambitions of Mochiuji he felt that a temporizing policy was possible with him, whereas the plot of Ujinori with Yoshitsugu directly threatened himself. An order in council was forthwith issued. Runs the substance of this precious document :

" Last month the Shin-Midō Mitsutaka, father
" and son, and the former Shitsuji Ujinori Nyūdō,
" planned a state of rebellion. The Kwantō as a
" whole joined them on the plea of injustice. What
" is the cause of complaint ? The tree with overtop-
" ping branches covers all in its shadow, but what is
" below is most important. Such an event was un-
" heard of in former generations. Now in brief the
" command is to be given to the Shōshō (generals).
" The decree is that the flag of the East be reduced
" to submission, and the baton (*fu-etsu*) is put
" in commission. Perchance all men of the Eight
" Provinces of the Kwantō are not at enmity. Those
" who are of kin quickly must notify their lord as to
" complaint. There is plainly a state of war. The
" provinces must submit. The people are at discord.
" 11th month 1st day (20 November 1416)
" Hatakeyama Owari no Kami Mitsuiye
" Koyama Ichizoku-chū
" Kawagoe Harube Taisuke Dono
" Satake Ikki Shūchū
" Chiba Taikin no Suke Dono."

This letter was circulated throughout the Kwantō, and the bottom promptly fell out of Ujinori's campaign. Norimoto from Echigo directed the forces of the Edo, Tōshima, and Nikaidō on Musashi. Ujinori, with his more immediate vassals and aided by his son-in-law Iwamatsu Mochikuni, drove these out of the province. But the Shōgun had spoken and his real strength was gone. The Yūki had always clung to Mochiuji, and the other Houses of Shimotsuke and Hitachi, the Utsunomiya, the Nitta, the Chiba, the Oguri, fell away from Ujinori. The Echigo army renewed its campaign. Mochikuni, a most conceited ass, felt that the Nyūdō had been gathering laurels at his expense, and he undertook to campaign on his own account. Perhaps the best course, for it ended in his surrender and composition with his suzerain. Ujinori was forced back on Kamakura thoroughly beaten in a campaign in which he showed good generalship against great numbers. The shouts of victory soon resounded in his rear. Then Norimoto issued peremptory orders to the Kwantō samurai to muster for the attack on Kamakura. All the Houses were now thoroughly frightened. There was no thought but to concoct some sort of complaint to gloss over their rebellion and to answer the summons of the Kwan-ryō. The army from Miyako, lead by Akamatsu Kazusa no Suke Yoshinori and Sakyū no Tayū Mitsusuke had been swelled to 30,000 by the addition of the 10,000 men of the levies of Mikawa, Tōtōmi, and Suruga under the Imagawa, father and son. The 12th month 2nd day (20th December) Mochiuji put aside all vacillation. If a lecher, drunkard, and roisterer he always showed the courage and obstinacy of the Ashikaga stock, itself sprung from the Seiwa Genji. On the 7th day (25th December) he was at Fujisawa. Here the huge army from the Kwantō, from Ōshū, from Dewa— 200,000 men says one scribe—blocked the way. It was through the kneeling contingents that the Prince rode. The faithful Yūki Shichirō Ujitomo, the now contrite Koyama, Satake, Oda, Chiba, Utsunomiya, Nitta, Doi, Tsuchiya, Shibusawa, Oguri, and many other Houses joined in this moving spectacle of belated sub-mission and reverential greeting to their lord—at the orders of Kyōto.

Then the Imagawa, Ōmori, and Katsurayama moved to the attack on the city. There was no serious resistance to be offered except at the Kehaizaka. This place of brothels was obstinately defended by the samurai under Chūmū no Taisuke, and the hard fighting was proved to later generations when skulls, bones, remnants of war harness were turned up in the peaceful operations of the farmer on the fields of the days of Meiji (1868—). Meanwhile Mitsutaka and Mochinaka were still holding feast and revel in the Ōkura palace, a fête continued ever since Mochiuji had been driven out of it and they had entered. As the smoke rose from the buildings fired by the advancing Imagawa, as the clouds of dust rose in every direction under the tramp of marching samurai, as the shouts rose to Heaven and shook the Earth, as the *konjichō* bird (causing earthquakes) flapped its heavy wings over the twice stricken town, the hearts of the good Kamakura people, accustomed as they were to such episodes in their lives, died within them. Women fainted, men cowered, little girls cried in their mothers' dresses, and little boys did those things they ought not to have done from sheer discomfiture. But the Kwantō was again loyal to its prince, and the people fled within to greet this stormy approach. The few who clung to the Inukake Nyūdō were equally determined to die in their tracks; albeit no other course was open to them in this old Nippon. When the blows fell on the outer gate of the Ōkura palace Mitsutaka and Mochinaka had already left it. Escape over the hills was impossible, but they succeeded in reaching Yuki no Shita. Here they were joined by Zenshū. His mansion at Inukake had been stormed by Norizane in person, and of the hundred defenders not a man was left alive. They died fighting to give Nyūdō the chance to escape. Chūmū no Taisuke, son of Ujinori, beaten at Kehaizaka joined them. Thus the four men met at the *Akabashi* (Red Bridge) of the Hachimangū. Hands were clasped in the final parting. " Entering the neighbouring monastery (which ? " sōsha ") " here they stabbed each other to death. Their wives, relatives, " and *rōtō*, to the number of forty persons cut their bellies open. " Infamous to posterity were the names they left." Thus sighs the chronicler. " For the present," can be added ; for such premature judgments in Nippon undergo official revision.   The unfortunate Mochinaka left a poem on dying :

" Though time of bloom shows many flowers,
" Then comes dispersion.   Lo ! the mountain cherry."

At least it has been fathered on him, and he was hardly old enough to father anything else.*

---

* The *akabashi* was also the place where Wada Yoshimori, henchman of Yoritomo, died fighting against the Hōjō clan.   His grave is just behind the Tenmatsu inn (marked by the post box) on the Wakamiya-Ōji.   The final struggle of his clan took place East and West of the Wakamiya-Ōji near the grave of Hatakeyama Shigeyasu.   The bodies were collected and buried close by, at the so-called Wada-zuka, marked by its pine trees and a suitable monument, on the road from Ōmachi to the Kaihin.   Only his son Asahina Saburō escaped—from Yuigahama by boat to Awa.   This was Yoshimori's son by the famous Amazon Tomoe-gozen, concubine of Yoshinaka and the spoil of Yoshimori, who captured her (no mean feat) in personal encounter at the battle of Kyōto.

CHAPTER VII.

The Plotting of Fujinami.

Such was the early and unfortunate ending of the enterprise of Ujinori. Trusting in the well founded suspicions of the weak Yoshimochi and the almost avowed ambitions of the Kamakura Kwanryō he had set the movement on foot, confident of an ultimate favourable issue. The powerful name of the Shōgun was sufficient to withhold for the time any movement of revenge on the part of Mochiuji; but it was matter of course that the fortunes of the Oguri House were seriously affected by these events. Now the inner government of the Kwanryō's immediate entourage was entrusted to three men: Isshiki Shikibu Shōyū Akihide, Yamana Kurando Ujiharu, and Oguri Hyoye no Jō Mitsushige. In his colleagues Mitsushige, as known partisan of Kyōto, always found opposition, open or secret. As said, however, the aegis of the Shōgun for the time being protected him and others engaged in the movement of the Inukake Nyūdō. At this point the weak Yoshimochi almost disappears from the tale, except to note the aftermath in Kyōto of the uprising. As soon as the news reached the capital that Ujinori and his partisans had been rewarded with death, it was of course "discovered" that Yoshitsugu was gathering soldiers to re-engage in rebellion. Yoshimochi did not let the "news" grow cold. The Sōkokuji was at once surrounded. Then a hunt began for the recalcitrant prince, who was found at last in the Kinkwō-In (hall) of the temple. Accounts vary. It is said that he was allowed to commit suicide; and again that by the order of his brother the Shōgun he was assassinated. At all events, in the sequel Yoshimochi did the proper thing; gave him the name of Yenshū-In (posthumous) with his own fair hands; and marked off one more relative as bagged. Yoshitsugu was twenty-five years old ; old enough according to Nipponese politics (and elsewhere) to be more cautious in his engagements.

It is one of the little ironies of the Nipponese conduct of affairs that nothing ever happens—except officially. A prince dies. Dead as a door nail? Nay, nay ; a grave turn of affairs is solemnly announced. With all the pomp and *formulæ* of the living the dead is conducted to his or her residence no matter how far distant. This is effected, with officials measuring the ground for the tomb, and the carpenters hammering together the box which is to be the last resting place. Then a serious issue is announced, and a few hours later the fact of decease proclaimed. This procedure is merely an extreme of what is carried throughout in connection with the great in Nippon. This falsification of fact, whether in history, a funeral, or a court function, no matter how patent the untruth, is supposed to hold good, as is obstinately taught and practised. Thus it was that shortly after the suppression of the uprising of Ujinori the Hangwan-dai Sukeshige was presented by his father to Prince Mochiuji, who graciously granted audience to receive the report as to the suppression of thieves in Hitachi and Shimosa. The prince received his old playmate with delighted countenance. Prostrate on hands and knees Sukeshige sing-songed his report to the suzerain. In reward the Prince gave him a sword beautifully ornamented with gold and vague promises of future preferment in his service. The whole court smiled and rubbed hands ; and everybody knew there was nothing of value in the whole performance except the weapon ; at least most of those present hoped so.

More serious matters than the wrath of the Kwanryō were hanging over the head of Sukeshige. When he was sent to Hitachi, the concubine Fujinami had high hopes of disposing of him, either in some unlucky fight with robbers, or by the fevers of the lowlands of Shimosa. Disappointed here the battles fought in the recent disturbance were looked to for securing the succession of the House to Manchō. When this failed her mind turned to more direct means to ruin the elder son with his father. She was on the watch for any opportunity, and of any kind that might offer. Now the 24th year of Ōei (1417) was the seventh anniversary of the death of Hatsuse, a most important feast in the Buddhist memorial services for the dead. Sukeshige had prepared elaborate *kinnotsu* (offering to the dead). With this he set forth to pray by the grave at the Bodaishō (family temple)—at the Fujisawa temple. Alone he entered his father's apartments with his offering. Mago Gorō had official duty to perform at the Ōkura palace and was absent. Fujinami appeared. Said Sukeshige—"To-day being the anniversary of " the mother's death Sukeshige humbly brings offering of the *kin-* " *notsu* to share with his revered father. Condescend that there is "no failure to receive it." Said Fujinami—"Respectfully received " from your lordship. The Ō-Dono without fail shall receive the " offering and partake thereof. May your honoured person enjoy " good health." Thus with mutual courtesy they parted. Fujinami ostentatiously placed the gift in the *tokonoma* (alcove).

In due time returned Mitsushige, to enter his apartments and put off his official robes to don more easy fitting garments. Before his eyes was the *kinnotsu* of Sukeshige. "Ah! To-day is the " seventh anniversary of the *hotoke* (spirit) of Hatsuse." Replied Fujinami, who just entered the apartment—"Yes, the young lord " himself brought the gift with the earnest desire that his father " partake of the memorial feast"—"That shall I do," quoth Mitsushige. "Few have a more loyal son, more filial in his obser- " vances, never failing in the seven proprieties. You yourself have "spoken of his affection for his younger brother Manchō, and his " respect and courtesy to yourself." The old man reached out a hand and picked up one of the cakes. Fujinami stopped him. "One moment; refrain!"—"And why?" said the astonished Mitsushige dangling the cake in the chop-sticks and turning to Fujinami. Said she—"Iya! Last night this Fujinami had most " unpleasant dreams, witnessing your lordship writhing in torments." She hesitated—"It is difficult to say, but in the dream your son " stood by smiling, and seemed to enjoy the pain suffered. Fujinami " does not feel at all sure of the offering. Deign not to partake "— " Nonsense," roughly answered Mitsushige. "This is mere filthiness " of tongue. Some maggot's egg laid in your woman's brain. No

" one is more devoted than Sukeshige, more obedient to every wish.
" What has he to gain by such a foul proceeding ? "—" Nevertheless
" refrain," begged Fujinami seizing his sleeve. At the moment a
little spaniel (*chin*) came sidling into the room. *Choro, choro,* he
danced up to Mitsushige. The latter still held the cake in his chop·
sticks, his arm dangling by his side. Jumping up the dog snatched it.
Mitsushige favoured the dog and watched it gobble the dainty.
Then pointing as it gambolled around the room—" See ! How
unfortunate and unlikely are your suspicions." The words were
hardly out of his mouth when the dog began to spin round and
round as in great pain. Then its eyes popping out of its head its
body stiffened. The legs stretched wide apart and gave way
beneath it. Then it began to spit out great gouts of blood. In a
few moments it was dead.

Weeping Fujinami sank to the floor. Stupefied Mitsushige
gazed at the corpse of the beast. Mechanically he repeated his last
words. " What has he to gain by such a foul proceeding ? " Burst
forth Fujinami indignantly—" What to gain ? Nay, he looks
" bitterly on any affection your lordship shows to my child Manchō.
" He fears that the younger son will gain his father's favour and be
" granted the succession to the House. Ah ! My unfortunate boy !
" Deprived of his father and in the hands of such an unscrupulous
" brother what fate is his ! No wonder Fujinami seeks to placate
" the hatred of this wicked man by submission." The eyes of
Mitsushige were on the beast and his ears open to the tongue of
Fujinami. " What a miserable scoundrel ! Thus to attempt the
" life of the kindest of fathers. Iya ! Even in the bitter strife
" between Etsu-Ō and Meitoku of Sō such infamy was not imagined
" between strangers. How so between parent and child ! " More
and more did the wrath of the hot tempered old man gather.
" Heita ! Heita ! " he called abruptly. At once at his lord's sharp
cry the *karō* appeared, followed by Imai Aigoshi of the guard.
Heita's eyes fell on the dog, then on Fujinami. He was prepared
for what his lord had to say. Mitsushige included beast and offering
in one sweep of his hand. Choking with rage he said—" See what
" consideration this unfilial and disloyal rascal has for the man who

Old Heita Interferes.

" gave him life. In all the Li-Ki (Book of Rites) of the sage of
" Morokoshi (China) there is nothing found to meet such a situation.
" The deed could not be imagined by Kōshi (Confucius). But
" Mitsushige is not too old to strike. At once—to this fellow's
" room!" He laid hand on his weapon to draw it forth. Imai
Aigoshi sprang forward and seized hilt and scabbard. It would
never do to allow his lord to draw his weapon in this affair.
Tanabe Heita prostrated himself in petition before his lord. " For
" the Waka-dono's (young lord) devotion to your lordship old Heita
" answers with his own body and life. Deign revered lord to hold
" your hand in this affair. This Heita feels sure that the matter
" can be made clear by the young lord." Mitsushige hesitated.
With grief he said—" Of the fact there is no question, Heita.
" Himself he brought the *kinnotsu*, which was placed there in the
" *tokonoma* in the sight of the household passing to and fro. His
" interest is patent. But Mitsushige will hold his hand. He is
" given to the charge of Heita. Let him be sought out. When
" found he is to be given no chance of prayer. Off with his head
" and bring it to me without delay. These are the commands of
" Mitsushige." In growing anger he left the room.

Tanabe Heita remained for a moment in thought. " Fujinami
" San knows more of this matter than anyone else," said he bitterly.
" My lord's orders—are the orders of my lord, to be obeyed." He
clapped his hands. " Bring *suzuri* (ink stone) and *fude* (brush),"
he ordered shortly to the page. Then Heita sat down and wrote
at length. Folding and sealing the scroll he turned to the waiting
Imai—" Imai, the Waka-dono is sure to be at the Yūgyōdera of
" Fujisawa. You must get there first ; otherwise my lord's orders
" will be carried out. The Ō-Dono as yet is very angry, and the
" young lord will make no resistance. This must not take place.
" Off with you at once, and give this letter to the young lord with
" the advice—from Heita—to go at once to Yūki in Shimosa.
" Earnestly urge it on him. Let the *rōtō* do the same. Heita will
" attend to his interests. He follows—none too quickly." Imai
lost no time. The clatter of his horse's hoofs was soon heard as he
gallopped out and took the road to the Butsukiridōshi, the deep cut

Sukeshige told of Fujinami's slander.

through the hills* leading past the temple of the Daibutsu to Fuji-sawa. Urging his horse he soon covered the five miles to the temple. The Kataoka brothers and Mito no Kotarō were lounging under the *ichō* tree before the *hondō* (main temple). A few words informed them. At once with Imai they hastened to the hill in the rear of the temple. Sukeshige was praying before his mother's grave. The solemn offering was finished. Informed that Imai Aigoshi had come he rose and went toward him. The retainer prostrated himself in tears before the Waka-dono. Said Suke-shige—" What has happened Tarō ? " Imai gave him an account of his father's great wrath and the advice of Tanabe Heita, to flee at once. Said Sukeshige—" But why should my honoured father's belly " thus rise ? What is the cause ? " With hesitating accent Imai told of the charge of poison. Sukeshige was thunderstruck. He was a guilty man to any eye. Then in firm tones he said—" The orders " of the Ō-Dono are the orders of my lord—to be obeyed. Fortu-" nately this is the year of the return of Hatsuse to her former " dwelling place. Together with her son she shall return to Meidō " (Hades). Thus my lord's commands are anticipated, without any " offence of injustice. He gave life, and has the right to demand " it." Seating himself on the steps of the grave he opened his gar-ments and drew his dagger. Ikeno Shōji sprang forward and seized the raised weapon. Kazama Jirō grasped the other arm. Thus the two big men prevented his suicide. Together the retainers prostrated themselves and plead with their lord to be in no such haste. Said Imai Aigoshi—" Would the Waka-Dono deign to " inspect the letter of the *go-karō*. Heita San is a man of wise coun-" sel ; his advice worthy of consideration." Slowly Sukeshige came to calmer thoughts. Heita plead strongly for the young lord's absence. If he should take desperate measures at this juncture all was lost and his name fouled. Surely Fujinami was at the bottom of the affair in behalf of Manchō. Deign to flee to Yūki, and Heita would see that the old lord's darkness of vision was lightened. " To " Yūki ? " said Sukeshige in some wonderment. A half smile

---

* Now tunnelled, spoiling this fine and ancient passage in existence a decade ago.

wavered on the lips of Imai and the *rōtō*. " May his lordship
" deign to learn that there live Tanabe Heirokurō and Heihachirō,
" awaiting the time when again they can prostrate themselves before
" their lord." Sukeshige gave a deep breath and looked at the
knowing faces of his *rōtō*. Some things were not always told to
their lord as responsible, and the loss of his two *rōtō* was of this
kind. Said Sukeshige—" Heita's counsel is to be followed. Imai,
" give him the thanks of Sukeshige. To Yūki ! " Now the reason
why the Tanabe brothers were living in Yūki in Shimosa forms a
tale apart.

CHAPTER VIII.

Kwannon Strikes Again.

In the early summer of Ōei 24th year (1417) the *rōtō* of Suke-shige were reduced to eight by the disappearance of the Tanabe brothers. At the Inamuragasaki *yashiki* it was known that old Tanabe Heita had a lengthy interview with the Ō-Dono. The details soon came out owing to the noise created by the event; but the whereabouts of the two men was not known, and both Mitsushige and Sukeshige remained in convenient ignorance as to this minor episode in their household What had taken place was the following. Heirokurō and Heihachirō had gone down to the beach of Saka no Shita to watch the fishermen draw the nets. This daily event performed they followed the shore along the Maebama,* and on some little commission of their father visited the Kwōmyōji and one of the *ōshō* (prebends). Returning through Zaimokuza they crossed the Wakamiya-ōji, the long avenue leading from the Hachimangū to the sea. Now here there is a little triangle formed by the avenue, the brook, and the Musashi-ōji (or Hase-kōji) which crossing the Geba-bashi leads somewhat deviously to the Hase Kwannon. This favoured plot of ground has always catered to the lighter necessities of man, except the large and massive stone lined well at the corner of the two avenues. To-day cakes, tobacco, fruit, biscuit, paper o all kinds and uses are sold. At the time spoken of it was occupied by a *saké* shop, the Yūkiya, kept by one Denkurō. Native of Yūki he was well known to the Tanabe. They at first refused his invita-

---

* Yuigahama. Yuigasato (Yui village) was then a thick.y populated quarter. The "Kamakura Taikwan" cites the "Adzuma Kagami" as here being located the *yashiki* of "Ōe, Okazaki, Maki, Nakasawa, Itomi, Tsuchiya, Wada Sakai, Hatano, Nagae, Kawano." This refers to the first half of the 13th century.

tion to enter, but pressed by the obsequious *teishu* they went into
the shop to spend a few moments. The host produced *saké*. The
fish, present of the *sendō* from the new catch, was excuse for further
stay. Just out of the water it was fit for the chafing dish or even
for *sashimi* (sliced raw). While the preparation was under way the
three men sat down in the rear of the place, to drink *saké* and look
out on the pretty garden of Denkurō which bordered the little stream
close by. It was gay with peony, and the arbour of wisteria already
showed the purple and white of its long clusters of flowers. There
was every excuse for delaying the return.

While thus engaged a samurai entered the inn. He was a
huge, ill-looking, scowling fellow. His knit brows, huge dirty buck
teeth, a frowsy beard, and a long pointed nose made him anything
but a pretty object. Calling the *kozō* (waiter) he growled—" What
" has this wretched cook-shop to furnish to-day ? Be quick, and see
" that you have some dish fit for a man such as myself "—The *kozō*
grovelled before such lordliness. "With fear and reverence : your
" worship can be furnished with fish cooked in sauce *(shōyu)*, with
" bonito or *tako* (squid) as salad. *Tai* (carp) is fresh and ready for
" roasting, or eels for stewing with rice and gravy. Moreover the
" brand of *saké* is of the best. Would your worship deign to patro-
" nize the list ? "—The samurai was not slow to accept the invitation. Nothing was omitted, and his appetite was as huge as his
person. He stuffed and drank. Then drank again. The drinking
was particularly to his taste. Appetite comes with eating. Much
more does thirst come with drinking. *Two shō* (3 quarts) of *saké* did
this human hog guzzle before he rose to leave. At this sign of
repletion the watchful *kozō* gently glided before him, blocking the
way with prostrated form. "And what now ! " quoth the big man
in well-feigned amazement—" Your worship's bill, for wine and
" food. Would your worship deign please to regard the scroll. May
" your worship deign to be pleased with the service of one so humble
" as myself." Thus the *kozō*, with the pertinacity of a *kozō*, kept
blocking the way with the unrolled bill, a full two yards in length.
The samurai was not pleased with his humble services. In great
rage he streched forth one long leg and removel the bill from the issue

by this simple process. " Pay ! " quoth he—" Assuredly," answered
the *kozō*. " Food or liquor ordered in the house is to be paid for.
" Perchance your worship has mistaken the Yūkiya for a *yashiki*,
" but it is a mere *yado* (inn) for paying guests." Roared the samurai
—" Ignoble rascal. You are bold enough to be impertinent. Pay !
" Plainly you are green to the Kamakura town. Never yet has
" Suzuki Gorō, the Ko-Tengu*, paid a bill ; least of all to a dirty third
" rate cook-shop. The *kerai* of Isshiki Dono honour those they
" patronize. Get out of my way or take the consequences." The
kozō stood his ground. " The house is for travellers. With *tengu*
" it does not do business. Your worship has eaten and drunk with-
" out stint. Now deign to pay the bill." The samurai gave one
deep " Ah ! " Then grasping the *kozō* by the neck he throttled him
until his eyes stood out. With a coarse laugh he hurled him to the
end of the room and made ready to stride forth. But the boy was
game. Springing up in rage he seized a long pole and again barred
the way. With tears he blurted—" Kichirō too can do something
" in the fighting way. Take care of yourself, Tengu." But he was
no match for the fighting man. The pole was brushed aside.
Thrown to the ground the big man bestrode him. Breaking the
pole, with one piece he proceeded to administer a sound drubbing.

    At his cries Denkurō came forth. The Tanabe brothers stood
at the entrance to the apartment watching the scene. Denkurō
prostrated himself. " Your worship is well known. Deign to pardon
" the boy, who has but recently come from Shimosa, and does not
" know the town and its clientele. Hence he served you. Truly he is
" innocent of offence." Denkurō's explanation but fanned the
wrath of Suzuki Gorō. " Iza ! He shall take his first lesson then in
" knowledge of the town. As for yourself, guard your tongue rascal,
" to avoid similar treatment." He raised the stick. Denkurō
leaned forward and dared to touch his arm in renewed petition.
Straightway the samurai launched his fist full in the inn-keeper's
face, and the latter rolled over and over to the end of the room.
Disgusted Heiroku came forward, followed by Heihachirō. Said

---

* Hobgoblin living in the mountains. Ko=small ; i.e. " human " as here
used,

Heiroku—" Such conduct is most unseemly for a samurai, although
" just what is to be expected from a kerai of Isshiki. It is for them
" to swindle and bully the shop-keepers of the town, to the dishonour
" of our caste. Here you have stuffed, gobbled, and guzzled away
" until your guts are fairly bursting. Pay what is owing and leave.
" Surely never again will service be given "—" Mind your business,"
shouted Gorō. " It is no part of a samurai to side with a tradesman
" in a quarrel, especially one not protected by his House. Let them
" go to Yūki Dono. You too want a taste of the Tengu's arm "—
" It is the part of a samurai to protect the weak," said Heiroku.
" We are doing a good deed in preventing your carrying such out-
" rageous conduct to extremes. You forget yourself. Deign to
" pardon the boy and pay the host. This is the proper course "—
" Thanks indeed for the advice. Deign to receive my humble com-
" pliments." Doubling his fist Suzuki Gorō struck a savage
blow at Heiroku. The latter dodged. His foot landed with a
thump in the big body of Gorō. His fist lodged with a smack
between Gorō's eyes. Back the latter went into the open to land in
a heap. His head met the stone curbing of the well with a crash.
Heihachirō leaped on him and pressed him down. Heiroku stood
over them. Said Heihachirō—" Ideya ! Brother you have struck
" hard. Oya ! Oya ! See ; why the fellow is dying ! " Suzuki
Gorō began to vomit blood. The eyes rolled back until nothing but
the whites were seen. Then he turned his head feebly to one side,
gave a short wheezy gasp and died. Heirokurō was highly disgusted—" What a weak *tengu* is this ! What now is to be done ?
" Never mind ; I take the matter on myself and will make report to
" my lord ; then await the consequences. Do you Heihachirō keep
" silence. Denkurō will say nothing, and none will ever know of
" your presence. You are not involved "—" Nay brother," said
Heihachirō, " you are the elder. It is for me to take your place
" and assume responsibility. Deign to allow me to do so." But
Heirokurō was firm—" It is my affair, a quarrel in a tavern. More-
" over the fellow had stuffed himself to overflowing. Sudden death
" could explain all. Do not be anxious." Denkurō timidly touched
his arm. As they turned to him the man's alarm was evident on

his face. But he was a cool collected fellow. His business required
it. Said he—"Absence so long in Hitachi, honoured sirs, makes
"Kamakura new to you. The affair cannot thus be composed. The
"Ko-Tengu was a prime favourite of Isshiki Akihide, his right
"hand man and tale-bearer, bringing his lord all the tattle of the
"wine-shops. For nearly three years he has levied his tribute on
"the shop-keepers of the city. If Denkurō had seen him enter he
"would have attended him himself, fed him well, and dismissed
"him in good humour stuffed with some idle tale of gossip. But
"now flight is necessary for all; and without delay. It is merely a
"matter of closing shop. That is done every day now in these dis-
"turbed times. Be assured that Denkurō knows the ins and outs of
"the Isshiki *yashiki*. Yūki Dono will not move a finger in the
"affair, and it would merely be trouble for your lord to face out the
"affair. Isshiki Akihide will move heaven and earth to avenge his
"favoured *rōtō*. But everything will be well. In Yūki this Den-
"kurō is well known. What he will not do in Kamakura my honoured
"master will do in Yūki town. There it will be perfectly safe to
"live."

Denkurō was so earnest, the advice seemed so good, that it was
at once adopted. At night fall the shop was shut up. A neighbour
was summoned, and the body of Suzuki Gorō was pointed out to
him to make report. Forthwith the Tanabe brothers, with Denkurō and the *kozō* as guides, made their way to Yūki in Shimōsa.
Here a wine shop was opened. Heirokurō and Heihachirō tied up
their cues and adopted the costume and occupation of *bantō* (attendants). They made a very arrogant pair of waiters. But if the
shop lost in one sense, it distinctly gained in another. The wine
was good and cheap, the service fair and quick, and no kind of
petty cheating of guests half seas over was practised. The clientele
therefore was of the best and most paying kind. When the shop
was first opened it had its experience of the bums and dead-beats of
the place. If one visits the town of Yūki in these present days he
finds a dull country town, of but little interest even to the travelling
bantō. In the days of the Yūki and Koyama it was the great city
north of Kamakura. Yedo, the fishing hamlet in the marshes of the

Sumidagawa, had not yet attracted the attention of Ōta Dōkwan. More than a generation passed before he gave it some importance by building a castle on the hill behind it. But Yūki was the goal and centre of all the feeble commerce of the time, and with Ōshū and Dewa this was of national importance, for traders with gold and furs went even as far as Kyōto. Strangers therefore swarmed to Yūki. When the new shop was opened the unsavoury part of the gay world, "the door-breaking fellows and vagabonds," thought for a time at least to find free quarters for wine and women. Thus they early invaded the *sakéya* of Denkurō. Loudly and merrily they called for refreshment and caroused. Gravely were they served. It cast something of a chill over the roisterers to watch the quick precision and energy of these big *bantō* of the host Denkurō. Then Heiroku brought the bill. Said the most impudent—"Iza! Hang it up *botchan* (youngster.) To-day we are "out of funds. *Ototoi oide.*"*—"He who eats and drinks, pays— "here, in one way or another." Such was the answer of Heiroku. As pay was not forthcoming he proceeded to shake the fellow out of his existing wits. Then standing him on his head he passed him on to Heihachirō for similar proceedings, with every disposition to repeat the process with the next man. The roisterers in alarm managed to make up the sum owing. Never again was the house of Denkurō thus favoured. As said its clientele so gained by this purging process that it was as wide-spread as the decent element of the town permitted. From being considered cold and supercilious the *bantō* of Denkurō came to be regarded as particularly reliable young fellows. Moreover they constantly practised their fencing in the side yard of the inn, and many were the townsmen who came to witness it. The younger element came to look up to them as leaders and protectors from the roughs. Wide spread was their title of *sensei* (teacher). The older element was always secure of safe escort if their time in the tavern was overstayed, and they had to return home in the darkness of the night.

It was for this reason that Tanabe Heita had recommended

---

*Come the day before yesterday=the Greek kalends, the coming of the cocklicranes; but cf. Rabalais I. 49.

Yūki as dwelling place for his young lord.   Yūki Ujitomo was but
a few years older than Sukeshige.   He would never believe the ill
rumours set afloat as to his friend.   Living here Sukeshige could be
kept in constant touch with Kamakura and what occurred there.
Of the journey thither but little has been preserved.   However it
was on this occasion that Sukeshige first met the man who later
had so much influence on his life.   Lord and retainers did not
always travel together on this leisurely journey to Yūki town.
Sukeshige would send them ahead, in scattered companies of two or
three, to meet and report to him the local conditions at some village
to be passed through.   One day he was urging his horse along the
Musashi plain, having made a detour and stop at Hirai in Kōtsuke.
To all intents and purposes he had lost his way, with nothing but
the mountain ranges to guide him, and a net-work of trails with an
obscure village as goal.   Of the Musashino it was said in those
days :

> " Moor of Musashi, flooded by moonlight;
> " Hill there is none; grass, naught but grass."

And the native scribe amends this :

> " Moor of Musashi, flooded by moonlight ;
> " Hill there is none; naught but house eaves."

in reference to the great city of Yedo—Tōkyō of much later date.

Sukeshige had planned to meet Mito no Kotarō and the
Kazama brothers that night at the village of Yotsuya, "Four
Houses," which well describes these hamlets on the moor.   All day
he had gone without food, and his horse also had nothing but the
unsavoury bamboo grass withered by the winter cold.   Faint with
hunger and thirst, a stumble of the animal threw the knight prostrate.   Miraculous to say, where his elbow struck the ground a spring
gushed forth, at least so tradition of later date explains its presence.
As he quenched his thirst there came tramping the moor with
steady stride a vigorous priest, an oldish man, attended by a single
disciple.   Seeing the faint condition of the knight he at once produced his wallet and food.   Better acquainted than Sukeshige with
the moor his *deshi* was sent to a farm house, within a long call of

the unlucky tumble. Here a bundle of hay was secured for the animal, and the priest insisted on replenishing the knight's wallet from his own food supply. Said he—"To him who treads the "Buddha's Way all life is dear." As Sukeshige gave him earnest thanks, and marvelled at his presence in such a lonely spot, far from temple and cloister, the priest smiled—" Not so far from temple "and cloister, for the whole of Nippon is the parish. This humble "priest is Yūgyō Joa, whose duty it is to succour distress wherever "found ; for whom the affairs of this world are as naught. For him "are neither cares, nor joys, likes nor dislikes. Only to him it is a "duty to aid the injured and unfortunate, whether they be inclined "or disinclined—a principle of vast importance. And you, respected "Sir ; deign to grant Joa the favour of name and home." Bowing in reverence said Sukeshige—" As for my insignificant "self, I am from Hitachi province, Kojirō Sukeshige, son of "the Hangwan Oguri Hyōye no Jō Mitsushige." The priest held up his hand in wonder—"How marvellous indeed this "our meeting ! No relations now are of Joa. The priest of Buddha "has left the world, and no longer has parent, brother, nephew. "But in the secular life Joa was the younger brother of Mitsushige, "Sakon Michinobu by name. On reaching early manhood the "weapons of war were discarded, to assume the armour of the "Buddha and to tread his path. Marvellous indeed is this "meeting. Surely our lives are brought together by the action of "some *karma*." With kindly direction and salutation priest and samurai parted. Instructed as to his road Sukeshige reached Yotsuya-mura and his anxious *rōtō*.

At the Daigyōji near Oyama the *rōtō* assembled for their entrance into Yūki town, now not far distant. It happened that on this day the riff-raff of Yūki were thirsty, unhappy, and ill-tempered, after their kind. It was the suggestion of a neophyte that the Yūkiya and refreshment be sought. On this aspirant they all turned fiercely. Said one—" Tarōbe prefers to drink standing, but not on "his head. Heiroku-San has too strong an arm." Said another— "And this Kenjirō has no liking to be as dice in a box, shaken by "the fist of Heihachirō-San." Said a third—" Here comes game.

The Reception at Yūki Town.

" Perhaps it will pay the tax of the stranger's entrance into Yūki."
Nine men wearing deep straw hats came along the narrow road
which served as high way into the big town. " Fair game ! " was
the unanimous verdict of the gang of roughs, and they drifted
toward the new-comers, blocking the way. " Take care what you're
doing," said Ikeno Shōji, as one man tried to shove him aside into
the rice-field—" See to your staff there," said Kazama Hachirō as
another brought it into close contact with his head. Cries went
up—" What impudent fellows are these to force their way in where
" they are not wanted. But every outside block-head thinks that
" Yūki town is public pasture, to give him a living. Out with them ;
" or else let them pay the tribute of entrance." Thus a contest of
shoving and pushing began, the samurai defending themselves
with no particular difficulty against the roughs. Sukeshige said—
" Be gentle. Dont enter the town with a battle, if it can be avoided." The words were hardly out of his mouth when actual fighting
ensued. A fellow raised his fist to strike Mito no Kotarō as the
smallest man in the band of strangers. Kotarō promptly hit him
between the eyes. Falling backward his staff struck the head of
Kazama Jirō. Jirō promptly grasped the fellow by the back of the
neck and sent him flying into the cold mud of the neighbouring
rice field. Then in rage the roughs joined battle. This was of
short duration. Safety was soon sought in flight. Laughing
Sukeshige and his *rōtō* continued on toward the town. Meanwhile
a self-appointed messenger of evil hastened to the Tanabe. " Sensei !
" Sensei ! Strangers are invading the town. People in fear are
" fleeing, and climbing to the roofs of the houses, and barring the
" doors. Aid us, Sensei ! Aid us ! " Said Heiroku—" Something is
" wrong. The townsmen are to be helped brother." Taking stout
poles they issued forth, the crowd respectfully making way for
them. Space opened before the strangers, and the Tanabe *kyōdai*
thus unexpectedly found themselves in the presence of their lord.
Said Heiroku—" Here's a state of things (*taihen*), brother ! We
" can only make apology forthwith to our lord." Prostrate, with
face on hands they addressed the Waka-Dono. " Pray pardon this
" gross impertinence and disrespect in opposing your lordship's

"entrance to Yūki. Our stupid selves had no thought of your "lordship's presence, except as in Kamakura town." Meanwhile the crowd waited for the pulverisation of the foe. It was amazed and discomfited—"The strong to the strong; the weak never find a champion." Certainly it was not so in this case. Said Heirokurō scowling—"Make apology to our lord at once, or suffer "punishment from all. Such disrespectful greeting is not to be "tolerated"—"Ah! Their lord! Apology and obeisance to the "revered lord of our honoured *sensei*;" and the crowd making obeisance dispersed to their homes, talking and magnifying the wondrous discovery that the *bantō* of Denkurō were samurai, as had long been suspected. Then the laughs and smiles disappeared from the face of Sukeshige as he held consultation over the prejudices and difficulties of the Ō-Dono, and the vile accusation against his son. "Alas! This is a wicked affair," said Heirokurō. "But "here your lordship is in safety and easy communication with "Kamakura. Our father will do everything to disabuse the "mind of the Ō-Dono. Meanwhile there is nothing to do but "wait on the course of events." Thus in the 25th year of Ōei (1418) Sukeshige was living in Yūki town with his *rōtō*, there to await the unsealing of his father's eyes and the dispelling of his prejudice.

Years passed; not favourable years for the fortunes of Mitsushige in Kamakura. The Shōgun Yoshimochi plays little part in this tale, but the nature of the man had great influence on the fate of Mitsushige, and of others who had engaged in the uprising of Ujinori. Here is an instance of court life in Kyōto. In the 9th month of Ōei 27th year (October 1420) the Daiju (Great Tree= Yoshimochi) felt uncommonly unwell. Now-a-days he would be ordered a course of "waters" and disagreeable salts. In his day and case not salts, but spirits were invoked on the principle that like cures like. So on the 15th day (22nd October) the Urabe no Kanenobu and Shintō priests held a special service in the palace, before a special shrine duly and elaborately erected to the Seven Buddhas of the Yakushi Seizū. All the priestly furniture of most elaborate character, cups, flowers of wondrous shapes, mirrors, flags were arrayed before the altar of sandal wood. Incense burners adorned with birds, sparrows, tortoises, and other beasts (except cats), consumed without stint costly and rare perfumes. The seven Nyorai were to be worshipped, and the *kuge* and *buke*, arrayed in white *hitatare* (robes) knelt in long lines, to pray and supplicate the gods for their lord's swelled head and liver. Reverently did Kanenobu invoke the Seven Buddhas of Shingon. The air lay dead and heavy, yet the flags waved and rustled as in a breeze. Smoke rose to the nostrils; an evanescent perfume was noticed by all. Then the Ommyō Hakase (professor of astrology) Sadamune incontinently tumbled over in a faint. This bad example was followed forthwith by Shirohashi Dainagon Kanenobu Kyō, Uramatsu Sangi Yoshisuke, Hino Sangi Arimitsu, Kanshūji Sachūben Tsuneoki, and the medical doctor Miya Uchi no Shōsuke Kōten. Now here are at least three privy councillors of the palace (Sangi and Dainagon) to funk this Shōgunal performance on the plea of being choked, dizzy, and faint. Great was the confusion and fright among *buke* and *kuge*. Those overcome were carried out, and the hall thus purged Kanenobu passed around restoratives to counteract this evil manifestation due, as he said, to the malign prayers of the affected men. At this no more dared to become affected. The Imperial doctor, the Tenyaku no Kami Sadamune, was arrested and put to the torture as remedy for his affliction. At last under proper and prolonged application of this stimulant he confessed his guilt. The diviner (*urabe*) was confirmed; and the medical man banished to Sanuki. The other guilty men got off more easily. In disgrace they were entrusted to the charge of the Kwampaku Mitsunori Kō, and for long were not allowed to appear at court, but *were* allowed to live in Kyōto. Meanwhile Kanenobu had prayed and danced for five days; the Shōgun Yoshimochi had abstained from strong liquors; the headache was removed. Great was the mercy of the gods!

Such was the man Mitsushige had to fall back upon. Meanwhile the foolish tongue and intrigues of Fujinami were creating difficulties for him. Sukeshige was still above ground. After months she learned that he was in Hitachi. Nothing could be gained from the Ō-Dono in running him down. In fact she was now treated with marked disfavour; but after all she was the mother of Manchō. Fujinami decided to move higher for influence. Summoning one Kajiguchi Jirō, the head *sendō* (boatman) of the Oguri House and a relative of her own, a foolish prattling old man, she began to tell him tales of the conduct of Sukeshige. With a band of thieves he had sought refuge in Hitachi, and fellows of the kind were flocking to his standard. It was said that his real intentions aimed at the prince himself, ambitious of being a second and successful Taira Masakado; and in his unbridled anger and pride he would not hesitate to attack his suzerain, who thus was in daily danger. The old man did just what she expected. This news was soon the talk of every barber shop and bath house in Kamakura, and the Isshiki *kerai* with joy brought these tales to their lord Akihide. Great was their welcome. Akihide allowed the stories to accumulate until he had quite a pack of well elaborated lies. Then he went to the palace and made full report to Prince Mochiuji; adding nothing, for this was unnecessary and undiplomatic with such full material to hand, and easy confident appeal to his fellow councillors, who of course were dosed with the same town talk. Said Isshiki—"The son would not so act without " the consent and support of the father. "This obscure quarrel, the " basis of which no one knows, is a mere blind." Mochiuji ordered the old daimyō to be summoned. Knowing the animus of Isshiki he did not believe too much in the tale, but it was a convenient handle to his growing anger and confidence. Said he—"Surely " you, his father, cannot be ignorant. This is difficult to believe. " The matter is town talk. What is this alleged difference between " Sukeshige and yourself?"—In answer Mitsushige had to finesse. His own growing certainty of having been deceived forbade in justice even reference to the real cause. His dismissal was almost curt. Disgrace was foreshadowed.

He left the palace pained and thoughtful. "Fujinami's tongue " is at the bottom of this. So bitterly does she hate Sukeshige, and " so ignorant is she of the undercurrents ruling this place. A " woman's tongue has ruined all." The situation was serious. But a few days had passed since the Prince had descended on the

Satake of Hikigayatsu. In the battle which ensued the leaders of the clan had all cut belly and their samurai were dispersed. Plainly Mochiuji was settling accounts with the more prominent recalcitrants in the affair of Ujinori. "Ah! If Sukeshige was but "at hand to take the burden of these affairs." His mind was long since disabused. He now admitted it and turned to this filial son for support. As matter of fact Sukeshige was then riding hard toward Kamakura town, summoned by old Heita who much disliked the complexion of affairs. A few days later Prince Mochiuji sprang his trap. He was now ready to make an active move against this old traitor Mitsushige. "Since he so loves Kyōto, let "him return thither; that is, his head. But he must expose his "bias to the council." The last scene was carefully arranged. The debate was opened as to the relations with the Shōgun. Prince Mochiuji heavily inveighed against Yoshimochi—the "Kubō-sama!" It was he who was at the bottom of the uprising of Ujinori. It was he who kept the Kwantō in constant discontent with its lord. The first month (23 Jan.–22 Feb. 1422) of the present year he had ostentatiously visited his brother Gien, head of the Tendai sect on Hieisan and its hosts of priests. He threatened resignation, and to put in his place his drunken and impotent son Yoshikazu. This was to the disgrace and decline of the fortunes of the House. Neither priest nor drunkard should conduct its affairs. Let the Kwantō contingents be summoned, and a march be made at once on Kyōto.

Mitsushige did not fall in the trap. He saw it plainly enough for the prince was over-vehement. The old man made his last dignified remonstrance to the youthful lord whom he had guided for so many years; since the Prince Mitsukane took him in favour for his boldness at the Kwannondō. Said he—"The suzerain is well "advised; but the matter has another side. If the Shōgunate be "assumed by violence, instead of the sixty-six provinces being "united under one government, double pretext will be given to "split them wide apart. The Kusunoki and the partisans of the "South Court are still strong and have root everywhere. With the "division of the Ashikaga House comes their opportunity. 'The

" hair blown by the wind shows the gaping wound beneath.'
" Great is the fame of your lordship. But only the greedy would
"advise the suzerain to make this move." He spoke with copious
citation of precedent and quotation of the lore of China. Thus he
put his position plain to all men. When he ceased Mochiuji
dismissed the subject and the council. Then he gave audience to
the expectant Isshiki Akihide and Yamana Ujiharu Said Isshiki
bluntly—" Oguri Dono is a crafty old traitor. The man is con-
" stantly sending inside information to Kyōto. There resides his
" suzerain, and he is a mere spy on our lord. So deep is the fellow
" that your lordship will never get a more open acknowledgment
" than in this defence of the Kyōto interests." Yamana spoke
much to the same effect. He was less courageous than Isshiki in
wickedness and slander. But the mind of Mochiuji was made up.
"The Yūki will not refuse to act. This has been ascertained.
" With the Momonoi and Nikaidō let the Inamuragasaki *yashiki*
" be at once attacked, and the traitor Mitsushige put to death. His
" head is to be brought for inspection. The father despatched, the
" head of the son is easily secured. A messenger is to be sent to
" Hitachi Province with this order."

When Mitsushige entered his *yashiki* there came before him
old Tanabe Heita. The *karō* prostrated himself before his lord.
Astonished Mitsushige learned that Sukeshige waited without,
with petition for admittance to his presence. Said Heita—
"The Waka Dono comes unaccompanied. His *rōtō* remain at
" Gokurakuji." Agitated and touched Mitsushige gave orders that
he be admitted at once. Sukeshige entered and prostrated himself
before his lord and father." " Humbly this Sukeshige submits
" himself to his lord's will. He has no wish to live under his father's
" displeasure. Innocent though he be of any offence, yet is it an
" offence to live against a father's will. Deign to express this will
" in person, and Sukeshige obeys, gladly giving up life." Said
Mitsushige—" Long, beloved son, have all suspicions as to any
" misconduct been dispelled by our faithful Heita. The sin is to be
" laid nearer home." He took his son's head in his hands and
kissed it. " My beloved son ! " The old man wept. Thus long

they remained silent in this close contact. Sukeshige sprang up
with fire in his eye—" How remiss and thoughtless ! Heita has
" sent bad news to Yūki. Your lordship is threatened. Life ! It is
" not life sought, but death fighting with his lord against these
" slanderous rascals." Said Mitsushige—" Yes, the blow cannot be
" long withheld. But how parry it ? " He told Sukeshige in full
of the council of the day and his lord's open disfavour. " A few
days since the Satake paid for their offence......... " ; he was interrupted by the entrance of old Heita, who respectfully handed him an
arrow. Attached to it was a letter. Said Heita—" A man loung-
" ing opposite shot this arrow into the door-post of the outer gate.
" Will my lord deign to give his orders." Mitsushige opened the
letter. It said—" Respectful notice to Oguri Dono. At dawn the
" Yūki, Momonoi, and Nikaido, march to attack him."

Silently Mitsushige handed the letter to Sukeshige. Both
looked at Heita. Then said Mitsushige—" This is no time to play
" the coward. Do you, Sukeshige, act as *kaishaku* (second). Forth-
" with this Mitsushige shall cut open his belly. Then follow me to
" *Meido*." Sukeshige bowed as one prepared to obey his lord
and father. Heita interposed. " Deign, revered lord, to listen to
" the words of old Heita. We have grown old together, and your
" lordship knows that Heita would never counsel a cowardly course
" of action. For the young lord to commit suicide would in any
" event mean the ruin of the House. Truly it would be a dog's
" death (useless). The Nippon of these days is too full of uncertain-
" ties to make such a course advisable. Your lordship's position is
" by no means desperate. The Oguri belong to Shinano no Kuni,
" are direct vassals of the Shōgun. Once a vassal, always a vassal.
" Such was the rule laid down by the great Yoritomo himself ; and
" severe was the punishment of Ōba Kagechika for his revolt. First
" deign to see what course Kyōto will adopt. Oguri castle is strong.
" The lord Utsunomiya Mochitsuna, long threatened himself, has
" been urging an alliance. Let order be given at once to Kajiguchi.
" Deign my lord to take boat to Edoguchi and thence to Oguri castle.
" The Waka Dono with Heita and the *rōtō* will defend the *yashiki*.
" We will die fighting if necessary, but the Waka-Dono shall pass

" safely through the enemy, to join your lordship at Oguri "—
" Heita, your counsel always is good. Be it so. Sukeshige, follow
" well his advice. Heita is old and experienced. Let Kyōto speak
" Such is the decision of Mitsushige." The old warrior's fighting
blood was up. With the darkness of night he, the women of the
household, and some samurai as guard, were on their way to Edoguchi at the Sumidagawa.

Tanabe Heitayū the *karō* of Oguri, was not long in making
preparation for the expected attack. Bundles of hay and straw
well soaked in oil were placed in different parts of the building.
Without stint the valuable fluid was dispensed like water. Then
the dawn was awaited. The foe was not long in making its
appearance. In front came the Momonoi. Behind them were the
Nikaidō. The Yūki formed the rear guard. A mighty shout of
battle was raised ; answered fiercely by the *rōtō* of Oguri. Arrows
flew like rain. Many of the assailants fell. The Oguri did not
escape unscathed. Their ranks were sadly thinned. Thus for several hours the unequal contest raged. On the suggestion of Yūki
Ujitomo the attacking force withdrew out of range for rest before
making one united attack. Then the *yashiki* was again approached. From the rear the position could not be assaulted in
force. The three clans were compelled to march up the steep
hill, their lines mixed and confused in the fishing village of Gokurakujimura. But now all was silence. Not a sign of life
was seen, not an arrow discharged. Cautiously they advanced.
Suddenly a great column of smoke rose, bright tongues of flame
were seen licking the roofs of the buildings. Plain it was that hopeless of defence the *yashiki* had been fired and the defenders sought
refuge in death. With a shout the Momonoi samurai rushed into
the flames and smoke, to take such prisoners as they could, to anticipate the *seppuku* of the lord of Oguri whose capture had been
emphasized in the orders of the prince, and to do what looting the
occasion offered. But hardly were they entangled in the maze of
burning buildings than the Oguri, lord and retainers, charged
through their ranks. Cutting and slashing they advanced in a com-
pact body. With the common soldiery they numbered a bare

fifty men in all. The *rōtō* were prepared to die in effecting the escape of the young lord. Before the fierce attack the Momonoi divided and fled to all sides. In the smoke and confusion they were without leadership before this unexpected attack. Then the second line of the Nikaidō was met within the narrow gateway, where the numbers of the Oguri counted as many as the enemy. These fared no better. Charging down the hill the Oguri went through them as a knife through paper. As for the Yūki, these hesitated. As the Oguri approached, as if in fear a lane was formed through the ranks, and thus Sukeshige and his attendants rode through to the hills of the Gokurakuji and Fukuzawa. In a trice the flames of the fishermen's houses rose to join the smoke rising heavenward from the *yashiki*. The Yūki soldiery had closed their lines and ran hither and thither to extinguish the flames. They thus blocked very effectually the disappointed and eager pursuit of the Nikaidō and Momonoi. Great was the confusion and division of council. In a rage the Momonoi, Wakasa no Kami and Sanuki no Kami, abandoned all thought of pursuing an enemy who had departed whither they knew not. As the brothers rode back to Kamakura said Nikaidō Dono—" Since when has Ujitomo gone to bed with a " fox ? He is loyal and blunt, but more stupid than crafty." Meanwhile the Yūki continued their righteous task of organizing and aiding the fishermen, and of covering the Oguri rear in their flight.

As Sukeshige clattered into Fujisawa he heard a shout in the rear. Pulling up his horse he looked back. Close behind came a single *bushi*, his *kerai* streaming far in the rear. Frowning Sukeshige recognized the horseman as Yūki Ujitomo. He rode to meet him holding out his war-fan. " Great is the reverence and fear for " the honoured friend of the Yūki House. But this is a public affair " Yūki Dono. Be sure that we will earnestly defend ourselves." Ujitomo laughed—" Bravely said, respected Sir ; as befits one of " your courage and reputation. The arrow letter, however, was shot " by a *rōtō* of the Yūki House, and the *kerai* not only gave pas- " sage to the Oguri, but are now earnest in confusing the Momonoi " and Nikaidō to aid in effecting the escape. But beware Oguri " Dono. Deign to give the respectful salutation of Ujitomo to

" Mitsushige Dono. It is the Isshiki and Yamana who are at the
" bottom of this affair, and they are well prepared. In a few days,
" if not already, an army will be on the march to Hitachi. Re-
" spected Sir deign to be on guard." Said Sukeshige—" Great are
" the thanks and reverence owing to Yūki Dono for this kindness.
" With life this action shall never be forgotten. Deign to accept
" these acknowledgments of Sukeshige, who speaks for his House.
" Report is to be made to my father." Thus they parted. Yūki
to rejoin his *kerai* and ride back to Kamakura. Sukeshige hastened
on to Hitachi. The words of Ujitomo were exact. He preceded but
a few days a powerful force marching under the command of
Uesugi Shigekata and Isshiki Naokane, and acting by direct order
of the Shitsuji Norizane. Of these battles little has been preserved.
With the aid of Utsunomiya Mochitsuna the forces of Oguri were
more than a match for the too hastily levied army of Isshiki and
Uesugi. The place was not strong but was well garrisoned. Oguri
castle, with an enclosure of 4000 tsubo (3½ acres), stood on a mound
in the plain with the Hitachi hills close at hand. To the South,
distant barely ten miles, was the mountain mass of Tsukuba.
Standing thus on level ground, undefended by cliff or river, its main
defence lay in moat and castle and the lack of cover to the enemy.
The assailants were repulsed many times, and in determined sallies
the garrison fought several pitched battles inflicting severe punishment. It was in one of these sallies that Ikeno Shōji Sukenaga
sent his name ringing through the land. In the dead of night he
succeeded in entering and firing the enemy's camp. The Oguri
rōtō made a fierce sally. In haste and confusion the siege was
abandoned on the following day, and the foe retreated in confusion
to Kamakura for solace and further counsel.

Mitsushige knew that the end could not be long delayed. He
summoned Sukeshige, and in the presence of Heita gave his final
command to this filial son. Sukeshige made respectful protest. He
pleaded the strength of the defence, his desire to share his father's
fate in a glorious death. But Mitsushige was not to be moved. The
Shōgun was sending aid, but it was in the shape of an army coming
to assist Mochiuji in the suppression of the Kwantō rebels. His son

must live to perpetuate his name and assert his innocence, to avenge his uneasy spirit on his enemy Isshiki Akihide. Such was his charge. With tears and grief Sukeshige withdrew to Yūki at his father's command. Here it happened that he was seized with a high fever, just as Mitsushige learned of the approach of Prince Mochiuji, commanding in person a large army and coming to attack Oguri castle. His *rōtō* carried Sukeshige off to safe quarters near Nikkō-san. The news and arrival of Prince Mochiuji coincided so closely that Mitsushige had no time to make safe disposal of Fujinami and Manchō. The castle was closely invested on all sides. Mitsushige and Mochitsuna fought bravely, but the end was certain. The time for death had come. The 8th month 15th day (19th September, 1423) the enemy prepared for the final assault. Mitsushige mounted a *yagura* (wooden tower) near the walls. Opening his war fan he shouted —" This Mitsushige dies, slandered before his lord by wicked " vassals. He is innocent of all offence. Now receive the final " discharge of arrows." Then he withdrew. The *kerai* of Oguri opened the battle from the walls. As the enemy swarmed within the now blazing mass of the castle the old daimyō seated himself on the mats and cut open his belly. Utsunomiya Mochitsuna did the same. Tanabe Heitayū followed his lord in death as in life. As the chronicler says; " the loyal died fighting, the cowards fled." Oguri castle had fallen.

The aftermath of this affair was not without importance. Sulking and angry Prince Mochiuji returned toward Kamakura. The Kyōto army had learned the news while in Suruga. They did not cross the Hakone pass. Fearing to be attacked rather than received by the allied House its commanders marched back to Kyōto. Mochiuji still remained in camp at Ebina,* growling and threatening his cousin the Shōgun ; firmly convinced, at least so pretending, that Yoshimochi was the instigator of these rebellious vassals. It looked as if he would march westward and precipitate a rupture. Yoshimochi was not afraid, but he wanted peace. Sōfuku Seidō, one of his priestly counsellors, was sent to the Kwantō in Ōei 31st year 3rd month (April 1424) to

---

* Kōza district, Sagami no Kuni (province).

argue with Mochiuji. The prince at first jeered at him, and refused all accommodation. Sōfuku came and went, and returned again. His council called to the memory of Mochiuji the effect of the Shōgun's last call on the Kwantō soldiery. This remonstrance, and its source, had effect. To the reminder of Sōfuku that Yoshimochi and Mochiuji were as father and son the prince now gave readier ear. By the 9th month (23 Sept.—23 Oct.) peace was finally established between the Shōgun and Kwanryō. Sōfuku Seidō returned to Kyōto satisfied ; Mochiuji to Kamakura in triumph. Before this, Ōei 30th year 2nd month (13 March—11 April 1423) Yoshimochi nominally had abdicated, inducting his drunken son into the office of Shōgun. Yoshikazu held it for three years of feasting and riot. Then he died, Ōei 32nd year 2nd month 27th day (13 March 1425), in an alcoholic delirium, leaving Yoshimochi again to assume the weary office with its ceremonial.*

---

* In the Ashikaga Bakufu (Military Government) the Shōgun Yoshimitsu had established a practice of delegation, thoroughly Nipponese in precedent and bound to give excessive power, and hence rivalry in ambition, to a few selected Houses of the vassals. He established : 1, Himself as Kubō-Sama (a strictly Imperial title). 2, the Sankwan or Three Houses ; Buei (Chiba), Hosokawa, and Hatakeyama, clans. In these alternately lay the right to be named Kwanryō (formerly Shitsuji) of Kyōto. 3, the Shishoku or Four Offices ; Yamana, Isshiki, Kyōgoku (Satake), Akamatsu. These alternately had the right to head the Samurai-dokoro (War Department) as Bettō. 4, the Takeda and Ogasawara alternately superintended the practice of the Kyūba (military arts). 5, the two Kira, Imagawa, Shibukawa, became commanders of divisions. (*musha-gashira*). The Ise House took the office of chancellors, to transmit State reports (Sōja). These were the *Shichi-gashira* (Seven Notables).

This form of Government was imitated in the Kwantō, up to the downfall of the ruling Ashikaga House before the powerful Uesugi. Mochiuji's rebellion primarily was due to the support given by the Shōgun to this powerful House. Just as the Uesugi in their turn saw to it that Kamakura should not oppose the interests of the Kyōto Shōgun.

1. The Kubō-sama, or Kwanryō.

2. The Shitsuji (Kwanryō). The Uesugi of Yamanouchi were descended from Norifusa ; and the Uesugi of Ōgigayatsu were descended from Shigeaki. They occupied the office alternately, and were known as the Ryō-Uesugi.

3. The Sankwan ; the Kwanryō of Kamakura, together with the Kwanryō of Ōshū, and that of Dewa. These two latter were descended from Mitsunao, brother of Ujimitsu.

4. The Hachigata (Eight Notables); Chiba, Koyama, Naganuma, Yūki, Satake, Ōda, Nasu, Utsunomiya.

As with the Emperor, the Shōgun disappeared in the power granted to his vassals. His power and resources were completely dissipated, and the long history of the Ashikaga is a continual struggle to assert the Shōgunal power; or of the great vassals over its exercise. If the arrangement was bad for Kyōto it was still worse for Kamakura. With time the sins and oppression of the great Houses were all repeated in the Kwantō, and with far more room for their exercise. With the fall of Mochiuji the Kwantō was left to itself, and profited by the situation. Peace was only restored by Hideyoshi. It was a period of nearly two hundred years of confused and deadly armed strife among a race which particularly delights in a fight, and in which for nearly eight hundred years civil government, as distinguished from military government, never figured.

PART II

THE ADVENTURES OF SUKESHIGE
AND TERUTE.

" But what do you think, O king? If one man were
" to seize hold intentionally of a fiery mass of metal
" glowing with heat, and another were to seize hold of
" it unintentionally which would be the more burnt?
" The one who did not know what he was doing.
" Well it is just the same with the man who does wrong.
" He who sins inadvertently,!O king, has the greater
"demerit."

Questions and Puzzles of Milinda the King.
(Rhys-Davids.)

CHAPTER IX.

The Meeting of Sukeshige and Terute.

Thus did Oguri castle and its lord meet with ruin. Five days later the retainers had the news at Utsunomiya. For sake of cousinship its lord and the abbot of the Nikkō Futaara had given an uncertain protection. But the hunt for Sukeshige now would be earnest and remorseless. Their lord was still shaken and enfeebled with the fever. There was no opposition on the part of Tomotsuna, brother of Mochitsuna when the Tanabe and Kazama departed with their lord, nominally to Nikkō-san, really to the hot spring of Kawaji in the Shioya mountains of Shimotsuke. Here the weeks passed. The fever disappeared, the painful and tottering steps were changed to longer walks amid the brilliantly painted hills in their autumn foliage. Thus was health rapidly restored. One day Tanabe Heirokurō appeared before his lord. Sukeshige noted the exceeding gravity of his face. The brave fellow prostrated himself in salutation. " May his " lordship deign to pardon the folly of this Heirokurō. Knowing the " weighty task before their honoured lord it has been agreed to await " his full recovery before making report and receiving his com- " mands."—" Ah ! " said Sukeshige drawing a deep and painful breath. " Then there has been news from the Ō-Dono." Heirokurō sadly shook his head. There were tears and anger in his face. " Alas ! Honoured lord the news is most important." He told in detail all that had happened on the fall day of the 8th month. Sukeshige bounded to his feet. " The villain Akihide ! Now the time " has come to carry out the mission of the Ō-Dono. The scoundrel's " head shall appease the wrath of the revered Sire. There is but " one course. To Kamakura ! "

That night all slept at Nikkō-san, the *kerai* now united under

their lord and the *karō* Gotō Hyōsuke.   This latter had remained
at Utsunomiya to keep in touch with the latest phase of affairs.
Sukeshige was granted a long interview with the lord abbot of the
temple, an ancient and prescriptive right of office in this Utsunomiya
family sprung from Fujiwara Mitsukane.   One of the *hachigata*
(Eight Notables) of the Kwantō the lord of Utsunomiya held a
peculiar position.   Naturally no love was lost between himself
and these ambitious Isshiki.   Said the abbot—" The restoration of
" the Oguri House is possible, even if difficult.   With the head of
" Isshiki Akihide, petition can be made to the Kyōto Shōgun, and
" the eyes of the Kwantō Kwanryō unsealed.   ' A man and the
" murderer of his father are not to live under the same Heaven.'
" This is the command of the sage Kōshi (Confucius).   But Kōshi
" was of the world.   I, who follow the path of the Buddha, have
" long abandoned all worldly interests.   As to this no advice can be
" given.   Seek out Joa Shōnin.   Great is his sanctity, and he is
" related to the Oguri House.   There is much at stake for good
" and evil, a *karma* of wide-reaching effect now and in future
" existences."   With shrewd and kindly smile the old man cast his
careless seeming eye over the eleven stalwart men before him.
Things augured badly for Akihide.

Thus it was that towards the end of the first month Ōei 31st
year (February 1424) they were near their goal.   They had travelled along the base of the mountains, avoiding the highways of the
Kwantō, and disguised as farmer samurai (*gōshi*).   The hills and
plain directed them along the uncertain paths, but as they approached the northern capital this guidance was lost.   Now they travelled
by night, resting by day in some one of the many caves carved by a
people ancient and now unknown ; or else a better rest was found in
one of the many shrines on the mountain and country trails.   They
were now but a few miles from Kamakura, and for the day hid
within the famous caves a bare two *ri* (5 miles) from the busy city.
Nor was the scene much different from to-day.   Kamakura had
still a large population.   Transport was difficult, confined to the
backs of men and pack-animals.   The country in its immediate
neighbourhood of necessity was under the highest cultivation.

Around the ancient Ōfuna, and extending on all sides, was the same sea of rice field girdled by the pine clad hills with their network of intricate valleys. Now these can well be likened to a tumbled and confused mass of *takō* (octopus), the arms of which represent the long, winding, and divergent valleys; the suckers the many shorter offshoots into the hilly mass. To march into Kamakura by dead of night past the *yashiki* at Yamanouchi was out of the question. Sukeshige and his company therefore plunged into the hills, intending to approach from the direction of Fujisawa. Such was the idea, better intended than carried out. The start was made in a thick fog, not improved by the darkness. Soon they were climbing and descending interminable hills. Swinging in a wide circle as they thought they walked and walked. Instead of the expected houses of the great city there were more valleys and hills, not seen but felt in the ascents and descents monotonously succeeding each other.

Hours thus passed. Dawn came, but with it no raising of the fog. Wearied out and hungry they stood in the pine forest on the top of one of the never-ending ridges. Below all was clouded in mist. Said Sukeshige—" Ah! How empty is my belly. No " matter what its dangers, gladly would Sukeshige hail the sight of " the city "—" And which city your lordship reaches is no certainty," growled Hyōsuke. " Truly one would think to be nearer Miyako "(the capital) of Yamashiro than Miyako of Sagami. It is not "entirely past the time of nuts, but these mangy peasants have " grievously neglected all due respect to their betters taken un- " awares." Said Kotarō—" Here is *onbako* (wild kale)." Broke in Shōji—"Do you take us for rabbits, respected Sir? Ideya! At " least one could breakfast on the rabbit; if present. But for the " weed, we are not touched with the frog's distemper. Besides it is " withered and of the last year's crop." Said Hyōsuke—" The fog " lightens." He looked around. The look of grievous hunger was re- placed by a smile. With a finger he pointed to the right through the wood. Before their eyes was a rough stone known to all. It marked the grave of the Kurando Ushōben Toshimoto, who in Go- Daigo Tennō's time had cut off his head with his own hand in

obedience to the august order of his master in Kyōto. Below them
to the left were the roofs of the Kaizōji. The Oguri *rōtō* looked at
each other, as if undecided to laugh or be angry. With one movement all plunged down the hill to reach the road on the Kehaizaka
close at hand.

As they stood for the moment, to take counsel as how best to
enter the city, *dotsu, dotsu, dotsu* along came the palanquin of two
women, with bearers and train of attendants. Standing by the side
of the road, in appearance farmers and not squatting bare-headed,
up came one of the guard. "Rude fellows ! Where do you come
"from?   Do you rascals know no better than not to doff head-gear
"before your betters. Down on your hams or off with your heads."
As he spoke he seized a pole from one of the attendants, and with
no gentle sweep knocked off the hat of Sukeshige. In a rage the
Oguri *rōtō* at once laid hands on their swords. Shōji grasped the
arm of the rash assailant with such force that he howled with pain.
The guards of the palanquin stood uncertain whether to attack these
rough looking fellows, or to run away abandoning the litters. Then
from the side of the one in the rear rode up a samurai. Said he to
Sukeshige—"Pardon this rude fellow. Evidently you are strangers
" to the city in the rough garb of travel. This clumsy clown knows no
" better than not to be civil. Follow in our train. In short order intro-
" duction will be given to proper accommodation. Such is a duty owing
" to new-comers."   Sukeshige at once grasped the advantage of this
introduction, this passport into the city. " Reverential thanks for
" the kindness thus deigned to strangers. It is true that we are
" *gōshi* come from Aizu in Iwashiro. Come to see the sights of the
" capital we have made a pilgrimage (*sankei*) to Fujisawa Tōtaku·
" san. Careful was the direction of the priest at the Yūgyō-dera,
" but in the fog the way has been lost. Thus we stood uncertain
" whether to go forward or backward. Deign to pardon any rough-
" ness in our party. As countrymen the ways of the city are new.
" With gratitude the command is obeyed."   Taking the hat from
the now obsequious *yakunin* (guard) he with his party lined the
road, to follow in the train of the litters. Thus they wound down
the steep curves of the Kehaizaka road. At the head of the valley

stood a fine *bessō* (villa). Here the train entered with the litters. A *yakunin* came forward and bowed with respect. " If the honoured " strangers, come to see the sights of Kamakura town, deign to " follow, they shall be conducted to the best resort for the " purpose. Here every opportunity to spend both time and " money profitably is granted. Thus with apology and rever- " ence former rudeness is purged, and the master's pardon " secured."

Next door to the bessō was the front of an inn—the Tomimaruya —a truly palatial establishment. With such introduction the hosts, Kichiji and Kichirō, bowed to the *tatami* with forehead on the two hands. " Gōshi from Aizu, the land of gold, and lined with it !" No welcome was too warm for such guests. Said Kazama Jirō to Ikeno Shōji—" This matter looks none too well ; this ready intro- " duction. Why not say a word of warning to the *go-karō* ? " Said Shōji—" As for the *karō*, if he knows not Kamakura, then " none do. As for our lord, it is time for him to rest, worn as he is " with travel and anxiety. As for ourselves, the belly of this Shōji " is empty as a drum. May the *kami* send food and drink, even " at the hands of thieves. Yumiya Hachiman (God of the bow and " feathered shaft) grant this prayer (Kimyō Chōrai) !" Said Kazama Jirō—" For food and drink, *kimyō chōrai*. As to the " rest may Hachiman-Sama turn a deaf ear. We have cut loose " from the fraternity not so long since as not to be well acquainted " with the methods of thieves." With such talk the party was in- troduced into a large room with a dais, a truly splendid apartment looking out on a beautiful garden with a pond in the centre. Backed by the circle of hill close] surrounding the valley the scene was as peaceful as if a thousand *ri* removed from the bustling city. As matter of fact this quarter of the Kaizōji was noted for its pleasure houses, its cook-shops, its night gaiety.* No place was more famed than the establishment of the brothers Kichiji and Kichirō. It was the rule to keep the *rōtō* of the different Houses somewhat apart, too close contact breeding frequent quarrels. Hence the Inamuraga- saki *rōtō* were not familiars of this quarter of the town so close to

* " Kamakura Taikwan " p. 81.

Yamanouchi. Hyōsuke knew it by reputation and occasional visitation; but with the Isshiki and this branch of the Uesugi he had had but little business to transact.

Some simple order given for the breakfast and the company settled down to rest. Hyōsuke went out into the town to gather news. Sukeshige turned over a scroll picked out of the *todana* (closet) of the apartment. Shōji squatted close by, respectful listener to the sing-song reading of his lord. From time to time Sukeshige cast an eye distraught into the garden perfumed with odour of the plum blossoms. This was separated from that of the neighbouring *bessō* by a hedge of *hagi* (lespedeza). As he gazed a girl appeared on the other side of the hedge. She cast a look up into the apartment. Too far off clearly to make out the features Sukeshige had no difficulty in seeing that she was of extraordinary beauty. Something familiar about her walk and pose puzzled him. Advancing to the hedge she hung thereon a *tanzaku* (roll of poem paper). Then with another glance upward, in haste, almost in flight, she disappeared toward the house. Said Sukeshige—" Shōji " please get me the *tanzaku* the girl has just hung on the hedge of " *hagi*. It is idle curiosity, but the desire to know its contents " seizes me." Replied Shōji—" Your lordship's command is heard " and understood; forthwith." Descending he was soon back again with the scroll. Sukeshige unrolled it, with admiring eyes and exclamation at the exquisite brush work. "Truly here is the " hand of an artist! Now as to the content; doubtless this is as " beautiful." The scroll ran:

" Flower laden the plants are dyed, plum tree of spring;
" Bending 'tis the autumn *hagi* holding back my sleeves."*

As his lord made no sign of reading this aloud Shōji held up his hand. Said Sukeshige—" What is it? "—" Our lord is very " reticent. On this mission of vengeance, treading on the tiger's " tail, will he not deign to let the *kerai* know the contents of the " scroll? The introduction to this place has been out of the com-

---

* *Sakishi yori iromie somete ume no hana ;*
  Aki hagi nabiku sode no tsumazuri.

Terute hangs up the *Tanzaku*.

" mon. But it is the merest common-place that a woman is
" the cause of all trouble among men. Why not divulge the con-
" tents of the scroll? Shōji humbly makes petition." Sukeshige
laughed—" Such a poem in such a quarter of the town is only
" unusual in its perfect execution." He read it to the *kerai*, now all
attention. " Will your lordship deign to explain the poem?"
persisted Shōji respectfully. "No great task," said Sukeshige
with indifference. " A man is attracted by the beauty of a
" woman; the woman by the fine appearance of a man;
" hence follows love; hence the reference to the flowers. The
" bending sleeves imply consent. That is what the poem
" means "—" Plain invitation indeed in such a place," grumbled
Shōji. Then seeing his lord's evident inclination to pursue the
intrigue—" May our lord deign to summon the girl. But Shōji
" with fear and respect beseeches that he be on his guard. Wine
" and women in this resort, and in our lord's mission, find little
" place." Sukeshige accepted the implied rebuke of his retainer. " If
" bull-headed Shōji is the mirror of loyalty. The matter is a trifle.
" Let it pass unnoticed." Mito no Kotarō did not think so. " Too
" great seriousness arouses suspicion. In the pleasure quarter the
" custom of the place is to be followed. His *kerai* are ample guard
" for our lord."

Thus urged by inclination and advice Sukeshige had Kichirō
summoned. This man was the younger and active partner of this
gay resort. Said Kotarō—" Doubtless the beautiful girl who has
" just hung the *tanzaku* on the hedge is some *tayu** of the
" quarter, so dazzling her beauty. The chief (*ō-gashira*) desires to
" make her this small present of gold dust. Let fish and wine be
" served, and a summons be sent her to attend." Kichirō was
puzzled. That there was some mistake he saw; but he was
quick to profit by it. The distance to the hedge was none too
close, and he had in the house a very beautiful girl by name Rei no
Kaoru from Miyako. His face took on due gravity. " It was a

---

* The highest class of hetaira. Cf. de Becker's "Nightless City" p. 45.
The title belongs to a minister of State, a very high court official; here used it
is an anachronism; it was used by the *jōrō* much later.

" great imprudence on her part.   The girl in question is the daughter
" of my brother Kichiji, who seeks for her a *muko* (adopted son-in-
" law) as she is the only child of the house.   But such munificence
" will doubtless move him to consent.   Deign to permit Kichirō to
" consult his brother.   The answer shall at once be forthcoming."
Then he backed out of the room on all fours, joy and avarice grasping his soul.   He found Kichiji in consultation with an old woman,
one Tamate, from the neighbouring *bessō*.   In the business of the
house she was no hindrance, so he described the whole affair to
Kichiji.   Kaoru was summoned to be coached in her part as *ojōsan*
(daughter of the house), and Tamate condescended to act as nurse.
The two women went off to prepare Kaoru for the banquet.   Meanwhile the Oguri *rōtō* also had their own tasks.   Gotō Hyōsuke had
returned with important news for his lord.   The Isshiki, Akihide and
Naokane, were still in Hitachi, arranging their personal interests in
the province.   Their return must be awaited, and the rôle of bumpkin
squires promised to be prolonged.   Yūki Dono had much to communicate to his lord.   His *karō* was now preparing the scroll, for a
personal interview was dangerous.   Paper could be burnt and leave
no sign.   Only the safe transmission was involved, and that was
easy.   Ikeno Shōji was to get it at the cook shop of the Suzukiya at
the Wakamiya-ōji.   Thus at the feast which followed the huge man
was conspicuous by his absence.

The feast was not marked by moderation.   On the banquet of
fish and delicacies the men fell " like tigers on sheep."   Their breakfast
had given but little scope to satisfy the hunger and insufficient food
of the past week.   The wine flowed freely, and all partook freely.
The dancing girls posed and sang songs to fire the warrior's heart
and loosen the gold of Bandai's slopes.   When Kaoru appeared
Sukeshige was in no mood for exercising particular discrimination.
Besides she was indeed a beautiful creature.   Rei no Kaoru was
famed in Kamakura town.   Twenty-two years of age, her hair
piled up in intricate rolls upon her head and fastened with nine
gorgeous golden jewel adorned *kanzashi* (hair ornaments), the oval
face framed in the black mass, the graceful sloping shoulders and
slender neck, a true race heritage of the Japanese woman, in her

gorgeous robe and sash she was a vision of beauty. The dance was over. She retired from the apartment. Tamate took Sukeshige by the hand to lead him to the lady. The *rōtō* went forth as if to see the sights of the town—except Hyōsuke. With stealthy step he followed his lord, to glide into the neighbouring apartment unobserved. Here he awaited developments.

It was not Kaoru who was waiting to receive the Aizu *gōshi*. This was indeed the lady of the *hagi*. If Kaoru was beautiful this girl was dazzling. Her long hair framing the oval of her fair face streamed nearly to her feet. The high brow, the proud and noble look, the small and sparkling eyes, the shapely hands and feet, the every movement of unconscious grace and conscious position betrayed the lady in the land. Tamate prostrated herself. Said she—"Tamate brings his lordship. It is " for my lady to crown the task and ascertain the truth. But " once, and that years back, has Tamate seen her lord. Terrible " is the risk. Beware." Abstractedly the girl touched the handle of the dagger in her bosom. Hyōsuke watching through a crevice loosened his sword. A most intense astonished look was on his face. When Tamate withdrew the girl approached the drowsy Sukeshige to rouse him. Intently she examined every feature, taking his head on her knee. The result was a sigh. "Hand- "some; yes! So was my lord. But surely this is not the man. "Sukeshige Dono was a man of high courage; not a lecher and " wine-bibber, as is this drunken fellow. But are men one thing in " their homes, and another in their pleasures? Alas! I have come " to sacrifice myself to my lord. It is not him. Having made offer " to another man pollution follows. Death alone remains." She drew her dagger. Close behind Hyōsuke drew his sword ready to make a spring as the arm was raised. Instead it was Sukeshige who caught the girl by the wrist. She struggled to free herself. " Nesan; what are you about! Ah! The lady changes shape." Said the girl weeping—"Deign to free me. Death must follow in " payment of the mistake rashly made. Surely I shall kill myself. "To none but my lord Kojirō Sukeshige shall I belong. Lady "Kwannon, aid me!" Sukeshige took the dagger and examined it carefully. He was thinking. "Death and life come to all. The "Aizu *gōshi* would not prevent you. Who is this Kojirō Suke- "shige?" Her breath caught in little sobs the girl made answer— "In folly I listened to the report of my nurse Tamate. This "woman's son, Ikeno Shōji, is retainer of the young lord of Oguri, "and to-day returning from the all night service (*okomori*) at "Fujisawa in a hatless man she thought she recognized Sukeshige. "Then the idea came to mind to seek an interview. The *tanzaku* "was hung on the hedge, anticipating a summons to the house. "Tamate was in waiting, and when Kichirō sent for Kaoru ar- "rangements were made to take her place. Mistaken, death must "follow. I am Terute, daughter of Satake Atsumitsu, lord of Ōta "in Hitachi. Espoused in early years by the young lord of Oguri, "the House of Satake extinguished by my father's unfortunate end, "with my mother I set out for Hitachi. Ōta was never reached. "In a battle with thieves my mother was killed by an arrow, and "this Terute was carried off. Soon found and restored to Yoko- "yama Tarō, years were spent at a fief at Tōshima, recently granted "to him. Then he came to live in this quarter, apart from all the "*yashiki* of Kamakura. Thus life has been passed. Terute dis- "honoured must die."

Truly she was a beautiful woman, and in her grief most moving. Sukeshige smiled. "And the proof thereof? Sup- "pose that this Aizu *gōshi* really be Kojirō lord of Oguri; what "proof that this lady is Terute?" She looked at him keenly, hope revived. A tinge of colour deepened to a blush. From the *mamori-bukuro* (charm bag) of red damask hung around her neck she drew forth a little image of Kwannon, less than two inches high. "This was on the *hachimanza*** of Shinra Saburō Yoshi- "mitsu, brother of Hachiman Tarō Yoshiiye. From the ancestor "Yoshimitsu it came to the Satake House, and from birth Terute "has carried it. Here is the scroll of the Satake House." She drew it from her bosom.—"Her ladyship indeed! What marvel!" Hyōsuke stood over them as one rapt. Then prostrate he made obeisance to the Terutehime and his lord. "Deign to pardon the

---

* The metal knob on the crown of the helmet.

"rashness of Hyōsuke in being ready to strike in his lord's behalf.
" But eyes and mind held his hand, and more and more the features
" of her ladyship came vivid to the sight.   The little girl grown to
" woman stood revealed."   Then turning to Sukeshige; " indeed
" my lord 'tis all true.   Not only the hereditary Kwannon and the
" scroll, but the eyes of Hyōsuke answer for the story of her
" ladyship.   It is the Terutehime, daughter of the Satake House.
" The memory of the years there spent pierce the veil of the past."
Thus spoke Gotō Hyōsuke, *karō* of Oguri Sukeshige, in youth a
page in the *yashiki* of Satake Atsumitsu under his father Gotō
Makabe Genzaemon.

Sukeshige holding the hands of Terute gazed long and
earnestly.   The little smile wavering on the lips of both betrayed
the joy at this meeting.   Sukeshige made no secret of his admiration.   The eyes of Terute, in which tears still glittered, sought
the *tatami*.   Said the knight—"Terute has shown her Kwannon,
" the Lady Merciful.   Deign to look.   Sukeshige offers proof."   What
he held forth was the little metal image of Hachiman, the *honzon*
or tutelary deity of Mitsushige which the worthy daimyō had
always carried with him, even on such a peaceful mission as a cherry
flower viewing.   Terute noted that a lock of hair accompanied it.
Said Sukeshige in answer to her inquiring look—"Both were
" brought by the messenger from Oguri castle.   With the head of
" Akihide as offering it finds burial at Fujisawa.   But for the present
" happy issue—Hyōsuke, the *rōtō* are to be summoned, for there is
" need of counsel."—" At your lordship's orders ; "   and the *karō*
withdrew, leaving husband and wife in earnest converse.   This
time it was the head of Terute which rested on her lord's knee,
and the fragile body quivered as she poured out to him the tale of
her painful life, and Sukeshige consoled past woes as best he
could.

Hyōsuke came upon a curious scene.   In the apartment all the
men were gathered in uneasy converse.   They had been telling
ghost stories to wile away the time, and nerves were a little on edge.
Said Kazama Jirō—" This affair goes too readily.   The welcome is
" too warm in this mercenary place.   Jirō would stake his head that

" our lord's companion passed in the garden a moment since. It is
" a fox and badger business." Said Shōji—" Foxes and badgers
" belong to the hills, as Kazama Dono well knows. As for welcome
" it is always warm to the new-comer. The matter of the woman
" is serious. Never were there two slyer and more villainous faces
" than those of the brothers of this Tomimaruya. As for the girl being
" the daughter of either, it is a palpable lie. And this nurse ? "—
" Our lord accompanied her in the passage way. She did not enter."
Thus spoke Mito no Kotarō. Just then the screens opened and the
old woman appeared. Shōji sprang to his feet with open mouth
and standing hair. He drew his sword. " Truly apparitions appear.
" My honoured mother, Tamate, this Shōji knows to be far
" distant in Tsukuba's hills. See ! This thing ! Get you hence
" spectre, or feel the edge of Shōji's sword." As he advanced
upon her the old woman laughed. " Son, raise not your weapon
" against her who gave you life. The matter is easily explained."
She turned and spoke to Hyōsuke who had entered and
stood just behind her. " Great is the joy and relief of Tamate
" at finding her son Shōji. His absence from the rōtō at
" the feast alarmed her. Assuredly her ladyship is in company with
" her lord. Tamate, on the news of the ruin of the Oguri House,
" left the village at Fujishirogawa and came on foot to Kamakura
" to get news of his lordship and her son. The way was long and
" weary, but the peasants were charitable. However the road was
" lost in the hills. Thieves robbed Tamate of the little provision
" carried. Nothing remained but cold water, and that is no food
" for the aged. Powerless I lay down to die. Then the lord of a
" train of samurai came by. At his orders I was brought to Kama-
" kura, to act as nurse for his daughter Terute. Here has Tamate
" lived, in the besso next to the Tomimaruya." Shōji made deep
obeisance—" Deign mother in your loving kindness to pardon your
" rash son for drawing his sword against you. Thinking you far
" distant this Shōji took you for a spectre. What folly ! " Tamate
laughed as her son embraced her—" A mother's forgiveness is easily
" secured. Besides there are spectres, and still worse. Your lord
" summons you to council ? "—Hyōsuke nodded assent. Briefly he

explained matters.   Thus all were gathered in consultation with their
lord and the lady Terute.

Said Sukeshige—" The meeting with Terute has been most
" fortunate.   Alas, that Sukeshige has to treat her as a younger
" sister, being on this mission of vengeance."   Tamate made exclamation—" Younger sister !   Surely after these years of marriage,
" and thus unexpectedly reunited, that would be cruel indeed."
Terute looked down, smiling and a little pained.   Kazama Jirō
came forward—" Our lord and lady have a duty to the House.
" Why not perform it ?   May our lord deign to accompany the
" kitanokata.   The kerai will keep watch.   Let the future take
" care of itself."   Said Hyōsuke—" Kazama Dono speaks well.
" Condescend my lord to give ear to what he says.   The House is
" important in many ways, and your lordship's mission is danger-
" ous."   Sukeshige hardly needed more than suggestion when
Terute timidly addressed her lord—" The object is to kill Isshiki
" Akihide, thus to tranquillize the spirit of the Ō-Dono ; an easier
" task here than elsewhere."   Said Sukeshige in astonishment—
" How so ? "—Answered Terute—" Akihide and Yokoyama Tarō
" are as fish and water.   Akihide is a constant visitor.   If my lord
" deigns to be patient he is sure to give him a meeting under favour-
" able conditions.   The escape to Fujisawa is close at hand, and
" petition can be made to Kyōtō to restore the Oguri House.
" Nowhere is your lordship safer than here at the Tomimaruya."
Sukeshige was overjoyed at his good fortune—" Akihide fairly
" walks into the net.   Off his guard, and seeking his pleasure, the
" traitor shall lose his head.   So be it."   Thus were matters arranged for the future.   With dawn Terute left her husband's side to
return under the guard of Tamate.   Prostrating herself in parting
salutation said she—" Deign, my lord, to exercise great care.   This
" is no friendly place, this Kamakura.   Above all distrust any good
" offices of Yokoyama Tarō.   Carefully avoid his discovery.   An
" easy path lies through the hedge, and Tamate to-night shall guide
" you.   Earnestly, my lord, Terute prays that you be on guard in
all things."   With this she took her leave.

CHAPTER X.

THE PLOTTING OF YOKOYAMA SHŌGEN.

"*Naruhodo!*" Said Sukeshige. "Then Yokoyama Dono
"has these five sons in his train at this place." Said Terute—
"Such indeed is my lord's dangerous position, the necessity for
"being so carefully on guard. This male issue of his concubines in the
"Tamagawa fief has been brought up in utmost secrecy in Musashi.
"Only of late years has Yokoyama Tarō thus openly established
"himself. The eldest is Tarō Yasukuni, then follow Jirō Yasutsugu,
"Saburō Yasuharu, Shirō Yasutaka, Gorō Yasunaga. The two last are
"but boys, the eldest being sixteen years. Whether my father knew
"of issue hidden away in the recesses of Musashino, Terute knows
"not. Assuredly my mother knew nothing. Never mention did
"she make of them." There were tears in the lady's eyes as she
gazed into the peaceful garden, the plum blossoms shining like
silver in the moonlight, the little *ike* (pond) darkly reflecting the
knotted tree trunks. With one long sleeve she furtively made as if
to wipe away these untimely witnesses of grief. Said Sukeshige in
low tones—"You say she died in battle?"—"Aye!" answered
Terute. "Great was the dissatisfaction in the Satake fief at Ōta
"at the transference to the charge of the Isshiki. Gotō Makabe,
"who had been *karō* of the House in his younger days, gathered
"some of the vassals and offered resistance. But Akihide had the
"suzerain's commission and the important aid of Kamakari Hyōbu,
"a disloyal vassal of the Satake. Great was the disorder in the
"fief. Yokoyama Tarō had determined to establish himself in
"Hitachi, to be close to the interests of the Satake House. Under
"the protection of the *rōtō* my mother and I set out, while Tarō
"Dono went to Tamagawa to summon his sons and settle matters

" in Tōshima, for by some influence his former fief had been restored
" to him.   Camping at Kohagi in Musashi we were attacked by
" highwaymen, or hangers-on of Kamakari's forces, for they were
" little better.   A stray arrow pierced my mother's litter and
" deprived her of life.   I was carried off to sell in Kamakura.   The
" news, however, soon reached Yokoyama's ears.   Great was his
" wrath, and great was his influence with Isshiki Akihide.   Kama-
" kari was soon forced to surrender my person, but my mother
" found a lonely grave on the moor.   Tarō Dono found his presence
" necessary at Tōshima.   After some years, on the summons of
" Akihide, he removed from Musashi to the capital.   To Yokoyama
" is owing gratitude for his ready interference, but the knowledge
" of his carelessness in not preventing my mother's death has kept
" him from pressing too earnestly marriage with his son Tarō.
" Truly, my lord, great has been the anxiety of Terute in the
" matter."—" And yet you bid me depart early !   Surely I too
" press you hard."   Terute looked down—" Not so my lord.
" But thus surrounded by enemies the position is too dan-
" gerous to linger.   Yokoyama Dono has never wished you
" well, and the power once in his hands has freely expressed his
" dislike and hate.   Treacherous and wicked himself his sons
" equally inherit his evil qualities.   Tarō is sluggish, cowardly, and
" a hypocrite. Jirō is greedy, blundering, and a hypocrite. Saburō
" is violent, brutal, and a hypocrite. Shirō is a spy ...... "   She
stopped, laughed a little, and held out her hands ; " all hypocrites,
" the trait common to all, varied by other evil qualities.   It is now
" near dawn.   Your lordship's presence is not to be suspected.
" Yokoyama and Akihide, as said, are as fish and water.   This is in
" your favour now ; against you if Yokoyama should suspect the
" object of your mission in Kamakura."   She ceased.   Sukeshige
took her in his arms to wipe away this grief in one final embrace.
Then lightly he pushed open the *shōji* and stepped through the
open *amado* into the garden now darkening with the waning
moon.   A few strides brought him to the hedge and he passed
through.   He thought he heard a cry, and stopped to look around.
Not a sign of life.   All was silent and peaceful.   The hills surround-

The Lovers' Tryst.

ing the Kaizōji cast a heavy shadow. Stepping rapidly he soon
reached his quarters.

Not so unobserved as he thought. This mooted marriage was
indeed a danger to Terute. Object of desire to the two brothers
Tarō and Jirō this was her real safety. It was something more
than any esoteric feeling of regret that made Yokoyama Shōgen
(he had shaved his head) assume the more neutral attitude of
indecision. For years he had intended Terute for himself, but
Akihide resolutely avoided all action tending to re-establish the
Satake House, and Shōgen was dependent on Akihide. Then arose
this affair with Tarō and Jirō. Jirō he loved, and was unwilling
to disappoint. Tarō was the elder, yet he was equally unwilling
to forward his views with Terute. Tarō Yasukuni had reached the
limit of his patience. "The girl has someone else in her head.
"Who can it be but my brother Jirō? For a younger brother thus
"to poach on the premises of his elder is not to be permitted. To-
"night Tarō shall visit Terute for the last time. Willing or un-
"willing she will of necessity accept the accomplished fact." With
such amiable intentions at midnight he slipped out into the garden.
Strategy would give him entrance to Terute's pavilion. His progress, however, came to a sudden halt. A man's figure made its
way through the hedge at the bottom of the garden. As one assured
of his way the stranger approached the *amado* of the pavilion. A
panel was slipped back and he entered. In rage Yasukuni crouched in the shadow of the hedge to take counsel with himself. Who
was it thus to visit Terute? Surely it was his brother Jirō—adul-
terer, thief, beastly villain. It was he who had anticipated his marriage; had thus forestalled him with the beauty. Not daring to
approach her through the house he sought this unsuspected access
through the garden of Kichiji. Thus did Tarō spend the hours,
watching, waiting, execrating the fortunate Jirō.

Meanwhile Jirō was as impatient as his brother. "Terute shows
"me anything but favour. Surely this dullard Tarō has captivated
"her. Women have no sense in such matters. She prefers the
"braying of this ass to my honoured self and known appetite; I
"who gain everything I really set out to obtain. Surely great

" would be her gain in sharing with me. It would be a merciful
" deed to anticipate this foredoomed cuckold. Does not the Buddha
" say—' with opportunity, and secrecy, and the right woo'r, all
" women will go wrong; aye, failing others, with a cripple even.'
" To-night shall see the matter settled." But Jirō was less decided
than Tarō, and he had to pass the apartments of father and brother.
It was near dawn when ambition spurred him forth to gain the love
of his lady. As he approached in the now darkened garden he had
just time to drop to the ground. The panel opened and a man
appeared. Tarō? No! This, Jirō saw at once. Of the farewell
he could hear but little in the low tones of parting. The familiar
address, the loving tenderness, the man himself; these important
details were open to him. To avoid detection he drew into the
shadow of the hedge and followed along it to see where the intruder
went. The man disappeared into the neighbouring garden. Jirō
thrust forward his head into the aperture. Crack! With rage he
grasped in silence his assailant. With equal anger his assailant
grasped him. Timely recognition prevented any proceeding to ex-
tremities between such loving brothers. Tarō! Jirō! Said Jirō
in explanation—" Unable to sleep I was walking in the garden.
" Hearing voices in Terute's apartment I approached, but before
" reaching the *amado* they opened and this man appeared. Who
" can he be?" Thought Tarō—" You are a liar and a hypocrite.
" You intended to anticipate me with the girl who is to be my wife.
" Hate this stranger as I do, your discontent is the one redeeming
" feature of my own disappointment." Aloud he said; " his features
" I saw well. The man is not of Kamakura." Said Jirō—" No;
" he talks through his nose, as do the Aizu *gōshi* lodged with Kichi-
" ji. But what has Terute to do with such a fellow?" Tarō
rubbed his sconce, then slapped his knee as if inspired by the act.
" Aizu *gōshi*; no! This fellow must be Hitachi Oguri, Sukeshige
" the son of Hyōye no Jō Mitsushige. Was not Terute at one time
" betrothed to him?" Said Jirō—" Surely 'tis he! Hence their
" familiar talk and address. She called him ' my lord,' ' farewell
" my lord.' He can be none but Oguri. His tall figure, confident
" walk proclaim it. Our father must be told at once."—" He alone

" can settle this affair." Thus spoke Tarō ; glowering inwardly and outwardly he accompanied his brother to the rooms of their father.

Shōgen heard this story with quickening alarm and attention. "Had he a mole under the right eye?" he asked Jirō. At the affirmative answer; "surely it is he! It can be none but Oguri "Sukeshige. But the truth is easy to ascertain. Summon Kichiji." Said Shōgen to the crouching inn-keeper—"There is report to be " made as to these new-comers, these Aizu *gōshi*. What manner of " men are they? Tell no lies. Answer correctly." Said Kichiji— " With fear and respect : there are eleven men in all, one acting as " the *Ōgashira* or chief of the company. This man is at least " twenty-five years old, strong in figure and somewhat arrogant " in manner. The rest obey him. The oldest is at least " ten years his senior. The rest of the company are much " of the age of their chief. One in particular is a huge fellow, " only approached in size by two others evidently brothers. The " smallest is spare, square, a very active strongly built man, of not " more than five *shaku* (feet) if so much." Said Shōgen—" The " older man has a scar through the cheek ; the hair of the giant " curls? "—" Your lordship describes them as exactly as if before " you." Said Shōgen—" To-night prepare supper for this Shōgen " and his sons. Let it be served in the neighbouring apartment. " Be silent."

Yokoyama Shōgen turned to his hopeful progeny as the *shōji* closed on the retreating form of Kichiji. "That it is Oguri there is " no doubt. The man with the scar is his *karō*, Gotō Hyōsuke ; " the big man is Ikeno Shōji ; the small active man is Mito no " Kotarō. This affair is most important. If these be the men, " though under the ban, to attempt to detain them would be most " dangerous. Any one of them is worth a dozen men. Together " they are an army. The position is most difficult. Meanwhile to " wait for to night. Assured of their identity plans can be made to "entrap their lord. For your own sakes carefully avoid any " quarrel." Yasukuni and Yasutsugu left their father's presence with all gravity added to hypocrisy before this dangerous foe. Shōgen had spoken more hopefully than he felt. For the Oguri, lord and retainers, he had no misguided contempt. His position was not an easy one. Akihide and his brother Naokane were absent from Kamakura. To apply to the Shitsuji Norizane was easy and out of the question. The Isshiki would feel no gratitude at such a move, and Norizane was the last person to whom Yokoyama wished to direct attention to his honoured self. Indeed the Shitsuji was not unlikely to warn Sukeshige indirectly that his presence was known. Kamakura swarmed with soldiers and *toritsugi* (constables), and yet the hands of Yokoyama were tied as to the arrest of these proscribed men. Evidently in this dangerous affair he must rely on himself ; and on guile. Fortunately he was a master-hand in such practice.

That night a noisy supper party held high revel in the apartment next to Sukeshige and his *rōtō*. With wide open *amado* the garden streamed with light, and the expected visit to Terute was impossible. " What a rude, noisy set. Truly these drunkards consider none but themselves." With regret Sukeshige thought of the quiet interview thus thwarted. He looked out for a moment. Figures passed to and fro in the garden as if the sun, not moon, was shining. The uproar showed no sign of diminution. Meanwhile Shōgen felt sure that nothing human could find rest near their banquet; and he felt inspired by the wine absorbed. He would face Shōki the demon-queller himself. Why not Kojirō Sukeshige? With loud expressed excuse he left the feast. Then his stumbling steps were heard on the return. Passing his own apartment he threw open the *shōji* and staggered into the room in which were gathered Sukeshige and his *rōtō*. " Iza ! Accept the apologies of " this humble person. But the *saké* cup is a bad guide. It points " to Gokuraku and leads to Jigoku.* Deign to pardon such rude " intrusion.........But who have we here! Surely is not sight " honoured with the presence of Kojirō Dono? Alas ! Respected " Sir, survivor of the ill-fated House of Satake grievously has Shōgen " felt the unhappy fate of your honoured sire, your own woes. " What can bring you hither ? But whatever it be this meeting is " most marvellous and happy. Deign to accept the humble services

* Paradise ; Hell.

" of Shōgen, his aid whenever required." Thought Sukeshige—
" Here is a mess! Accident has effected for this fellow what design
" might have failed in doing. However, to give a fair answer; it
" is honey, not vinegar, which is needed to meet his wiles......With
" fear and respect: merely to find out how matters were in Kama-
" kura, the possibility of the re-establishment of the Oguri House,
" and to take the counsel of friends as to its best acconplishment has
" brought Sukeshige to Kamakura.   It is with gratitude that Yoko-
" yama Dono is numbered among them.   Accept reverential thanks."
Prostrate in salutation the two noble lords roundly lied to each other.
Said Shōgen—" In such case a closer neighbourhood is good.
" Besides in Shōgen's charge is Terute your wife.   Long years have
" you been separated.   Deign at last to consummate the marriage,
" to bind the connection.   This is the earnest prayer of Shōgen."
Answered Sukeshige—" At your lordship's orders.   In the condition
" of the House it would be out of place to appear openly in Kamu-
" kura, but the hospitality of Yokoyama Dono is accepted and with
" grateful thanks."   Thus with appointment for the following day
Shōgen took his leave.

As arranged, on the next day Sukeshige and his *rōtō* issued
forth in state in answer to the urgent invitation of Yokoyama
Shōgen.   In the *bessō* of this latter all preparations had been made
to receive them.   The Oguri *rōtō* looked in each other's faces.
Wonder was but politely concealed at the magnificence displayed in
this mansion.   Costly woods, the *fusuma* of silk and painted by
master hands, a scroll landscape on silk with flying birds signed by
Chao Yung famed even in Nippon* in the *tokonoma*, showed not
only wealth but taste.   Shōgen, with four of his sons behind him,
received the young lord of Oguri with greatest unction and respectful
cordiality.   Many were the bows, deep the sucking in of the
breath, interminable the compliments exchanged as to health and
weather.   This ceremony lasted nearly half an hour.   Then said
Shōgen—" To come to the earnest matter of our meeting: let

---

* The son probably of the famous Tzū-ang; himself littérateur and
painter.   In the time of Yoshimitsu there was much contact with China, and
importation of Chinese art.

Terute be summoned." Now Terute had passed a very unhappy night. The unexplained absence of her husband-lover, his dangerous position amid these hidden foes, gave this summons an evil meaning. It was with cast-down impassive face that she presented herself before Shōgen. Prostrating herself—" Father, hum-" bly with fear and reverence : deign to give command to Terute." —" Umu ! " sucked in Shōgen. " Truly in one married, or to be " so, here is modesty ! Years ago your revered father betrothed you " to Oguri Dono. Deign to look. Here he presents himself, and yet " Terute graces him not even with a salutation." With the same equipoise Terute raised her eyes to behold her lord. The massive forms of Ikeno Shōji and the Kazama brothers, of the Gotō, the Tanabe, the Kataoka ; the ever keen restless glance of Mito no Kotarō gave confidence even in this den of thieves. Who could face these men in battle ! Certainly not Shōgen and his sons. Respectfully she made obeisance before Sukeshige. Respectfully lord and retainers saluted her ladyship. " My lord has been long " absent. The revered command of my father is to be obeyed." Even Shōgen admired such aplomb. It ran in the family.

Then said Shōgen—" Nine times is the *saké* cup to be exchang-" ed. This is a joyful occasion. Let *saké* be served to all." The company withdrew to the banquet hall where the wine was to be served. In a separate apartment Sukeshige and Terute, in the presence of Shōgen and Gotō Hyōsuke, of Jijū wife of Yoko-yama, faced each other. Nine times the cup of *saké* passed between them. Thus did Shōgen, as in all willingness, sanction the former contract. From his worthy progeny came no sign of protest. They knew their father well. Surely he must be certain of his game. Then the wedding party adjourned to the banquet hall. Here the company awaited them. A fine banquet of fish and wine was served. All the delicacies of sea and moor, easily procured in Kamakura town and the Kezai quarter, were produced. As the feast neared its end Shōgen turned to Sukeshige —" But passing " clouds are the misfortunes of the Oguri House. It would be " good for Terute during this trouble to remain under the charge of " my humble self, if such seems well to your lordship. The House "restored she can join Sukeshige Dono in full confidence." Now Terute thus formally contracted in marriage was as safe as a mouse in a mill. Truly Sukeshige felt that Terute and himself had misjudged this Yokoyama Tarō. His soul swelled with gratitude. "Yokoyama "Dono, as ever, shows his kindness and readiness to engage himself "for friends. The offer is accepted with reverence and thanks. "Terute und.rstands the position of Sukeshige and the Oguri House. "Without doubt your lordship's fair offer inspires her too with grati- "tude." Terute bowed, with no particular impress of joy. "With "fear and respect: her lord's commands are as from Heaven. The "wife's part is to obey. Deign to receive the humble thanks of "Terute." This was the nearest she could come to protest. Shōgen half turned a shoulder. Sukeshige had a slight wrinkle in his nose. The Oguri *rōtō* felt much like the *kitanokata*. These surroundings, this welcome. they distrusted.

Said Shōgen—"The matter is unimportant, thanks superfluous. "But it emboldens Shōgen to ask a favour of Kojirō Dono"— "What is in his power to do, that shall Sukeshige do," was the reply. Then said Shōgen—"Your lordship's reputation for horse- "manship is widespread. Now there has been presented to me a "wild horse; a fine beast equalled by none, but my cowardly "fellows fear to ride him. Useless to Shōgen will his lordship deign "to receive the animal and grant an exhibition of his powers." Said Sukeshige—"To hear is to obey. These powers are small but "at your service. This is small return for the favour granted by "your lordship." Shōgen turned to Tarō Yasukuni—"Conduct "Oguri Dono to the stable of Onikage. From this exhibition learn "to display greater courage yourself." Yasukuni bowed to conceal joy and amusement—"Will his lordship and company deign to "follow." Sukeshige and his *rōtō* at the tail of Yasukuni began the ascent of the hill behind the *yashiki*, known as the Kehaizaka. At the top Yasukuni turned to the left. A short distance brought them before a stockade of stout tree trunks. This enclosed a flat piece of ground on the mountain top. To the right, in the Sasuke valley, could be seen the *yashiki* of Uesugi Shigekata. Yasukuni in his present company looked almost longingly at its roofs. Before

them rose the big pines of Genjiyama. Said Yasukuni—" My
" honoured father gives this Tarō little recommendation for courage.
" Humbly he admits his fear. This is the stable of Onikage, but
" your lordship can readily manage him, a mere wild horse. Deign
" to excuse my insignificant self." Sukeshige well concealed his
half contempt. " With fear and respect : the command of your
" honoured sire is to be obeyed. The talents of Sukeshige are
" trifling. Apology is needless." Swinging back the bar of the gate
to give them admittance Yasukuni incontinently took to his heels
down the hill. The rōtō looked after him in some wonder.

Stationing the Kataoka brothers at the gate as guard against
surprise Sukeshige and his company advanced into the paddock. It
was a large place, some 70 or 80 ken square (480-520 feet), covered
with long dry suzuki* through which the new grass was pushing
its way. A huge pine tree stood near the centre. The stable
(koya) was at the further end. All was silence. Advancing
toward the barn they had nearly reached the tree when Sukeshige halted. " What a filthy stench ; but whence comes that
noise, Shōji ? " There came to their ears a moaning sound,
kii, kii, kii. Grumbled Shōji—" Surely my lord there is nothing
unusual here, unless it be this nag of which so much mystery is
made. He made his way toward the tree through the mass of
tangled weed. On reaching it —" fushi ! " he exclaimed. At his
call the others hastened up. Wretched was the object before them.
A man, naked and starved, was tied fast to the foot of the tree. His
hair was white, the head fallen to one side, the face cadaverous.
His painful slow breathing gave the impression that death was close
at hand. " How pitiable ! " said Sukeshige—" What could the
" man have done, what crime committed, to be so treated ? " The
rōtō gazed. The place was covered with bones of men. The fresh
limbs and trunk of a human corpse lay close by, knawed in places.
At the orders of Sukeshige the bonds were cut, the man raised and
supported. At the presence of other men the glaucous eyeballs
showed signs of life. Said Shōji—" Take courage and tell your

---

* Eularia Japonica. This grass blossoms in long, beautiful, feathery
plumes.

" tale. Our lord is merciful and means you well. A sword cut
" would be mercy to such a doom." The man's eyes opened in a
fear-stricken horrible stare. The look fell full on Sukeshige. A
gleam of joy seemed to enter this stricken soul and give it strength.
" 'Tis the young lord of Oguri! Surely the *kami* (gods) have sent
" his lordship in this extremity. Alas! Humble though I be, yet
" long has the search been undertaken for the *himegimi*. The moun-
" tain is no longer leaf-clothed, but vengeance comes to hand as
" gift of the gods. This is Dosuke, retainer of Atsumitsu Dono. It
" was by no accident that his lordship perished in the Katasegawa.
" Struck down and netted in the water by Yokoyama Tarō, this
" villainous man thus killed my honoured lord. Seeking safety, and
" to carry the news, Dosuke leaped into the stream and escaped by
" swimming. But only to fall into the hands of Isshiki Akihide.
" Before decision was reached opportunity for flight presented itself.
" Refuge was sought in Musashi. Here Dosuke lived in hiding,
" seeking how best to avenge his lord on Yokoyama Tarō, how to
" get the ear of her ladyship. But the gods were unfavourable.
" Not long since it was learned that Shōgen, as he was now called,
" and his daughter were living at Kamakura Kaizōji. This latter
" could be none other than the *himegimi*. Thither Dosuke made his
" way, to see her ladyship in secret; but instead he fell into the
" hands of Shōgen. With joy he haled me to this place and had
" me bound. 'Ah, rascal! Perish you shall; but not by the
" mercy of steel or rope. Remain here, living food for Onikage.'
" Thus for some days has Dosuke lived, strangely neglected by the
" horse; and driven by hunger, more by thirst, to share at times
" the horrid meal of the horrid beast. Refrain my lord from further
" adventure here. This animal is powerful as a thousand of his
" kind, and surely will dash you to pieces. For this reason has
" Shōgen sent you hither, as others have been sent." The voice
now strong suddenly collapsed. Only gurgles and whispers came.
Exhausted by the effort Dosuke sank back an inert corpse.

Lord and retainers looked into each other's faces, amazed and
horrified. The mask was stripped from Yokoyama Tarō and his
always deadly intentions. Sukeshige grasped his sword and gnash-

ed his teeth. " Ah, the villain !   The scoundrel ! "   He leaned over
the man and examined him.   He was dead ; as much so as any of
the severed masses on this execution ground.   Said Sukeshige—
" Unfortunate Dosuke !   But the *kami* have been kind in unsealing
" our eyes.   Ah !   This fellow, Yokoyama Tarō !   His head shall
" be presented at the Yellow Fountain (Kwōsen in Hell).   Dosuke
" shall make report to his lord in Meido."   He half drew his weapon.
Shōji laid a respectful hand on the scabbard and knelt.   " Deign
" my lord to refrain.   First comes the appeasing of the wrathful
" Spirit of the Ō-Dono.   This performed, the head of Isshiki Aki-
" hide offered to his Spirit, the task of killing this miserable thief is
" easy.   May our Lord be pleased to reflect."   With a sigh
Sukeshige thrust back the weapon.   For a moment he remained in
thought.   " The affair is complicated.   Terute can no longer remain
" under such a roof.   She knows not that the hand of Shōgen
" secured her father's death.   But Shōji is right ; thoughtful and
" loyal.   Mere courage and angry vindication are here worse than
" useless.   The present farce is to be carried through.   Now for
" Onikage ! "   Followed by the *rōtō* he strode toward the *koya*.
Now the bad habits of Onikage, as is carefully explained by the
chronicler, were due to the evil disposition of his master Shōgen.
Furnished with no food but the writhing bodies of men, the un-
natural taste of the beast had been fostered and developed.   With
ordinary fodder Onikage was as any other horse, except in his superlative qualities.   There is a saying of the Nipponese that " the
thoroughbred horse knows the expert rider."   The sound and
smell of men aroused the animal.   As the door of the stable was
thrown wide open Onikage presented a fearful sight.   " His
ears were like the green cut bamboo, his eyes shone like a hundred
mirrors."   The huge animal, six feet from ground to saddle, reared.
The slaver floated like foam from his mouth.   The eyes glared red
and deadly.   Brave as they were the Oguri *rōtō* shivered, their hair
stood on end.   Ikeno Shōji dared to step before his lord.   Sukeshige
stood in admiration.   " What an animal !   What legs, back, and
" withers !   And the fineness of the head !   The sage himself (Kōshi)
" could well find profit in his company."   Boldly he stepped forward.

Springing up he grasped the forelock of the horse, pulled down his head, and looked him in the eyes. These lost their fierce glare. As if recognizing a beloved master they took on an almost human look of affection. Onikage neighed and whinnied. Said Sukeshige—"Rope for bridle; never was there a finer beast. Shōgen "and his sons are cowards. That is the secret. For such an ani- "mal no better use has been found than to terrify the helpless." Mito no Kotarō brought rope and a bit. Sukeshige leaped on the horse's back. "Now to the *yashiki;* to see out this scoundrel's "game. Fortune, not he, has given Sukeshige an invaluable ally." Thus they went forth on their return.

Shōgen felt assured that all was over. Sukeshige was killed, the *rōtō* scattered in flight. Then Yasutsugu presented himself before him, his hair disordered as in rage or fright. "Respected father "surely this man is a demon. Here he comes riding Onikage. "What is to be done?" Shōgen went forth. Sukeshige and his *rōtō* were just entering the court of the mansion. Onikage paced like a lady's mare. No pussy cat could have been gentler. He fairly purred.* Shōgen was all smiles. "The lord Oguri has "not belied his reputation. Deign to look. Humble preparation "has been made, the court prepared. Will your lordship deign to "mount the ladder?" Said Sukeshige—"At your honoured com- "mand. Let a ladder be brought and preparation made." Dis- mounting he gave Onikage in charge to Kazama Hachirō. Enter- ing the *bessō* he awaited Gotō Hyōsuke. The latter soon made the journey to and from the inn. Then Sukeshige appeared for the exhibition. He wore an *eboshi,* a light blue *shitatare* (cloak), and a gold hilted sword. The crest of white *kikyō* stood out resplendent on the robe. Saddled and bridled Onikage was brought forward by the Kazama. Grasping the reins of blue and red Sukeshige leaped into the saddle. Gently he paced the animal around the enclosure, made him rear and curvet. Meanwhile a ladder some thirty feet in length had been brought. Ikeno Shōji took his place in the centre of the courtyard. Yokoyama and his company looked

---

* *Neko no mitai na.* With the dreaded Onikage the direct support of the native scribe is needful.

The Might of Ikeno Shōji.

on, in doubt which of the two, lord or retainer, could accomplish such an unheard of feat. Sukeshige rode up to Shōji. "Is all ready?"—"Fear nothing, my lord. The ladder is as the highway itself. Ride up with confidence." Several times Sukeshige brought Onikage up to the ladder. Shōji held it as if embedded in rock. Gingerly Onikage put first one foot, then another, forward; then he drew back. Sukeshige aided him with voice and rein. At last the noble beast entered on the task. Fore legs and hind legs carefully planted he rose up the rungs. Shōji gently tilted man and horse. Now they were at the centre. How were they to descend? As if the ladder and its weight were merely a halberd held in hand. Shōji gently lowered the other end of the ladder to the earth. With circumspection Sukeshige encouraged and teased Onikage into making the descent. As horse and man reached ground they tore off in a mad gallop around the enclosure, sending sand and pebbles in a hail as if a storm had broken loose. Mad applause burst out. Even Shōgen, with panic and death at his heart, could not refrain from joining. Master and man, there were none like them. Sukeshige brought the horse to a halt before Shōji. His own retainer he could offer no praise but this. The *rōtō* all bowed to the strong man in silent salute. Sukeshige rode before Shōgen who stood on the *rōka*. "The command of Shōgen Dono has been "performed. The exhibition itself is a trifling one. Is there aught "else Sukeshige can do at your honoured will?" Said Shōgen, sullen and willing to bring him to shame by failure of some sort— "Let the *go-ban* be brought. Deign to mount thereon. With "such a huge animal the feat will be unequalled"—"Reverentially "your lordship's command is heard." In a rage Sukeshige rode off to his *rōtō*. "Iza! The fellow's impudence! Mount the *go* "board; who ever heard of such a feat! Not this Sukeshige; but "to try it. 'To manage the legs is as dressing a lady's hair.' " The *go* board then was brought and placed in the middle of the court. Now a *go* board is a square of less than sixteen inches, a massive block of wood mounted on stout legs.* How to get the

---

* Actually $15\frac{3}{8} \times 15\frac{3}{8}$ inches: $4\frac{1}{4}$ inches thick: total with legs $8\frac{3}{4}$ inches from the ground. *Go* is a difficult game, misnamed "Japanese chess." The *kikyō* is he flower platycodon grandiflorum.

Onikage mounts the *Go*-Board.

beast up? Sukeshige cudgelled his brains. Gingerly he approached it and drew back several times, to give the horse an idea of the nature of the task expected of them. Then boldly riding forward the horse's fore hoofs were planted on the board. Gently Sukeshige urged him forward to descend. Now the back hoofs mounted the board. Working on the two reins Sukeshige made him rear. Like a cat Onikage sank on his haunches. Together came the fore feet on the board. The almost impossible task was performed. Then as if carved stood man and horse; Sukeshige standing in the stirrups as if erect; Onikage his fore legs stiff, the back legs bent as if to spring. The onlookers rose to their feet in wonder. Then the horse reared. With a mighty plunge Sukeshige brought him to the ground. Another mad gallop and a gentle trot; dripping with sweat horse and man stopped in silence before Yokoyoma Shōgen.

The latter could hardly speak from wrath and fear. What could he do with such a man, such men? He was too gloomy to praise. " The reputation of Kojirō Dono lags behind actuality. It " would be beyond reason to ask more of your lordship. Deign to " receive humble thanks for such an exhibition." The words were cold and coldly spoken. Said Sukeshige—" Deign to grant a little " respite. An early dismissal is the request made with reverence to " Yokoyama Dono." Thus they separated. Oguri and his *rōtō* returned to the inn to take counsel as to the news of the day, the course to adopt toward the Yokoyama. Shōgen retired to his apartments, likewise to cudgel his brains as to how to deal with this enemy. Surely his affairs were at a fine pass.†

---

† As to the *go*-board—Homma Mago Shirō performs a similar feat, described in the Taiheiki-*Maki* 13. (I P. 384 Hakubunkwan Ed.).

CHAPTER XI.

The Waters of the Tamagawa.

Shōgen, with arms crossed and head down, was as a wooden image, in that eastern pose supposed to be given to thought or nothingness—the contemplation of his navel. A shadow was cast on the *tatami* in the sunlit room; someone prostrated before him. Raising his head he could not restrain a cry of joy. "Ah! 'Tis "Saburō. Never was your presence more opportune."—"Honour-"ed Sir, with fear and respect : Saburō comes to make report as "to matters in Būshū Tamagawa." Yasuharu slily observed his father. Informed as to all that had occurred during his absence, himself a hidden witness of the feat of Sukeshige in riding Onikage, he waited for the older man to unbosom his fears, to seek his advice. Of all the sons of Shōgen this was the one to whom he held most, with no little admixture of fear. Saburō Yasuharu in face and form displayed the low brutality, the coarse strength, the savage ill-temper which made him less fit instrument than worthy partner in his father's exploits and prosperity. Yasukuni was dull and cowardly. Yasutsugu added greed and conceit. This fellow was neither dullard nor coward, nor was he any more scrupulous than his worthy parent. The first two sons were of the issue of one mother. This fellow had been got by Shōgen out of a country wench named O-Nabe (stew-pan). Yasukuni and Yasutsugu made some pretence to the position of samurai. This fellow was little better than the *ya-kunin* he headed. He was the chosen instrument of Shōgen and Akihide for any particularly dirty work. Hence the joy at seeing this promising branch of the family tree.

Shōgen explained matters to him. "Akihide and Naokane "are away from Kamakura. If this be made a public affair it is

" necessary to report it to the Shitsuji Norizane. This is out of the
" question. For Shōgen to attack the fellow openly would not only
" make a stir, considering the known relations of the Oguri and
" Satake Houses, but success would be dearly bought at the cost of
" much bloodshed "—Yasuharu eyed him almost with contempt.
Said he—" There is a way, and an easy one. Poison him."
Bright hope gleamed in Shōgen's eye ; an inquiring eye—" Poison
" him," repeated Saburō. " Namban-doku* put in the saké will do
" the work. If these fellows do not die of the poison forthwith,
" paralysis ensues within twenty-four hours. Helpless they can be
" bound, their heads struck off, and great will be the reward from
" Prince Mochiuji." Shōgen clapped his hands with joy. " Domo !
" Saburō surely there is more than your mother's word for being my
" son. Such rare intelligence ; such readiness ! " Saburō smiled
grimly. It was another score on his elder brothers. They were the
stumbling blocks to his desire, for he had the same kindly feeling
toward Terute, rendered more hopeless by his being the junior, and
more hopeful by his own ingenious unscrupulousness. Said Shōgen
—" The matter is easily arranged. Invitation to the return banquet
" will shortly arrive. As soon as it comes, see Kichiji and Kichirō.
" Make all arrangements for the deed." Thus ended this short and
important council of father and son.

Rei no Kaoru was dressing for the feast to be given by the Aizu
gōshi to the lords of the neighbouring bessō-yashiki, Yokoyama
Shōgen and his sons. To this she was summoned as dancer in the
first place, as beauty in the second place. It would have been
difficult to determine in which she shone pre-eminent. For a
moment she passed into the inner room to secure some ornaments.
Voices struck her ear through the plaster partition. One was that
of a man whose pursuit she hated, Yokoyama Saburō. It had been
a relief to know him absent from Kamakura. Something was said
of the Aizu gōshi. At once the girl was crouched, her ear close to
the flimsy wall. Saburō was speaking—" Aizu gōshi is mere pre-

---

* South barbarian poison : the reference is either to China, or an anachronism of Momogawa. Tradition refers these scenes to the Kamakura Gongendō.
Some writers transfer it to a Go-ken-mura, a country hamlet.

" tence. This fellow is no other than Oguri Sukeshige. The rest
" are his retainers. The objections to seizing him openly are evident.
" On your part you do not want your house to be a battle field.
" Obey the order given, and you shall not only profit directly but be
" favourably mentioned to the provost Naokane. Besides as *kerai*
" of our House it is your duty to follow this order. You run no
" risk. The antidote to the poison is at hand ; *umeboshi* (pickled
" salt plums) rubbed into a paste with fresh blood of toad or frog.
" This taken causes vomiting ; and purging restores to perfect
" health." Said Kichiji—" The command of our lord shall be
" obeyed. But how escape injury to the others ? " Said Saburō—
" Everything has been arranged. In drinking with the lord of
" Oguri none partake except my father, already fortified against the
" drug if opportunity to avoid the challenge does not offer. The
" *saké* has already passed freely in the feast and wits are clouded.
" None will observe whether the same wine is served to the *rōtō* as
" to ourselves. The signal for giving the poison is to be the appear-
" ance of Kaoru in the dance. Do not fail to act with energy "—
" With reverence is the order heard and understood." Thus spoke
Kichirō. A rustling, the sound of *shōji* pushed aside, and the men
left the room.

For a moment the girl remained crouched, frozen with
horror. Everything in this cowardly deed revolted her, including the man suggesting it. In a moment she was seated, inditing
a letter of warning. She folded the scroll into small compass.
Then the thought struck her—how transmit it? The time was
short, the feast was in progress. Eyes were observant, and any
messenger would be stopped and questioned. To warn Terute was
useless. This supper in the pleasure palace was no pastime for the
lady. She would not be present. She could rely on none but herself. Thinking busily she finished her dressing. As anticipating
the call by error she stepped into the corridor, coming face to face
with the brothers of the Tomimaruya. In procession they were
bringing the *saké* as if some special offering. Kichiji showed some
surprise at the presence of Kaoru. " The *tayu* is in haste. Does
" not Kaoru wait a summons ? "—" Danna (master) the page has

The Waters of the Tamagawa.

"already come.   The guests clamour for the dance. Such is the
" command of Saburō Dono."—" In such case follow us," grumbled
Kichiji.   The two men were too intent on their dangerous game to
look more clearly into the matter.   Besides who knew the occasion
better than Saburō Dono.

The feast was at its height when they entered the room.   The
saké had indeed circulated freely, and few were in condition to
observe circumspection.   The brothers of the Tomimaruya prostrated themselves before Shōgen and Sukeshige seated at the
head of the room.   " Deign to receive this saké, Awamori of
" Akune*.   To the greatness of such guests alone is such liquor fit.
" Poor though the efforts be to entertain, condescend to savour of
" such merit as this wine pretends."   Filling a cup Kichiji boldly
raised it to his lips and drank as test.   Then the wine was poured
for Sukeshige and Shōgen.   As Sukeshige took the cup in hand
Kaoru came forward.   " Deign honoured lord to put aside the
" wine.   First comes the dance ; then in all propriety the wine.
" Condescend to favour the mizu no kuruma (water waggon)."
She opened her folding fan and posed for the dance.   Sukeshige
put down the cup.   Shōgen frowned, and took advantage of the
attention riveted on Kaoru to pour out the full cup beside him.
Kaoru danced divinely.   Then she sang :

" On lofty moor of inmost Tamagawa ;
" Forgetful traveller : he dips and drinks the water ! "

Now there are many Tamagawa (Jewel Rivers) in Nippon ;
but one is famous, or rather infamous.   Thus Kōbō-Daishi, the
great apostle of the ninth century, made the poem to warn travellers
against drinking the poisonous waters of the Tamagawa of Kōyasan
in Kii Province.   Sukeshige was not slow to take the warning.
Surely this wine was poisoned.   He glanced at the cup of Shōgen.
It was empty.   If poisoned it would not have been drained.
Slowly he reached again for the cup.   As he did so, in an awkward

* The very best (saijō) awamori of Akune. Awamori=arrack, more
alcoholic than saké. Akune is a large town in the north west corner of Satsuma,
Shussui (De-mizu) gori ; noted for its fine saké in ancient times and now, says
that excellent guide book the Shinsen Meishō Chishi Vol. X p. 597 (Saikaidō).

movement the long sleeve of Kaoru swept too close and dashed it from his hand. The wine was spilt on the *tatami* before Suke-shige. In confusion the dancer sank at his feet. " Nay ! " said Sukeshige. " It is but an accident. Let another jar be opened." He made as if to raise the prostrate girl. As he did so Kaoru slipped the letter into his hand. In confusion at her awkwardness she made as if to retire, but Sukeshige demanded again other wine. He had no suspicion that any plot went beyond himself. Kichirō now appeared with a second flask of the precious *saké*. He had neither the courage nor confidence of Kichiji ; especially confidence in Yokoyama Saburō and his antidote. It was with white face that he stomached the poisoned wine under the keen glance of Sukeshige. The latter turned to Shōgen with full cup. Shōgen leaned toward him with a little smile, and touched his lip to the full cup. " One moment and Shōgen rejoins the company." Thus on press of necessity he rose to leave the room. Sukeshige bowed and in doing so poured the wine into his bosom. Then tilting back his head he made as if to drain the cup to the dregs.

When Shōgen returned he found his host very red in the face. Groaned Sukeshige—" Ah ! Something has disagreed with me ; my " chest feels as if of lead. Breath comes with difficulty. Iya ! The " stomach, how it rumbles and twists ! What pain ! What pain ! " Deign my lord to excuse this Sukeshige for the moment. He re- " turns at once." Said Shōgen—" Surely your lordship's indisposition " is trifling. Such valour, one who can ride the famous Onikage, is " not to be tripped up with dinner and a little *saké*. A moment " and all will disappear. Take more wine." But feebly smiling Sukeshige excused himself and left the room staggering and sway-ing. Hyōsuke noting his lord's indisposition joined him. They stepped into a room close by. Said Sukeshige—" The awkward- " ness of Kaoru was no accident. Here is a letter. Surely the wine " they gave me was poisoned." He tore open the scroll. With pale face Hyōsuke read over his shoulder. The scroll ran— " Yokoyama Saburō has given the Tomimaruya brothers *namban* " *doku* to poison the lord of Oguri and his *rōtō*. If not death, " paralysis ensues ; unless *umeboshi* rubbed in fresh blood of frog be

" taken within the sun's circuit. The dance is signal for the deed.
" None are to escape. Deign, honoured lord, to leave this place at
" once. The name and mission of Oguri are known."—" And *rōtō* ! "
said Sukeshige. He looked anxiously at Hyōsuke. Said the latter
gloomily—" Hyōsuke and his brother have drunk twice since
" Kaoru began her dance. Shōji has tippled like a whale ; the
" others less so. The poison as yet does not act. Deign my lord
" to return ; and this hive of scoundrels shall be cleaned out before
" death ensues." He laid hand to his sword. Sukeshige detained
him. " Not so ! At once to Fujisawa. The Shōnin, Joa, will
" know what to do, how to save all. Here comes the scoundrel."
He threw himself on the floor as in agony. Hyōsuke leaned over
him as in anxious solicitude, and the better to conceal his growing
wrath. Said the *karō* to Shōgen—" What is to be done ? My lord
" is in great suffering. Surely he cannot be left thus." Shōgen
could hardly conceal his glee. His game was assured. He would
make it surer, under the direction of the astute Saburō. " Convey
" your lord at once to the apartments of Terute. The indisposition
" is but a passing one. Doubtless a little nursing under the care
" of his wife will effect a cure. Women are a great antidote to
" wine." He sneered.

Thus the party broke up. Under the direction of Shōgen the
rōtō carried their almost unconscious lord through the hedge to the
apartments of the astonished and alarmed Terute. Sukeshige's
face was almost purple. Some of the others were notably pale.
Hyōsuke had dropped the hint of their dangerous position. With
his game thus bagged, under his own claws and ready for immediate dressing, Shōgen left to make his final dispositions. Out of
sight Sukeshige was on his feet at once. The convenient knot com-
pressing his throat was released. The blood again took its free course.
It was the paleness of anger which now tinged his face. " No time
" is to be lost. Sukeshige, warned by Kaoru, threw the wine away.
" But the *rōtō* have drunk. The antidote is to be sought at once.
" Ah ! Here comes the rascal again. Like any carrion bird he
" will not leave the feast out of sight." He half drew his weapon,
but it was a woman's form which emerged from the darkness. Rei

no Kaoru prostrated herself before them. " Deign to pardon my
" awkwardness. There was no time to warn the *rōtō*. Yokoyama
" Saburō only brought the poison just before the dance. But escape
" must be made at once. The Yokoyama retainers are assembling.
" Tarō and Jirō will shortly be here to secure the heads of those they
" consider dead men. Condescend my lord to escape at once.
" Deign to grant the humble prayer of Kaoru that she be allowed to
" accompany the lady Terute. Return I cannot; except to meet a
" cruel death." Weeping she sought the feet of Terute. Gently
the lady took the hand of the singing girl. " Deign my lord to
" take this girl. Shōgen will do no injury to Terute." Said Sukeshige—" All must go. Let there be no delay. Terute could not
" remain under the roof of the murderer of Atsumitsu. The Shō-
" nin will give aid." Onikage, bridled and saddled, was brought to
the *rōka*. Then stepped forward the Kataoka brothers. " With
" fear and respect: will our lord deign to grant a petition "—" What
" is it?" said Sukeshige—" To allow us to make a defensive
" fight against the Yokoyama. Assured that your lordship is dead
" or dying within the few minutes gained in thus obstructing them
" means much." Said Sukeshige—" Be it so." The party left the
yashiki of the Yokoyama by the mountain in its rear. Terute and
Tamate rode the mighty charger, as gentle under the touch and
guidance of his master as a kitten. Kaoru clung to his tail. Thus
the huge horse, followed by the *rōtō* plunged into the wood, to
scramble up the steep slope and seek the road and refuge of Fujisawa
Yugyōdera.

Meanwhile the Kataoka brothers made ready for the battle.
Shōji and everything inflammable were piled together in one apartment. The entrances were carefully inspected ; the means of flight
as well as fight. Then they waited for the foe. There was no indecent haste. It was now midnight. Several hours had passed since
the deadly deed was committed at the Tomimaruya. As Saburō
Yasuharu said—" The matter will keep. As the hours pass the
more helpless they will become." But Yasukuni and Yasutsugu
were impatient. Action was not to be entirely left to the younger
brother. Besides to fight with the dead or dying was perfectly

safe. Saburō however refused to risk his skin in the encounter.
"Attend to the matter. Saburō awaits the more propitious time."
Demanding some thirty men from his father, as in a huff he rode off
on his own business. These fellows could burn their fingers in an
attack on the desperate Oguri *rōtō*; not he.

The Kataoka heard the tramp of many feet. Throwing open
a panel of the *amado* the brothers looked out. They were in
shadow; the garden was filled with moonlight. "Naruhodo!"
said Katarō." Is not this Tarō Dono? And Jirō Dono also!
"Truly our lord is honoured at this inquiry as to his health, even
"by a visit so out of season. Your lordships come well attended."
—"Let there be no further talk. Your lord has been poisoned
"with *namban-doku*. To spare him suffering this Tarō and Jirō
"come uninvited to secure his head. Make no resistance. Besides
"the *rōtō* also will surely die. Nothing can save either he or
"them." Said Katarō in great rage—"Oh, you scoundrels! It is
"true indeed that our lord has been foully poisoned. His dead
"body lies within. But it is Tarō Dono and Jirō Dono who shall
"announce his presence to Emma-Ō. Take the warning arrow."
From the shadow followed a rain of shafts. Half a dozen of the
Yokoyama retainers "pitched head first into the potato patch."
Yokoyama Tarō, with an arrow through the arm, lost all appetite
for fighting and withdrew. In anger shouted Jirō—"Forward!
"These fellows are half dead already. It is an easy task to kill
"them." But it was no easy task. Dropping the bow the Kataoka drew their swords. The space was narrow, the contest not so
unequal. A number of the enemy fell, slashed by the merciless
strokes of the brothers. In confusion the foe drew back to take
counsel. Plainly the assailants were too numerous long to maintain
the position. The Kataoka dragged the bodies of their quondam
foe into the pile of combustibles. A damask robe, the one in which
Sukeshige rode Onikage, was thrown on the edge. As Jirō
counselled another attack in front and rear smoke was seen to rise.
Despairing of successful resistance these invalids had fired the
pavilion. Anxious to get the head of the lord of Oguri the band of
Jirō dashed forward. They were too late. The place was a see-

thing mass of flame, and it was work enough to save the *yashiki* it-self from the conflagration.

Meanwhile Sukeshige and his company had reached the top of the hill. Even as they stood there a faint light arose, then the blaze of the building on fire in the valley below. Hastily Sukeshige pushed South, past the stone of Toshimoto, to get into the Fujisawa road. As he did so a band of some thirty men rode out of the shadow and blocked the passage. Who could they be? Their leader was a young man of twenty-five years or less, truly an ugly fellow, squat and black. He wore a purple belly guard. His halberd adorned with silver rings whirled round a head bound with a towel (*hachimaki*) as for battle. A cloak of damask on his shoulders gave him some pretence to leadership, for otherwise he was a very coolie (*ninsoku*). Sukeshige did not know him. This was Kamakura, not a mountain wilderness. So he rode forward seek-ing quiet passage—" Probably there is some mistake here. We are "travellers on our way to Hakone, Deign to let us pass." The man laughed savagely—" Iza ! Sukeshige Dono does not escape in " this easy fashion. Yasukuni and Yasutsugu have no more wits " than they can spare. Saburō Yasuharu is not such a fool. He sus-" pected an attempt at escape. But the game is up. Be wise and " stick out your head." Sukeshige was prompt to take the cue. He had this man's character from Terute. A whispered order and the Kazama in charge of the women disappeared in the forest to the left They were to act in strict obedience to Terute's orders, as one knowing the ground. Then drawing his sword Sukeshige charged forward. Now seven men against thirty is a more than uncertain fight. The Yokoyama *kerai* swarmed around Onikage, to drag the rider from the steed and finish him. The resistance the Oguri *rōtō* could offer was much diminished by their rapidly weakening con-dition. The poison was having its effect. Even Ikeno Shōji was but little better than half a dozen men. With a huge cedar pole, torn up in the forest, languidly he swept off the assailants like flies. Pertinacity and numbers might have gained the battle. But Oni-kage was a host in himself. He had been left out of the feast. Biting, kicking, plunging, with flaming eyes and steaming nostrils, the mighty horse cleared a space around him. The Yokoyama *kerai* drew off to try the chance of arrows. Then crashing in their rear came the Kazama brothers, sent to the rescue by Terute's order. As the rascals broke in flight for home they were met by the Kataoka, descending the Kehaizaka in their retreat. With one accord, headed by the judicious Saburō, they took to the woods, hastily climbing the wooded hill to the South.

The Oguri, lord and retainers, were safe and united ; but weakening. Where were the women ? Said Kazama Jirō—" Close by : ".at the Zeni-arai well.* At her ladyship's orders we came to the " aid of our lord "—" To their rescue ; then to retreat to Fujisawa." All turned over the hill, much in the track of the thievish *kerai* of Yokoyama. On reaching the cave dedicated to Benten they burst in, Sukeshige leading. In the darkness of the large cavern there was no sign or sound of anyone. Stars and moon shed an uncertain light into the centre through the cavity in the roof. Shōji stumbled over a body in the dark corner near the well before the shrine of the goddess. " Ah ! The hands of Shōji are wet." Smelling them—" Blood ! My lord there is some foul business here." He raised and brought the body before the opening. It was that of Tamate, her throat cut from ear to ear. Not a sign of the younger women was found anywhere. Shōji returned, to stand gloomily beside the corpse of his mother, his face in his hands. All pitied him. Tears stood in their eyes ; keen was the feeling for the loss of this comrade whose devotion was known to them. Said Sukeshige—" A cowardly deed ! " Thus to make war on women ! Terute and Kaoru evidently have "been dragged off by the Yokoyama retainers. What will be their " fate ! " Lord and retainers with hands on their swords made as one movement toward the mouth of the cave. Sane counsel interposed in the person of Ikeno Shōji himself. He knelt before Sukeshige— " Deign, my lord, to consider the uncertainty of such an enterprise. " Whether her ladyship has been taken to the Yokoyama *yashiki*

---

* Money washing well. The effect is as with the oil in the widow's cruse. One becomes wealthy. The zeni-arai-ido is easily reached from Sasukegayatsu or the top of the Kehaizaka, a pretty walk. The well is in the cave of Benten, marked by many *torii*.

" is not known.   Attack is one thing, defense is another ; and both
" with people forewarned, and in Kamakura town itself !   Take
" counsel of the Shōnin.   Deign to be guided by him."   Tenderly
Sukeshige laid his hand on his retainer's shoulder—" Even in grief
" Shōji shows restraint.   How vengeance moves you before this
" corpse is known to all.   Be it so."   Then a grave was dug by the
uncertain light of pine-wood torches, and in it was laid the body
of Tamate.   Standing beside it the men clapped their hands and
recited a *nembutsu*.   Marking the place with the cedar uprooted
by Shōji they took their way to the Tōtakusan Fujisawa.

It was five o'clock in the morning when the Oguri, lord and
retainers, entered the enclosure of the Yūgyō temple.   Fastening
Onikage to the Ichō tree before the *hondō*, leaving his *rōtō* in the
charge of the priests, and some badly needed their care, Sukeshige
sought an interview with Joa Shōnin.   With tears in his eyes he
narrated the events which had brought them to this terrible pass,
and begged his assistance.   Joa made minute inquiry as to the
banquet and its progress.   " There is no great danger for the men.
" The antidote mentioned is powerful against other poison.   Doubt-
" less this is the case also with this *namban-doku*.   Plum trees are
" more numerous at the Tōtakusan than at Hachimangū itself.   Hence
" the *umeboshi* is a superfluity in the pantry.   As for toads and frogs,
" the ears of all but the deaf can testify to their presence."   Summoning a disciple he gave directions for the preparation of the drug.
The *rōtō* were brought to the rear of the *hondō* (main hall) as the
safest hiding place, and there quartered.   Then Joa Shōnin counselled Sukeshige.   " Under the care of my priests there need be no
" misgivings as to these men.   As to Terute nothing can be done.
" Whether alive or dead, whether at the bottom of some pool in the
" Katasegawa or in ocean depths as is only too likely, or in the
" hands of Shōgen, this Sukeshige is equally helpless.   Chaste and
" faithful, loving and self-sacrificing, living a life free from blemish,
" it is hard to believe that Kwannon will not favour her, in the next
" existence if not in this.   This Joa is in position to make inquiries
" and ascertain the truth.   Be patient.   For Sukeshige it is best
" to leave this place.   Go to Yahagi in Mikawa province.   There

" take counsel with your relations the Asuke.   Thus in time the
" restoration of the Oguri House can be effected.   Deign thus to
" act."   The advice was good, its source inspired.   The next day
Sukeshige, mounted on Onikage, rode westward.*

* Shōnin has been interpreted—preacher, evangelist.   As with Nichiren etc.
More properly it is the title of honour of a high ecclesiastic.   As these were
associated usually with monasteries the term prior or abbott seems appropriate :
but the *shōnin* also had relations of episcopal functions with the laity—i.e. bishop.

CHAPTER XII.

The Rōtō* of Oguri.

The temple of the Shōjōkwōji, the Tōtakusan of Fujisawa, then as now was one of the most influential foundations in Nippon. The Jishū (Ji sect) had been established in the latter half of the thirteenth century by Ippen Shōnin (Ochi Michihide) ; who, when barely out of swaddling clothes, at seven years of age, had shown that apocryphal precocity of the Nipponese and started a course of theology beginning with Tendai doctrines at the Kaikyōji of Tōkuchiyama in Iyo, running through the teachings of esoteric and exoteric Shingon (mainly charms and nonsense), Jōdo, and Nembutsu, and ending up by establishing his own peculiar preaching of the Buddha's " Wheel of the Law " in this Ji sect. In the fourth generation from this worthy Donkai Shōnin founded the parent temple of the sect here at Fujisawa. More popularly it is known as the Yūgyō-dera (temple of the travelling prelate), from the peculiarity that its head, known as the Yūgyō Shōnin, continually travels from province to province, preaching the doctrines of the sect, performing miracles when occasion offers, and in so doing visiting with great impartiality the temples both of his own and rival sects travelling in the Buddha's footsteps. When death approaches, the great wooden lotus kept in the front of the *hondō* or main temple at Fujisawa close

---

* The term *rōtō* (郎黨) refers more particularly to those retainers attached to the personal service of their lord ; the officers of his immediate service. The term does not differ much from the commoner *kerai* (家來) which is used in place of it, and often out of place. *Kenin* (家人) is the distinctly higher term, equivalent to vassal. A great House like the Uesugi would have important but subordinate Houses in this vassal relation. The subordination is to the House not the man. For the development of *Rōtō* and *Kenin* see Ariga's " Dai Nihon Rekishi " II Chap. 54 Section 4 (pp 5, 6).

their leaves. At this miracle and sign notice is sent forth, and the holy preacher returns to the temple, to make his departure from this existence, perchance happily to Nirvana, such is the great holiness of these men. Of this temple and its priest the following anecdote is told.

In the ancient days of one of these earlier Shōnin,† the worthy preacher then being on his home circuit, it was noticed that every day there came to the preaching at the *hondō* a very beautiful lady. Her soft demure glance chastely sought the ground. Her willowy form bent in prayer before the altar. Nothing but a beautiful oval face appeared beneath the *zukin* (mantilla) which concealed head and shoulders. Her contributions to the cash box were weighty. Every day the worthy Shōnin distributed among the zealous the Semmai-dōshi no Myōjō (1000 ups—1000 downs), charms to secure health and happiness in this world and the next. Invariably he smiled and passed over the outstretched hand of the lady. But great was her persistence and repentance for whatever was her offence. Finally the Shōnin relented, and into the hand of the fair penitent passed the longed for charm. Congregation and lady left the temple with deep reverence to place and priest. For long the Shōnin sat in deep revery. Beside him sat in reverent patience the attendant disciple (*deshi*). The Shōnin raised his head and turned to him. " Go to the hill behind the temple. There will be found " a dying fox. Return and make report." Alas! Had the Shōnin lost his venerable wits, or had they merely " gone visiting," as centuries later with that lay disciple in a distant and barbarous land. But it is the place of the Buddhist disciple to obey, not to question. Rising and saluting, and passing the Shōnin with his right side toward him, the disciple did as he was bidden. To his amazement, on the hill behind the temple he found a fox dying ; in its mouth, tightly held, was the *myōjō*. In fright he hastened back to the temple and made report to the venerable teacher. Said the Shōnin—"The beautiful lady, so constant in attendance and

† Eikyō (1429-1440). Here Momogawa places the tale. Inquiry at the temple showed less bump of chronology than the scribe. The little pamphlet issued by the temple authorities makes Ippen Shōnin attribute his inspiration of the Ji doctrines to the Kumano Gongen.

" devotion, is this fox. Without doubt in the next life her piety
" will be rewarded by birth in human form. Great is the mercy
" and the efficacy of the Buddha ! Gather the disciples, and make
" a grave for the body of the fox on the hillside." This was done,
and to this day the legend remains as part of the stock of temple
lore, although the actual site of the Kitsune-zuka (fox-mound) in
these degenerate days has been forgotten. At least the vast graveyard on the hill behind the Yūgyōji has an original beginning.

Such was the sanctity of these holy men that their preaching
could thus secure a human birth even to being in the form of a beast.
Joa Shōnin enjoyed exceptional influence. To him had fallen the
early spiritual guidance of Prince Mochiuji ; his conversion to the
way of the Buddha. The affairs of men no longer attracted from him
anything but benevolence. When Oguri castle fell in flames, when
Oguri Hyomonjō Shigefusa of the younger branch, involved in the
ruin of the House, cut belly to anticipate the vengeance and army
approaching his fief in Musashi, Joa made no sign of slightest anger
or attachment to the world. To the sly remark of a courtier seeking
favour, that " the Shōnin had all the apparatus to secure the dead a
" happy issue in the next existence, and the living against their
" ill-will ; " replied the worthy bishop—" Joa has abandoned
" the three worlds.* The deeds of men work out their own *karma*,
"and none can prevent. The Way of the Buddha (Butsudō)
" diverges from the Way of the *bushi* (Bushidō). It is the part of
" Joa to aid the unhappy. There his mission ends." Prince
Mochiuji, a little fearful of his teacher's resentment, was enthusiastic over such complete renunciation of worldly affairs.
Isshiki Akihide, departing for his new conquest in Hitachi, thought-
fully chewed the cud of contemplation. He read deeper. The rash
courtier got a glance of sour disfavour from the prince ; hence from
all present. He went home in grievous uncertainty whether he
would not be ordered to follow the example of Shigefusa.

With the arrival of the Oguri *rōtō* Joa Shōnin at once took
energetic proceedings. While the men were being dosed and purged

---

* *Sanze* or *Sangai*—Yokkai, region of desire ; Shikikai, region of love ;
Mushikikai, region without love or desire.

he ordered his monks to make a great pyre of wood in the temple enclosure. Then all the available hair was sought and gathered in one mass. This was no small quantity, for it was a common offering of women, too poor otherwise to contribute to the temple's support, in some cases ready to make this greatest of offerings from religious enthusiasm. Hence the years had brought a huge mass of such offerings. Everything in readiness the Shōnin waited. His patients were getting along rapidly. The illest man of all had been Shōji, as the one absorbing the greatest quantity of the poisonous drug. But the vomiting, the purging, the feeding on rice-gruel, the now heavier meals, at the end of two days had made them as good as ever. Their appearance was ghastly, their strength great, their rage grown to giant proportions. Meanwhile the Shōnin's fears and expectations were realized. His inquiries had been fruitful. He had learned and transmitted to his guests, for report to their lord, that Terute and Kaoru had been carried off by the Yokoyama *kerai*, and were kept closely confined in the charge of the Tomimaruya brothers. So much the priests of the Kaizōji could tell him. Nothing could be done for them—at present. Now Saburō on his return had reported to Shōgen the meeting and battle with Sukeshige. Said Shōgen—" He must not be allowed to escape. Doubt-" less he has sought refuge with Joa Shōnin. This is an easy matter " to ascertain." Said Yasutsugu who entered at the moment— " Easier than thought. The Shōnin has already made report of the " presence and the poisoning of the Oguri, lord and retainers. The " matter is town talk. He has been granted the bodies for burial by " the prince, who is displeased at the method of their ending, but will " do nothing."—" Eyes surpass ears," said Shōgen sententiously. " Saburō, do you take fifty men, go to Yūgyōdera, and secure evi-" dence of their death."

Thus it was that on the afternoon of the third day Saburō Yasuharu at the head of fifty men rode into the temple precincts. Fortunately the ten men in the *hondō* knew nothing of his presence ; Saburō only suspected theirs, and as yet was inclined to exercise politeness. Joa Shōnin anticipated him. Warned of his approach he met him at the head of his monks. The chants rose, the censers

were swung, the acolytes carried bunches of grave sticks (*sotoba*).
On Saburō making announcement of his mission Joa was all holy
unction. "Alas! It is too true that these violent men sought
"shelter here in the arms of the Buddha. But past hope they are
"all dead to the Lord of the Lotus. Their tablets now are being
"written, to be placed in the Tablet Room (*Sekii no Ma*). Bad
"and rebellious their wicked spirits are now to be exorcised. Thus
"tranquillized their evil wills will be purged and they will gain
"seats on a lotus. Violence breeds violence. Their punishment
"reaches them in the present existence. You, honoured Sir, have
"come just in time to head the procession. The pyre has already
"been fired. When its heat has departed the white bones are to be
"gathered and interred with all respect. Deign to lead the chorus."
Saburō was completely taken in. The task was congenial and
suited his object. With all due hypocrisy he dismounted and with
his *rōtō* joined the procession to the blazing pyre. Joa led them to
the windward side. He and his monks with their fans drove the
stench into the faces of the Yokoyama, lord and retainers. It was
a stench surpassing all stenches; a stench of burning hair, of ancient
hair and hair oil. Saburō fumed and choked. He prayed in terms
most profane and impolite. Joa too prayed.—"These men were
"men of war, of carnal war; men given to the Six Passions and the
"Hundred Evils. Once names in the flesh, now they are mud.
"Namu Amida Butsu! Namu Amida Butsu! Innumerable spectres
"of hell and sea, evil ghostly beings, forthwith enter on the Way of
"the Buddha, to attain Nirvana and forgetfulness of the deeds of
"men. Namu Amida Butsu! Namu Amida Butsu!"—"Namu
"Amida Butsu!" chanted the monks vigorously fanning themselves and the Yokoyama. "Namu Amida Butsu!" groaned and
choked these rascals. "*Nan to kusai na* (How they stink)!"
chanted Saburō in lower tones. Fortunately the service came to an
end; hence without indecent interruption. The Shōnin, to remove
him from the *hondō* and the subject, turning to Saburō in courteous
terms urged him to take refreshment in the prior's hall. Saburō,
now convinced, was ready to see Kamakura again, but courtesy and
the desire to get the stench out of throat and nose counselled ac-

ceptance. He dismissed half his train. With the rest he would ride
the short distance to the city. His men lost no time in obeying orders.

Meanwhile as evil luck would have it a youthful and brain-
less acolyte, one Chinami by name, thought that the Oguri *rōtō* should
be apprized of their danger. So he came flying to the rear of the *hondō*.
Here they were busily preparing for the start westward at night-fall.
Blurted out the fledgling—" Ah, honoured Sirs! Your affairs have
" come to a pretty pass. Here is Saburō Dono with fifty men come
" from Kamakura to seize you. Pray the Buddha to give you other
" forms, to turn you into fox, or badger, or snake. Any miracle is
" possible to the Lord of all the Universe." Shōji, who was polish-
ing his sword, raised his head. His eyes blazed like suns in his
white cadaverous face. Without a word he was outside and had
leaped from the rail to the ground. Hyōsuke called—" Shōji!
" Shōji! You will ruin affairs and put the Shōnin in a pass with-
" out issue." But Shōji was deaf. There was nothing to be done
but seize their own weapons and follow him. Saburō already was
passing in front of the *hondō* when the huge man, his disordered
hair like the mane of a lion, his face blue and corpse-like from recent suffering, burst into his path. " Ah, you villain! Poison was
" fit food for my lord, that in this cowardly way you sought to send
" him hence. The knife was for a woman's throat! But Emma-Ō
" in hell was stern. ' Where is the head of Yokoyama Saburō.
" Get you back to Earth, you fellows. With that in hand return
" for judgment. Sacrifice is to be made to the Yellow Fountain.
" Your band is incomplete.' Thus spoke the King. Dastard, stick
" out your head! " Joa Shōnin was aghast. How avert this catas-
trophe? He interposed his voice, not his form. " What vision is
" this! Avaunt ye ghosts! Already has this Joa made exorcism
" in full form. No longer is your presence to be tolerated on
" Earth's surface. Get ye hence! " And he meant it. Would
that the Oguri *rōtō* were in Tōtōmi or Dewa, or anywhere but in
Fujisawa! Such rash and reckless men! Saburō was not deceived.
He laughed bitterly. " Ah! The Shōnin is a diplomatist. But
" matters are not so conducted. These men make open proclama-
" tion of their presence. Seize and bind them."

This was easier said than done. Saburō spoke bravely for the Oguri were between himself and the gate in the high wall surrounding the temple enclosure. Odds of two to one against them were small indeed. Swords were drawn. The priests fled to every side. The battle was joined without delay. Little chance did the Yokoyama *kerai* have against these picked men. If the faces of the foe were corpse-like and without strength, their own efforts were sapped by deadly fright at the words of Shōji. Had not these men really returned from the dead, the Under-World? Most of them were soon cut down under the well directed blows of the enemy. Only two escaped in flight and confusion toward Kamakura. Hyōsuke and his companions respectfully drew aside to permit the duel between Ikeno Shōji and Yokoyama Yasuharu. Whirling his halberd Yasuharu rode at him to cut him down. Shōji roared with ferocious glee. " Ah ! Poison is a safe weapon ; not so steel in the open " field. But such a death is too good for a coward." He thrust his sword back into its scabbard. Lightly he dodged the onrush of horse and rider. Seizing a huge gravestone close by, as Saburō turned again to attack him he hurled the mass full at him. The weapon interposed was snapped as if of wood. Borne down by the weight Saburō came to earth, his brains and blood staining the ground. For a few seconds the limbs moved feebly under the great stone. Then the body lay inert.

Joa came slowly forward. The *rōtō* prostrated themselves before him. Said Hyōsuke—" Venerable Sir, the deed has been most " rash and thoughtless. There is but one thing to be done. Bind " us forthwith, and send us prisoners to Kamakura. Such is the " humble petition. Such assuredly would be the command of our " honoured lord. Deign to issue the order. Gladly do we offer our " limbs to the bonds." Joa smiled. " That would be a desperate " remedy. And beyond repair. But Joa, it is to be trusted, has " more expedients than to necessitate adopting it. Truly you are " men of fearful power. It is a field of death. Joa indeed has left " the world, but by another and fairer route. However this affair " makes more urgent the departure. Such disguise as there is will " be furnished. Travel by night, rest in the forest by day. Since you

Ikeno Shōji kills Yokoyama Saburō.

"petition for the order of Joa ; this it is." Then the monks in haste brought forth garments, white, black, and grey. The mighty men of war were clad in the robes of fasting shavelings. Tall men, the robes were short. For the warrior's belt was substituted the seamless *obi* (girdle) of the priest, and in this most incongruously stuck two swords. Monk and layman burst into laughter as they looked at the outfit. Then with deep reverence the Oguri *rōtō* said farewell to the Shōnin and his monks of the Yūgyōdera, and betook themselves to the road leading westward over the passes of Hakone to Mikawa. As for Saburō and his dead retainers Joa made small bones about the matter. With night at hand these were carried off some distance to the hills on the Kamakura road. Joa said nothing, and the rumour spread that the Yokoyama had been attacked by one of the bands of thieves swarming the hills of the Banyugawa. Prince Mochiuji still spent most of his time in camp, his army yet undisbanded. Such fellows had a fair mask. The two men who escaped to Kamakura were wild with terror. They told a tale of a battle with ghosts, in which steel was used and whose presence was gravely denied by the stately prior and his monks. Suspected themselves of collusion with the robbers they were then put to the torture, with all the ingenuity of the times and race. Whether they paid the penalty of cowardice or crime no one pitied them in the well deserved punishment for their offences. Thus they confessed everything desired, from the well corroborated stench of the funeral pyre at Yūgyōdera to their own iniquities. They died on the cross, and their suspense and sufferings thus ended.

Meanwhile the Oguri *rōtō* did not get far on the way to Mikawa. At the top of the hill, outside the temple, Mito no Kotarō with all solemnity squatted by the roadside. For a little they waited his approach, then returned to ascertain the cause of delay. With obeisance to the *karō* said he—"With fear and respect : deign to "present the humble petition of Kotarō to his lord, excuse and "request for leave of absence. Kotarō goes no further." Said Hyōsuke—"Respected Sir, why in this manner ? The difficulties "of one are the difficulties of all. Deign to open your mind to us "that consultation can be held." Said Kotarō—"For my part I

" return to Kamakura, to offer congratulations to the brothers of the
" Tomimaruya, Kichiji and Kichirō. Rewarded by our lord with gold,
" rewarded by Yokoyama, rewarded by the Kwanryō himself doubt-
" less through his officers, truly they are subjects of a congratulatory
" address. Kotarō would join in this. Nay ! Bringing their heads and
" leading the Lady Terute by hand it is his design to present himself
" at Mikawa to his lord." Said Hyōsuke—" On the matter there can
" be no difference. It is for the performance of all. Difficult for one
" man to accomplish, for all it is feasible. At once then to return
" to Kamakura ! " Thus did the journey westward meet with an
early check. With eager minds all hastened toward the capital.

This time Hyōsuke made a different and bolder entrance.
They were dead ; ghosts. He pushed his way directly up through
Yamanouchi Quarters were to be sought in some cook-shop of
Ōkura or Yuki no Shita, far enough removed from the Kaizōji quarter
to escape any observation, yet not so far as to be unable to act with
rapidity and energy. Darkness covered the strangeness of their outfit.
Hyōsuke approached a place favourable to the design, situated on the
Wakamiya-ōji. The plot of ground facing the wide avenue was the
site of numerous inns and cook-shops wedged in between and behind
the great *yashiki* which lined the sacred road to the sea. Here was a
small but attractive inn, the Suzukiya, its main recommendation
being the evident idleness at the time of host and staff, and the
capacity of their own party to occupy all the attention of the staff and
kitchen. To Hyōsuke's inquiries said the *teishu*—" Deign to enter
" honoured Sir. By chance the night is dull, the company scant.
" The whole house is at command. Condescend to honour this
" humble place with your presence." Hyōsuke made sign to his companions to enter from the outer darkness. At the sight of the incon-
gruous company emerging into sight the teishū and servants were
seized with terror. Such big fellows ! Such garb ! Surely they were
highwaymen meditating some fearful deed. The *irasshai* (deign to
enter) broke into a stutter of fright. It was Hyōsuke rather than
the host who conducted them to an apartment in the rear. Here
the *karō* gravely addressed the frightened man. " The alarm of
" the *teishu* is without cause. Doubtless he takes us for mountain

" robbers meditating or having accomplished some desperate deed.
" Dismiss such idea.   Nikaidō Dono has just died, and at the Hōkaiji
" memorial service is being held.   We are Nikaidō *kerai,* and for
" the past night and day have been held in close company in prayer
"and a stinking apartment of the temple.   In pity some of the
" *shoké* (minor priests) gave us these robes to conceal the warrior's garb
"and escape from the temple precincts.   We have come thus far to
" seek food unobserved after this fast.   At dawn we return to prayer,
" better fortified for the performance."   With joy and relief the
host prostrated himself in apology and fearful reverence.   Hyōsuke
stopped the growing list of dainties on his lips as afforded by this
fortunate house.   "The best that sea and hill affords.   Look!
" Here is gold.   Take this as security."

Then, as said Hyōsuke and the chronicler, " did the gods of
happiness dance."   The maidens, reassured, brought the feast
prepared.   Hyōsuke spoke with truth as he remembered the past
hard and meagre diet at Fujisawa.   All ate tremendously.   Shōji
fed himself and the snake too.   Ten times did the huge bowl, like to
the bowl of Benkei at the Koshigoe Mampukuji, pass to the rice tub to
be filled.   The house staff looked on in fright, the cook sweated and
worked to supply the appetites of these ten heroes.   It was as if
Yoshisada and his army again had come to town.   At last repletion
was reached.   The *teishu* presented himself.   Said he—" With fear
" and respect : honoured Sirs the hour is late, the fires drawn.
" If nothing be commanded, deign to permit the house to go to rest."
Said Hyōsuke—" Nothing is needed but hot water and the roasted
" wheat (*mugi*).   All can retire."   Then bedding was spread.   The
hibachi with its carefully nourished spark and steaming kettle was
brought in.   Then with low obeisance the *teishu* and his staff of
maids disappeared ; an occasional voice in the distance, and soon
all was silence.

Faces grew stern.   Hyōsuke explained the plan for action.
Adjoining, almost joining, in the rear the Tomimaruya and the
yashiki-bessō of Yokoyama Shōgen there was a small barn (*koya*)
familiar to all in their residence and journeys between the two houses.
Said Hyōsuke—" Shōji is to start before the rest.   Find entrance in

"some way to the *koya*, and gathering material for a fire be in
"readiness for a signal to start the conflagration. This will be
"given by one of our company ; or the swarming of the neighbour-
"hood will be sign itself for action. On our part we will break
"into the house from the front, rescue her ladyship, and put all
"within to death, even to a kitten. Such is the course to be
"pursued. Deign, respected Sir, to depart forthwith on this mis-
"sion." Ikeno Shōji made ready, to enter earnest protest and to
perform the task. With revential obeisance said he—"Will not
"the honoured *karō* condescend to modify to some degree this
"order ; allow someone else to carry out this task in Shōji's stead ?
"Truly practice makes perfect, and becomes monotonous. At the
"Inamuragasaki *yashiki* it was Shōji who set fire to the building and
"applied the torch to the fishermen's huts of Gokurakujimura. At
"Oguri castle it was Shōji who torch in hand burst into the enemy's
"camp ; the others carrying naked swords. Now again it is Shōji
"who is selected to play fire-bug. Deign to consider............"—
"These eminent recommendations for a task in which there can be
"no slip," finished Hyōsuke. "As *karō* the order comes as from
"our lord. Deign, dear Sir, so to regard it. In truth to no other
"is such an essential part of the plan of action to be entrusted. At
"Inamuragasaki it was made plain that Shōji Dono could handle
"torch and sword with equal care. At Oguri-jō the tale of heads
"carried back to the castle by your honoured self equalled that of the
" rest of the company united. Hyōsuke feels assured of success with
"such aid. Be sure that Shōji's sword will find work to do, as well
"as the torch. The retreat with her ladyship is thus secured."
Thus ended this little controversy within the ranks.

There was a *go* board in the alcove. Shōji went to the closet.
Within was a box containing the *go* counters. Lovingly he fingered
them. "Go-ishi (stones) of Shingū. 'It would be a shame for the
"*teishu* to lose a single one of such beauties, soft as a woman's
"hands." Carefully he piled them together. Then the box was
partly filled with ashes. Live charcoal from the *hibachi* was
imbedded therein. Shōji put the box carefully in the bosom of his
dress. Sliding the *amado* he stepped out into the inn garden. A

minute later he passed into the dark lane to take his way once again to the Kaizōji valley. Passing to the rear of the Tomimaruya he was soon before the *koya*. This was locked by staple and padlock. Shōji examined the fastening. Going to the *ike* (pond) he dipped therein his *hachimaki* (head towel). Returning he wound it round the staple and began to twist—*giri, giri, giri, giri, giri*. A moment, and lock and bar were in his hands. Shōji glided within. It could be said that Kichiji and Kichirō had foreseen such mission and provided the best of material to hand. The *koya* was a storage house for all the old rice bags, straw wrappings of the bundles of charcoal, dried and worn out bamboo poles, and other such combustible rubbish. The worthy brothers were ready to gain in various ways, and no source escaped them. From the maid who entered the gate, to the charcoal bag fit to go forth on the refuse pile at the rear, an honest *mon* (fraction of a farthing) was to be turned. To be sure Kichirō sneered a little at these tricks. He was younger and of freer hand. But there was not much to choose between them. Both not only would coin the farmers' daughters into gold, but the farmers themselves into copper. Equally businesslike Shōji went about his task at once. A little pyre was soon collected. Convenient to hand he started a fire with his live charcoal. Then he squatted like Fudō-Sama, glaring out into the darkness, his sword across his knees instead of being held erect. Thus he waited the signal for action.

As the temple bells boomed the first watch after midnight, the hour of the ox (1-3 A.M.), Hyōsuke and his companions followed close in the track of Ikeno Shōji. The whole city was wrapped in sleep as the silent figures passed along the road from the Jūfukuji leading to the Kaizōji quarter. It was tolerably well known what they would find in their path. The Tomimaruya, as with all such places, would be dark and silent. Only the two watchmen at the door, guard against thieves and fire, would be awake or partly so. Hyōsuke approached the door of the pleasure inn and knocked. Replied a voice in some irritation—" Who is without? Are you so " ignorant as not to know that all is closed at this house. Admit- " tance there is none until broad day. Deign then to return."

Replied Hyōsuke—"Learn that the case is exceptional. This day
"our lord Yokoyama Saburō visited Fujisawa Yūgyōji and is
"returning late. Here he intends to rest. Open at once. Re-
"freshment is to be provided. Anything further his lordship
"commands will await his early arrival. Delay will be to your
"disadvantage." Hyōsuke spoke with much truth, for the head of
Saburō accompanied them. The name of Yokoyama was all
powerful at the Tomimaruya. Former *kerai* of the worthy Tarō
Yasuhide the brothers at all hours were at his behest. Besides, was
not this matter of Kaoru cause of recent anxiety to their masters ?
What were the intentions of Yokoyama Dono in reference to this
affair ? Would he withdraw his favour and support ? Plainly
neither he nor his were to be irritated. Active submission was
to be shown. Slowly and sleepily one of the men drew back the
bars and swung open the heavy door. As he did so Hyōsuke
drew his sword with an upward sweep. "Atsu !" was all the
fellow had a chance to say. He fell, severed in two parts from
ribs to neck. His companion started to flee, only to be cut down at
the first step by Daihachirō. The Tanabe brothers guarded the
front, the Kataoka the rear exit. The other five invaded the house,
cutting down all they met. Some fell rising from sleep. Others
fled, only to fall by the swords of the Tanabe and Kataoka.
Kichirō heard the tramping of feet, the cries of alarm and death.
"Water-blister rascals !* he thought. Probably they were men of
the lower class of retainers, *ashigaru*, out for a frolic and bent on
thievery. He seized the oak staff at his bedside, and nearly naked
sprang into the corridor. Here he came face to face with Mito no
Kotarō. Kichirō stared at him as a ghost. The *kerai* of Oguri
wasted no words. A sweep of the sword and the protecting arm
thrown up was severed. Head and body parted company. Thus
died this wretched man. The blood spurted over the silken panels,
dyed the *tatami* soft and white as the finest cotton wadding.
Kotarō paid little attention to his victim, except carefully to identify
him. Then he went on, to enter every room in search of her lady

---

* *Mizubara gurai wa shite yatsu de gozaimasu kara.*

ship in the one case, or of victims in the other case. Such was the method of all.

Meanwhile Shōji was sucking his thumbs, with such patience as he could command. " Surely the *go-karō* is not entirely reasona-" ble. Truly all the wise are wrong. To play with fire is but " tedious. The least that Hyōsuke Dono can do is to give Shōji a " certificate of patience to offer humbly to his lord. He promises that " the sword shall find action. It stands fair to rust in the scabbard. " Ah! The *rōtō* are at work." Shōji rose, and in the darkness advanced to the door of the *koya*. Just then a man lightly clad came running, evidently seeking escape through the garden. As he passed the *koya* a pole tripped him up. In an instant Shōji was on him. Rising he dragged his prisoner to his feet. A gleam of great and ferocious joy overspread the face of Shōji. Kichiji gasping with exhaustion and terror gazed at his captor with the lack-lustre expression of one already half-dead. " Iza! The *go-karō* promised well. Oh, " you miserable filthy scoundrel! But Benten-Sama has all kinds of " luck at her disposal. It is your turn to taste of the wrong kind. " What shall be done to the scamp? Any ordinary death is "unseemly. Of course of that you are yourself assured." He paused, as if awaiting answer from the terrified Kichiji. The latter merely rolled his eyes and gurgled. Shōji held him up, the left hand clasping his throat. He drew his sword. With the blade he touched him, now here, now there. " These ears; they listened to " the counsel of Saburō Dono. Why not to the sentence of Emma-" Ō? These lips which have lied to our honoured lord; how can " they lie to the king of the dead! This nose which still reeks with " bloody perfume (*chi no kaoru*); is not the blood of Kichiji still " more precious? These hands which bore the poisoned cup; made " useless by their trembling. These eyes, without the other features, " how useless! What a funny face! *Sans* eyes, *sans* nose, *sans* "jaws, *sans* hands, *sans* everything! Ideya! The sword of Shōji " is not to be polluted by such a scoundrel." The grasp on the throat tightened, the eyes and tongue of Kichiji stood out horribly. The fingers of Shōji met. With one savage twist he broke the neck of the wretched fellow and threw the corpse to the ground.

The Burning of the Tomimaruya.

As he did so the smell of smoke, the glare of fire, came to his own very perfect eyes and nostrils. Looking up it was obvious what had happened. His precious fire had got out of bounds during his colloquy with Kichiji. The *koya* was ablaze. Like a flash of lightning the fire ran beneath the straw eaves of the great house. Thick volumes of smoke were rising through the burning roof. Then a bright blaze shot up to heaven. A hand was laid on his shoulder. Said the somewhat irritated voice of Hyōsuke— "Could not Shōji Dono wait the signal but for a little?"—Said Shōji; "Truly apology is to be made for this result, but this fellow "intervened, and in talk with him the fire escaped notice. Deign "to accept this explanation, honoured Sir"—"A good one; more "than good," said Hyōsuke. He and the *rōtō* examined the body of the innkeeper. "Shōji Dono has spared steel. A worthy method "with such a scoundrel. Our own work pressed, and gave small op- "portunity for selection. None have been allowed to live. But what "is to be done? Her ladyship is nowhere to be found. The place "is aroused and swarms with people. See! The *yashiki* of Yokoyama "is involved." This was the case. The temple bells, the fire bells, were now loudly clanging. The Tomimaruya was a blazing mass, and fire was spurting in jets through the roofs of the neighbouring houses. The Yokoyama *kerai* and servants in confusion ran to protect the *bessō*. Withdrawn to the hillside the Oguri *rōtō* watched the progress of the work. The shifting wind in this maze of converging valleys was sending flames and smoke first to one side, then to the other. With satisfaction they noted the hopelessness of the effort to stay the spread of the conflagration, to save the *bessō*. Then deciding that they could but regret part of the mission unaccomplished, and make report to their lord as to the other part, carrying the head of Yokoyama Saburō they left Kamakura, this time to make their way in all haste to Yahagi in Mikawa province.[*]

---

[*] As to Shōji's one-sided colloquy with Kichiji, says Momogawa (pp. 71-72) —"*to mimi wo soide—'kono mimi de motte Saburō ni iitsukatta ka ...... kono kuchi* "*de motte isai shōchi to itta na'* ; *to ago wo sukkari kiriotoshi—'tsuide ni kono hana* "*wo kitte ore ga Kenchōji no toshi no ichi ye uri ni yuku. Mimi, hana, ago, ita nado wa* "*dō da ?......iya omoshiroi kao ni natta. Ningen wa hana ga nakute, mimi ga nakute,* "*kuchi ga nai to yoppodo okashi na mono da na.*" The *kōdan* writer has not been followed in all strictness.

PART III

THE MISFORTUNES OF TERUTE AND SUKESHIGE.

"Brahman! Why do you ask an unconscious thing,
"Which cannot hear you, how it does to-day?
"Alive, intelligent, and full of life,
"How can you speak to this so senseless thing—
"This wild Palâsa tree?"

The Body—
"Covered with clammy skin, an impure thing and foul,
"Nine apertured, it oozes, like a sore."—(The Buddha).
　　　　　Questions and Puzzles of Milinda the King.
　　　　　　　　　　(Rhys-Davids).

CHAPTER XIII.

The Lady Merciful.

Joa Shōnin in one way had been correctly informed as to the fate of the Lady Terute. The rascals of Yokoyama in their flight discovered the presence of the women in the cave of Benten at the Zeni-arai-ido. By order of Yokoyama Saburō the unfortunate Tamate was at once punished with death. The two younger women were dragged off down the Sasukegayatsu, and thus conveyed back to the *bessō* to await the judgment of Shōgen. Saburō was careful not to restore the missing hand-maid to Kichiji and Kichirō, and thus Terute and Kaoru were relegated to an apartment with no exit beyond door and roof. The most important decision was as to Terute. The second day lapsed she was summoned to the presence of Shōgen and drily told that the fate of Sukeshige was sealed, his death by poison assured. The next day, by consent or force, she would become the wife of Tarō Yasukuni. Protests were unavailing. Determined not to undergo such fate Terute was conveyed back to her prison and unfortunate companion. Kaoru was left as prize to the claim of Saburō Yasuharu, with death as issue. As this worthy had departed on his mission to Fujisawa, the twain, lady and dancing girl, thus once again found themselves together.

For Terute this night was little troubled with sleep. With pain she watched the tossing of the worn and bruised Kaoru, for the girl had been roughly handled. In the middle of the night she noticed an unusual stir in the house. Between the cracks of the closed *amado* it seemed very light without. What had happened? She went to the *shōji*, pushed them aside to make some inquiry of the *kerai* placed on guard. He had disappeared. Instead there poured into the room a thick volume of smoke. Loud cries were now heard on all sides. The guard gone Terute now dared to push back the *amado*. The Gongendō, given the holy name in derision, was in a blaze. Kaoru now also was awake and joined her. The dancing girl was light on her feet. In a moment she was out on the roof. Holding Terute by the hand she sought refuge as far as possible from the rapidly advancing flames. The two women escaping attracted little attention. Many were doing likewise. Nay! Willing hands aided them down one of the many ladders which gave access above to those fighting the fire. Seizing the hand of her ladyship Kaoru dragged her along into the gathered crowd. Women hastily dressed in their gaudy garments were fleeing in every direction. The girls thus escaped without notice into the foot path leading past the prison cave of Kagekiyo. Here Kaoru diverged from the road to the Kaizōji and hurried Terute along the foot path leading to the Engakuji at Yamanouchi. From the top of the hill the girls looked back. The sky was ablaze with light. The Kaizōji quarter was now a mass of flame. Up both valleys the conflagration extended. In the midst, as if lighted by day, stood out the grave of Kagekiyo, the unfortunate *rōtō* of Yoritomo. Its stone arches yawned ironically amid the glare. Kaizōji needed the water cure as badly as Kagekiyo himself.*

Fortune had favoured them. In flight the girls turned back into the Kenchōji and climbed past the Hanzōbō shrine into the country north of the Ōkuragayatsu. Ignorant of these intricate hills they were quickly lost. Day dawned and they wandered and rested alternately, following the vague directions of the peasantry to be quickly lost again. Wearied out by such unaccustomed exercise it was nearly noon when they came out through the woods into a broader highway. In both directions they looked steeply down

---

* This Kazusa Shichirōbei Kagekiyo, 3rd son of Kazusa no Suke Tadakiyo, accompanied Wada Yoshimori when the latter was [sent up to the Daibutsu of the Nara Tōdaiji by Yoritomo in Kenkyū 6th year (1195). Kagekiyo figures as representative at this *kuyō* or memorial offering. He was brought back by Yoshimori in disgrace. Later he was transferred to the custody of Yata Tomo-iye. Failing a pardon he refused all liquids and died. So says grave history ("Kamakura" of Ōmori Kingorō). Tradition points out this cave as the place of his imprisonment and death. "Apocryphal." comments the Bungaku-shi Ōmori.

through an artificial cut in the rocks. From a tea shed just opposite came forth an old woman. " Ah ! What beautiful girls ! Honour-
" ed ladies you look weary. Doubtless you have deigned to escape
" from the fire at Kaizōji. Enter within and it will be a privilege
" to give a service plainly both require." The woman spoke in kindness. Said Kaoru—" Truly your ladyship nothing
" could be better. We can go no further without rest, and may
" learn something of the fire and what has taken place." Turning to the old woman ; " respectful thanks for the shelter kindly offered.
" And this place ; what may it be called ? " Said the dame—" This
" is known as the Asahina *kiridōshi* (road cut by Asahina) † For
" many years humbly we have served wayfarers ; mostly trades-
" men, never such beautiful company. All—husband, son, daughter
" in his train, have left this *oba* (auntie) to keep the house ; and
" have run to the fire at the Gongendō. Deign to enter." She brought hot water for their feet and dried them herself. Then they were shown into a small but clean room in the rear, looking out on the cliffs towering above and showing the steeply dropping road beyond. Then she left them to prepare the needed food.

After the meal Terute and Kaoru overcome by weariness slept. It was late afternoon when they awoke. Voices were heard. The outer shop was filled with a noisy excited crowd discussing the events of the night and day. All sorts of surmises passed as to the origin of the fire. Some said that a drunken guest had knocked over a lamp in the Tomimaruya. Another man claimed it as the act of an abused scullion maid. Said a third—" Kikyō-San speaks well,
" but the fire had a more important origin. It is said to have been
" started by ghosts." The company exclaimed in loud wonder.
" Yes, by ghosts. It is known that Saburō Dono recently poisoned
" the Oguri, lord and retainers, come to Kamakura to avenge the old
" lord Mitsushige on Isshiki Dono who had slandered him to Prince
" Mochiuji. Although the *kerai* of Saburō have confessed that
" mountain thieves killed their lord on his return from Fujisawa, yet
" many believe their first tale of the ghosts of the Oguri *rōtō ;* and

† Famous son of Wada Yoshimori. He accomplished this feat "in a night."

" such attribute the fire at the Tomimaruya to a kindred vengeance."
Said another—" Truly these Kamakura samurai are terrible fellows
" since even ghosts can commit such havoc." Sceptics interposed.
Interminable was the discussion. Then: came panting up the hill
a middle aged fellow, his arms stained blue by exercise at his dye
tub. "Ah! Obasan! Have my worthless son and your honoured
"daughter as yet returned.?" To the old woman's negative—
" What a night! With my son Tomoiye,—hard at work at the
" tubs all day, we prepared to rest well. But all night it has been
"a task to carry our goods far off from Ōgigayatsu to the hillside at
" Sasuke, for none knew where the fire would stop. As you know,
" the *obasan* of the house is very helpless and very greedy. To me
" fell the task of carrying her and her money box on my shoulders—
" and heavy were both of them! With this burden we had the bad
" luck to run into the train of the lord Isshiki Naokane. Prostrate
" went my humble self, and the *obasan* went nose and box into the
" mud of the ditch close by. It was only their hurry and amuse-
" ment that prevented her being cut down by the *bushi*, for one
" took it on himself to be very angry. Luckily he did not see the
" box. And they tell a terrible tale in Kamakura town. It is said
" the lord Isshiki was attacked at the Saikyō bridge by the ghosts
" of the Oguri *rōtō*, and that his lordship lost his head. Whether it
" be jest or not, truly the *norimon* (litter) passed in great haste."†

At this corroboration of his tale the more credulous of the
gossips plumed himself and smiled with satisfaction. The captious
were silenced. The crowd were uneasy. Mirth and gossip ceased.
One by one they settled their score and departed. Said Kaoru to
Terute—" Unfortunate has been the lot of your ladyship. Assured-
" ly it was the *rōtō* of Oguri who attacked the Tomimaruya in the
" night, in search of your ladyship and vengeance. What is now
" to be done?" Terute thought for a time. Then she said—" I
" have heard my lord say that near Mutsuura at Nojima there
" lived one of the Oguri *rōtō*, Mito no Tamehira. As this man's

---

† The Monjushō (Law Court) of the Bakufu was close by. Hence the name
of Saikyō-bashi, Judgment Bridge." It is between the Hase road and the present
palace (Go-Yōtei), close by the road diverging to Sasukegayatsu.

"brother, Kosuke Tamekuni, was *karō* of the Satake House, if he
"could be found doubtless news of my lord's whereabouts can be
"ascertained and all will be well. Let us inquire the way to
"Mutsuura." Calling the worthy dame they sought to pay their
entertainment and get directions. The latter the old woman readily
gave. "'Tis late ; but hasten a little, and before full night Nojima
"can be reached. As for this poor meal, deign to accept it. The
"recommendation of such honoured ladies to their guests will be
"ample recompense. Doubtless soon you will return to the
"Gongendō." Firmly she refused any compensation. With this
somewhat doubtful compliment, better understood by Kaoru than
Terute, they took their leave and began to descend the pass to
Kanazawa.

Now, as the chronicler says, the hardest task of either Terute
or Kaoru had been slowly to pace the beach at Yuigahama and pick
out the tiny sea shells, much as Japanese women do to-day. Or
else to measure with idle tread the garden or polished *rōka* of *bessō*
or pleasure palace. Their night's walk had worn them out. It was
with difficulty that they progressed. It was full night when hardly
able to crawl they came across the flat into the little fishing village
of Nojima. As they stood uncertain what to do, a woman came up
to them who had been eyeing them from head to foot for some
minutes. Said she—"It is plain that these honoured ladies are
"strangers here. Doubtless you have deigned to flee the fire at
"Kaizōji. At this fishing village there is no fit place for such
"guests. Humble I keep the ferry here. On the other side is my
"house. At one time an inn, now it is a poor place, occasional
"stopping place for vendors of face pastes, rice powder, combs and
"other toilet notions ; or of the traders in baskets, *miso*-strainers,
"and such coarse stuff. The accommodation there is better.
"Deign to honour my poor house." Terute did not like her looks.
Her eyes deep-set glittered almost ferociously. White hair prematurely framed the coarse face of a still young and vigorous woman.
However, what else was there to do amid the darkened houses of
this remote sea-side village ? Assenting the two girls entered the
boat. The woman pushed off with sturdy oar. Taken by the

beauty of the scene, the black outline of the hills sharp against the lighter darkness of the starlit sky, the fitful shining waters framed therein, the sea beyond with its islets lighted by the moon just rising above the horizon, they paid little attention to the woman at the oar. A matter of ten minutes landed them on the other side of the inlet. Entering the house they were shown to a room. Then prostrating herself said the woman—"The house is poor, but with " money anything can be bought, *saké* or fish. Deign to give your " commands." Neither wanted anything but rest. However for the good of the house fish and *amazaké* (sweet wine) were ordered. To pay for them Kaoru inadvertently brought forth a little bag of gold with the Chinese coins then current. At the display the woman's eyes opened and shut with ecstasy. Her fingers twitched. She almost tore away the piece offered for the purchases. " Ah ! " The feast shall be worthy of the recipients. Truly this is a poor " fishing village, but lobster and bull-pouts can be had, and though " it may seem boasting the cooking shall be fit for a great house." Going outside she called her son, a pretty vigorous boy of a dozen years. " Go within and talk to the honoured guests. Be careful " not to lose sight of them." With this she ran off as hard as she could.

Her mission, however, was not simply to get supplies. Near the Kinryūji, with its huge stone on which flew down the Myōjin of Mishima, she knocked at the door of a house. A man appeared. " Gentarō-San ; and your master Kotaka, is the honoured Sir " within ? "—" Ah ! It is Fujinami San, the mother of Mutsuura. " Much is it to be regretted, but the fire at the Gongendō took " Kotaka San to Kamakura. It is late, but he has not yet returned. " Deign to wait a little." Said Fujinami—" That is impossible. " The matter will not keep "—" How regrettable ! " said Gentarō—" There is power for Gentarō to act in the master's absence. " Propose the business to me." Fujinami grinned. Much better was this affair with Gentarō than with Kotaka San. The latter was considered greedy and hard in his loans to the peasantry. In every way money, or what would bring money, was an object to him. In this affair she had thought to tempt him by the magnitude

of the bribe. Said she—" In truth there is a prize come to hand,
" manna from heaven.* Two girls of wonderful beauty have
" come to the house. It is evident that they have escaped from
" the fire at the Kaizōji of Kamakura. They are on their way
" to Yūki, but it is plain duty to restore them to their owners.
" Pay me well for them." Gentarō wrinkled his nose—" A
" filthy business, Fujinami San. What would the master say?
" To buy in this case means to sell elsewhere and cheat the owners.
" To sell girls is something he would not deign to do. But money
" is needed for his purposes. As you say, to restore these runaway
" girls to their occupation is a virtuous deed. Two hundred kwan†
" is the price agreed upon." Fujinami cried out. She fumed and
raged. " Two hundred kwan for each. Both are beauties, though one
" is unsurpassed." Said Gentarō coldly—" The matter is only taken
" up to oblige Fujinami San. Even then it must be masked in the
" report made to the master. Accept or not as you please ; or go
" elsewhere with the bargain." This Fujinami could not do. She
had neither time nor other customer. The bargain was struck. She
had not even the prospective satisfaction of opening the eyes of Kotaka San to the nature of his bargain, for she thoroughly believed
that the speech of Gentarō was mere hypocritical by-play. What
nonsense to be finicky about the virtue of a girl in this fishing
village ! So it was agreed that before the second watch (3 A.M.)
Gentarō was to be in waiting at the Setō-bashi with his boat. Said
he in explanation—" This is no matter to bring directly to the dan-
" na's notice. He shall have the money and gloss the circum-
" stances afterward as best he can—and does. As for the girls, they
" must be got away from Kamakura and the district as soon as pos-

---

* Momogawa uses the expression—*kanro wo hiyori Ten kara*. *Kanro*—sweet
dew which falls from heaven in the reign of a virtuous sovereign ; really an
insect excretion found on fruit trees. Cf. Brinkley's Dictionary : as usual. It is
a pity this comprehensive book has been allowed to go out of print.

† Twenty *ryō*=twenty dollars : (200000 *mon*). A goodly sum for the time.
Coinage in Ashikaga times was Chinese. Gold dust in paper bags sealed, or
bullion in easily cut bars also was in use. See Munro's "Coins of Japan pp 86
o 99; 186, 187.

"sible. Gentarō can arrange that part of the affair." Thus they parted.

Now it being the worthy Fujinami, though no mention of Yū-ki had been made by either Terute or Kaoru, she thus thought to emphasize the flight of the two *jorō* from the Gongendō and silence any scruples of Kotaka, and perhaps of Gentarō. Of the latter, however, she had too much knowledge to attribute excess in this way. With her purchases she made her way back, revolving in her mind various expedients to get possession without delay of the gold carried by Kaoru. Now the reason why the dancing girl was thus wealthy was as follows—There was an old fellow, one Hamaguri (clam), *bantō* or clerk of silk dealers in Kamakura, and their bank as far as current funds were concerned. It was his practice before going among the hamlets and little towns of upper Musashi to collect the woven silk from the farmers, to visit the Kaizōji quarter for its amusements, and while there to pass the time in a sort of Nirvana and practical worship of the god of wine. During these few days of unconsciousness he would entrust his valuables to the sober care of Kaoru; and his confidence was never misplaced. Unfortunately for him he had neither been informed of the plots of Yokoyama and the Tomimaruya, with which the time of his visit coincided, nor of the intended vengeance of the Oguri *rōtō*. One thing was certain. Ha-maguri San was as silent as his namesakes, and never reappeared at the shop of the Ikkyō brothers. His Nirvana extended from drunkenness into eternity, and the firm having ascertained his whereabouts had to shrug their shoulders, confound the two hundred *ryō* of gold dust he carried with the melted gilding of the Tomima-ruya, and carry it to the account of profit and loss. It was this gold which excited the covetousness of Fujinami. Thought she—" Aid " must be obtained. This girl is to be killed. Gentarō San can " well be content with the other. Ah ! Toda of the Tennin-maru " (Ship " Angel ") shall help me. He can dispose of the body, and " none be the wiser."

Meanwhile a scene not without interest was taking place at the abandoned cottage. Obeying his mother's directions the boy had entered the apartment of the ladies. Prostrating himself he made

salutation. Said Terute—" He is just the one of whom to make
" inquiries. What a fine fellow ! One feels in sympathy with him ·
" Deign to tell me, young master—is there not a man living here-
" abouts named Koshirō Tamehira. But alas ! Probably he goes
" by another name. As *rōtō* of Oguri he would conceal himself."
At this injudicious remark Kaoru was frightened, the boy widely
amazed. He touched the sleeve of Terute—" ' *Rōtō* of Oguri ' ; how
" comes it, *nesan,* that you speak of the *rōtō* of Oguri. Ah ! You
" deign to have a tiny mole behind the right ear. And you are very
" beautiful. Often has my mother spoken of the wife of Kojirō Su-
" keshige, the Terutehime of the Satake House. She too had a mole
" behind the right ear. It is Terute, in very truth ! " In joy he
clapped his hands. Then said he to the frightened women—" Dont
" be afraid. Dearly do I love my elder brother Kojirō. I am Man-
" chō, son of Fujinami. Ah ! Nesan, Fortune itself has brought
" you hither." Then his brow knit in a frown—" Wait ! Manchō
" is not so sure of that. My mother has spoken thus often enough,
" but never in kindness. Deign for the time being to say nothing, until
" her feelings can be ascertained. Deign to conceal your identity."
As he spoke the *shōji* was pushed aside and Fujinami appeared.
The end of the conversation, carried on in a low tone, had escaped
her. The first part she had heard. " The hated wife of Sukeshige
" has come here ! She lies in the hand of Fujinami ! Sell her to
" Gentarō ? Never ! Death shall be her portion. Vengeance for
" me, a double dose of gold to Toda. Gentarō can whistle for
" his bargain. Any excuse will do for him. The colour of the
" hair has changed (a horse of another colour). No hand but
" Fujinami's shall seek her bosom. Now to feign ignorance." She
entered the room to announce the service of the evening meal, then
left in haste as one pressed. Manchō with boyish exhuberance and
joy acted the inn maid. Fujinami remained without, ear intent on
any scraps of conversation, but she gathered nothing. The meal
disposed of she entered again to counsel rest. Wearied, and willing
later to get the report of Manchō, the proposition was eagerly accepted, and soon mistress and maid were lost in sleep and uneasy
dreams.

The Demon of Gold and Hate.

Fujinami, like many mothers, thought she knew her son. She knew very little about him. His reticence was aided by her sharpness, for she did not intend him to forewarn her as to the personality of the guests. She sent him to bed in the work-room and trusted to the gentle breathing of assumed slumber to prepare for the business on hand. Toda of the Tennin-maru was not long in making his appearance. He was a huge lumbering fellow. Puffed out in the wadded *kimono* of winter which as yet wrapped up his huge limbs he was in appearance a very *Niō*; one of the *Niō* of the Sugimoto Kwannondō, or the Kōtoku-In, particularly hideous and descended to the fishing stage. Said Fujinami bluntly—" The pur- " pose is changed." Toda's face fell. He glowered. The woman laughed—" Toda gets double instead of single; the same as to the " task. It happens that this wench is the wife of Oguri Sukeshige, " he whom Fujinami so hates. She too shall die, but by my hand. " To Toda remains the disposal of the bodies. The gold shall be " divided between us." Said the man—" Whether as burden " bearer, or to strike the blow, give your orders." He held out a hand like a ham. Said Fujinami—" No, the hand to kill must be " mine. Wait here. Fujinami will report the deed as done. First " they must sleep soundly. Let the first watch of the night (1 " A.M.) strike at the Kwannondō of Mutsuura. Here is *sake*. Par- " take." Taking her kitchen knife (*deba-bōchō*) she went outside. " *Giri, giri, giri*, the grindstone flew round.

Manchō wide awake listened in horror to this talk. " What " a crime! Nesan surely will perish by the hand of my mother. " The wife of my elder brother! Manchō too is his vassal, to " interpose his body on his service." Slipping from under the cover he stole into the corridor and made his way to the room of Terute. In haste he shook the girls, first Terute, then Kaoru. " Honoured " ladies you must leave. Most unfilial is the conduct of Manchō, " but a wicked plot is on foot to end your lives, the one to secure the " gold, the other to satisfy hate: Nesan, my mother has recognized " you and intends to kill you. Toda of the ship " Angel " will cast " your bodies into the sea, food for the lobsters. In haste away; " seek the Setō-bashi. From there turn to the left and make for the

" hills not far distant. The right leads along the flat to Nojima.
" Driven into this corner you will surely perish with none to aid, for
" all will support Toda and my mother. Turn to the left, without
" fail." Urging them he slid back the *amado* and fairly pushed them
into the moon-lit road. Listening to the *bata bata* of their feet he
smiled with satisfaction. " And Manchō! Never can he survive
" such a shameful thought; never can he face his elder brother."
He went to the *andon*. Putting his little finger in his mouth he
bit off the end. With the bleeding stump he traced on the paper of
the lantern :

" Remembrance to the sight ;
" A mark, methinks, as left in running water."

He hesitated. Ah! His mother hated Terute. Extinguishing the
light he lay down in Terute's bed. Then he pulled the cover over
his head.

Meanwhile Fujinami had prepared her cutlery. She stole in
bare feet along the corridor. Gently pushing the *shōji* she found
the *andon* extinguished. So much the better! Softly she approached the bed of Terute. Gentle breathing of one in sound sleep
was all that was heard. Fujinami pulled back the cover. The white
throat glistened in the dimness. She straddled the body. Then
the sharp knife at a single effort sank deep. The cry was stifled in
a flow of gore. A tremor or two and the body beneath her was
quiet. The head had almost been severed from the body. Fujinami grunted, *sub voce*, with satisfaction. " Now for the other wench.
" But why not rob her? Gentarō San will be satisfied with the
" girl. What regard will be paid to her long tongue? It is better
" to sell her." She withdrew, then softly called to Toda—" For
" one the deed is done. Take the body now. But first bind the
" other girl and carry her to the boat of Fujinami. She shall be
" sold to Gentarō San who awaits her at the Setō-bashi. The gold
" we divide." Toda nothing loath entered the apartment boldly
with his lantern. What if the woman did struggle or make an out-
cry? He was Toda of the Tennin-maru. Men did not trifle with
his strength. He went to the bed near the *shōji*, but there was no
Kaoru. At his cry of astonishment and alarm Fujinami came

running. She found him standing by the bed once occupied by
Terute. The lantern exposed the face of Manchō. The poem
written in blood on the *andon* told the truth of the affair. With a
cry between wail and rage Fujinami sank with clasped hands on her
knees. " Ah ! Such infamous wretches, scum of scoundrelism.*
" The vile bitch has made Fujinami murder her own son. What
" is to be done ! What is to be done!" Toda touched her shoulder
" —Mother, surely they and the gold cannot be far off. Why not
" ...." Fujinami was on her feet enraged. " True ! At once
" to seize her. Successful all the gold is yours. Do you go one way ;
" Fujinami takes the road to Setō-bashi." Like a demon she
sprang out into the night. Toda prepared to go the opposite
direction. Along the street of the village came the man who
posed as husband of Fujinami, one Urabe Kenjirō. He was an
old and surly fellow, as yet strong. With a gasp Toda thought of
Manchō. He slunk off in the dark to his own abode.

Meanwhile Terute and Kaoru painfully stumbled through the
night along the horse path which led to the Setō-bashi. They had
reached a cutting in the road. On one side the seven little Jizō
(god of children) looked blandly and stonily down on them. On
the other the apes of the Koshinzuka (monkey mound) seemed to
mock them. Steps of a person running rapidly were heard fast
approaching. Kaoru stood in front of Terute to defend her if
necessary. In a moment Fujinami was upon them. Her eyes
glaring she brandished the knife stained with the blood of Manchō.
" Out of the way girl ! The life of this wench is mine. Let Fuji-
" nami have her. Deign not to prevent." Said Kaoru—" Woman
" are you mad ! What has her ladyship done that you should try
" to kill her ? What evil has ensued that thus you should ill-treat
" peaceable travellers ? "—" Shut up ! " bellowed Fujinami, blind
with rage. " The blood of Manchō cries for vengeance. This is
" the hated wife of Sukeshige, the filcher of my boy's life basely
" taken by her guile. What ! You are still obstinate to defend
" her ? " Kaoru tried to seize her hands, to hold her. Peasant by

---

* *Nikusa mo nikushi*—says Momogawa. None of the *kōdan* writers spare in-
vective at this point.

origin, by nature, returned to her former life Fujinami had a man's strength. Kaoru struggled, crying out to Terute to flee. Fujinami flung herself on her, plunging the knife deep in her side. The unfortunate woman fell backward. Fujinami bestrode her. " Ah ! " Bungler and interloper. Take that ! And that ! And that ! " Savagely she thrust the blade into the defenseless breast. Kaoru gently sighed. Then her spirit fled in this defense of the lady. Fujinami sprang to her feet. " Fool ! One forgets." She took up the pursuit, sure of success. On the road, between the Bentenjima and the Setō no Myōjin, she reached her victim. The long hair of Terute wound around her hand she stood over her to strike. Prayed Terute—" Why so angry mother ? Am I not your son's " wife ? "—" Yes ; you jade ! As such this death is too swift and " easy for you." Fujinami thought for a moment. " Ah ! Close " by here ! " Dragging her by the hair she came close up to the bridge. In ancient days this inlet ran deep into the valley to the foot of the hills, half marsh, half lake according to the state of the tide. A short distance from the road was a little wayside shrine (tsujidō). Close by at the edge of the water stood a huge pine tree. The tsujidō still stands, probably much as it did in those days. The pine is misrepresented by a mere degenerate sapling. Here the wood-cutter, husband of Fujinami, conducted his daily task. Faggots and slivers of wood lay thick on the ground.

Seizing the hands of the half fainting Terute, Fujinami bound them tight behind her back with the end of a rope she found lying on the ground. Then she coiled the strand around her victim. She approached the water. The pine tree caught her eye. "Ideya ! I shall burn the slut." Dragging Terute to the foot of the tree the free end of the rope was cast over one of the huge boughs. " Kii, kii, kii," wailed Terute. Fujinami mocked and sneered as she pulled her clear of the ground and left the body swinging. " Umu ! You would go to Yūki Hitachi. " Yuki no Shita-chi it should be. Now the himegimi stands in " her proper place, elevated above the crowd. Truly a high place " and sharp eyes are needed to discover the whereabouts of your " lord, now in the halls of Emma-Ō, bound as yourself. Hence

"you go to join him. Badger! Fox! Hussy! Truly the fate
"of *jorō*, at beck and call of every low fellow who paid your
"master money was too good for you. May you find rebirth in
"the form of an animal; cat that you are, wench!" Busily she
sought the pine branches and slivers. Even in her rage she did
not dare to touch the tempting faggots of Urabe. The old man
had still a strong arm. But the fat branches of the tree answered
well. Pine needles covered the ground. Though a little damp
from recent rain a fire was soon started. Thick black smoke
poured up in a heavy column, in which darted bright flames
rising high to the trunk of the pine. Fujinami tried to see the
progress of her operation, but the smoke was driven by the wind
right into her face. Hither and thither she sprang, throwing
more pieces of wood on the pyre. The wailing of Terute grew
fainter and fainter. Then it ceased altogether. Said Fujinami—
"'Iya! Surely it can be taken for granted that in all probability
"this pernicious wretch is dead.'" She began to kick apart the
burning mass. Suddenly a bright light illumined the place.
Fujinami was thrown on her buttocks as by some heavy hand.
As she stared there stood out against the black sky the massive
tree, "the rope worn as to a gossamer thread, and suspended therefrom a very tiny object of curious shape." Gasped Fujinami—
"The *hotoke* (spirit) of Terute! Surely this is no place to remain."
The sound of an approaching oar brought her to her feet. "Gen-
"tarō San! He must not find Fujinami here." Throwing her
skirt over her head she plunged into the darkness of the trees en-
closing the shrine of the Setō no Myōjin.

Terute came to herself. Her head was heavy and painful.
She looked around her in dazed fashion. She was seated on the
steps of a shrine. A huge pine stood beside the little temple which
was surrounded by a dense grove of *koyamaki*, *ichō*, and *matsu*. The
fitful light fell on a *fukuishi* (lucky stone) close by the entrance
to the island precincts of a shrine evidently dedicated to Benten
Sama. The Setō no Myōjin!" Terute put her hand to the charm
bag at her neck. "Ah! The Kwannon Sama is gone. It is to
"Kwannon Bosatsu that the life of Terute is owing. From her

" shrine at Mutsuura she has flown down to my rescue.   Kwannon
" Sama ! Kwannon Sama !   Deign august one to receive the fearful
" and reverential thanks of this humble Terute."   A light shone
round about.   Terute heard the fall of metal at her feet.   Stooping
she picked up the tiny metal image thus miraculously restored.
Imprudent she held it close before thrusting it into her bosom.   At
her face thus illuminated an exclamation was heard from the grove.
" Unlucky is this Fujinami ! But surely vengeance is only delayed."
The woman flew forward.   Terute sprang down the steps of the
shrine and ran out into the road.   This time she was determined
on death rather than to fall into the hands of the enraged fish-wife.
Reaching the bridge she jumped up on the rail.   All was pitch dark
below.   " Namu Amida Butsu ! "   She sprang into the blackness.
The upraised knife of Fujinami met nothing but air.   The woman
herself was thrown violently against the bridge by the force of
her blow.

    Gentarō, in waiting below the bridge, heard the fall of a body on
the deck of the boat.   Promptly he drew the intruder below.   By
the lamp he made careful survey.   " What a prize ! Truly a woman
" of wondrous beauty.   Doubtless this is she who was promised by
" Fujinami.   But has she not come herself to enter Gentarō's
" service ? The old woman has made a bad bargain."   He went
on the deck to cast off the mooring.   Fujinami already was at hand.
" Gentarō San ! Gentarō San ! Deign to hand over the girl who has
" just escaped. Thus will you do Fujinami a great favour. After all she
" amounts to but little."   Said Gentarō—" Nay, good wife ; treasure
" trove.   You agreed to make sale, and the lady herself has chosen
" to accompany Gentarō, as you see.   She has abandoned your com-
" panionship.   She refuses acknowledgment.   She recognizes no
" obligation.   She no longer makes you her go-between.   Good
" bye, from both of us.   Good bye ! Good bye ! "   The cunning
rascal had severed the rope with his sword and the boat began to
drift away.   In rage Fujinami shouted —" Gentarō San ! Honoured
" Sir ! Deign to return.   The woman is the wife of my hated
" enemy, Oguri Sukeshige.   Deliver her into my hands for death
" and Fujinami is Gentarō's slave.   Kotaka Dono will do anything

" for old Urabe, and Urabe shall milk the money bags of Kotaka for
" Gentarō's own. Deign to give her back for death." A heavy
hand laid on her shoulder made her turn in fright. Behind her
stood Urabe Kenjirō. The real name of this man was Gotō
Makabe Genzaemon. He was the father of Gotō Hyōsuke and
Daihachirō. The old man's eyes blazed with wrath, his drawn
sword was held in his hand. For a moment he stood, ear intent
for sign of returning oar. Then he turned on Fujinami. " Misera-
" ble woman! You, once associated with the old lord Oguri Mitsu-
" shige! Who yourself nursed Kojirō! Thus you plot injury to
" my lord's House; have sold her ladyship to this unprincipled
" scoundrel and into a life of shame. Prepare at once to make the
" journey to the hall of Emma-Ō." Fujinami clasped his knees
and plead for life. But he answered—" Your son lies dead, his
" throat cut from ear to ear, doubtless sacrifice in the place of the
" *himegimi*. In the River of Souls he needs a guide. Go wicked
" woman, to join him." The weapon descended. The head rolled
to the end of the bridge. Wiping his sword on the dress of Fujinami with a kick he sent the body into the water. Then Makabe
Genzaemon turned his back on Mutsuura, to take up the search for
the *himegimi* on which this sudden and lugubrious light had
been shed.

Gentarō gently sculled down the inlet. The words of Fujinami rang in his ears. He balanced all the possibilities. " The
" arm of Kotaka Dono is long, his power is great." He eyed
Terute, now seated in the bottom of the boat, dazed and weeping.
He could get a small fortune for her. Perhaps Fujinami lied ; at all
events to be able to say so on her own testimony, to plead ignorance.
Avarice overcame prudence. Said he—" Be not afraid, lady. There
" is no one to injure you. Instead your life again shall be a round
" of pleasure. Doubtless you are from the Gongendō of Kama-
" kura." Thought he, " surely she will not expose her true name
" and condition in the present state of the Houses of Satake and
" Oguri. She will lie." Here he was on safe ground. Terute
answered—" My name is Kohagi, from Hitachi province. Deign,
" good Sir, to restore me to my home in Yūki with one Makabe

"Genzaemon, well known in the town. He will amply reward "such favour." Said Gentarō—"This shall be done, lady. But "Gentarō has matters away from Mutsuura. Other hands will "ensure your safe delivery. Truly fortunate has been this "escape from the hands of Fujinami." He lied, and lied unctuously. At Nojima was awaiting him his co-partner in more than one black business. The boat of Umpachi was gently sculled alongside. Gentarō drew him apart and put him in possession of the facts. "For three hundred *kwan* she is yours, a noted "beauty and without friends"—"That is hardly true," replied Umpachi. "Neither in Yūki nor in Kamakura can a market be "found for such goods."—"Yūki I grant," said Gentarō ; "and in "Kamakura the burning of the quarter will make such women a "drug on the market for the time being. But you lose nothing on "that account. In Kyōto a thousand *kwan* can easily be had. "The terms are cheap." Thus they bargained and chaffered over the person of Terute. Finally Umpachi produced two hundred *kwan* in gold dust. "She must be taken to the Nakasendō towns. "Great is the expense and delay. Perhaps even to Miyako. Deign "to accept this sum and lose yourself in the crowd of Kamakura." Gentarō carefully examined the seals on the little bag of gold dust. Said he—"The sum is received with respect and thanks. But "Kamakura likewise is no place for Gentarō. He goes to Ōshū." So the worthy pair came to land and departed on their separate ways.

Meanwhile Mito no Kosuke, *karō* of the Satake House posing as Kotaka Dono and usurer of Mutsuura, returned to his dwelling. He had gone to Kamakura to sift this tale of the Oguri *rōtō* and the fire at the Gongendō. Seated before the *hibachi* he found a tall priest. This man's hair was reddish, his face frightfully scarred and seamed. "Ah ! Kosuke ! It was thought to find you at Kamakura town." "—From there have I come, brother. But why eye me so in-"tently ? Has anythiug been learned as to the search ? The task "of squeezing these peasants is ungracious, this outside taxation. "Have you, honoured Sir, aught to impart ?" The priest sighed— "The affair is serious, brother. What report has Gentarō made ?"

Kosuke was surprised—" Gentarō? The fellow should be here. " From me he has no mission." Koshirō's face lightened—" The " tale is thus spread abroad by the confession of Toda of the Ten-" ninmaru. Last night Fujinami sold a woman to you through " Gentarō, who paid for her two hundred *kwan*. This woman was " the *himegimi* for whom so long we have sought. Fujinami her-" self thus told Toda, who bragged of his readiness to kill her, as it " was through her that Fujinami killed her son Manchō. In " drunkenness Toda let out the tale ; and in the hands of the *machi-* " *bugyō* (magistrate) and under the torture it lost nothing in the " telling. To-day he is to be crucified at the Nojima ferry, sport to " all travellers with the bamboo saw. The severed head of Fuji-" nami has been found at the Seto-bashi, and Makabe Genzaemon " is suspected of killing her. The kindness of the old man in sup-" porting this unworthy woman has been misplaced. Mean-" while the presence of *rōtō* of Oguri is suspected and strict " search is to be made. Action is to be taken at once. Thus " Koshirō makes report to his elder brother." Both men re-mained with bowed heads. Great was the misfortune. Thus to find, thus to lose the Terutehime, sought through all these years.

A little sigh of pain roused Koshirō. He raised his head. His brother, bared to the waist, had thrust the dagger into his side. Koshirō would have sprung forward. The outstretched hand of Kosuke stopped him. " This is the one way out of the affair for " Kosuke. The scoundrel Gentarō in his name has sold her ladyship. " Never could she be looked in the face. Hard has been the task to " press from these unwilling people the funds necessary for this " search. Take the thirty *ryō* thus amassed. On Koshirō now de-" pends the prosecution of the task. Search out and ransom her " ladyship. Deign to make report and clear the name of Kosuke." He drew the dagger across his belly and fell forward. Koshirō stood over the body, tears in eyes, face drawn with grief. Baring his sword he severed the head from the body, to find honoured sepulchre at some wayside shrine on the Kamakura road. The money secured he adjusted his robe, slipped the deep straw hat over

his head, and with bell and staff stepped forth again into the world
in search of his lady.*

---

* The temple of the Mi-kawari no Kwannon, who came to the rescue of
Terute, still remains to-day at the western end of Mutsuura—Kanazawa, close
to where the Kamakura road comes in.

The Setō no Myōjin at Kanazawa was founded by Yoritomo in gratitude
for the god's favour at the original shrine of Mishima. It was during the fes
tival and the absence of his sons that the house of Taira Hangwan Kanetaka
was attacked by Yoritomo's orders, and his head secured. This was the curtain
raiser to the battle at Ishibashiyama, and Yoritomo's ultimate success.

CHAPTER XIV.

The Misfortunes of Terute.

This Mito no Koshirō Tamehira, younger brother of Kosuke Tamekuni, himself was a retainer of the Oguri House in the younger branch. To indicate something of the man's character this tale is told. When the Isshiki at the head of a large force set out for Oguri castle, the minor fief of Shigefusa in Musashi Hyōmon was taken on the way. The affair, sudden in its inception, found Shigefusa unprepared. Forthwith he cut open his belly, his retainers were scattered, or found service with the older House. Koshirō Tamehira determined on a more summary vengeance. He sought death; but Isshiki Akihide should accompany him. What had been done once, could be done a second time. Naokane at that time was conducting his unsuccessful campaign against Mitsushige. Akihide still lingered in Kamakura. Tamehira came to the city. On a night when it was announced that the great lord would make a *sankei* he hid behind the *ichō* tree of the Hachiman shrine. When the torches announced the approach of the palanquin to the steps a man sprang forth with drawn sword. Proclaiming name and title Tamehira summoned Akihide to stick out his head. The *kerai* who came to the defence were cut down like weeds. Everything prospered at the inception of the journey, but an arrow transfixed both arms of Tamehira and rendered him helpless. Akozu Heima,. the archer and in command of the Isshiki *rōtō*, had him bound. Then Tamehira unwilling and struggling attended the *sankei*, an object of wonder to the on-lookers. Returned to the *yashiki*, Akihide himself examined him in the garden. Oguri castle was stiffly holding out but its doom was certain. The great desideratum was to learn the whereabouts of the young lord Sukeshige,

known to have gone elsewhere. This man probably knew. Tamehira was obdurate. A plague on these torches which illuminated
his own wrath and despair, and the darkness which concealed the
face of Akihide as he reviled him for his cowardly slanderous tongue,
for his daring to propose such treachery, so very natural to the lord
himself by his own practices. "Now strike off the head of Tame-
"hira. The mission has failed. That is to be regretted ; not life."

With this amiable intention he was remanded to the
prison. Meanwhile cooler thought gave Tamehira the idea to
finesse. Why lose his vengeance, throw away life? When the
guard brought food he expressed his repentance. "The lord
"Isshiki has offered to promote the humble Tamehira to be
"*kerai* of the Ashikaga House. What a fool he has been!
"But the tongue of such a low fellow is to be disregarded.
"Much to be regretted are the suspicions thrown on his lordship's
"sincerity. Sukeshige Dono is now concealed at Yoshida-machi
"near Fujisan. His hiding place however is obscure. None can
"act as guide but this Tamehira. Deign thus to report to his lord-
"ship. His decision is accepted with gratitude. Let him judge by
"the event." Tamehira spoke with such fear and regret that his
captors were gulled. Akozu made favourable report of him, and
his bonds were removed. He was well fed. With all honour and
strict guard, in company with a party of the Isshiki *kerai* he set out
for Yoshida-machi at the base of Fujisan. The Isshiki *kerai* were
not noted for sobriety. Tamehira was noted for a strong head. He
was the best of good fellows. Soon popular his challenge to a
feast, on this desolate mission away from Kamakura town and its
pleasures, was readily accepted. Tamehira, on the verge of failure
and entrance to Yoshida town, eluded his drunken escort. The
people of Yoshida, rough mountain folk, jeered at them and recommended the ice of the Kōri-ana (Ice cave) for their aching heads.
They had to return empty handed to Kamakura. Their officers
were decapitated. The rank and file were reduced to the peasantry
by their angry lord. His affairs took Akihide out of Kamakura,
and Tamehira made preparation to enter it. Handsome, he now
proceeded to undo Nature's handiwork for better success of his

mission. Infusion of burnt sea-shells bleached his hair. Acid and the branding iron seared his features out of all recognition. His wounds healed, thus disguised Tamehira took up residence with old Kajiguchi Jirō, once head *sendō* of the Oguri House, and now living at Enoshima Ryōshi-machi. He passed as his son, recovered and disfigured by small-pox, most filial to his supposed parents. Thus he aided Kajiguchi in his daily task, and kept a sharp eye on events in Kamakura, waiting the return of Prince Mochiuji with the Isshiki lords in his train to the Kwantō capital. The Gongendō fire brought Tamehira to the city, its supposed origin to Mutsuura to hold council with his brother Kosuke. Here he had heard of the tale of Toda extracted under torture. Realizing its importance to his brother and old Makabe he had waited the *karō's* return to make report. Such was the man who had gone forth to search for the *himegimi*, to settle accounts with Gentarō whenever he met with him.

Meanwhile the Lady Terute continued her unwilling journey through the Nakasendō towns westward toward the capital. This Umpachi was a most complete scoundrel. Appreciating the great value of his prize, dreading the escape or recognition of the lady, much of the time he dragged her along by night. By day he would put up in some miserable inn or farmer's house, and giving out that his charge was crazy he would tie her to a post, while curled up at her feet he sought such slumbers as his terror allowed. Not only escape, but a more drastic remedy, was beyond the reach of Terute. Naturally under this treatment she did not thrive. At first Umpachi had intended to make the long journey to Miyako. Here he could sell the girl for at least a thousand *kwan*. But he became alarmed for his purchase. She ate hardly enough to keep her alive, her eyes lacked lustre, her face had the pallor of ill-health. In this spring of Ōei 31st year (1424) the rains had been unusually heavy, footpaths bad and dangerous, the peasants unwilling and exacting to all who could not demand service. Umpachi was stingy ; he and his charge often struggled for miles through mire and along the dangerous cliffs of the passes. On reaching Aohaka in Mino province Umpachi was glad to compromise matters. He was worn

out, more with watching than actual weariness.　Gladly he sold Terute to Manchō, keeper of a large pleasure house at this town which
marked the coming together of the two streams of travel of the Tokaidō and Nakasendō of old Nippon.　Manchō gave five hundred
kwan for Terute, and flatly told Umpachi that he was over-paid at
the price.　" As for the lady it will take weeks to rest her body.
" Your reasons, respected Sir, for coming by the mountain road were
" doubtless strong.　Deign to accept this price."　Umpachi accepted.

In those days Aohaka was a noted place in the records of
Nippon.　Here Yoshitomo sought refuge after his defeat by Taira
Kiyomori, only leaving it to find death in Ōmi.　The princess Yasha, his daughter, sought death in the neighbouring Kabusegawa ;
Yoritomo his son, coming like another Japhet in search of his father,
was here captured and sent to Kyōto, to delude the acute Kiyomori
with (perhaps) simulated stupidity.　At the beginning of the fifteenth
century Aohaka was a flourishing town, a centre of traffic.　As such
it became one of the important post towns between South and
North, Capital and Kwanto.　Manchō's establishment, the Yoro-
zuya, was the most important in the place.*　Well satisfied with
his new purchase he paid the greatest regard to the well being
of Terute.　Under such treatment her pristine beauty soon shone
in all its splendour.　But when the time came for him to
profit by all this care he met with disappointment.　Terute
absolutely refused to act as did the other maids of the inn ;
to be lady in waiting to his guests.　Manchō was justly proud of the
bevy of frail beauties, inn-mates or inmates, which gave his place its
reputation.　But here was a true queen of them all—later they gave such
women the high sounding title of *Tayu*—who refused obstinately to
enthrone herself.　Manchō could match Umpachi as a brute.　Like
this latter he trembled for his shekels.　If he used force with the
girl it would kill her, or she would kill herself.　Said his wife O'
Nagi—" To-day I boxed her ears well for her obstinacy and the

---

* There are said to have been " no inns " in the days of Mediaeval Japan.
However—after the battle of Dan-no-ura (1184) the Taira ladies and women
were sold in numbers to the brothels of Shimonoseki.　Aohaka (Green Grave)
is just a little East of Tarui on the old Nakasendō road.

" jade nearly went into a dream. Be careful. Persuasion is to be
" tried, or the loss of all this money is to be feared. Try the counsel
" of the other women. These girls all have some motive for entering
" the house. Knowing what brought her here it can be decided
" what action to take."

To Manchō the advice seemed good. Summoning a girl named
Seiryū (green willow) he laid the position before her. " Find out
" the reason for her persistency. You, who add such lustre to the
" house by beauty and accomplishments will add to the considera-
" tion due you from the house. Great will be the profit of the house
" if Kohagi and Seiryū are known to entertain its guests." Seiryū
smirked at this little compliment. She hardly regarded Kohagi as
her understudy (shinzō).* Naturally the other women took the conduct of the new arrival badly. Seiryū was entirely willing to forward Manchō's object. " Many are the ways by which girls enter
" the ' nightless city.' It would be a matter of great good fortune to
" succeed in this object. Master, with fear and reverence the best
" shall be done to secure your end." Betaking herself to the room
of Terute, still lodged as one of the great ladies of the house, she
gently pushed the *shōji* and entering prostrated herself in a salutation half mockery. Terute's greeting was kindly and reserved.
Seiryū opened her mission with little circumlocution. " Truly
" Kohagi San your reason is difficult to fathom. To choose a life of
" hardship and abuse instead of one of luxury and pleasure is strange.
" The consideration of the master will not last forever. If you refuse
" to take the place of waiting maid in the inn he will certainly adopt
" harsher methods. It is not for the interest of the other girls that
" such an example be given. We can conceive of no other
" reason than an obstinate adherence to an engagement with some
" man, lasting during the present existence." She laughed and
eyed Terute sideways ; " Dear lady, you are quite old enough
" to know that a man has no assurance of either fidelity or
" fickleness on a woman's part. In maidenhood this Seiryū also

---

* " Nightless City " p. 55-57. The *yarite* p. 59 was the " manageress,"
" female hag." This book is a complete and scientific study of the Edo Yoshi-
wara as found in the original documents and descriptions, therein cited.

" was bound to a man. When he tired of me, and sold me to
" this Manchō, I anticipated that the change would be terrible. In
" truth variety adds spice to pleasure. Seiryū is well satisfied. Be
" advised and abandon this obstinacy." Said Terute—" With fear
" and respect : the words of Seiryū San are heard. It is true that
" a vow keeps Kohagi from any pollution of her person. Gladly will
" she undertake the harsher tasks in exchange." Seiryū, nettled at
her failure, took her departure to report to Manchō. Said he—
" Thanks are due Seiryū. She has opened a way to success. If the
" other tasks be not performed then Kohagi is to do her duty as
" lady in waiting to the house."

Rubbing his hands he summoned Kohagi. Readily she admitted the exactness of the report made by Seiryū. Said Manchō
blandly—" It is easy to see that it is impossible for you to remain
" eating off :your head. You shall be transferred as desired to the
" private uses of the inn. But your duty will be that of a maid
" of all work, no longer that of a lady. Umu! Umu! What shall it
" be? What duty can be found? Ah! Yajirobei and Kidahachi,
" their services shall be transferred elsewhere. Besides, they are
" most graceless idle scamps. To Kohagi falls the duty of maintain-
" ing the service of bath and stable." As Terute bowed in respectful
assent and joy—" There are seven tubs to be filled with water. Each
" tub requires five buckets (tarai) of water ; that is thirty-five buckets
" in all. Allowing for spillage this is eighteen trips to the Kagami-
" ike (mirror pond). Here the river water is muddy ; that for the
" bath must be clean. The water of the well is too hard to use with
" soap. It must be brought for the washing. An inn has much of
" this to do, seven baskets full. This also is part of your task.
" However the Kagami-ike is but five chō from here (⅓ mile). Then
" wood is to be cut for heating the baths. This also is Kohagi's
" task." As Terute bowed, eager to begin this weighty business—
" Deign to wait a little. The horses are not to be forgotten. For
" these, twelve in number, grass is to be cut on the mountain side.
" There it is best, not by the roadside. Unfortunately the mountain
" lies the other way from the Kagami-ike. But at all events even
" Kohagi could not carry water and grass at the same time. Grass

" and water go well together, but not with Kohagi." In silence
Terute listened. She knew little of the actual work of house-keeping.
She knew enough of its details to know that this conscienceless
scamp was mocking her, was practising on her this subterfuge to
force her to comply with his wishes. Said she—" The command
" is heard with reverence and understanding. The task shall be
" accomplished, or Kohagi abandon her present way of living."
Thus she took her leave.

With her heavy burden of buckets at the end of the carrying
pole Terute came to the Kagami-ike. O'Kabe, the bawd of the house,
(*yarite*) acted as guide. Manchō regretted the concession, but the pair
had already departed. At the bank Terute staggered, one of many
times. The pole in falling lightly grazed the foot of O'Kabe. Angered
the older woman raised her arm. The open hand struck Terute
a heavy blow across the face, knocking her down; this too one of many
times in her life in Manchō's house. " An awkward slut ! Truly
" the master is wise. Half a dozen times have you fallen with the
" empty tubs. How can you carry them when filled with water ?
" Soon you will be brought to reason. Remember your bargain."
Jeering she took her leave, to report to Manchō the certain success
of his scheme.

In despair Terute rose and stood beside the pool. It was a
pretty place. Surrounded by low hills crowned with cedar there
were open glades on its banks now bedecked with the flowers of
summer. A little shrine stood part way up the hillside. Its *torii*,
two stone *tōrō* (lanterns), a flight of stone steps, gave it some preten-
tions. Dazed the girl looked round her. " Ah ! Truly misfortune
" governs the existence of Terute. All is evil. The hand of
" everyone is against her. No kindness is anywhere to be found.
" The task is impossible to carry out, and this bad man thus thinks
" to entrap me. But 'Kohagi' will indeed abandon her present
" life. Kwannon Sama ! Kwannon Sama !" She wound her
tasuki (shoulder cord) firmly about her wrists, drawing the knot
tight with her teeth. With hands raised in prayer she made ready
for the plunge. Then a light appeared to shine in the centre of the
pond. Greater and greater grew its intensity until the brilliance

The Vision of the Lady Merciful.

filled the whole place. A figure beautiful, graceful, imposing, of a woman formed in the midst. Said a voice—" It is not for Terute " to kill herself. True it is that in a former life deeds have been done " to be compensated in this existence. But all shall turn out well. " Faith and chastity has its reward. Remember the words of " Kwannon. All shall be well. Terute must live." A gentle breeze arose across the surface of the pond. A delicious perfume as of the mountain lily spread through the air. Then the vision became fainter and fainter to the wondering girl. She fell on her knees. " Kwannon Sama! Kwannon Sama ! " But the cry now was one of hope restored, of triumph. Lightly she rose to her feet. Hands freed she eyed the task. Bravely the buckets were filled to the brim. Then placing the pole across her shoulders, lo! the weight was as a feather. Distance itself was annihilated. As if spoken she found herself at the door of Manchō's inn. And so with the fire wood. A touch of the axe and this was split into fragments. Amazed was O'Kabe a few hours later to enter the bath room and find the tubs filled and steaming, a temperature the perfection to the most exacting and exhausted.

Thus every day was the task of Terute met with precision. To the mountain she had gone, full of faith inspired by previous experience and with the praise of the Lady Merciful on her lips. Uncertain she stood before the lush grass of early summer, very uncertain how to use the sickle in her hand, certain that in some way use would be found for it. As thus she stood the sound of a flute was heard—*hiu, hiu, hiu*. Kohagi the serving wench was also Terute the great lady. At the sweet strains tears came to her eyes, remembrance of happier days. As she looked a lad riding a cow came round the shoulder of the hill. He was the musician and divinely did he play. Coming up to Terute he was quick to note the tears of sympathetic feeling. " Ah! Nesan too likes the sound " of the flute." He laughed deliciously, musical as the instrument itself. " But why are you on the mountain ? " Said Terute— " Alas! These baskets are to be filled with cut grass. But how " to cut grass is beyond my skill. What is to be done ? " At her trouble the boy was sympathetic—" Of that Nesan evidently your

" honoured self knows little.   Deign to let me have the sickle."
Springing down he took the instrument and earnestly went to
work. Soon the grass was cut, the baskets filled. " And now
Nesan, whither are they to be taken ? "   At the answer of Terute
he sucked in his breath with amazement. " Naruhodo ! To
" Aohaka ?   But it is full twelve *chō* (nearly a mile) from here, and
" this alone would require five or six trips. Besides you are hardly
" of the build to carry aught but your own beautiful self.   But here
" is my cow, a wonderful burden bearer."   Forthwith he piled the
baskets on the cow. Then Terute was placed on the baskets. The
boy leaped on the neck of the patient beast, totally disappeared from
sight beneath the protruding mass of fodder. Yet in a trice the
journey was over, the baskets bestowed at the stable of Manchō.
Said the boy—" Nesan at this hour you shall find aid on the
" mountain. Be sure that it is gladly given." As Terute gave her
thanks with deep obeisance cow and boy took a radiant female
form and flew off into the brilliant West. Laughing and crying
Terute prostrated herself in earnest prayer to the powerful and
beneficent goddess. She stretched out her hands to the fast departing sun ; easy in mind, assured in heart, that it would rise again and
with it bring her the aid of the Lady Merciful—as it did in some
form, of peasant, carrier, pilgrim, or village youth.

What should he do ? Manchō was in a quandary. O'Nagi, at
the girl's evident confidence and exhuberant spirits, counselled harsh
measures. " Has she not broken the contract under which she
" entered here ? Why hesitate to do the same with her ? "
O'Kabe aided her powerfully. Manchō still feared the event of
such proceeding. Besides he was a little wounded in his pride
that Terute should thus get the best of him, doing the work of
two strong and lazy men with such a frail body. He would
give his brains one more chance. So he sat down to cudgel them
before cudgelling Terute. Days and months had passed since the
girl's entrance into the house. Summer had passed into winter
now nearly at an end. The other women lolled away the hot
season in cool and shaded apartments. In winter warmly clad
they sat in sunny rooms with southern exposure, warming themselves

at the brazier. These were the true delight and profit of Manchō. Terute had undergone the heat of the sun in summer. Now she passed the winter clad in a single thin garment, working from dark morning until late into the night at tasks fit to strain two men. The New Year was close at hand, the house full of guests. Terute was busy with her bath tubs which were in great demand. Carefully she went from one to the other to see that all were full, the water of proper temperature. She approached one which seemed to need fuel. Bending down she stirred the fire, adding her little bellows to the natural draft. A splash notified her that the tub was occupied. " Ah ! An honoured guest. With fear and respect : humble " apology is made for intrusion." She raised her head, looking up. The man looked down. " Atsu ! Terute ! "—" Sukeshige ! " At that moment the daughter of Manchō, Hanako, approached with the bath robe to be donned on emerging. Said Sukeshige rapidly in a low tone—" Terute here ! But this is no place for explanation. " Deign to come to-night to the Haginoma (Lespedeza room) where " Sukeshige is lodged." Terute made sign of comprehension.

After months of waiting the season had brought its opportunity to Manchō. Terute was returning from the bathroom, her brain in a whirl at this unexpected meeting with her lord, this unhoped for chance of escape. What had brought him here ? Plainly he was no passing guest of the house. He was lodged in the private apartments, the daughter of the house attended him in person. Openly to send to any woman in the house his command was natural in such case. Yet thus secretly he summoned her to his apartment. Plainly none of the other women served him. The voice of O'Kabe broke into her thoughts. Sneering and falsely smiling she summoned her before Manchō. This worthy spoke, his face cast down, so secure was his triumph, so great his anger. " It " is the custom, Kohagi, to observe with great exactitude the forms " of the New Year. Thus is the favour of the *kami* secured during " its continuance. You are ordered therefore to go out into the " town and buy the *nanamono* (Seven Articles). These are *komatsu*, " *madake, ebi, daidai, yabukōji, kombu, noshi*.* He handed her a

* *Komatsu*=young pine trees for the door front ; *madake*=bamboo ; *ebi*=

chōmoku mon and turned his face aside to laugh as Terute thanked him. "*Kashikomarimashita.*" She made humble obeisance of leave and took her way to the door. O'Kabe and some of the girls lounging at the entrance mocked and jeered as she passed. Manchō was so pleased with his discovery that he had not hesitated to impart the cream of the jest to the *yarite*, and she to the others. All rejoiced at the master's sharpness of wit.

Once in the street Terute hastened to get out of the reach of these ill-natured voices. Taking her way into the town she came to a halt to consider the matter. What should she do? Ignorant as she was of the uses of money she knew well enough that the paltry fraction of a " cash " was worse than nothing. Mechanically she turned and made her way to the little temple of Kwannon standing on the hill above the Kagami-ike. Slowly she climbed the steps and clapped her hands in prayer. As she did so footsteps were heard climbing upward. In a short time there stood beside her an aged priest. Terute turned to him with eyes full of tears. Said the priest—" Nesan, surely you are in difficulties. But who in Aohaka " does not know of the devices of Manchō to secure the services of " the maid he bought from Umpachi? He jeers at himself, and " the matter is town talk, known even to a poor wandering priest. " What now is his plan? " Said Terute—" He has sent me forth " to buy the *nanamono*, with but a *chōmoku* to purchase them. " Nay! Thus late in the day; for if the *yakunin* (constables) " seize me in the street after the temple's evening bell, the *machi-* " *bugyō* himself will condemn me to the life Manchō has determined " on. Ah, good Sir, surely the fate of Kohagi, is sealed." Bitterly weeping she sank at his feet. The priest protested in wonder. " A " *chōmoku mon* to buy the *nanamono!* A wicked plot; but it can be " circumvented." Terute looked up in hope; the priest down in benevolence. Continued he—" Take the coin and go to the

---

lobster; *daidai*=bitter orange, a large sized variety; *yabukōji*=a plant with small red berries; *kombu*=edible seaweed, *laminaria; noshi*=red and white wrappings for gifts. " *Kashikomarimashita* "=Respectfully heard and understood. The New Year, old style, began near the end of January, or even February (as late as Feb. 22nd. thus extending into March). Oei 32nd year it **began 20th January (1425).**

"mountain close by beyond the *ike*. Here the village boys are
" playing. For the coin gladly will they get you all the *komatsu*,
"*yabukōji*, and *madake* needed. Keep enough for yourself and
" take the rest into the town for sale. With the money secured go
" to the farmer's houses just outside the town and buy *daidai*.
" These will find ready sale, and with the money the *ebi* and the
"*kombu* can be bought in the fish market. Keep enough of the
"cash " to supply yourself with *noshi* for the gifts. Thus will you
" have honoured the command of the master Manchō. Come!
" Deign to follow to where these lads are playing. A priest is good
"at driving a bargain." Obediently Terute followed his guidance
and direction. As if inspired the village boys dispersed to gather
pine, bamboo, and the red-berried plant. Supplied with these
Terute made thankful obeisance to her priestly adviser. Slowly
he went on past the turn in the road and disappeared, the girl half
expecting that he too would depart heavenward. Surely he was as
a Buddha met in Hell. Then she betook herself to town. Safely
was the threshold of Manchō's house passed as the temple bell
boomed the evening hour. Black with rage O'Kabe ushered her
into the presence of Manchō and O'Nagi. Surely they had their
victim safe. Who of the many bidders would pay highest for her
favour? Off with this scullion's robe! O'Nagi was going over
the finest and most expensive robes in the house-chests.

Manchō's lips were pursed with rage as Kohagi presented herself, followed by the house *bantō* and *kozō* carrying the *nanamono*.
He no longer contained himself. " How is it Kohagi, that with but
" a single *chōmoku* you have made purchases costing several *yen ?*
" The lobster alone is many times the value of the coin. Answer
" and speak the truth. Do not lie, for surely you have some concealed
" lover to furnish you. You are cheating me, robbing the house
"of money." Said Terute—" Truly, honoured master, the matter is
" simple. For the *chōmoku* the farmers' boys gathered *komatsu*,
" *madake*, and *yabukōji* on the mountain. These have been bar-
" tered or sold for the other needed articles. Hence Kohagi succeed-
"ed in accomplishing the task."—" And the money you made;
" surely you can prove your acuteness by its display ? "—" Nay,

"master; what money was left was put in the box at the Kwan-
"nondō of the Kagami-ike at the end of the village." Manchō
roared with passion. He leaped into the garden, and seizing
Kohagi threw her on the ground. " Oh! You thief! Your earn-
"ings belong to your master whom you have robbed. The *komatsu*
"belonged to the owner of the mountain. Surely the *machibugyō*
" will condemn you to servitude, if not death. But Manchō shall
"anticipate the punishment. Take this! And this! And this!"
His pent up wrath burst forth. Falling on the unfortunate girl
brutally he belaboured her body with his fists. Then he began to
kick her. Even O'Nagi protested. "Manchō Dono, consider!
" You are destroying your own property. Punish her, but more
" gently. Be careful not to strike her face. Kick her legs and beat
"her back. Thus satisfy your wrath and spare your pocket."
Manchō was well satisfied with the advice. The pleadings of
Terute were answered by blows, administered under the skilled
direction of the two hags and his own heat of passion. O'Kabe
was prepared to leap down and give more direct aid. Instead she
gave a cry of terror. Manchō heard a fierce snort at his ear, a
warm breath on his neck. Then he was seized by the waist, lifted
from the ground, and shaken as a cat does a rat. Emerging from
a stable close by Onikage had approached the pair. It was in the
mouth of the powerful brute that the human brute pleaded
for an aid his men did not dare to give. Summoned by
O'Kabe they swarmed, to be dispersed by a savage kick to
any coming too near. Then Onikage, gingerly dancing, came
towards the curb of the well in the centre of the inclosure. The
brains of Manchō were evidently destined to besprinkle either its
interior or exterior. At this critical juncture a voice in commanding tone was heard. "Onikage! Onikage! Up to mischief again?"
The samurai spoke to his mount. The horse gently put down the
groaning Manchō on the ground, battered and unable to move with
one hoof of Onikage resting on him. "But what is wrong?" asked
Sukeshige. He spoke as much to the horse as the by-standers.
Manchō answered—"Ah! Sensei Dono, this is a wicked animal
"you have. Deign to fasten him more securely, or allow him to

" be sent elsewhere. This woman was sent to buy the *nanamono* " and has robbed me. It was in punishing her that Manchō has " suffered such injury." Sukeshige eyed the confused senseless heap of the unfortunate Terute. Some brawl of this not over-reputable house; no affair of his to pry into too far. " How did she rob you?" he asked. Manchō explained matters. Once started in the fullness of his soul he laid bare his whole bitter experience with Kohagi, her obstinate chastity, his own schemes to pollute it. Now it was anger, now pity, that took possession of Sukeshige at this tale of woe. The Hangwan seated himself in judgment on the curbing of the well. His eye was cold ; every question was a stab. Finally he said—" That you have suffered no wrong is plain to any " just person. On the contrary the plot is a most wicked one. In " bringing you the *nanamono* she has amply repaid any duty owed " your house, for to send her forth with a *chōmoku mon* was to " deride her. As for the mountain land, all know it to be public " property. If any have to complain, let them go to the parents of " the boys who secured the plants, to the priest who advised this " course." Then abruptly—" plainly the woman is not for you. " Deign to put a price on her. Sōtan Sensei himself shall bid."

At the name of the famous man and artist of the district Manchō wriggled in respect ; he would have sat up, if he could. " Truly the sum paid for her was five hundred *kwan*. She is " worth double that, but such a bad bargain Manchō is willing to " part with at cost price." Said Sukeshige—" For the picture of " Narihira Ason the temple gave this Sōtan as gift three hundred " *kwan*. That much can he offer you. Here it is. Accept the " bargain." But Manchō was obdurate ; his refusal was emphatic. —" Nothing less than cost for an article purchased is permissible. " The *machibugyō* is friendly to the house. He will regard the " matter differently." Sukeshige sighed—" Ah ! And so recently " your manner was very different. Greatly is it to be feared that " Onikage must have his own way." He made a sign to the horse. Manchō, once more suspended by the girdle, felt the pressure of the animal's teeth on his spine. He screamed in terror. The horse gently shook him. Sukeshige laughed. Then O'Nagi came forward. "Deign master to consider. Your rescue is impossible, "your life is precious. Fate has many turns, and Sōtan Sensei can "repay Manchō in other ways than coin." The gentle voice of Hanako plead in kindred terms. Besides she had real pity for this girl; just as she had some contempt for the other venial inmates of the house. Truly she plead earnestly and prettily. Sukeshige himself thought so. Sullenly Manchō gave way. "Be it so. Let "those present witness the bargain. For three hundred *kwan* the "girl belongs to Sensei Dono. Let all anger be put aside." At a sign from Sukeshige the horse released his victim. Manchō came to ground with a thud. Sukeshige passed the bag of gold dust over to Mankei the *bantō*. Said he—"Let not thought of your wounds "give concern. A bath, and a sovereign salve possessed by Sōtan, will "make you as good as new in an hour. The horse shall be more "securely tied. Please order the women to take charge of Sōtan's "purchase. Truly she seems to need care, much more than your- "self good Sir. She has been most roughly treated." Manchō grunted consent. He was awed by his guest's name; his ambition aroused, hence his resentment was abated. Kohagi was picked up and carried off unrecognized by Sukeshige, much more concerned over his night's appointment and the conduct of Onikage. Himself he lead the equine champion to his stall.

CHAPTER XV.

SŌTAN SENSEI.

How was it that Sukeshige, under the name of Sōtan, was thus found at Manchō's inn? Aside from the accident of his presence his rôle had been determined by the exigencies of the politics of the time. As said Yoshimochi in Ōei 30 year (1423) had made earnest efforts to come to terms with Mochiuji in Kamakura. To avoid any offence to the Muromachi Bakufu in Kyōto it was decided that the *rōtō* of Oguri should be scattered through the various towns between Fuchū (Sumpu or Shidzuoka) and Ōtsu, to keep an eye on the situation easily ascertained on this travelled route. Sukeshige himself, accompanied by Mito no Kotarō, had gone to reside in Ayame village not far from Aohaka. Here he posed as a poor teacher of painting and writing. Meanwhile the Asuke brothers of Yahagi kept watchful eyes on matters in Kyōto, for it was very uncertain how far the accommodating mood of Yoshimochi would go in satisfying Mochiuji.

Though adopting the priestly name of Sōtan the artist was as one not yet completely conforming to the priesthood; the scholar not the cleric as not yet having shaved his sconce. The student's robe suited him well, the deep hat in which ordinarily he went abroad concealed his unshorn head, but often as not he assumed the dress of a *samurai*, and it was generally understood that he and his companion were *rōnin* (masterless men), which after all was near enough the truth. Mito no Kotarō made a most unpriestly acolyte, and worse *bantō*, for his master. His manner of soliciting customers was such as rather to frighten the loose coin from their pockets, than to act as magnet to it and the owner's sympathies. In these sales the plan was first tried of putting the sketches in a basket hung outside the house. The purchaser made selection and left his present. This proved more satisfactory to the buyer than the painter. Sukeshige could not keep pace with his clientele. Then to place these works of art more favourably Kotarō went to the various neighbouring towns and villages to effect their distribution. It is to be added that these drawings had their mission. Before the days of Sukeshige, and in much later times, they were used as a cipher to spread abroad information as to the whereabouts of a much wanted person. Thus the famous thieves Kumasaka Chōhan, Tsukushi no Goroku, Ishikawa Goemon, a range from the days of Taira Kiyomori to those of Toyotomi Hideyoshi, gave information to their bands as to their hiding place and intended raid. The notices were posted as mere pilgrim's offerings—the *senja mairi no fuda* (1000 shrines pilgrim's ticket) found at every shrine even to-day—and a favourable substitute for carving one's initials, the motive albeit being religious, as some of these artists in public places also evidently believe as to their own efforts. By these pictures Sukeshige got a great reputation in the district of his residence. His favourite subject was chickens. There were " chickens roosting on trees, picking up food under the stacked rice-straw, roosting on a mortar and crowing;" and we are told that at the Kitano Temmangū of Kyōto is a notable one in which the feathers plucked from the bird seem actually falling to the ground.*

The name assumed therefore by Sukeshige was well known. One day a man appeared as messenger from the lord of the district. The commission was to paint a picture of Narihira Ason, the famous poet and Don Juan of Nippon, for the temple of Kokuzō Bosatsu at Aohaka. Sukeshige undertook the task with pleasure. He showed the nobleman standing with hand outstretched and pointing to a flock of wild geese flying across the moon. This work of Sōtan Sensei, dimmed by age is yet to be seen. So exquisite was its beauty that crowds flocked to the temple to see it.

With the very pardonable purpose of witnessing the effect of his work, and having the added excuse of enjoying the plum

---

* An eagle painted by Sōtan is finely represented in the "Painters of Japan " of Arthur Morrison.

blossoms and their fragrance, then bursting into bloom in the temple grounds, Sukeshige with Mito no Kotarō in attendance set out for Aohaka Kokuzō Bosatsu. Entering the temple they stood apart watching the people and listening to the criticisms, usually expressed with understanding, art being an inborn faculty of the race. The work was much appreciated, the comments flattering. As they prepared to leave there came up the temple steps a young girl of eighteen or twenty years, in company with an older woman who from her dress was evidently the mother. The girl was very pretty, the face a pure oval, the eyes sparkling, and the fresh colour of youth tinging the ivory pallor of the complexion. As she and her mother stood before the picture her admiration was very evident. "Ah! Truly the artist must have painted himself in Narihira Kyū. How handsome he must be! How "fortunate to have such a man for a husband!" Said the mother —"Girls of your age, Hanako, should leave such matters to the "parents. It is not for them to think of husbands. Their heads "are too light, their experience too small. Surely they would "introduce none as son-in-law into their father's house but a "most worthless idle fellow, chosen for his looks." The girl bowed her head in mute unwilling assent. As she looked up she caught the eye of Sukeshige. Now there was no particular likeness between the *kuge* (court noble) of the portrait and the samurai standing near by. But Sukeshige had been drawing that morning, and leaving Ayame-no-sato in some haste had not noticed an ink smudge made in a moment of abstraction under the jaw. The quick eye of Hanako caught it, the idea flashed across her mind at once connecting the man and the painting. Then she blushed as red as the plum blossoms without, and in some confusion followed her worthy parent down the temple steps to the park.

In leaving they had to pass a tea shed where some half a dozen young samurai were ensconced, drinking *saké* and making remarks more or less rude as to the crowd swarming the grounds. At the sight of the girl and her mother one of them gave a shout. "Iza! "What luck! What is wine without *tabo;* and here is a pretty "wench indeed. Come old woman! We are lonely without the

The Meeting of Sukeshige and Hanako.

"spice of a petticoat. Your daughter for our service! Give her at
"once and make yourself scarce. She will be honoured by such
"clients." In fright the women drew back. "With fear and
"reverence: deign good Sir to pardon us. My daughter is young
"and has nothing to do with such matters. Please excuse this
"rudeness in refusal." The samurai was in a towering rage.
"What! A town wench refuses the invitation of such company!
"When the fish comes not willingly to the hook, then the net is to
"be used. Let us seize the girl at once." He sprang up. His
companions did the same. In fright Hanako and her mother cast
themselves at the feet of Sukeshige then close by. He had dismissed
Kotarō on a mission, and was leaving the temple grounds to find
Onikage and ride homeward. Said he—"What is wrong here?
"What injury do you fear?" For the moment Sōtan Sensei disappeared under the habit of the Hangwan. Said the mother—"We
"have committed no offence, beyond refusing my daughter for the
"service of these men, who threaten to carry her off and put me to
"death. Deign, honoured Sir, to hear our petition, to grant us
"protection." Sukeshige stepped forward—"Respected Sirs, these
"women have asked protection. This it is the duty of a samurai
"to give. Deign to accept the apology offered for rudeness in
"refusal. No woman unwillingly should be forced to serve.
"Consider that such action is unworthy in those of the military
"caste." The men were in a great rage. "Who is this fellow, thus
"to shove his elbow into other folk's affairs? Besides he is a
"stranger, a man without support. To accept this apology is beside
"the mark. It is necessary to punish this impertinence. As for
"the girl, she shall suffer worse than if she had submitted quietly.
"Kill him! Kill him! Kill the old bawd! Seize the girl!"
They came on all sides to attack Sukeshige. The knight did not
take the trouble to draw his sword against these drunkards. Besides bloodshed in the temple grounds was a serious matter, fatal to
his own affairs. The first man went flying with a kick. Sukeshige
seized a second by the elbows, and with him knocked down a third
in no gentle fashion. A fourth, too close for comfort, received a
very hard fist between the eyes, seeing more stars by daylight than

he had ever seen by night. A fifth made a sweeping slash at Suke-shige to cut him down. Sukeshige leaped the weapon, and seizing the fellow by the waist sent him flying some thirty feet. The sixth ran away. Painfully rising the rest followed his example. Never had such a fellow been seen in Aohaka.

As Sukeshige received the thanks of Hanako and her mother, prostrate in gratitude, a considerable company rushed into the gate. A man of fifty years, or thereabouts, headed them ; evidently a rich plebeian of the town. Wife and daughter cast themselves on the neck of Manchō, brought to the rescue by news of the disturbance. The innkeeper earnest in thanks solicited the attendance of Suke-shige. " With fear and respect : condescend to accept humble " salutation. Occurring in the temple grounds this can be made " a most serious affair. Doubtless these fellows will so represent " matters to their lord that search will be made. But report " shall be made to the *machibugyō* (magistrate) and his good offices " secured. Deign to accept the hospitality of the grateful Manchō " for a short time. The house of Manchō is yours honoured " Sir. Condescend to enter." Sukeshige had little taste for any-thing but to get back to Ayame-no-satə and receive the report of Kotarō, gone to Tarui to get the news of the capital. How-ever there was much in what the man said. To disappear for a few hours was no disadvantage, especially if any consequences and search into this affair were to follow. Reluctantly he agreed to accompany the host. Himself leading Onikage, to escape further notice and because the animal was very intolerant of strangers, he was thus conducted to the inn of Manchō which was not far off. Evidently it was a place of first importance, its owner a rich man. Sukeshige was conducted to an apartment facing the garden on the rear. This was shut in on one side by a high wall against which stood cherry trees as yet leafless. In the centre was the usual fish pond overhung by a willow. Dwarf trees, curious shaped lanterns of stone, the tiny winding rock bound path of an artificial mound, decorated the ground. On an island in the centre was a little Inari shrine, of prime importance to the women of such an inn as that kept by Manchō. But in these private apartments there was

little to show the nature of his business. Refreshments were
brought. Lavish was the attention, deep the gratitude of parents
and daughter. Hanako in attendance was as the shadow of Sukeshige, and by no means a disagreeable one. Then the bath was
announced as ready. Conducted thither by Hanako herself Sukeshige was rubbed, and scraped, and soused. While her charge
comfortably stewed within the tub the girl stepped out for the
moment to have the robe in readiness for his exit. It was during
this critical moment that Sukeshige and Terute had their unexpected interview.

His progress to the bath had enlightened Sukeshige as to the
main business of his host, and that Manchō's place was not merely
one of the large busy inns with free and easy service such as was
found in these post towns. How did Terute get into such a place?
How to get her out again? Great was his abstraction during the
banquet which followed. This was most elaborate ; fish of various
kinds, lobster from the distant sea, preserved alive in salt water,
saké the fragrance of which was incentive to unlimited drinking.
All desire of Sukeshige to get away had departed. He made a polite
but most absent-minded guest, his thoughts on the approaching interview with his wife. It had required much urging from Manchō
for him to prolong his stay until morning. Now he rejoiced at such
good fortune, and most decidedly unbent in his manner. The
banquet over he was conducted back to the room on the garden, the
so-called *haginoma* according to the tablet hung within. While
reclining and answering and asking questions of Hanako the house
was disturbed by an unusual uproar. Frightened cries were heard.
Thinking that perhaps his whereabouts had been traced by the
recent foe Sukeshige rose and went forth. Instead of samurai he
found that it was Onikage in action. As said he played his part out
of pure sympathy for the misused girl. He had no reason for a stay
beyond the importance of preserving the incognito of his real rank,
and ascertaining the fate of Terute and how to remove her from this
place. Peace made with his host he early asked permission to retire.
This was readily received. Manchō had his particular plans for
this night, unknown to Sukeshige ; Hanako had her own particular

plan for the night, unknown to Sukeshige and her father ; O'Nagi was so nettled over affairs that she wanted time to consider matters. whether to get rid of this inconvenient guest as quick as possible, or follow the hint dropped in her ear by Hanako and already half approved.

Midnight came ; the inn at last was silent. Terute, who had lain as one totally prostrated, gently rose from her poor couch. Her nurses had soon left her. The *haginoma*, which chamber was it ? Of the inner apartments she had but casual acquaintance, and dared not ask. Gently she stole forth to wander the corridors, to seek some indication of her lord's whereabouts. Surely he would be awake, show some sign of guidance. In these wanderings at last she reached the garden in the rear. A hedge of *hagi* ran to the wall at the end. She was on the right track at last. She stepped into the garden. Cracks in the *amado* showed the room opposite to be dimly lighted.

Sukeshige as he watched heard the gentle tread of a woman shuffling along the corridor. It could be none but Terute. Taking his *haori* he threw it over the *andon* and plunged the room in a dim light. Gently he opened the *shōji*. The steps ceased. But now they seemed to come from the garden. He opened a panel of the *amado*. The moonlight flooded the room. Just then a woman glided out of the darkness of the corridor. Taking her by the hand Sukeshige drew her within and gently removed the *zukin* concealing the downcast and blushing face of Hanako. So astonished was he that he stood clasping her hand, both of them unconscious of the little anguished gasp from the shadow of the garden. Suke-shige slowly pushed together the *shōji*. " The daughter of Manchō " Dono ! Is not this Hanako ? Surely this is no place for her to be. " Deign lady to retire. Great would be your parents' grief to know " of this conduct. Sōtan cannot accept such gift." Said Hanako— " Nay, Sensei Dono, accept the thanks and humble apology of " Hanako for intruding on your presence. She has gone too far to " go back. Earnest is Manchō's wish for a son to husband his " daughter. Deign to remain here in Aohaka, to accept the service " of my humble person ; a service so gladly given to him who

The Tryst in Manchō's Garden.

"saved Hanako from harm." Weeping she sank at his feet.
Sukeshige puzzled and annoyed was at a loss what to do. And if
Terute should come! Hanako certainly would make a scene, the
danger would be very great.

One source of embarassment was soon removed. Again the
shōji was pushed aside. Awakened by O'Nagi on his daughter's
exit from their room Manchō entered with severe countenance.
His wife followed him. "Iza! Sōtan Sensei this treatment is
"hardly fair. Hanako is not as one of the maids of the inn, at the
"service of any, even of the Sensei Dono. Since the matter has
"gone so far deign to consummate the marriage. Gladly does
"Manchō receive as *muko* one so distinguished. Wife, bring forth
"the *saké* cups. Let the wine pass in recognition of this bond of
"husband and wife. Sensei Dono cannot deny the accomplished
"fact." Sukeshige was half angry, half puzzled. What should he
do? To resist was to precipitate a disturbance, to expose his real
identity. Besides he must gain entrance ; he must see Terute. Of
her intrusion now he had little] fear. Anyone near at hand could
recognize the moment as unpropitious. *Amado* and *shōji* were open,
the room visible to all. Manchō and his wife had acted with
intention. With resigned gesture he seated himself before Hanako.
As he did so there was a shuffling of many feet without, the cry of
a woman. Sukeshige sprang up. There was something familiar
about the voice. But Manchō intervened. Hanako seized his
dress. Manchō went to the *amado*, looked out, then closed it.
"Some woman carried off. Be sure none too unwilling. The
"matter shall be looked into to-morrow. Now for the present busi-
"ness." Reluctantly Sukeshige again sat down. The *saké* cups were
passed. To the great lord this was a small matter, the taking of a
new concubine. Sukeshige really meant well to the girl. Besides
in such a place as Manchō's these temporary bonds were common,
lightly assumed, lightly broken the next day. Where there are two
parties, there are two wills and can be two intentions. Thus did
Hanako, the flower maiden, enter on the hard service of her lord.

It was after dark when Mitō no Kotarō returned from Tarui
with important news for his master. To his surprise his lord had

not yet returned to the house at Ayame-ga-satō. None had seen the *sensei*. Reasonably assured of meeting him he therefore started forth on the Aohaka road, to reach the town itself without any sign of Sukeshige and Onikage. After wandering hither and thither, making discreet inquiry, after midnight he gave up the search and started homeward on his return, hoping to find his lord already before him. He had just left the town when he heard the cry of a woman from the rice fields. The moon was still bright. A band of men could be seen coming along the *dō-bashi* (narrow road) between the fields. Clumped together they evidently were carrying some-one. Again the woman's cry rang out clear. " Are ! Are ! Help ! " Help ! " Forthwith Mito no Kotarō advanced into the foot-way. Here a little bridge covered with earth and turf crossed a more pre-tentious stream. In the middle of this Kotarō took his stand with outstretched arms. As the fellows came up they eyed him with anger and astonishment. A big fellow who seemed to be the leader said —" *Mowa !* Where has this fellow sprung from ? ' Dropped " from the sky like bird's dung, or burrowed from the ground like " a mole ? ' You low cur get out of the way. You obstruct the " passage. Thus will you escape a punishment we are too busy to " administer." Kotarō jeered—" *Doka !* This is brave talk from " your kind. As for your business it is plain enough. You are " thieves, and have carried off this woman to sell her. Passage " here is none. Off with you at once. ' This is for a mantis with " his scythes to face the Imperial chariot, or to cleave a rock with " a hen's egg.' " At this the rascals were greatly astonished and enraged. The big man prepared for action, summarily to toss Kotarō into the brook. A follower touched his arm, as if uncertain as to his hearing. " Is the fellow drunk, chief ? What does he " make speech about ? " Said the chief—" It is a matter of no " moment. Some stuff about a man's thighs and a Court " carriage, and to leave the smock for the swag ; moreover to re-" lease the woman. However he is but one. Into the brook " with this brave mongrel ! This will damp his courage."*

* Takarai in his *kōdan* plays on *tōrō* (mantis) and *tōrō* (lantern). *Tōrō ga ono wo motte ryūsha ni mukō ga gotoku, keiran wo motte taiseki ni ataru ga gotoshi.* The

Putting down their burden on the ground they made a rush at Kotarō, the big fellow in the van. His bulk obstructed the others. Dodging under him Kotarō grasped him by the elbows. With a sweep he was held over the head of the knight, sending his more immediate followers to right and left head first into the rice fields. The next moment the fat fellow was wallowing and plunging in the deeper water below. Kotarō did not wait for the attack of the others. Jumping into their midst he dealt blows and kicks to right and left. Willing and unwilling they too were soon wallowing in the mud up to their middle. But one fellow did the *bushi* strike with intent; so hard as to drive his head into his shoulders. His companions picked him up and stood him on his feet, shorter by a couple of inches. " Oya ! How queer Tomiye " looks thus shortened. Comrade how do you feel ? " Tomiye was very uncertain as to how he felt or where he was. Was he on Fujisan or Shumisan, in Ōmi or in Yomi ?† Truly he did not know. Seeing his condition they looked in fright for aid from their chief. He was seen making off as hard as he could across the rice fields, spattering mud and water in every direction. His followers were not slow in taking the hint and the same general direction back to Aohaka.

Kotarō approached their victim and leaned over to untie the rope wound around her. As he did so their eyes met. " Atsu !" exclaimed the knight. " Kotarō Dono ! " said the lady. Kotarō was rapidly at work releasing her. In wonder he exclaimed— " How comes your ladyship here at such an hour, and in Ao- " haka ! Truly the *kami* (gods) have been kind in granting " Kotarō the favour of this task. Deign to accept the service and " the idle curiosity of this Kotarō. Returning from Tarui it was " expected to find his lordship at Ayame-ga-sato. Doubtless how- " ever he has long since returned." Said Terute—" Do not trouble " with further search. He is now at the house of Manchō in " Aohaka. Much is to be told, and the return of these men with

---

chief's answer—*Tōrō* (lantern) *no mae de ono wo motte itan da, onna wo yokosane-he uchi wa ke-he-ran to iu da.* 213.

† Shumisan=Buddist " Sumeru." Yomi=Shintō Hades.

" others is to be feared." Kotarō thought likewise. No time was to be lost. As Terute was in no fit condition to walk he took her on his shoulders, and as fast as he could he made his way to safety in Ayame-ga-sato. As the lady unfolded her tale Kotarō pursed his lips and sucked in his breath in wonder and thoughtful consideration. Said he—" The news from Tarui is most serious. The Asuke " brothers feel sure that an attack is hanging over them on the orders " of Kyōto. His lordship must be informed. After the events of " this night it is impossible for Kotarō to approach Manchō's house. " What is to be done ? " Finally it was agreed that Kotarō should go to Aohaka the next day ; to go as near as possible and spy out any chance to communicate with his lord. A stranger, trouble could be made for him, for Terute had recognized Mankei in the big man of her assailants, of whom one at least had been seriously injured. Moreover to connect the rescue of Terute with his lord Sukeshige was of doubtful issue. So early on the following day he betook himself to town, leaving Terute in full possession of the house, and of nothing else. Kotarō was a man and a samurai. What he wanted was either supplied, or supplied itself.

Thus Terute was left to herself. The thought came to her— " Ah ! This is the commemoration day of my honoured mother's " death (*chōdo shōtsuki mei*). A prayer must be said. Doubtless " there is a temple near-by where a service can be held." But she had not a *mon* ; herself, her hair included, belonged to her lord. Perhaps there was money in the house for offering. She hunted high and low, in every nook and cranny. Not the impress of a coin even in the dust, which was thick enough in these bachelor quarters. Not a thing of value was to be found. Sukeshige and Kotarō had their swords and horses ; they valued little else. Just then, *chishi, chishi, chishi,* came the tinkle of a bell approaching along the roadway. Terute peered out. A Shūgyōsha Kōmyō Henjō Jūbō Sekai, (a pilgrim, haloed, universally illuminated in this ten sided world), an exceptionally holy man came opposite her. Terute made salutation as the deep straw hat like unto a huge mushroom turned toward her as if in contemplation. " Deign reverend Sir to " enter. This day is a memorial feast of the dead. Condescend to "say a prayer for their well being." The priest bowed. Terute brought warm water for his feet. Putting down the *oi*,* removing the straw sandals and bathing, he entered the house and was shown into a room where was set up a temporary altar (Butsu-noma). The lamps were lighted; the incense sticks soon smoked. Then the priest produced his scroll. Striking his little bell he began to intone a mass for the dead. "Namu Amida Butsu! Namu "Amida Butsu!" The service over Terute bowed in thanks. There were tears in her eyes. "Reverend Sir, truly it is cause of shame "that there is nothing here to offer but hot water. But the master "is gone and I am alone. For the kind solicitude for these "honoured bones deign to accept thanks. It is all there is to "give...........But there is this mirror. It is of little value to any "but my humble self. However, deign to accept it." From her bosom she pulled out a little Eight Dragon mirror and passed it to the priest. Taking it he examined it with care, sucking in his breath. Then he examined Terute with equal care. In spite of his seamed face, his red hair, Terute found something kindly in the scrutiny. She was not afraid. She felt an iron support near her. Why, she know not The priest turned to the Butsudan. Reverently he took out the *kaimyō* of Satake Atsumitsu, that of her ladyship his wife. The little scrolls trembled in his hands. Deliberately he replaced them. Then he rose and went to the bottom of the room. The wondering eyes of Terute followed him. Prostrating himself, his forehead on his hands, spoke Mito no Koshirō. "The long search is over. Truly this is her ladyship, Terutehime, "heir of the Satake House. Mito no Koshirō would make report to "his lord." Said Terute—"Mito no Koshiro! That it is Terute "who speaks is true. Here is the Kwannon carried by Shinra "Saburō on his helmet; here the scrolls of genealogy. How come[s] "it that Koshirō Dono seeks Terute?" Then Koshirō made report for his brother the *karō*. For the suicide of Kosuke he made apology. Would her ladyship deign to accept the expiation. "All

---

* A box with legs carried as knapsack by the wandering *yamabushi* (a sort of hedge priest of genuine clerical ordination). It is figured in "Benkei." **Vol. II. 287.**

"had paid dearly for their crime. The heads of Toda and Fuji-
" nami adorned the ferry crossing at Mutsuura. The dishonoured
" corpse of Gentarō, traced by himself to Yūki, was food for wolves
" on the slopes of Ashiōsan. Himself he had sought out her lady-
" ship, to serve her to death, to secure the restoration of the Satake
" House." Tears of lady and retainer mingled in this tale of these
sufferings through the long years. Joyful was the meeting.

There was a sound of voices outside. Thinking them to be
of travellers demanding pictures of Sōtan Sensei, Terute went forth.
Curiously enough these little temple offerings had gained the reputation of being a charm against fire, an insurance. Kotarō
had informed Terute as to their way of living. Visitors
did not surprise her. Koshirō, remained within, heard cries,
the voice of Terute calling for help. Outside he found her
struggling in the grasp of a big fellow. Mito no Kotarō stood
by helpless. Several *yakunin* looked on grinning. Said the big
man to Kotarō—" You are a thief, fortunate not to be charged with
" your misdeeds. This is the second time we meet. I am Mankei,
" *bantō* of Manchō. This woman has run away from the inn.
" Back she goes. Ah ! Beauty, you have an interview in prospect
" with the master. You will be compelled to serve by the order of
" the *machibugyō* himself." Kotarō could have wrung his hands
with rage at this abuse and his own impotency. Not a word could
he or Terute say, not a hand move, as to the previous ransom of
Terute, without wrong to their lord. The priest interposed. At the
sight of rosary and bell Mankei and the *yakunin* showed respect.
He demanded to have the matter explained. Said he—" The
" woman is entitled to her ransom. The Buddha bids his priests to
" aid the unfortunate. She is unwilling to accompany you. This
" foolish cleric will ransom the lady." He took Mankei aside. For
a poor priest he was certainly well supplied, but that was none of
Mankei's business. Sharply did they chaffer and bargain. Mankei
put two and two together. His master had three hundred *kwan* in
hand from the false ransom of the Sensei. The priest offered as
much more. Strange to say none are sharper and fairer to the interests of their employers than these fellows. Mankei was an

honest pimp. The bargain was struck. The *yakunin* witnessed it.
With threatening look at the enraged Kotarō the *bantō* of the inn
swaggered off with his attendants. Koshirō and Kotarō lead Terute
within.

Kotarō eyed the new-comer askance. " Aid from a strange
" hand is never grateful. Reverend Sir, humble thanks are due
" from Kotarō in behalf of her ladyship. Deign however to ex-
" plain such generosity. The sum is a large one." Terute smiled
through her tears. Kotarō, puzzled at the evident acquaintanceship,
looked from lady to priest. Said the latter with assumed dignity
and severity—" The sum is large ; to be recovered, it is hoped, with
" usury in another form. But, Sir and nephew, rather should your
" honoured self explain how such a rascal dares to call Mito no Ko-
" tarō a thief." No longer able to contain himself he burst into a
chuckle. Kotarō in amazement made obeisance to his senior.
" Umu ! Who would recognize Koshirō Dono under such guise.
" Your presence is most opportune. And my revered father ? "
Koshirō raised his hand. Terute gently touched the sleeve of Kotarō.
He understood. For a moment he covered his face with his hands.
Then suavely—" Deign, honoured Sir, to let Kotarō hear how the *karō*
" of Satake met his end." At the tale of his uncle Kotarō remained in
thought. " Report is to be made to my lord. According to his
" decision lies the fate of Kotarō." But Terute protested—" Oguri
" Dono can have none but commendation for the brave deed of
" Kosuke. His expiation of offence was excessive. The *karō* of
" the Satake House had committed no deed to deserve rebuke.
" His judgment on himself has been too severe. His lord has no
" complaint to make. On the contrary masses in commendation
" and for the rest of his spirit are to be said." Terute spoke
simply, with the dignity of her position. In gratitude Koshirō
and Mitō no Kotarō bowed to the ground at the commendation
of the departed Kosuke.

Then earnest counsel was held. Said Koshirō—" For Kotarō
" to approach Aohaka is useless. This Koshirō can seek out the
" whereabouts of Sukeshige Dono and give him notice. Mankei
" has no grudge against the priest. Even if detected the priest

" will not be connected with the samurai. Deign, your ladyship,
" to write a letter. Koshirō will be the bearer." Forthwith
Terute sat down to write. The scroll finished Koshirō set forth
on his mission. Terute could give him few directions how to
proceed. Her life at Manchō's had given small opportunity but
for the daily tasks, the beaten path to lake and mountain. Koshirō carefully examined the front of the place. He even ven-
tured to enter for an alms. Well received he ascertained that
at least this part of the establishment did not harbour Sūke-
shige. From the vague vision of her last night in the place
Terute could tell him something of the scene of the capture.
Evidently she had been followed in the house, for her captors
grumbled harshly as to the hunt she had given them. A
garden furnished with pond and trees, enclosed by a wall with
postern gate, had been the scene of the assault. Carried through
the gate the fields behind the town were soon reached. The
rescue by Kotarō had followed. Koshirō left by the front to
seek the rear. His eye soon marked the wall, the trees rising
above it. Not a chink or cranny was to be found. Placing
his *kongō* cane against the wall he stepped up. Carefully he
peered over the top. Luck favoured him. Sukeshige was standing on the *rōka*. He seemed sad and dispirited, as one worn
by fortune and battle. He was in a great quandary. Eager
to leave Manchō's place uncertainty held him there. Departure
meant departure from Ayame-no-sato. He could not remain so
close to Aohaka. And yet he had no news of Terute. Without
such he did not dare to leave Ayame, and so was held to Aohaka
and Manchō's inn. As he mused a letter wrapped around a stone
fell at his feet. He picked it up and raised his head. A man
disappeared promptly behind the wall and Sukeshige heard the
shuffle of approaching steps. At a glance he noted the hand-
writing of Terute. Quick as he thrust the scroll into his bosom
it was noticed by Hanako. She plead to see it. Sukeshige
refused. When she pouted a little he explained it as an un-
finished poem. Said he—" None but a vain author, and few
" are otherwise, would dare to show such a writing before it

" had been ground and polished so as to shine like a mirror.
" Deign to have patience, and allow Sōtan to be the Sensei,
" not the poet. When perfected you shall give judgment there-
" on." She was always a little afraid of him, and a caress
with the promise satisfied her.

As soon as he was again left to himself Sukeshige eagerly
ran over the contents of the scroll. Terute wrote not only a
very beautiful hand, but the contents of the letter were critical.
Sukeshige admired the one, formed rapid judgment on the
other. He must leave Manchō and Ayame at once. Plainly
affairs were coming to a point in Miyako. He could not
compromise the interests of his cousins, although the Shōgun
had an axe to grind with the Asuke on his own account. None
attended, dared to attend, Onikage but himself. At Hanako's
sleepy remonstrance when he left her side, he said that he
heard the horse restless in the stable. Satisfied she was asleep
again before he left the room. Onikage was soon lead out.
Pushing open the postern gate Sukeshige mounted and gallopped
off to Ayame. Tender was the meeting of husband and wife.
When Terute told of her experience with Fujinami, the latter's
fate, the lord of Oguri sucked in his breath. " My mother
" sold you, knowingly, to this scoundrel Gentarō! Truly she
" was a wicked woman. Through her slander great was the anger
" of my father toward Sukeshige. When the castle fell it was
" thought she had perished. Neither Sukeshige nor the rōtō
" had tidings of her flight. The kami have punished this
" wicked woman. As for this Sukeshige, an idle mission has
" brought important issue. The Shirohata Jinja of Aohaka
" is noted for its efficacy in rewarding prayer. To test its
" benevolence, secure fortune in war, and union with his wife,
" Sukeshige made his petition before visiting the Kokuzo Bosatsu
" temple. The meeting with the daughter of Manchō has
" followed. The glorious god is not to be neglected. Thanks
" are due. Decision is as follows : Ayame-no-sato is to be
" abandoned. At dawn Sukeshige and Terute will seek the
" presence of the god. Koshirō and Kotarō will make all ready

"for departure, the one to Ōtsu with notice to the retainers
"to gather at Yahagi castle, the other to Fuchū with similar
"notice. Unfortunately the matter of punishing Manchō must
"be postponed. Truly the fellow has been most wicked in his
"conduct. Moreover, not satisfied with the ransom of Terute he
"has tried to steal her, and once more a ransom has been paid.
"The day of his punishment will come. More important matters
"press."

The following day Sukeshige, accompanied by Terute, undertook the *sankei* to the temple. No matter how well intentioned
the pilgrimage was rash. Hanako quickly grasped the fact that
Sōtan Sensei had fled. The girl naturally connected him with a
woman. When therefore Mankei reported that Kohagi lived with
a samurai at Ayame, and a servant reported having seen Sōtan
and Kohagi at the Jinja (shrine), she at once concluded that to
find Kohagi was to find Sōtan Sensei. Accompanied by her
mother and Mankei, and without notice to Manchō, she set forth
for Ayame-ga-sato. The discovery of her missing lord was easy.
Sukeshige eyed the pair, prostrate in obeisance, with indifference.
The fresh beauty of Hanako had staled on him in these days.
Terute, with such kindness as a woman could find in such case,
was not disposed to salve matters for the girl. Hanako eyed her
with hate and indignation. Sukeshige listened to her pleadings,
but it was Koshirō who made answer. His dress as priest was
discarded for the time being. Once more he was the samurai.
Mankei eyed him with wonder and misgiving. Koshirō addressed
himself to the mother—"Good dame, these matters are not so
"plain as they appear on the surface. Deign to wait their expla-
"nation. You and your daughter will then be satisfied. Judgment
"yet remains to be given." Kotarō smiled at this cryptian
utterance. Terute could not restrain a half movement of pity.
After all these were insignificant people caught in the wheel of
great interests and bound to suffer. Sukeshige was a sphinx.
Continued Koshirō—"It is best for you to return home. Think
"no more about the matter. Your honoured daughter is yet very
"young. Unfortunately Sōtan Sensei is compelled to pronounce

"the formula of divorce." At these words Hanako wailed in grief. The mother bounded up in rage—"Hanako, this is to "act foolishly. This man has a stone for a heart, thus unkindly to "treat you, to prefer the serving wench. Nothing is to be "gained here." Hanako would have thrown herself at the feet of Sukeshige, in petition, but her mother and Mankei dragged her off. Scowling the latter returned, to say to Kotarō— "Twice have Mankei and this *yarō* (low fellow) met. To "fight on a narrow bridge is one thing; on broader ground "another. The third time Mankei will act differently." Kotarō sprang to his feet. Mankei, slowly and with difficulty, gathered himself together on the opposite side of the road. Grunting with pain, his hands held to a broken rib, as best he could he tottered off to make report to his master, fully convinced that it would have been proper to do so before coming to Ayame-ga-sato.

On their departure Sukeshige emphasized his order. "There "is no time for delay. Koshirō and Kotarō are to depart at "dark on their missions. With Terute this Sukeshige leaves "at dawn. Man and woman travelling together cause no sus-"picion. Yahagi is not too far to reach before dark. Onikage "can well carry the double burden for the twenty *ri* (fifty "miles). Consultation is to be held with the Asuke brothers." In haste preparations were completed. At dark Koshirō and Kotarō made obeisance to their lord and lady and departed to West and North. Onikage, ready saddled, was lightly fastened at the side of the house. Sukeshige and Terute went to their rest of a few hours before starting. Suddenly Sukeshige sat up. Says an adage of the Nipponese—"the sleeping knight is roused by the sound of the bridle bit." Sukeshige awoke Terute. "Preparations are to be made at once. A band of men are "approaching by the road." Everything moveable was gathered into a sort of barricade. Wherever there was a flimsy wooden door Sukeshige tore it from its groove. The *andon* was extinguished. Then came a beating on the *amado*. Loud voices called on them to surrender. The broken wood fell inward with a crash.

Putting Terute behind the barricade Sukeshige stepped forward.
"Oriya! What conduct is this good Sirs, thus to break in at
"night, thus ...... "—"Shut up!" was the sincere and unceremonious reply. "Present yourselves to be bound forthwith.
"This is the guard of the Daikwan (Lord's Bailiff) Hikawa Jin-
·" roku, come to seize Oguri Dono and his wife Terute. Your
" presence here is known to Miyako. The innkeeper of Aohaka,
" Manchō by name, has given a full description of both of you.
" Unsuspicious he has harboured the woman and been cheated
" by the lord. Surrender at once and give no trouble." Said
Sukeshige to this gentle summons—"That the innkeeper has lied
" of purpose is evident. This girl was ill-treated and ransomed
" in the presence of many persons. As for this Sōtan he is
" well known."—"Words are useless. Surrender or suffer the
" consequences of resistance. Men; forward and seize them!"
At the order of Jinroku half a dozen sprang over the *rōka*.
To drive them off in confusion was quick work of the sword
of Sukeshige. Heads and limbs, parted from their original owners,
lay on the ground. Groans of the wounded, shouts of the unconvinced at a safe distance, turned the quiet night into the
uproar of a great gathering at odds with itself. Jinroku shouted
his order—"Withdraw and use your bows. This man is noted
" for his strength and skill with the sword. His head sent
" to Miyako will be evidence enough of your earnestness.
" Shoot down both man and woman." Truly the fate of Sukeshige and Terute seemed determined. Seizing a broken *amado*
Sukeshige sought with this indifferent protection to spring upon
the foe. At this juncture aid burst upon the scene from the
shadow of the house. At the appearance of Sukeshige in the
open Onikage dashed forward, easily breaking his light tether.
Kicking, biting, plunging, he broke and scattered the body
of archers. In a trice Sukeshige was on his back. Terute ran
to him and was drawn up behind. In anger and regret Hikawa Jinroku laid hands on the robe of Sukeshige. With a
sweep the shining sword descended. Cut in two Jinroku rolled
to the sides of the roadway. Spurred on by voice and rein

Onikage dashed through the opposing mass of *yakunin*. A few
random arrows were discharged into the darkness in the direction of Yahagi, of the Great Ocean, of Limbo. The thunder
of hoofs grew faint. Grumbling the constables picked up their
wounded and the dead leader and departed for Aohaka. The
rest were left for daylight. Ayame-ga-sato again sank into its village
peace.

At this news Manchō could only gnash his teeth in regret
and terror. The revelation of the identity of his serving maid
and Sōtan Sensei had made him wild with fear. To none
would the sight of the head-box of Sukeshige have been more
agreeable than to the miserable innkeeper. Like the toad before
the sickle he could only await the vengeance of the famous
Oguri *rōtō*, sure to fall on him for his treachery to their lord,
his abuse of their lady. Every stranger, every wandering priest,
gave him the chill of suspicion. Meanwhile other misfortune
was at hand. At least he had the palliation of the uncertain
connection of Hanako with Sukeshige. Anxiously he guarded
and nourished the ailing girl, hoping for some indication of
its fruit. Then one night his misery was consummated. In
the morning Hanako was missing. Her body was drawn up
from the deep waters of the Kagami-ike, and her fate explained. Crazed by grief, by her abandonment, she had fled
in the night, to seek by suicide relief for the suffering of her
mind. No merciful hand of man or goddess had intervened ;
and thus ended the earthly existence of the unfortunate flower
maid.

CHAPTER XVI.

THE BATTLE OF YAHAGI; AND THE JOURNEY OF
MITO NO KOTARŌ.

Of these matters Sukeshige at the time knew nothing. Yahagi and the security of its walls were reached before night. Here lord and lady found warm welcome. Once more Terute was lodged as befitted her condition. The days passed, in this short breathing spell, during which the Oguri *rōtō* gathered at their lord's summons. The fief of the Asuke at Yahagi was of considerable importance, guarding as it did the ford of the river on the main road to the North. It was this fact which made the state of affairs more dangerous for them, gave greater inducement to Yoshimochi Kō to carry matters to extremes. The ruin of the Oguri House, root and branch, seemed to be a principle with the Ashikaga House. However, while the warriors held council, Terute in company with the lady of Jirō Nobuyoshi wandered the garden within the castle precincts. In the river flowing close by, Jorurihime, beloved of Prince Yoshitsune, had drowned herself. On this very hillside the lovers had met and parted in their brief wooing, the lady to watch the knight as he and his train splashed through these waters on the perilous journey North. The evenings were passed in reciting to *biwa* (guitar) and *koto* (harp) old tales from the Heike Monogatari, or the many ballads later collected in the form of Joruri Monogatari. One night, after such pastime and a banquet of fish and *saké*, they had retired for the night. Uneasy in his sleep Sukeshige stirred and woke. Surely there was some presence in the room. He rubbed his eyes and stared on all sides. A tender wailing voice, *kii, kii, kii*, rang in his ears. The *andon* burnt dimly. Then beside it a form began to take shape. Vague, ill-defined, at last the robes of a woman could

be made out. Then the slender figure, the face concealed by long
hair, was evident to sight. With wide-open mouth, heart chilled
and nerves tense, Sukeshige watched the uncanny form as it glided
and undulated in the air as if to approach the couch. Surely it was
an apparition. It had no feet. He half rose—"What want you
" here, vile wretch! Why come to accost this Sukeshige? Get
" you hence spectre!" Taking the hard pillow he hurled it vigorously at the object. With an anguished cry at this harsh reception it
disappeared. The sound of wailing faded out " as a bell in the
night carried further and further away." Sukeshige turned
almost roughly as the aroused Terute touched his arm. Then gently
he explained the vision. Both puzzled over the matter, its bearing
on their fortunes. Day broke after a night of little sleep.

Then came an express messenger with decisive news. The Muromachi Bakufu had outlawed the Asuke brothers. Imagawa Ryōshun and his son Nagatada were on the march from Suruga. A decision was to be reached at once. Sukeshige and his *rōtō* sought an interview with the lords of the castle. The Asuke, Jirō Nobuyoshi and
Saburō Nobuhira, sat facing the lord of Oguri. Behind them were the
rōtō. Said Sukeshige—"The hatred of Prince Mochiuji to the
" House of Oguri is based on the slander of Isshiki Shikibu Shōyū
" Akihide and Yamana Kurando Ujiharu. The House is innocent of
" all offence. But although the Yūki and Utsunomiya have made
" earnest representation to the suzerain he refuses to listen to them.
" Nothing but the destruction of the House satisfies his anger. Surely
" in such hands the office of the Kamakura Kwanryō is bending to
" its fall. But the times are not propitious. The cause of offence
" being this Sukeshige, deign to bind us with rope, lord and re-
" tainers eleven men, and send us to Kamakura. Thus all em-
" barassment is to be avoided. The House of Asuke is preserved.
" Condescend to grant this our petition. Otherwise it is our duty to
" cut open our bellies." Jirō Nobuyoshi consulted with his brother.
Then he made reply. " To act in such manner is not for the Asuke
" brothers. Our Houses are allied by blood. The sacrifice of one
" would not secure the safety of the other, and the deed would stink
" in the nostrils of men. Moreover there is other cause of offence to

" the Shōgun beside the presence of the lord of Oguri at Yahagi.
" For him to cut open his belly at this juncture is not befitting.
" Deign to allow the matter to be left to the fortune of war. Our
" pillows in line we will die in battle together if the *kami* so ordain ;
" escape together if such be our fate. The Imagawa, father and
" son, can be approached with argument. If such fail, and the
" orders of the Kubō Sama admit of no excuse, then battle is to be
" joined. Deign respected Sir to accept this counsel, and join the
" forces of Oguri to those of the Asuke in the coming strife."

Such issue could be foreseen. Sukeshige bowed in acceptance and thanks. His *rōtō* made deep obeisance to the lords
of Yahagi. Then the women and children were sent out of
the castle ; many of them to Miyako, to find safety among relatives. Terute, in the charge of Mito no Koshirō, was sent to
Ōtsu in Ōmi ; to await the result of the negotiations with the
Imagawa. Only the fighting men remained to meet the coming
attack. The negociations came to naught. Ryōshun answered that
the orders from Miyako were explicit. The Asuke and the allied
House of Oguri could surrender and wait the issue of an appeal to
the Shōgun. Privately he sent word to the Asuke, complimenting
them on their courage and advising them of the hopelessness of such
appeal. Hatakeyama Mitsuiye had urged particularly that the
heads be sent to the capital for identification. No pardon was
possible.

Ōei 32nd year 1st month 20th day (8th February, 1425) the
army of the Imagawa appeared before the castle. Ten thousand
men followed the standard of the Suruga chiefs, levies mainly of
Suruga and Tōtōmi. Within the castle eight hundred men maintained the defence. The first day's fighting was not unfavourable.
All day the great force of the enemy was held to the opposite bank
of the Yahagigawa, unable to cross in the face of the rain of arrows.
Ryōshun grimly waited for night. Meanwhile a strong force was
marching up stream. Crossing the river in the dark some miles
above, at dawn he turned the flank of the enemy and drove them
within the castle. The whole army crossed in the progress of this
movement. Yahagi-jō was closely invested on all sides. To take

the place by assault was early tried, but so close were the ranks that heavy loss was suffered. The war arrows pierced the serried host, killing those in the van, wounding those in the rear. At evening a sally was made against the discomfited and retreating foe. Fierce was the struggle, great the carnage. The Oguri *rōtō* in the van the garrison burst into the ranks of the enemy's rear. It was a battle with swords. The fight became a series of scattered duels in which one side knew the ground, the other was uncertain and confused. Before the Imagawa could send aid many of their best men, over-matched and outnumbered, were cut down. Then Nagatada rode to the rescue. Jeering the Yahagi forces came together and slowly withdrew up the slope. The enemy did not dare to follow in the dark, and the fight was over.

The following day Ryōshun adopted a different plan. It was the *yagura* (wooden platforms) erected within the castle walls which plagued his men so greatly in the assault. On rollers these could be transferred from one place to another to meet attack. By day Ryōshun closely invested the place. At night, instead of retreating to his camp, his son Nagatada with a large force was sent to seize a little hill which rose within long arrow range in the rear of the fortification. Unfortunately the garrison was not large enough properly to provide for too extended a defence. Much had to be intrusted to the natural strength of the knoll and the easy defence by day with the aid of the castle's fire. Minimizing his loss by this night attack Nagatada rushed the place in the dark. Its defenders were put to the sword. The next morning, 23rd day (11th February), the far-shooting arrows, or *tōya*, began to rain into the castle inclosure. If incapable of extended battle line the garrison was too great for the narrow precincts. All day shelter was sought under such protection of shields and hoarding as could be improvised, but great was the loss. Council was held as to what to do. There was no dissent. It was death on the battle field, or safety by cutting a way through the enemy. During the day numerous attacks of the enemy were repulsed, every preparation made for the sally in force. The chances of escape were excellent. But the design was anticipated. The afternoon was waning, the garrison engaged in repulsing a more determined attack than usual. In the castle was one Toita Nagatoshi. He had been at one time a *rōtō* of the Asuke. For cause he had disappeared, but at this crisis in his lord's affairs had reappeared. His excuse seemed plausible and he was again enrolled. Really he was engaged to the Imagawa, and there was nothing in his lord's prospects to confirm his renewed allegiance. In the confusion of the attack, disregarded amid the garrison, he found opportunity to set fire to the castle. Thick clouds of smoke began to rise from the inclosure. The Imagawa forces with a mighty shout vigorously renewed their efforts. The garrison could not remain within. The gate was thrown open. Promiscuous fighting took place at the posts of defence now closely beset by the enemy. Slashing to right and left the Asuke brothers and the lord of Oguri rode out into the midst of the foe. The narrow space between hills and river alone saved the scanty force from immediate annihilation. The enemy could not find room to bring his numbers into action. Thus for a time the defence held its own in the rapidly waning light. The battle became a series of detached fights against small and scattered remnants of the Asuke *rōtō*. The news soon spread that the brothers Nobuyoshi and Nobuhira had been killed at the ford ; likewise the lord of Oguri. Part of the foe were plundering the burning castle, others the farmers' houses of the village. Why lose the opportunity ? The fight slackened, the survivors of the garrison had their chance of flight, until the stern voice and discipline of Nagatada began to bring disorder out of confusion. But precious moments had been lost.

The news of the fall of Yahagi castle was not long in reaching Ōmi no Ōtsu, through which passed the express messenger of Ryōshun. The Bakufu was not so uniformly successful as to suppress news of its victories. In great distress for his lord, and in sympathy for his grieved lady, Mito no Koshirō set forth with Terute for the battle field four days after the contest. Argued Koshirō with his long experience—" In the darkness his lordship " and the *rōtō* had every chance to escape mishap. Deign not to " weep. Tears befit not the wife of a samurai. Doubtless tidings of "better purport will be obtained near the scene. Rumour always "lies. Such has been the experience of Koshirō." With this encouragement they trudged along the road by Biwa-ko. Terute had the plain dress of the *omairi* (pilgrim) of the lower class ; a white *kimono*, deep hat, sleeves trussed up, and the few needfuls at her back in a handkerchief or *furushiki*. Koshirō again had assumed his holy guise. He was in full rig as a Dai Jōmyōten Rokujū Rokubu (that is, pilgrim presenting or *promising* to present his autograph scrolls to the temples of Nippon's sixty-six provinces). Therefore he wore a mouse coloured *kimono*, white mits (*tekko*), leggings (*kyahan*), straw sandals, a girdle without seam (*maruguke*). He carried a bell and a *kongō* staff. In this latter was concealed a sword. On his back was the *oi*.* As they approached Tarui a group of farmers was noted in discussion on the road. At a sign Terute, as if wearied, seated herself by the road, Koshirō approached to learn the news. At last ! They were talking of the battle at Yahagi. Great was the pity expressed. The Asuke were popular in their fief, and their name for benevolence was wide-spread among these humble folk. Said one man—" Mattock and spade disagree......." Puzzled he scratched his head. Somehow things did not hang together. Said another in merriment—" Oribe San has heard the "parson in his sleep. His brains are mixed. Or has he too been "at Yahagi ? 'Few lose to many, 'tis agreed.'† However the "news is to be regretted ; though the country people far and wide "have secured much plunder at little cost from the victors, yet the "farmers of Yahagi have suffered and their women have been carried off." Said a third—" Then it is true that the lords have been "killed ? "—" True for the Asuke Dono. The lord of Oguri is said "to have escaped to the hills. At least the Imagawa are very "angry, and strict search is being made to secure his head." With this brave news Koshirō returned to Terute. Leaning over as if to adjust her *waraji* the lady concealed her tears and joy.

---

* The priest's dress had its esoteric meaning. It has been gone into in "Benkei" II p. 305 seq ; The Kwanjinchō.

† A touch of Momogawa—" *Kuwa wa suki ni kanawanai*," mattock and spade disagree : " *Kwa wa shū ni teki shi gatashi*," for few to oppose many is difficult.

Koshirō considered the situation—geographically. "That his "lordship would make his way direct to the land of Imagawa "Ryōshun is unlikely. Every road on the sea provinces will be "watched. Plainly he is hid somewhere in the mountains." He opened his hands toward the great mass of Central Nippon as if in despair. How hopeless was the search. Said Terute—"Call to "mind, Koshirō, that the Oguri first came from these hills. My "lord has spoken of the early fief at Hiraoka no Kumabuse in "lower Hina. Here is the guardian divinity, the *ubu no kami*, of "the Oguri, at the Take-no-Ya Hachimangū close by the Seirinji "(temple of the green-wood). Let inquiry be made there." Koshirō clapped his hands in reverence and joy. "Koriya! Your "ladyship is assuredly right. Sukeshige Dono can be nowhere else "than at the Seirinji. To go to Yahagi is useless. The way lies "straight ahead." Thus resolved boldly they set forward. It was a long hard struggle, this walk through the mountains of Shinano. Place and people were rough, noted from before the days of Kiso Yoshinaka and his mountaineers. Avoiding the more frequented Nakasendō the peasant trails were sought. Nights were passed in temples or farmers' houses under plea of pilgrimage through these parts. Toward the end of their journey night found them without shelter. Terute was exhausted, both were hungry. Mountain piled on mountain before them, "standing up like *tsurugi* (two edged swords)." With the last dim light of twilight they stood before a primitive *torii*. Said Koshirō—"Torii means temple or shrine, "small though it be. Your ladyship can go no further. Besides "these mountains are dangerous in the dark. Bear, boar, poisonous "snakes range freely. In the shrine close by the night can be "passed. Deign to decide to stop here." Willingly Terute assented. While she bathed her feet in a brook close by, Koshirō collected fire wood before the little shrine. With flint and steel he ignited the sulphur dipped slivers of wood.* Looking up he uttered an exclamation. To Terute's inquiry—"Ah! Fortune is with your lady-"ship. The light shows the name of the shrine—Take-no-ya

---

* ? Momogawa. Flint and steel were familiar to Old Nippon.

" Hachimangū, shrine of Hachiman of the bamboo arrow. The
" god himself has led your ladyship hither."

At this good omen both rejoiced. The *oi* was set down on the
verandah of the shrine. Food was produced and cooked. Then
Koshirō forced open the *kitsune-gōshi* (grating). Close to her journey's end Terute assumed her proper garb. Improvising such couch
as was possible the fire was extinguished and the grating closed.
They laid down to rest. In the middle of the night Koshirō woke
Terute. With finger on lip he pointed without. Bright lights were
close at hand on the mountain trail. If these were Ashikaga *tori-
kata* (constables) there remained but one course, suicide for both.
Lady and retainer were agreed. They would go in company to
Meido. The band was close at hand, themselves shut in the shrine.
Escape was impossible. Intently they kept watch through the
grating. The intruders soon appeared. Evidently they were but a
band of mountain thieves, and had been badly mauled at that.
Bandaged heads, legs, arms, groans, and much earnest wrath were
in evidence. Their leader was an active fellow, dark and hairy,
not particularly young. " A poor affair that ! " He grumbled.
Then he laughed as he regarded his arm in an improvised sling.
" Truly that young samurai at the Seirinji can strike hard. Kiichi
" San, he has broken your head with his pole. You should leave off
" the title of Emma or seek aid of your namesake. Jizō, the gentle
" Jizō no Take, has fared little better. His eyes are black, his nose
" twice its size, and his grinders badly lacking. The *rōtō* is as strong
" as his lord "—" Ah ! My arm hurts."—" Iza ! Surely the ribs are
" broken. A horse has kicked me "—" Yai ! The shins of Tozakai
" are beaten to a jelly." Thus went up exclamations of woe one after
another. At the orders of the chief plasters and bandages were in
preparation. Koshirō half drew his sword as several of the fellows
approached the shrine But it was evidently an old haunt of theirs,
of assured propinquity. They dived beneath it, to reappear with a
huge iron boiler and cooking utensils of various kinds. Meal and
medicament were soon being made ready ; bruises and bellies were
in course of repair.

Said the chief—" Who can he be ? For one man, with a

" single *rōtō*, to beat off our party of thirty men is beyond reason.
" The aid of the cowardly monks goes for nothing. The Seirinji
" *bōzu* are noted for their gallant battles, but it is with petticoats."
Sneered another—" Not so! The *bōzu* permit none but pages."—
" And the sex does not show beneath the costume. Ask the farmers
" round about as to their daughters whereabouts." This from a
third. Said a fourth gravely—" Slander not the holy men. To
" them the sex is of small account. Many of them can be safely
" trusted with any woman." All made merry. Said the first follower—" For such rich and lazy fellows not to contribute to the
" good cause is pitiful. The Nantō (South Court party) can yet
" raise its head above the treachery of this Ashikaga prince. He
" has not kept his word, this juggler. The august will is disregarded.
" Let us make a second attack. Has the chief turned coward
" at a few bruises?" Said the leader—" No! Deign to re-
" member that this Hiraoka in former times was the fief of the
" Oguri, then holding it under the name of Kanai, and des-
" cended from the stock of Taira Shigemori. The House now is
" in disgrace with the Ashikaga. The young lord is said to have
" escaped from the battle at Yahagi. Doubtless this is no other
" than the lord of Oguri, Kojirō Sukeshige. As for the *rōtō* he is
" not Ikeno Shōji, nor one of the Kazama. These are big men, as
" are also the Tanabe and Kataoka. Probably it is Mito no Kotarō,
" for he is not tall. Surely the knight is Sukeshige Dono. No
" attack is to be make on him." A chorus of praise heralded the
chief's decision from the more battered of the party. Sukeshige
came in for a share of it. None could speak too highly of his
prowess.

Open went the doors of the shrine with a bang. Koshirō stood
forth. At the sight of him the band sprang up in terror, ready to
flee, unable through fright to move. His six feet of stature crowned
with red hair, his seamed demon-like face, was it not the god himself in anger? Prostrate they went down before the shrine. Said
Koshirō—" Fear nothing. Your good will to the Oguri House has
" been heard by Mito no Koshirō Tamehira. Deign to accept thanks.
" But truly this is a poor way to find war funds—to rob temples and

The Meeting with Oniyasha.

" travellers. Says the proverb—' When thirsty drink not of stolen
" water.' Meanwhile let us all go back to the Seirinji. Doubtless
" satisfactory meeting can be held with my lord ; more profitable
" than the last one." He looked over the battered company with
satisfaction. Then he turned to the shrine. " Deign your ladyship
" to come forth. These men are friends to the House of Oguri
" ....Her ladyship, the Terutehime," he said in explanation. All
prostrated themselves in obeisance. Said the chief, his face on his
hands — " Deign to accept due apology for intrusion on his lordship.
" This is Kizukuri Hyōsuke Takatomo. Gladly escort is offered to
" the Seirinji, to ask pardon of Oguri Dono." Koshirō rejoiced.
He knew his man well. This Kizukuri had been *kerai* of the Yūki
branch attached to the fortunes of the South Court. As this House
was extinct he called himself *kerai* of Ujitomo, but really was a
rōnin. In his devotion to past interests he was irreconcileable. First
he had figured in Echigo, where he fortified himself on Myōkōzan
and put the district under tribute and terror. Later he did the
same at Kongōzan in Tango. Hence he was known as Kongōsan
Oniyasha. Now he was operating in Shinano, thus impartially
gathering tribute for his political objects, and living riotously and
pleasantly in the prosecution thereof. He gave orders to his followers—" Let those who had the impudence to attack his lordship,
" and the grace to receive the benediction of his hands, shoulder her
" ladyship. The rest are to shoulder the baggage. Forward to the
" Seirinji ! " He took a hand himself as one of the blessed. In an
improvised litter Terute thus was carried down the mountain.
Koshirō attended, in earnest talk with Oniyasha.

At Seirinji the monks were still busy, themselves attending to
broken heads. Sukeshige and Mito no Kotarō standing on the
verandah of the *hondō* (main temple) saw the lights approaching.
Again the thieves ! This was too much. This time they should
have a taste of the halberd. The two *bushi* advanced to the gate.
Up the slope came the band, carrying a woman in an open litter.
" Terute ! Koshirō ! Is this a matter of ransom ? " Thus demanded
Sukeshige. Koshirō came forward to make obeisance. He presented Oniyasha in due form. Prostrate the latter made humble

apology for his attack, explanation of its purpose. Said Sukeshige—
"Naruhodo! In your intent there is some justice. Doubtless the
"matter can be arranged with the priests. They would be glad to
"live in good understanding with such neighbours, to be free from
"disturbance. But what is to be done with Terute Dono? A
"temple is no place for a woman." Said Oniyasha—"Deign to
"remove to the mountain fort. There residence will be safe and
"convenient. The band is at your lordship's orders, now or when-
"ever the flag of the Oguri House is raised to avenge its wrongs on
"the Isshiki." Thought Sukeshige—"A good resource for a *rōnin*;
"a derogatory position for a feudal lord." He replied—"The matter
"shall be considered. Deign to return to Kumabuseyama. Answer
"shall be made, as also for the priests. The affairs of the House re-
"quire early action." With reverence the band made their salutation
and retired. The sound rejoiced at their escape; the wounded found
excuse for their injuries. Sukeshige, with Terute and his *rōtō*,
entered the temple to hold council. Seirinji lacked a *nyō-in* or
woman's hall for such pilgrims. Decision was quickly reached.
To live with Terute at the temple was unseemly; to go to the
mountain fort was impolitic. They would return to Yūki, doubtless
a centre for the *rōtō* scattered in the fight at Yahagi. With regret
Sukeshige learned of the fatal issue of the battle to the Asuke brothers.
With astonishment he heard the gossip picked up by Koshirō in
passing through Aohaka. It could not be helped. Said he—"To
"travel together through Suruga and Sagami is inadvisable. Mito
"no Kotarō shall go first, to await us at Yūki. Sukeshige follows
"after. Do you Koshirō accompany Terute on the sea road. Suke-
"shige will go on alone. But the interval between should be short
"and communication easy. Deign not to delay."

Not unwillingly did the monks see them depart. With Oniyasha reasonable composition had been secured; his support to the
monastery was more desirable than his opposition. The tribute
paid was very moderate. This effected, for them to harbour the
lord of Oguri was dangerous, and they took this natural if selfish
view. A boat was furnished, and the Oguri, lord and retainers
four in number, swiftly passed down the waters of the Tenryūgawa

until it emerged in the foothills near the sea. Here Mito no Kotarō hastened forward on his journey to Yūki, leaving the others to follow more slowly. Crossing the Ashigara pass he skirted the hills, pressed a boat into service on the upper Banyūgawa (Sagamigawa), and giving Kamakura a wide berth pushed on to the head of the broad bay which then entered far into the lands now covered by the great city of Yedo-Tōkyō and the rice fields of Chiba prefecture. In those days the mouth of the Sumidagawa was a wide extending swamp covering most of the low ground. Kotarō reached this Miyoshinohara (now Kanda) toward evening. He was hungry, thirsty, and tired. "Ah! The belly of Kotarō is empty. What is "to be done? Sign of house there is none. There is said to be a "fishing village hereabouts on the islands (Edo), but nothing is to "be seen but reeds. Besides Kotarō is no fish." He came out on a little lake nestled under the hills close by. "Water-ways are roads. "Men live on the banks." He followed the side of the pond for a short distance. Coming to a flight of stone steps he climbed up, to come out on an open space large enough to contain a shrine of modest proportions and in an advanced stage of ruin. For a moment Kotarō stood at the edge of the hill looking out over the sea of reeds and water extending North, East, South. Then he turned toward the temple standing amid the thick grove of pine which closely hemmed it in. An old blinking man was seated on the steps, giving him careful examination. Kotarō approached. "Venerable "Sir, deign to grant shelter and food for the night. Doubtless the "temple is in your charge. The traveller is wearied and hungry." The aged man looked him over. At his unfavourable manner said Kotarō—"Have no fear as to reward. I am in funds." He brought forth a little bag of gold dust, some copper coins. The old man's demeanour became cheerful and obsequious. "Deign, "honoured Sir, to wait before the temple. Food for your enter-"tainment shall be brought. You shall find full occupation." Without ceremony he made off down the steps and into the foot way, at a pace which startled Kotarō out of all consideration for his years.

Mito no Kotarō watched him out of sight; then he entered

the temple. It was not a cheerful place. It was a stench of stale and vile revelry rather than of incense which met his nose. Said he —" The belly must wait. Water is to be had everywhere—except "from this uninviting pond." Looking around he picked up an old *dobin* (kettle) ˋsquatted in a shallow vessel of hot water. It contained liquid. Kotarō put his mouth to the spout and drank. His eyes opened in ecstasy. Again he drank, and drank again. It was *saké* of the purest brand. "Surely my luck has been great. " No bad entertainment for such a broken down place. But what " is that?" A sound, *gutsu, gutsu, gutsu*, came from the depths of the temple. Kotarō approached the *honzon*.* Somewhat to the knight's astonishment lights were burning behind the altar. Perhaps it was some subsidiary shrine. Leaning familiarly over the bronze shoulder of a seated Binzuru he peered into the corridor commonly found behind the main altar of a temple, and which is often lined with subsidiary images of deities which cannot find place elsewhere, most promiscuously arrayed and often out of repair. Atsu! Here was a sight indeed. Opposite him lay sprawled a frowning Emma-Ō. The red paint, the huge uplifted eyebrows, the clenched fists, made a tolerable ugly presentment. Near by, in ungainly *negligé*, was a Shōzuka no Baba. Not far off was Meikyū-Ō. Hatsu-Ei-Ō lay beneath him with mouth wide open. Demons, red, white, and blue, were sprawled in various attitudes along the corridor. It was the music of their snores that had attracted his attention. Said Kotarō sententiously—" Fish and filchers go together. These thieves " have first tippled themselves into a drunken sleep. The feast " is not far off." Boldly he stepped into the corridor and over the

---

* *Honzon*—The chief idol of a temple, usually established on the altar. Shōzuka no Baba, the old hag who robs little children in the River of Souls, and pitilessly sets them to work. These worthies are wonderfully portrayed in gigantic proportions at the Ennōji (Arai-Emma-dō) near Kenchōji at Kamakura. Several at least, particularly the remarkable Emma-Ō, are the work of Unkei the 13th century sculptor. Binzuru was one of the sixteen *rakan* (disciples) of the Buddha. One day, as the object of the remark passed, he said to his neighbour—" Gad! What a fine girl." Since then he has been banished outside of the holy of holies, and is a sort of ecclesiastical hanger on—of jovial aspect.

Kotarō's Adventure at Ueno.

prostrate bodies. His enterprise was rewarded. At the end was spread an elaborate meal. The fish sent up its perfume to his nostrils, the rice tub smoked agreeably. Facing his hosts Kotarō squatted and proceeded to stuff himself. Then there was the *saké*, perfume to the nostrils equal to its taste to the palate. To the mind of Kotarō came his experience with Chikuma. The Gotō brothers were hardly likely to come to aid him on this occasion. What had been their fate in the battle? It was the one sad thought. Mind and body were satisfied and buoyant. What next?

Kotarō selected a piece of stiff paper and rolled it into a quill. He stood over the prostrate Emma-Ō and inspected him. " A poor " job, this rascal. Unkei would be ashamed of him. Doubtless he " is afraid to go to the Ennōji and gather a hint. He would leave " his carcass at the execution ground. And this Baba? No bad " job. The Baba of Ennōji is too kind. Her face and eyes, anxious " not harsh, do not repel little children. They would not run to " hide behind the rocks of the Sai no Kawara. As for the demons " they are well got up. But what a scrawny lot! Now for this " fellow." Bestriding Emma-Ō the *bushi* with no gentle hand thrust the quill up his nostril. The king of Hell snorted and sneezed, mumbled, then rolled over heavily in his drunken sleep. " How " about this one? " He tried the blue devil; with no better success. Angered Kotarō gave him a terrific cuff, first on one cheek, to be straightened up by a cuff on the other cheek. The fellow sat up with a roar. Emma-Ō and his fellow kings and demons, the Shō-zuka no Baba, slowly rolled open the eyes behind their hideous masks. Said the king of Hell—" What filthy scoundrel has " come here to disturb the feast? " His eyes wandered to the end of the corridor. Those of his band followed. In a moment all were on their feet in rage. " Gesu! The rascal has robbed us of " our banquet! What punishment is fit for such a miserable " scamp? " Said Emma-Ō portentously—" He has come to be " judged by the gods of Hell? Be it so. Emma-Ō hands down " the decision. Ears and nose shall furnish forth his provender. " His flesh, little by little, shall be stripped from his bones. De-

" licious the *sashimi** provided for the greedy wretch. Bound fast,
" other food there is none. Truly he shall share in this our feast,
" and himself provide the banquet. Such is the judgment of Hell's
" king. Seize him ! " Forward they sprang on the laughing Kotarō.
But the space was narrow, the light was dim, they were drunk and
in their own way. The two kings, Meikyū and Hatsu-Ei, cut down
each other ; and the blue demon finished the survivor. Aiming a
terrific blow at the elusive knight, Emma-Ō cut the Shōzuka no
Baba from hip to shoulder. " Hatsu ! " And the terror of mothers
and the nursery disappeared into the shades. Kotarō added
his own efforts to those of the drunken thieves. He stood over the
prostrate Emma-Ō, sole survivor of this band. " A most rash and
" unworthy enterprise. Kotarō has no excuse to make to his lord if
" thwarted in his mission. However the fellow cannot be left alive.
" He is the most infamous of the band." Severing head from body
quickly he took his way to the front of the temple. All was quiet.
Kotarō hastened down the steps and took the road which led northward, to get as far from the scene as possible.

He had not gone a hundred yards when steps were heard
approaching in the darkness. By the white hair Kotarō recognized
the bent old man, doubtless the out-post of the band gone to give
notice of his presence at the temple. He stepped in front of him.
As the fellow sprang actively away his body rolled by the roadside.
Kotarō leaned over and inspected him. As with the rest his
appearance was a disguise. The white hair removed, there lay the
body of a tall man, whose black hair contrasted strangely with the
get-up of his figure. Kicking the body into the ditch the knight
made the more haste. At some distance a light could be seen,
perhaps on the main north road. Here lodging could be found.
Surely his rest would not be disturbed in a place accustomed to entertain travellers. Kotarō approached and knocked. A woman's
voice answered. To his demand for lodging ready assent was given.
The door unbarred he entered. Two women made obeisance before

---

* Properly sliced raw fish taken from the live animal, which is cut with
skill in order to preserve life as long as possible. Far less consideration is taken
of this last named qualification than is thought.

him. Both were very beautiful; both were gorgeously apparelled. Seeing the fright in their eyes Kotarō looked over his own person. His garments were splashed with blood. He laughed—"Kowa! "Dont be afraid. At a temple below here some thieves made an "attack. It was in combat with them that the blood was spilled. "Deign to accept the explanation. They were a most curious set!" He went on to tell of his experience with Emma-Ō and the Baba. Said one of the women smiling sweetly—"With fear and respect: "honoured Sir you have been most fortunate. These belong to a "powerful band and this house is their headquarters. As this night "they are absent on a distant raid you are safe. As for ourselves, we "are from the Kamakura Gongendō. Returning to our homes after the "great fire of last year we were captured by these fellows and com-"pelled to enter their service. Deign to hear our prayer and take "us with you." Kotarō thought for a moment. He considered his lord's mission, and temporized. "The matter doubtless can be "arranged. Surely my lord would approve such action. You shall "be saved."

As he spoke there came hasty steps and a voice at the door. The women grew pale under their rice powder. Said the one who had spoken—"Deign to hide in the room yonder. Some messenger "comes from the chief. The band doubtless is returning." Conducting Kotarō into a darkened apartment at some distance she left him to rejoin her companion waiting silently by the entrance. Hardly had she gone than the knight followed softly in her wake. From the dark turning of the *rōka* he watched the women as they unbarred the door and gave entrance to a number of men, evidently thieves. They all stood at the *genkwan* (entrance). Kotarō slipped into the room adjoining, and passing from one to the other got near to listen. Said the leader—"Lady, terrible is the tale. Returning "by the Kwannondō we found Emma-Ō, the Baba, the Kings, and "the demons weltering in blood. The temple is splashed from floor "to roof. Nay more: the chief himself lies dead in the ditch by the "roadside. You must make a new selection for a lover from the "band." The women gasped—"Ah! Doubtless it is the wretch "now here who bragged of his exploits at the temple. Expecting

" your return he has been put off with fair words, and will stay the
" night." Said the head-man—" Show us to his lodging. The for-
" feit is to be paid at once, the chief avenged." At the heels of the
women the band trooped along the corridor. As they disappeared
around the corner Kotarō came forth. Shaking his fist in the
direction of the sirens he raised the door bar. The next moment he
was out in the darkness, flying for life whither he knew not.

The shouts of the pursuers were soon heard. The torches
showed his flying figure. In despair and exasperation he plunged
into a path entering the reeds. A yell of joy went forth. His capture and the slow revenge was assured. In those days this Asakusa district was a wilderness. Two hundred years later it was just
awakening to the life of men.* Kotarō came out on the banks of a
broad rolling stream. In the darkness the opposite shore looked to
be miles away. To-day Mukōjima is crowned in spring with a
glorious bloom. Then both banks were reeds. In this early spring
of the second month (March-April) the green growth was just
forcing its way up among last year's withered crop. The shouts
were drawing near. Something must be done. Kotarō stole along
the edge of the reeds. Then doubling back some distance he waited. The band could be heard at the river's edge. He leaned down.
Flint and steel were busy. Then a great flame went up. The
favouring breeze blew the fire straight down toward the river. He
could hear the shouts of the thieves taken in their own trap, cut off
and compelled to face fire or water. Let such escape as could.
Secure in his retreat Kotarō took his way back to the road ; back to
the house. No mercy was to be granted to the prayers of the faith-
less jades, cozening their deliverer with a false tale of violence
Both died forthwith. Then leaving the house in flames Kotarō
slowly went on his way northward, a little uncertain in mind as to
whether his justice had not been over-speedy. Perhaps the girls
had betrayed him in fright. However, *shikata ga nai* (no help
for it).

---

* Takarai here tells two interesting anecdotes of Iyeyasu at Asakusa; too
anachronistic for insertion.

CHAPTER XVII.

ONIKAGE SERVES HIS LORD.

At more leisurely rate lord and lady, attended by Koshirō, took their way northward. As precaution they travelled in separate parties. Koshirō and his lady in company; Sukeshige sometimes ahead, sometimes following, on Onikage. At Mishima town they lodged together before passing the barrier. Earnestly did lord and lady pray at the shrine of the Daimyōjin. Terute for shelter granted her at the subsidiary shrine at Setō no Kanazawa; Sukeshige for good fortune in war. Peculiar must be the efficacy of the glorious god. Had not Prince Yoritomo secured the head of the father, while the sons of Taira Hangwan Kanetaka joyfully attended and worshipped at the god's *matsuri* (festival) at this very temple? Had not Terute nearly lost her own head at the younger shrine? Koshirō too prayed vigorously, saw to every line of Onikage's harness and their own equipment, and carefully noted every face he met in town and temple grounds. In neither was there aught to disturb them. Then with dawn he and his lady set forth. It had been determined that they should take one of the lower passes, and descending the mountain by the Shichitōdō* be on the lookout for Sukeshige near Odawara town. As foot travellers this rough and little used trail gave every facility to escape any barrier, if such had been erected, at Senkokuhara. Sukeshige was to ride by way of the Gongen shrine. The barrier known to be at Yamanaka was easy to avoid. If Hakone† was barred, a way would be found to pass it. The situation was uncertain owing to the recent strain between the

---

* The ancient and collective name of the hot springs, from Yumoto to Sokokura—Miyanoshita.

† That is—Moto Hakone. The other village is the mushroom offspring of the Tokugawa barrier.

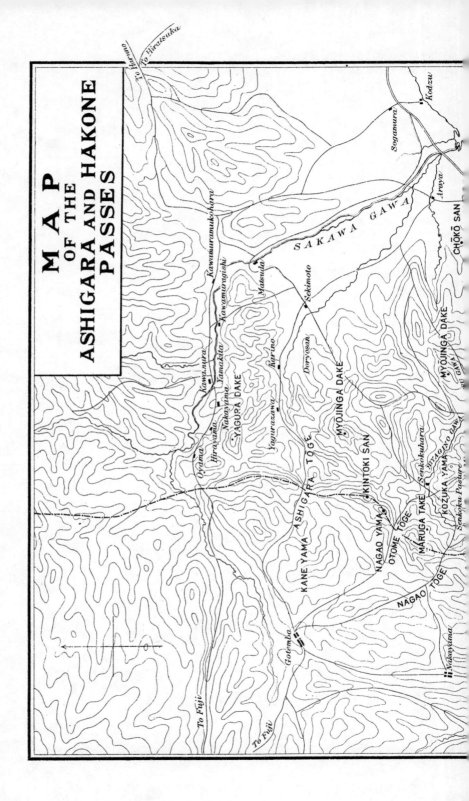

MAP
OF THE
ASHIGARA AND HAKONE
PASSES

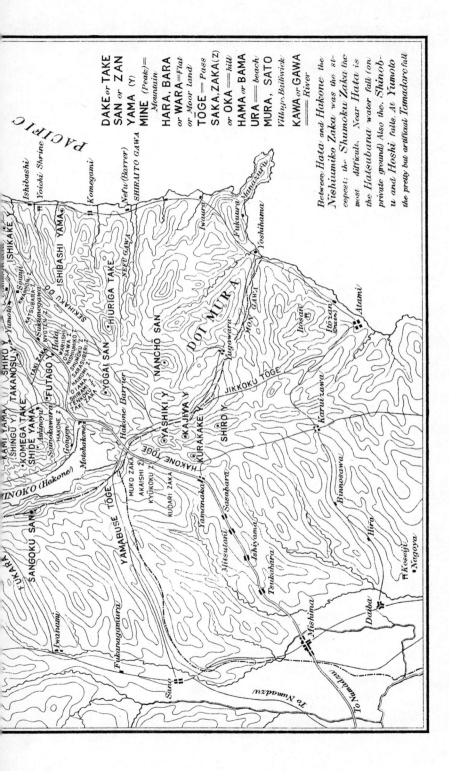

PACIFIC

DAKE or TAKE
SAN or ZAN
YAMA (Y)
MINE (Peak) = Mountain
HARA, BARA or WARA = Flat or Moor land
TŌGE = Pass
SAKA, ZAKA (Z) or OKA = hill
HAMA or BAMA
URA = beach
MURA, SATO Village, Bailiwick
KAWA or GAWA = River

Between Hata and Hakone the Nishiumbo Zaka was the steepest; the Shumoku Zaka the most difficult. Near Hata is the Hatsubana water fall (on private ground) Also the Shinobu and Hoshi falls. At Yumoto the pretty but artificial Tamadare fall

Ishibashi
Yoichi Shrine
Komegami

Nefu (Barrier)
SHIRATO GAWA

Iwaura
Fukaura Yunoizu
Yoshihama

Atami

ISHIKAKE Y
ISHIBASHI YAMA
Sōunji
Myōjō Z
YATSUBARA Z
Sukiunogoya
NYOTEN Z
MARISHI Z
OSAWA Z
OSHIUMO Z
SHUMOKU Z
HAKONE Z
SARASHIBERI Z
SHIRAMI Z
HARORI Z
TENBARI Z
TANWOKI Z
ZAKA

SEKIHAKU DŌ
HIURIGA TAKE
NEFU GAWA

NANCHŌ SAN

DŌI MURA

Itōsan
Itō-san (Onsen)

YOGAI SAN

Hakone Barrier

YASHIKI Y
KAJIYA V
KURAKAKE V

SHIRO Y

JIKKOKU TŌGE

Karuizawa

Yugawara
MON GAWA

KAMI YAMA Y
SHIKO Y
SHINGU Y
TAKANOSU Y
Yumoto
KOMEGA TAKE
SHIDE YAMA
TAKI ZAKA
FUTAGO Y
Sankokuwara
Ashinoyu
Gongen
HAKONE Z
Motohakone

INOKO (Hakone)

SANGOKU SAN
FUKARA

MUKO ZAKA
AKAISHI Z
KYŪKOKU Z
KUDARI ZAKA

HAKONE TŌGE

YAMABUSE TŌGE

Yamanaka
Susahara

Binnosawa

Iwanami

Fukanagamura

Mitsutani
Ishiyama

Tsukahara

Hira

Koseiji
Negoya

Suno

Daiba

To Numadzu

Mishima

To Numadzu

Kwanryō of Kamakura and Kyōto, and they dared to make little inquiry. Their route would take both parties close together and yet apart. Disaster to either would be gossip of the peasantry, quickly learned. But something is to be said of these famous passes.

Both are very ancient ; both noted in war and history from the earliest days of Nippon. Of the two the Ashigara pass at the base of Fujisan is the oldest. By competent authorities it is considered to be the Usuitōge of the Nihongi, not the pass so named near Karuizawa, and from which Yamato Takeru no Mikoto could not have looked back on the scene of his wife's sacrifice.‡ In these very early days before the reign of Kwammu Tennō (782 A.D.) there were no roads. If anything of the name existed they were mere indistinct trails of mountaineers. In spite of the activity of Fujiyama it was the Ashigara pass which took precedence. This offers much easier access than Hakone, and for long men did not notice that the latter was the shorter distance. But in Enreki 21st year 5th month (June 802) a road was formally opened which penetrated the heart of the mountain district. For foot travellers it was shorter and they could face its difficulties. To these the Ashigaratōge became distinctly unpopular. Besides the establishment of the shrine to the Hakone Gongen, perhaps in Engi (901-922) gave added incentive. The Gongen there worshipped were regarded as particularly efficacious ; and particularly necessary to propitiate on the passage of this mountain region. Before the days of the Edo Bakufu it seemed as if from spirit of merest contradiction the most difficult and dangerous route was sought. The trail hung high on the ridges, looking over precipitous cliffs and down steep slopes. Truly divine aid was needed in this dangerous place beset by sudden storms and savage men.

The passes were easily defended. Up to the inception of the feudal wars the Kyōto Government had free access, and Yoriyoshi and his son, Hachiman Tarō, in their wars with the Abe did their

‡ Kojiki p. 213. Nihongi I. p. 207 : Both chronicles refer to this country as in the hands of the Yemishi, or aboriginals. The Kojiki says Ashigara. The Nihongi—" Shinanu-Usui." But the Nihongi is here the less reliable and the more artificial.

284

fighting much farther North.   Minamoto Tameyoshi lost his head,
not only through the heartless wickedness of his elder son Yoshitomo, but through disregarding the advice of his younger son
Tametomo.   The latter wanted to hold the two passes.   With the
Kwantō behind them "not a man from Miyako would get through
alive;" and Tametomo viciously brandished his terrible bow.   So
much for Hōgen (1156-1158), at which period the feudal wars of
Nippon more properly shifted their centre from North and West to
this critical spot of the main island.   With the establishment of
Yoritomo at Kamakura in 1181 A.D. the popularity of route and
shrine took a bound forwards.   The Bettō of the Gongen shrine*
had given the defeated army of Yoritomo every aid.   Harboured by
him Tokimasa and his son found easy access to the roads of Kai
province.   With the Minamoto Shōgun's success he secured the
person of the man he most hated—at that time—Ōba Kagechika.
Greatly was the shrine favoured.   Regardless of politics the tradition descended ; for Hōjō, Ashikaga, Tokugawa did likewise.   But
the military side was not neglected.   When Yasutoki, in Shōkyū
(1219-1222), was marching on Miyako, the capable Masako and
her brother Yoshitoki saw to the garrisoning of the two
passes.   In Kemmu 2nd year (1335) Nitta Yoshisada and
Ashikaga Takauji fought fierce battles through these mountains.
In the uprising of Zenshū, Ōei 23rd year (1416), the Bettō
aided Prince Mochiuji.   In Eikyō 10th year (1438) Mochiuji vainly
tried to hold the passes against the army sent by the Shōgun
Yoshinori, advancing northward to chastise him.   Later both were
strongly held by the Hōjō of Odawara.   These latter much improved
the roads, especially the first of the name, Hōjō Sōun (Nagauji).
He did mōre.   He made the district fashionable, as well as the key
to the Kwantō.   Thus, as the chronicler says, both passes have been
in use since the days of Heianjō.†

---

* The tutelary deities here are Ninigi-no-Mikoto; Hiko-ho-hodemi-no-
Mikoto ; Kono-hana-sakuya-hime-no-Mikoto.

† Kyōto, founded 793. The capital, transferred from Nara to Nagaoka,
here at last (at Uda) was established until the days of Meiji. Then the Shōgunate counted for more than the Empire ; Tōkyō became the capital.

There is more to tell than the story of war. After Kamakura was founded the Ashigara pass fell into disrepute. The Hakone road was not improved. In those days the road ran much as now to Yumoto, a most ancient place. Across the river from Tōnozawa is Yusakayama. The trail climbed steeply to its summit, zigzagging through thick forest. Once emerged at the top glorious views of sea, mountain, and valley, thoroughly appreciated in these ancient days, were secured. The path continued along the ridge, crossing over the Jōyama (Shiroyama or castle mountain), where later in the sixteenth century the Ōmori had a stronghold. From here it crossed Takanosuyama and descended into Ashinoyu. Skirting the west side of Futagoyama it descended into the precincts of the Gongen temple. As to its further course in the middle ages, in the Ashikaga times, there is dispute. That there was a barrier at Yamanaka is known. This road through Moto Hakone leads into Izu. But the main trail is said to have skirted the north end of the lake (Ashinoko). A little earlier it had reached Ubago from Hakone Gongen-zaka by way of Moto Sai no Kawara (Ashinoyu?). From Ubago it crossed one of the lower passes, the Nagaotōge or Fukaratōge, into Suruga province, descending into Fukanagamura and joining the Ashigara road. Neither the present Tōkaidō by way of Hata, or the Shichitō roads to the hot springs existed, though probably rough trails led to primitive bathing places in the mountains. Thus it is known that in Ōei 10th year (1403) Yoshioki, son of Wakiya Yoshiharu the nephew of Nitta Yoshisada, fled from Mutsu to hide himself in Kiga (Miyanoshita). The Kwanryō of Kamakura, Prince Mitsukane, discovered his whereabouts and had him put to death—matter of record in the " Kamakura Taisōshi " and the " Sokokura Ki." Sokokura, it is to be said, is the ancient and parent resort of the district. Yoshioki is considered as the founder and first patron of the hot spring. In Tembun 14th year (1545) the later Hōjō organized the establishment and imposed regulations ; which means taxes, not decency. In the days of the Odawara Government, the famous Date Masamune was a noted patron and patient (Tenshō 1573-1591). From the days of the Tokugawa the manufacture of ornamental woodwork takes its rise.

Although not part of the present story the fate of this old road can be followed to its conclusion. Favoured by the later Hōjō of Odawara the district, strictly speaking, dates from them its present history. They did little to make passage to it easier. The road was bad, steep, and dangerous. But they popularized the hot springs, and fortified the passes. Hakone in the early days of the Tokugawa found but little favour. At first it was tried to suppress it, then to minimize its use. This merely made it the secret route for all who wanted to escape observation. Thwarted on this line the Edo Bakufu determined to use its facilities for their purposes. They began to appreciate it as the trap beyond excellence. With a complete change of policy Hakone was made the main road to Yedo. The old rough stony trail, with its long concealing bamboo grass adding to the difficulties particularly on the Mishima side,* was now to be improved. The new road by way of Hata was laid out. The descent by Yamanaka was the main road. On the order of Matsudaira Masatsune, in Genwa 4th year (1618) the people of Odawara and Mishima set to work on the construction of a road suitable for a great traffic. The Ashigara pass was abandoned. Says the chronicler shrewdly—" The Tokugawa liked to raise difficulties." Hakone had its difficulties. They added to these by a most complete barrier system. Travel was to be in every way watched and impeded. It was strictly a road for pedestrians. As late as 1863 (Bunkyū 3rd year) the Shōgun could not go by carriage to Kyōto for installment. At Hakone was established the greatest barrier of the many on this range and road. In fact the village had its being therefrom. Its hotels to-day are vestiges of the old rest-houses for the travellers awaiting inspection. Even in Ashikaga times there probably was a barrier—the Hakone Ashikawa barrier, said to be Moto-Hakone. The Edo Bakufu chose the site with triumphant precision. Yōgaisan with steep slopes rose on the land side to the South. The lake guarded by boats prevented evasion to the North.

---

* The upper slopes of the pass on the Mishima side traverse rough rounded bosses covered with bamboo grass. The forest begins half way down, now mostly removed and the ground under cultivation. On the Odawara side the forest runs far up into the range, except Mukōyama and the Ashinoyu district.

To complete the guard a line of barriers was thrown along the ridge —at Senkokuhara, Yakurasawa, Tanimura, Kawamura where the Ashigara route was joined. Thus access from Suruga was prevented. The Nefugawa-seki (barrier) was neatly thrown across the coast road from Izu. This guard was so efficient that the finding of bodies of travellers, lost in the complicated valleys and ranges during snows and storms in their efforts at evasion, was no unusual occurrence. This was of no small importance where it was desired to give an example. As the chronicler says—"In former times the barriers were the erection of the fiefs, concerned with no interests but those affecting their own narrow precincts. In Tokugawa times the barriers were national, the traffic impeded nation wide."

Hence they were hated. "Diaries, records, histories, all denounce them." Passports were a *sine qua non* and were designed to drive all into *this* net; hence the small importance of the other barriers. They were most minute in detail; for samurai, signed by their lord; for peasants signed by the *nanushi* (village mayor). Sometimes the countersign of the lord also was demanded. Arms were an object of search and trouble. Women and children of the daimyō *yashiki*, imprisoned in Edo, sought to escape to their home districts. East and West the double tide of traffic was given careful inspection, and hence often unreasonable detention. Here are some of the regulations, always harshly enforced :

1. Hats to be removed on leaving the barrier : (for identification).
2. *Norimon* (litter) doors to be left open : (for identification).
3. Women to show vouchers in detail : (their travel was much embarrassed in every possible way).
4. Women in *norimon* to be inspected by the women at the barrier : (to certify to their sex).
5. Wounded, dead, or doubtful persons, without certificates could not pass.
6. The regulations did not apply to Dōjōnin (Court Officers) or Daimyō ; but suspicious persons could be detained.

(These last two regulations were meant to be given catholic interpretation).

These rules were issued in Shōtoku 2 year 2 month (7 March–6 April 1712).

A pregnant woman gave birth to a female child *en route.* Alas! Her certificate read for but one female. She could not pass. Women must have permit of absence from the Rusu-Yakunin (furlough constable) and the seal of the *nanushi.* A lower daimyō had to climb out of his *norimon* on the passage of his superior. Hence the open doors of the *norimon* were an added source of irritation. There were redeeming features. The strength of the legs and arms of the Hakone chair bearers, the good cheer of the inns. Be it said that at the present day the former has waned and the latter is matter of dispute on the old Tō-kaidō road. The chair bearers were known as *kumosuke*—cloud assisters. Why? The scribe waxes eloquent and becomes vague. It is wise to follow his example and not rush wildly into "Things Japanese." In a few decades who can explain the "white wings" of the great American cities. Certainly not the dirty stained garments of the wearers. Of all this Edo world of fashion and travel the favoured resort was Tōnosawa. This now rather despised and pretty place was given the name Shōri-yama by one Shunsui attendant on Mito no Mitsukuni. In ancient days Gensoku Ōtei of Tōda (China) had sought seclusion with the beautiful princess Yokii at the Mountain of the Black Horse (Risan). In the healing waters of the bath the emperor's vigour was restored. Hence Shunsui, impressed by the scenery, burst into praise and named the bath of Tōnosawa, Shōritō; the place Shōrisan* It is still musical as ever, with song of *geisha* and strum of *samisen.* It lies shaded in the deep cleft of its hills, surrounded by the dangerous mountain stream as in the neck of a bottle; and, it is to be confessed, is one of the most attractive resting places in the valley.

It was by the trail leading down over Senkokuhara to Soko-

---

* *Shō*—superlative? *Shō=katsu* 勝.

kura, hence across the deep cleft by *tsuribashi* (hanging bridge
of bamboo), and down the valley to Yumoto that Terute and
Koshirō were climbing and stumbling to join Sukeshige at
Odawara town. Wearing *meseki-gasa* (concealing head-cover)
the knight left Mishima-Eki in the darkness and rode up the
mountain slopes of the Hakone pass, to cross it by Moto
Hakone and the Yusakayama road. The night was dark, the
sky heavy with clouds, the progress slow through the dark
forest of pine and cedar. Then the trail became steeper and
steeper, and even more rough. An occasional rumble and flash
showed the presence of the coming storm. Heavy drops began
to fall. Then the rain came down in sheets. Sukeshige could
not restrain a gesture of impatience. "Iza! The journey does
not start well. In storm and the forest no shelter is to be
found This Sukeshige is in for a ducking and a cold one.
"Surely no other person is out in such a storm." The icy
wind of the upper mountain blew drearily; the rain seemed
to penetrate and soak every thread of his garments. He shivered.
Pressing Onikage they climbed rapidly through the silent little
hamlet of Sasahara. The steeper grade surmounted he pulled
up the horse for rest and to get its wind. The violent gusts
had settled into a steady rain. Sukeshige sat stolidly on his
horse, his only protection against this icy bath being the overhanging pines and his deep hat. As he thus chewed the cud
of bitter reflection the sound of a flute suddenly floated through
the air, *hiu, hiu, hiu.* Sukeshige was startled. On this dreary
mountain road, amid the wild valleys, the thick forest, the
ragged slopes of these cavernous hills, the sound came as something uncanny, out of the way. "A flute heard in such a
"place! Who can it be thus to beguile the journey through
"the wilds at this late hour?" The sound came nearer, wailing rather than sportive. It seemed as if the mind, not human
lips, played a ghastly air on the reedy pipe. Sukeshige laid
hand to his sword. Then the flute player appeared painfully
climbing the steep grade out of the hamlet below. Nothing to be frightened at. A mere slip of a girl, fourteen or

fifteen years of age, nothing could be seen but the face peering out of the protecting *zukin*. She carried a white lantern at the end of the staff in the left hand. With the right hand she ran over the holes of the instrument applied to her lips. She stopped before the knight—" Are-yo ! With fear and reverence : " respected Sir, in garments soaked by the storm you will suffer " sickness. Deign to let me guide you to shelter close at hand. " The master with pleasure will furnish fire at which to dry " your honoured person, refreshment for your weariness. Con-" descend to accompany me." Sukeshige smiled—" Truly nesan " the invitation is kind. How comes it that the Danna will not " be angered at your being abroad so late? Perchance the " guest will share the rebuke." With some wonder he observed her. Her garments showed no sign of the storm. She replied, more to his glance than to his words—" More fortunate than " your honoured self shelter from the storm was found. This " has delayed the return from the master's mission. Joyful " and kind will be your reception." Thought Sukeshige—" At " all events there will be a fire at which to dry the clothing. " Ill might follow this soaking ...... Be it so maiden. Accept " earnest thanks for the kind thought." Following the girl he directed Onikage into the forest trail. Gently fingering the flute she advanced some distance along the mountain slope into a secluded dell. Here was a fence and a rustic gate. On entering within was found a cottage of considerable pretensions. The girl disappeared to the rear.

Dismounting Sukeshige tied Onikage beneath a cedar close by. Advancing to the house he was met at the entrance by a woman of some thirty years. In the dim light of the doorway it could be seen that she still retained the figure and looks of great beauty in girlhood. Prostrated in welcome more complete survey of features and expression could not be obtained. With apologies she ushered him into an apartment in which was burning a huge brazier. " Deign to wait but a little. The " master of the house has been ill. In a little while all will be " prepared for your reception honoured Sir. Meanwhile dry

" and refresh yourself. Truly such reception is very rude." With
deprecating acquiescence and apology for intrusion on his part
Sukeshige proceeded to attend to his more practical needs. With
garments drying before the brazier, refreshed in body he looked
around the apartment. It was really a magnificent piece of
architecture. The screens were of the finest silk, embroidered
by an artist hand with wild ducks flying across a reedy swamp.
The wood work of *hinoki* (chamaecyparis) was polished to show
every minutest grain of the structure. The fretwork of the
partitions was of Nature's handiwork and most intricate. The
devastating insects which thus carved it were master hands in
the grotesque. As he finished his inspection the sound of the
woman's garments was heard rustling along the corridor. Gravely
she bowed before him. "With fear and respect: deign, noble
"Sir, to allow me to act as guide to the master's apart-
"ment. You are expected. For this trouble the condition of
"an invalid can offer excuse." Sukeshige expressed his pleasure
at the opportunity of giving thanks in person to his host.
"The indisposition without doubt is but temporary; the obliga-
"tion rests on the guest. Deign to act as guide to the lord
"of the mansion." With this conduct he passed along the
corridor. The place was truly vast. Glimpses of gardens sleeping in the darkness could be seen. Though late the house
was open as at mid-day. Then he was ushered into a large
and brilliantly lighted room at the end of which was a screen.
At a sign to approach he advanced. The screen was withdrawn disclosing to view a lady. Her long hair trailed on the
ground. Her face turned away she seemed to seek something
on the ground. Sukeshige came close. Then she turned. With
amazement and horror he looked into the face of Hanako.
A smile, half bitter, half enticing, was on her lips. "Does
"shame enter the heart of my lord at his cruel treatment? Deign
"to dismiss it. Hanako is but the serving maid of her lord's
"pleasure in all existences. Deign to be seated. The couch is
"prepared; Hanako obedient to her lord's desire." She rose
and glided to his side, seizing his hand. At the touch a chill

went through Sukeshige. The eyes of Hanako, burning with passion, had a cruel wicked glare. On the beautiful face a lurking sneer of triumphant evil, sure of victory, played around the corners of the mouth, converting its tender curves into a hidden leer. Gently pressing her bosom against his arm she made as if to put her arms around his neck. Sukeshige was as one in a dream, trying to throw it off but less and less able to free himself. His fingers met the handle of his dagger. The touch of steel aroused him. With an effort he held the intruder at arms length—" Cursed Spectre ! Again you haunt this " Sukeshige ; or is it a lie, the tale brought to Seirinji by Koshirō ? " Did not Hanako drown herself in the Kagami-ike of Aohaka ? " Are you not a filthy ghost, a wretched phantom ? Hence with " you'! Away with your foul embraces smelling of the mould ! " With the drawn weapon he slashed fiercely at the detaining arms. As the fingers of the spectre sank into his flesh his own cry answered the wail of the evil vision. Sukeshige rubbed his eyes. Cottage, women, magnificence, all had disappeared. He was standing amid the dripping trees of a forest of pine. Tethered close by stood Onikage. Only a few drops of blood, oozing from two tiny punctures on the right hand, gave evidence of the truth of the experience.

Said Sukeshige—" Ah ! It was the ghost of Hanako who thus " misled me. What misfortune ! In what direction is the road to " be found ? Any guidance, even ghostly, would be welcome." Slowly he mounted Onikage. " At all events upward cannot be far " wrong. But the way is difficult for the horse." So it was. But the giant beast proved his mettle. He seemed as much cat as horse, climbing over fallen trees and stumps, scrambling over boulders. The top of the ridge was reached. Sukeshige looked down on the dimly gleaming waters of Ashinoko.* He had come out just beyond the post-town of Moto-Hakone. A lighted lantern showed the presence of barrier and guard. All the better was his journey through the forest. Descending he came into the road which climbed the hill to the hot pool of Ashinoyu. A *tsujidō* (wayside shrine) stood close by. As the gentle drizzle had begun again he

---

* Lake Hakone.

took refuge beneath its roof, giving opportunity to Onikage to rest from his labours. Thus man and horse remained while the minutes passed. As he prepared to mount and continue his ride torches were seen coming down the hill. It was yet an hour or more from dawn. Who was it thus to travel the pass at night with such a large company? There were at least forty men. In the midst was an oldish man carried in a *nagabō-kago*. As he came nearer Sukeshige by the light of the torches recognized him to be Yokoyama Yasuhide. "Hatena! Heaven has delivered him into my hand. Atsumitsu "Dono shall be avenged." He prepared to spring on him suddenly as the litter passed. But the sharp eyes of Shōgen detected the unusual size of Onikage standing in the darkness. "Who is that man? "Strange that Onikage should be in this place. Into whose hands "has he fallen?" On whispered instructions one of the train hustled the silent figure standing by the *tsujidō* as if to let the train pass. He peered under the hat. Before Sukeshige could cut him down he fled back in terror to the litter. "Oguri Dono! Oguri "Dono!" The frightened cries of the Yokoyama *rōtō* gave the news to Shōgen. Before Sukeshige could rush into the crowd he had sought refuge behind his train. Massed they prepared to strike at the spectre. The voice of Shōgen reassured them—"Don't fear. "No ghost will handle steel. Be sure you have a man to deal "with. The report of Oguri's death is untrue. The Shōnin has "played with us. No! No! To attack this fellow with the sword "is unavailing. He is a truly terrible man. Stand by Shōgen! "Shoot him down with arrows." Back on the hillside they fled. Trembling hands strung the bows. There was no recourse. To battle with so many was "like striking at the swarms of summer locusts in the rice fields with a flail." Putting spurs to his horse Sukeshige dashed past them in the darkness.

Encouraged by Shōgen the Yokoyama *rōtō* started in pursuit. Up the hillside the chase was not so uneven. At the foot of Futago-yama they had nearly reached him. Onikage was worn out by the rough scramble of the night. Passing the reedy pool at Ashinoyu the knight reversed the blunder that other and milder men have not seldom made since and in broad daylight. Turning to left instead

of right his course took him down the valley of Kowakidani, instead
of over the narrow shoulder to Takanosuyama. The pursuers gave
a shout of triumph. They would drive him into the bottle neck of
the Jakotsugawa and easily take him alive. The chase spread over
the grassy range. Down the pathless valley thundered the hoofs of
Onikage. The pursuers were being left behind. In those days the
two little streams met in a deep pool at the head of the pretty fall
whose beauties are so inaccessible to visitors to the present crowded
place of fashion and travel. Far down at Sokokura a hanging
bridge of bamboo (*tsuribashi*) was swung across the chasm and carried travellers along the meagre trail to Tōnosawa and Yumoto.
At the junction of the streams which form the Jakotsugawa is yet
to be found a primitive bath-house, but the place has much changed
with the dying volcanic activities of the district. The rocky barrier
has been removed, the pool drained. The fall makes a shorter
plunge. To its edge came Sukeshige and Onikage. The streams
were low and scanty. The waters barely tempered the fierce heat
of the pool. Steam rose in clouds. Forty feet beyond the opposite
bank loomed fitfully and steep through the vapour. Nearer approached the shouts of the pursuers beating the hillside. Sukeshige
leaned over the neck of Onikage. "Brave horse! You are beast.
"Sukeshige is a human being. Both have been made by Heaven.
"On Onikage rests the accomplishment of the vendetta of the Ō-
"Dono. The leap must be made. Make up your mind to it
"Onikage." The animal neighed as if in comprehension. Backing the horse as far as he could Sukeshige rode forward. Onikage
made a terrific spring. Alas! His efforts of the night weighed on
him. Down came man and horse into the boiling pool. Sukeshige
could not breathe in the stifling atmosphere, not even shout out as the
burning, scalding, torturing liquid drenched him. Onikage seized
the robe in his mouth. With a last struggle the noble animal
reached and scrambled up the bank. Then his legs spread wide
apart, his eyes glazed. He sank down, gave a heave or so in
attempt to rise. His head rolled backwards, and Onikage had gallopped his last ride.

    Painfully Sukeshige arose. Tortured as he was, half uncon-

The Leap into the Sokokura Hot Pool.

scious, he knew that he could not remain at this place. Feebly he felt for his cloak. It was gone. The raw air was torture to the burnt flesh, the garments a net of fire. Staggering he made off down the valley. How far he went he knew not. Strength gave out. Unconscious he rolled into the bushes by the wayside. The projecting roots caught the body, otherwise he would have gone to the river hundreds of feet below. This saved him. The Yokoyama *rōtō* were not long in reaching the river. The stiff upturned legs of the horse caught their eyes. " Ah ! He has tried to jump the pool. " Fool ! Bravely has he been trapped." The cloak of Sukeshige at the edge of the fall was soon seen. Plainly the knight had found burial within the boiling waters. The flesh would be melted from his bones. Assured as to his fate, yet to satisfy their master they further searched the road on both sides, down to the bridge and beyond. The cliff never came into their heads. Who could pass there and live ? Only birds. With the cloak as evidence they returned to make report to Shōgen. He shook his head. Nothing but the head of Sukeshige would satisfy him. Before he had been thought dead. Just now they had met him on the Hakone pass. But delay was not possible. He had an urgent mission to carry out from Akihide to the Imagawa in Suruga. Thus he went on his way unsatisfied.

Meanwhile Terute and Koshirō, crossing Fukaratōge had passed Ubago without difficulty. Who was there to trouble a man and woman on pilgrimage in these days of peace established with the Kyōto Shōgun ? They had crossed the bridge at Sokokura and were continuing down the steep valley to their appointed meeting with their lord. A little beyond the bridge, where the path skirted the precipice, feeble groans were heard. " Wa-n ! Wa-n ! " They looked in every direction ; naturally upward, the only place where aught but a bird could roost. Nothing was to be seen. Said Terute—" Look well, Koshirō. Perhaps aid is to be given to " some unfortunate. But the sounds come from the face of the cliff. " Has some bird human voice ? " She looked over and down into the tangled mass. Dawn had been succeeded by broad daylight. Just below the path, caught in the roots of the bushes was a body. From it came the groans. Koshirō tied his girdle and that of Terute firmly to a tree. Lowering himself he placed his feet under the prostrate form and gradually worked it with himself to the top.

Stretched out in the road Sukeshige slowly opened eyes pained by suffering and fever. In amazement Koshirō and Terute were leaning over him. Whispered Terute—" My lord ! Sukeshige ! " How come you in this plight ? What can have happened ? And " Onikage ? " With great effort the wounded man told his tale, in feeble disjointed whispers and a voice unrecognizable to wife and retainer. He told of the adventure with Hanako, the meeting with Yokoyama Shōgen, the fall into the boiling pool and the death of the noble Onikage. In anger Koshirō shook his fist at the vapour, rising into the calm clear sky over the shoulder of the hill. Said Sukeshige—" The future is to be considered. Do you Koshirō take " Terute to Yūki. Seek out Yūki Shichirō Ujitomo and give her " into his charge. The restoration of the Satake House will be se- " cured by him. Sukeshige is done for. His command to the *rōtō* " is to offer service to Yūki Dono, to guard the interests of the Lady " Terute." Tears came to his eyes, of helpless rage and pain at his condition, at this dog's death. Koshirō straightened up. " Nay ! " Matters are at no such pass for the lord of Oguri. Health restored " the vendetta of the Ō-Dono shall be accomplished, the Oguri " House restored to its honours. Is not Koshirō here ? Taking his lord " on his back shelter is to be sought until the cure is effected. Take " courage my lady. Do not weep. His lordship is at no such " desperate pass." Thus the brave *bushi* cheered his lady, his injured lord. Taking Sukeshige on his back, with Terute he proceeded down the valley. At Yumoto there was a primitive bathing resort. Here Koshirō could secure first aid for the suffering man, some medicament to allay his pain. To both lady and retainer the one feasible idea was to seek refuge at Yūki. Here alone was security enough to give the sick man rest and attention. Painfully they stole along the highway to the North. Avoiding Kamakura they entered on the Musashi plain and passed to the North of the wide bay which enters so deeply into it. Thus they reached a place in

Musashi known as Ichimenhara.* It was necessary to halt. The condition of the patient was too unfavourable. At first there had been great hopes. Sukeshige had rallied very positively from the terrible shock. The scorched flesh responded to the unguent applied. But there seemed to be something more terrible behind the effects of the boiling spring. In a few days dark reddish boils broke out all over his body. These suppurated and discharged a greenish pus which infected the sounder tissue in their neighbourhood. The itching was intolerable. Sukeshige scratched and scratched. The eruption spread. The stench was frightful. At every water-course lady and retainer, kneeling beside the swollen shapeless mass of his body, washed and cleansed these sores. But some alleviating salve must be secured. At the edge of the little village was a place, half inn, half farm-house.

Koshirō approached the *teishu* who stood watching them and their painful progress to his place. Said the *rōtō*—" Deign, good " Sir, to allow us to rest for a moment at your inn, to set down our " burden on the *rōka*. We are wearied, travelling to Yūki town " with this sick man. He is very ill. Perchance the town can be " reached before night." The *teishu* smiled — " Before night! " Honoured Sir not before to-morrow night, and at much better " progress than is permitted with such charge." He approached to examine the invalid. Great was his pity. Said Koshirō—" My " son has met with a sad accident. We have been living in Mino " province, Aohaka Zaiyuimura. Here the farmers possess the " finest rice land in Nippon, the best of *hatake* to grow their wheat. " But the district swarms with poisonous snakes. The farmers had " gathered to erect their bamboo screens, to light their fires, to raise " their shouts. Thus it is hoped to strike fear into the fearful beast " which haunts the village fields, killing man and animal meeting it " unawares. My son was *sensei* of the place, teaching the children " elements of writing, of morals, of the five duties of the upright " man ; doing the clerical business of town and individual. He had

---

* Kotesashigahara says another account. This place is about six miles south of Irumagawa in Irumagori, Musashi. Ichimenhara was a short distance north of Miyoshigahara, i.e. Kanda (Tōkyō).

" little trust in such primitive methods. Trained to the weapons of
" war he determined to face the scourge and battle with it. How
" secure the meeting? From his sleeping wife he took some hair.
" The hair of a woman when burnt in the fire attracts snakes. Then
" armed with his bow he sought the pond which the poisonous
" serpent was supposed to frequent. The hair was burned. In the
" night two blazing stars appeared, moving over the marshy waters
" of the pond. Standing firm my son took aim. First the left eye,
" then the right, was pierced. Heavy clouds gathered. With crash
" and rumble the storm broke. Happy at his victory my son dis-
" regarded the sheets of falling rain. The village freed of its foe he
" returned to his home. But next day he was ill. The following
" day so weak and giddy as to be unable to rise. Thus matters
" went from bad to worse. Wise men say that he has been struck
" with *gakiyami*, the disease resulting from the poisonous breath of
" the serpent. To remain in Mino was no longer feasible. In hope
" of cure or alleviation of his suffering the virtues of the Yūgyōdera
" were sought. In vain; advised by the monks now we seek our
" native town of Yūki. There to await the will of the *kami*."

The *teishu* sighed, " The tale is a sad one. But come within.
" This day at least no further progress is possible. Here we have
" an inn, all that this small place affords. But better could hardly
" be found. At the end of the garden, on the edge of the moor, is a
" detached cottage. This is at disposal for as long as desired. Other
" guests will cause no interference, in no way disturb the sick man."
Koshirō smiled with pleasure—" Thanks for this great kindness.
" Surely the *kami* have shown favour in leading us to this inn."
Said the *teishu*—" Deign to follow me." He conducted them to
the little cottage at the end of the garden. With obeisance the
order for refreshment was taken, and he departed to see to its preparation. Koshirō set out for the village to get the much needed
salve. Terute devoted herself to the necessary cares of Sukeshige's
swollen body, the endless washing, the constant anointing. Thus
the days of a week passed. The village grew rather proud of its acquisition. People came to peep at the man stricken with *gakiyami*.*

* This dreadful and mysterious disease of mediaeval Nippon is unidentified.

Koshirō had gone to the village with his little shells to be filled with salve. On returning he found the inn full of strangers ; samurai and servants in attendance on the occupants of two litters standing before the inn. Great was the running to and fro, the bearing of dishes of fish and flasks of *saké*. Koshirō determined to know who these great lords were. With no great difficulty he found the room set apart for the banquet. It looked out on an inner garden (*naka-niwa*) curiously decorated with pond and rockwork, lanterns, pine, maki, and bitter orange. It was an epitome of minute elegance in landscape gardening. Koshirō gently fingered a hole in the *shōji* and looked within. Hatena ! The man seated was Isshiki Akihide, idly fingering a scroll and from time to time looking into the garden. The enemy in this place ; her ladyship must know at once. But Terute was to find out in another way. Yokoyama Shōgen was not unblest with curiosity. Stopping in company with Akihide he was not long in learning of the case of *gakiyami* living at the inn. A man sick with *gakiyami* he had never seen. The disease was said to be one of the punishments of hell. Unkei had been favoured with the sight of the frowning face of Emma-Ō. He, Shōgen, now had an opportunity to witness this rare punishment of the nether world. Slipping into *niwa-geta* (garden clogs) he advanced down the garden to the *koya* at the bottom. Now there was little likelihood that he would have recognized Sukeshige. But as he came close up to the *rōka* Terute raised her head. Shōgen was at startled as Terute. "Umu ! Evidently she has been stolen by "thieves and carried off at the time of the fire at the Kaizōji. Again "she is in Shōgen's hands. Plainly the oldish man referred to by "the innkeeper is the thief, travelling the country with a beautiful "woman and a monster in the shape of the *gakiyami byōnin* (sick "man) ; thus making a living on the idle lust and curiosity of the "vulgar." He would reclaim his property, punish these rascals. Leaping forward he seized Terute by the wrists and dragged her into the garden. "Ah, you jade ! This is the return for the kindness,

---

It is not *raibyō*, or leprosy, familiar enough. The *gaki* refers to the inmates of the hell of hunger : *yami*—sickness. Hence the terrible nature of the affliction, and its supposed divine origin. Sukeshige's case is classic.

"the years of tender care. First you lavish caresses on the worth-
"less Kojirō. Now you travel the country with these mounte-
"banks. Surely such taste is most depraved. But you shall feel
"the wrath of Shōgen. As for this pimp and his monster, they
"shall die under the blows of the *rōtō*."

With a wrench Terute freed herself. Scowling she faced Shōgen. "Wicked man! For the tender care of early years gratitude
"would be owing, if such care was not the result of vilest purposes.
"Know, Tarō Dono, that this Terute is well informed as to all the
"past evil deeds. From the dying lips of Dosuke, cast out as food
"to Onikage, was ascertained the fate of Satake Atsumitsu, murder-
"ed by his brother Tarō. The *kami* have delivered this villain into
"the hands of Terute. My father is to be avenged." Drawing her
dagger from her bosom she made a quick pass at Shōgen. She was
a woman. Her weapon was for herself. Small was her skill in
other use. Shōgen laughed. Then frowning he looked her over.
"So to the ears of Terute has come the tale of Dosuke. This Tarō
"does not pretend to deny its truth. In his vengeance he glories,
"in the fall of the Satake House. Your own person is but object to
"further his ambitions. Once the fiefs restored Terute would have
"trod the road to Yomi (Hades). This Tarō killed Atsumitsu, he
"who jeered at his lack of skill before the Oguri, and put him to
"shame. Sukeshige has met his death in the hot pool of Sokokura
"........Or perchance this shapeless mass is the man himself.
"Knowing the secret of Atsumitsu's fate, vowed to avenge his death,
"this Terute shall die. But first the truth is to be confessed as to
"this fellow."

Leaping on her he seized and threw her to the ground. Then
he proceeded to torture her ; to compress her flesh, twist every sen-
sitive joint, press on every exposed nerve. Grimly Terute struggled
in silence. Of the *gakiyami*, the man stricken with *gōbyō*, punished
by the gods themselves, men had superstitious fear. For all Yokoyama's bragging, unrecognized her lord was safe. Then a powerful
hand seized Shōgen, drew him backward, and cast him heavily to
the ground. Koshirō stood between his lady and the assailant.
Said Terute—"Seize him Koshirō. His life belongs to Terute. This

"is Yokoyama Yasuhide, murderer of Satake Atsumitsu. Terute is "now to satisfy the spirit of the lord of the Satake House." Koshirō had not suspected the presence of Yokoyama. Had not his lord met him not long since, bound toward Suruga and in the Hakone hills! He took him to be some aging libertine, attracted by a pretty woman, and emboldened by the presence of a helpless invalid as the only defence. His guard was lax. Yokoyama was not slow to wriggle to his feet. He ran down the garden shouting for aid. It was an easy matter for Koshirō to overtake and cut him down, but the *bushi* grasped the situation. Said he to Terute—"This fellow "is with Isshiki Akihide. Their *rōtō* swarm in the house. My "lord is helpless. Taking him on her back may her ladyship deign "to escape to the moor at the rear. Koshirō will put up a defensive "battle." There was no time for discussion. Terute shouldered the helpless Sukeshige and ran away at the back gate into the moor. Koshirō prepared to defend the cottage. The enemy soon appeared. He stood forth—"Mito no Tamehira, *rōtō* of Oguri Kojirō "Sukeshige, presents himself. Come to meet the vile sycophants "and slanderers, Isshiki Akihide and Yokoyama Tarō, this Koshirō "represents his lord in battle. Cowards, advance and test the edge "of his sword!" Isshiki was brave for other people. A second time this fellow faced him. In wrath he ordered his retainers to cut down this man without support. "Bind the beggar, the man with "*gakiyami*; seize the woman!" The *rōtō* swarmed to the attack from all the eight sides of space. With gleeful shout Koshirō met them in the fight. Brightly gleamed the long sword as it swept the space before him. Great was the execution performed in his lord's name. Sukeshige himself at his best could hardly have done better. Five men lay dead. Others retired to nurse their wounds. Akihide fumed. Koshirō stood defiant. Then the cowardly and cooler headed Yokoyama strung his bow at short range behind the *rōtō*. Straight went the arrow to the defenceless breast of Koshirō. For a moment his arms spread wide. Then he tumbled in a heap. Thus died the brave knight in defence of lord and lady.

His head secured the little house was ransacked. Not a sign of woman or sick man. Said Yokoyama—"The man is helpless. On

"a woman's legs the pair have not gone far. At once to the chase.
"Bring back their heads." Off dashed the retainers, to scatter over
the moor in different directions. Terute had not gone far ; perhaps
five *chō*, not half a mile. Then her strength gave out. Helpless
she gazed over the waving grass of the moorland. The clump of
woodland was for her still distant. Besides, concealment in such
place there was none. The noise at the inn already could be heard.
Pursuit would follow. She wrung her hands in despair. Great
tears welled from her eyes. From grief she could not see. A voice
addressed her—" A woman and a sick man ! These doubtless are
" the objects of the chase of these fellows. Brave game ! " Terute
with her burden was crouched at the feet of a tall priest, a man
with strong, resolved and rugged face, of commanding presence. A
train of monks and *hōshi-musha* (priest soldiers) attended him.
Sturdy fellows stood silent beside the litter the *ōshō* had abandoned.
Up swarmed the *rōtō* of Yokoyama and Isshiki. Said the priest
severely—"What means this uproar ! Does your lord mean to
" attack the train of the *Ajari* of Kofukuzan. Look to it that un-
"favourable report of this conduct be not made to Prince Mochiuji."
The leaders were all apology. An attack on the reverend bishop
and his train was not dreamed of. They were in search of some
beggars, who had just caused a disturbance at the inn. It was suspected that they had passed this way. Said the priest coldly—
" All here are under the protection of the Ajari of Kenchōji, in his
" train. As your business is not with him get you hence and back
" to your lord. The apology is accepted." Disgruntled the fellows
could only withdraw. . Profound was the obeisance, deep was the
regret. The powerful Ajari of Kenchōji, favoured by Prince Mochiuji, was not to be trifled with. Had not the prince with his own
train fought the great fire of Ōei 21st year (1414) ? Insolent as they
were not even the *rōtō* of Isshiki dared to make further question.

The priest fingered his rosary of rock crystal beads. " The
" Ajari follows the Way of the Buddha. The Five Rules
" (*vs*-murder, theft, adultery, lying, intemperance) are to be observ-
" ed by his priests. As attached to his train this man and
" woman are to be aided. Thus no lie is involved." In low

tones he spoke to his disciples. Scattered words—" Oguri,"
" Joa Shōnin," " Isshiki Dono," " Satake " could be gathered. Wondering whispers arose. Terute felt herself the object
of pitying curiosity. The Ajari approached the sick man—" *Gaki-*
" *yami,* the result of offence committed in a previous existence
" (*gōbyō*) ! Truly lady the cure is difficult. Whither do you go? "
With tears Terute told her tale; the experience in the pass of
Hakone, the hard struggle to reach Yūki town, the meeting with
Yokoyama and Isshiki. Said the Ajari—" To go to Yūki would be
" rushing into the midst of the foe. Already having trodden on the
" tiger's tail has the escape been most fortunate. Besides no cure
" for this ill is to be found at Yūki. The outer body can be aided.
" Make infusion of the root of the *mokui,* a tea of its bark. Thus
" the flow of pus can be stopped, the sores dried. Washing is useless.
" It is only at the shrine of the Kumano Gongen that petition is to
" be made ; only in the healing waters of the Yakushi Nyōrai of
" Yunomine that the divine aid and a complete cure ensured. Deign
" to make the journey to Kii province. Recovery is certain." At
the joyful thanks and acquiescence of Terute—" Get the beggar's
" cart just passed on the road. Gladly will this fellow exchange
" garments. In such garb the journey is to be made ; the husband,
" drawn by the faithful wife over mountain and through dale, to
" find health." The *hinin* (outcasts) were soon found. The waggon,
a box mounted on wheels cut from a board, was confiscated. The
rags of the mendicant and his aid were exchanged for the garments
of the lord and lady. A rope was attached to the rude cart. Then
the Ajari asked for *suzuri* and *fude* (ink and brush). A placard
was made of a wooden stave. On it he wrote :

> " Anyone pulling this waggon, once shows filial
> " piety to ancestors, twice shows it to parents,
> " thrice secures loyal service from descendents.
> " You who aid in drawing this cart will secure
> " *bukkwa* (release from human existence). Yo!
>   " Kofukuzan Kenchōji
> "Oei 32th year 3rd month 23rd day (11th April 1425)
>   " Ajari (Seal)."

Prostrate in tears before the bishop Terute gave grateful thanks. Joy at the assured result made the terrible journey and task seem small. Thus she remained long after the prelate's train had passed from view. Then rising from the dust she grasped the rope. Thus began the long travail known as "the pulling of the *gakiyami-kuruma.*"*

---

* Yakushi is the saving member of the Buddhist Trinity; Dainichi, the Word; Amida the Eternal Buddha in Heaven. The first two are manifestations of Amida. It is a doctrine of Northern Buddhism—cf Eitel "Handbook of Chinese Buddhism"—Trikaya and Triratna.

CHAPTER XVIII.

The Epic of Terute-hime.

These events took place now nearly five hundred years ago. Tradition has only preserved in fragments the record of this journey of the five hundred miles over which a frail woman, sustained by faith, clung close to and accomplished an almost impossible task. Miracle has touched the case. In priestly record three days brought Terute and Sukeshige to the healing waters of the Yunomine Yakushi Nyōrai. The sober sense of chronicle notes the leaves of early summer on the trees, the signs of approaching spring at the journey's end. The affection and respect of an aging people have preserved the deed, the woman's name, as example to the succeeding generations.

The *gakiyami-kuruma* is first heard of at Itabashi on the Nakasendo.* Though passing through the central mountain district of Nippon the route offered advantages. The great rivers flooding the sea plain were more formidable barriers to the path of Terute than the steep passes of the mountain ranges. Besides, if there was the dragging up on one side, there was the descent on the other side. The approach of the vehicle always caused excitement. At its first appearance—" Aiya! Aiya! What comes here? Look Kamajirō! " What is it? He looks like *temmondō* (asparagus preserved in " sugar) "—" Iya! Rather Binzuru Sama. See how black is his face, " how white his hair. And the woman is a beauty. What a pity she is " a *hinin* (outcast)." Thus spoke a second man. As they came nearer said a third—" Nesan! Nesan! What is that in the cart? Is it human

---

* Now a suburb north west of Tōkyō; therefore close to Ichimenhara. But to reach the Nakasendō from Kotesashibara the North road to Itabashi would also naturally be followed; not cross country.

" or a wooden image? Brother, or uncle, or husband?" Answered
Terute—" We seek the healing aid of the Kumano Gongen. It is
" my husband. Suffering from *gakiyami* the Gongen alone can
" grant their aid. Hear our petition; deign not to detain the sick
" man." Standing by they read the placard on the cart " Ah!
" What a meritorious deed! What a faithful wife, thus painfully to
" drag the sick man along the mountain road! See Tarōzaemon,
" Tarōbe, Kyōzaemon; he who pulls once shows filial piety; thrice
" one gains a seat on a lotus. To work Tarōbe! To work Kyōzae-
" mon! Thus merit and entrance to the paradise of Amida is
" assured." Replacing Terute on the rope many a farmer lent his
aid to the task. Progress varied. On some days Terute advanced
barely the fraction of a *ri* (2½ miles) on her journey. Other days
several *ri* were placed to the credit of the accomplishment of the
task. Always she had little difficulty in seeing the starting place of
her day's journey from the resting place at its end. In the dusk
of a fall day Aohaka in Mino was reached. The first great obstruction of the Nakasendō hills was safely left behind, yet great fear and
oppression was on Terute's soul as she approached the place. To
pass in the night was dangerous. The curiosity and attention of
the *yakunin* would be aroused. Such as she and her charge courted
publicity and charity. To pass in the day she feared recognition.
Fortunately there was none. In beggar's rags, face smeared with
the mud of the road and streaked with sweat, concealed by the
deep straw hat, Terute was almost as unrecognizable as Sukeshige
himself. The condition of this latter was frightful. Sightless, deaf
to all sound, dumb to all speech, the unsightly flesh mummified in
some places, dropping off in others, all turned from too close inspection of such an object; nor would it have made any difference.

In the growing darkness the inn of Manchō was already ablaze
with light. Manchō himself was not to be seen. The worthy cit,
in the interior of his house, brooded over the loss of his beloved
child. Was it a first vengeance for ill treatment of the noble dame?
Ah! Why had he not put her to death before all this discovery?
At night he would start up in fright, thinking he heard the crash of
breaking wood, the cries of people in death agony, the smoke of

conflagration, the triumphant shouts of the fierce Oguri *rōtō* seeking out this Manchō for punishment. His lot was most miserable between his own fears and the savage hazing to which O'Nagi subjected him, as responsible for all the disaster, past and overhanging. Not so that of his women. With Mankei and the men attendants they thronged the front to watch the *gakiyami-kuruma* pass. The native scribe jests at their expense. Robbing their patrons they made compensation by pulling the *kuruma* through their part of the town. Said one—" Kanjirō, wheedled of his cash by my " guile, robbed travellers. His head now adorns the execution " ground. Thus penance is done for my part of the deed. I am " secure of *bukkwa*." Said another—" Chōyemon San murdered " his father to secure his farms and pay his debt to Manchō. It " was in my lap he rested his head. Thus I avert the ill-will of the " dead from myself." Such was their comment. Terute shivered. Did not such aid curse rather than assist the journey ?

Such were the misgivings, the discouragements, which began to crowd upon her as the physical strain and wretchedness more and more did its work, the material breaking down and overcoming the strength of the moral. More than once the mighty precipices of the mountain road offered a facile ending to the task, relief from present suffering. Now the deep and shining waters of Biwa-ko, the swift river flowing from it, offered the temptation. Terute resolutely put such thoughts behind. Death did not end all. It but meant separation from her lord, the unconscious wandering of aeons. Not in such way could both attain the paradise of Amida. The idea of the loneliness through time overpowered her. As yet she was strong enough ; but it was with a sigh that she turned from the swift waters of the Setagawa and again set at the task. Thus did the weeks and months pass. Spring had turned to Summer ; Summer to Fall. It was the end of the eleventh month (the present December and beginning of January). Worn almost to a shadow, hope drooping at last before the task of growing magnitude, at dusk Terute dragged her charge into Ōsaka town. The ground snow covered the flakes again began to fall fast. Ōsaka was then a very different place from the great and busy mart of the days of Iyeyasu.

Its renown was due to its temples, especially to the great Tennōji. It was part of this holy shore of Izumi and Settsu. The village was the Tennōji and its dependents, and little else beyond the importance of the watch and ward over the river approach by the Yodogawa to Kyōto. Terute advanced along the Teramachi, pulling with difficulty the little cart. The long cold white walls of the monasteries seemed as heartless as the falling flakes, piling up the snow which clogged the wheels of the clumsy conveyance. There was not a house at which to make inquiries in this ecclesiastical section of the village. To get an idea of such a place in these days one must go to Kōyasan, one of the two or three, and the most perfect, of the remaining old mediaeval monastery towns of Nippon. Here a little cluster of shops devoted to the sale of pilgrims' necessities and holy souvenirs is segregated in the midst. On all sides, extending to great distances, are the walled-in hundred monasteries with their thousands of monks living on the great endowments of past benevolence and piety; living, teaching, preaching well, to all appearances, according to the light afforded them.

At the great gate of the Anneiji, Terute could go no further. Pulling the *kuruma* into the shelter of the gate she sought to warm her frozen fingers, to collect her ideas half dazed with starvation and exhaustion. The numbing sleep in this storm and cold now seemed pleasant to this Terute. She came and knelt in the snow beside her dear charge. Brain whirling, giddy, she hid her face in the robe of Sukeshige. Then a sound of riot brought her to her feet. Along the road came laughing and shouting a band of beggars, riff-raff gathered from this mercurial western country, living on their wits and what fear could extort from the farmers on their established beaten route. They were discussing one of their chiefs, to whom they rendered a fearful obedience such as the Shōgun could not hope to secure from the most servile vassal. "The chief has buried his wife to-day. The dwell-"ing in the Kogarashi wood will be lonely. Surely he will not be "in a good humour." Said a second—"Koya San is a sturdy "fellow for his years. Another will soon be secured, of that there is "no fear. Nor will she have a bad situation. From Kyūshū, he

" is said to have been in former days a samurai. Probably he has
" committed some grave offence, thus to hide his identity under the
" guise of a beggar "—" Shut up! Perhaps he seeks occasion for
" vengeance. It is not safe to discuss the chief's affairs. These
" walls have ears." Said a fourth—" As for the woman she seems to
" be at hand. What a beauty! And in beggar's garb; she has no
" one to protect her, and comes under our law. Here is our wel-
" come from the chief." Said the first man—" But who is in the
" cart?" They approached to inspect these poachers on their pre-
serves. " Nesan, who is this man? Or rather what is this thing?
" It seems made out of sweet flavoured bean paste.* Is it human,
" husband or brother?" To Terute's answer—" How pitiable!
" You have no passports from the beggars' chief? But even beggars
" have bowels of compassion. In the wood at Kogarashi is a roar-
" ing fire and good shelter. There you shall be warmed and re-
" stored to life with a good banquet. Surely you shall have our aid."
He winked at his companions. " What a fine girl! Never should
" she be left with this rotten punk......Come nesan! Fortunately
" our chief is wifeless. You present yourself in the nick of time.
" This fellow is half dead already. The cold will finish him."

Rushing on the pair the *kuruma* and its contents were kicked
over into the deep snow. Terute was seized by vigorous arms and
carried off down the road, crying for an aid which only the cold
monastic walls answered. With their progress to the wood was
heard the sound of a bell. In the road appeared an old priest. He
wore a grey kimono heavily wadded for winter use, was ringing his
bell, and chanting his prayer. " Namu Amida Butsu! Namu
" Amida Butsu!" Deliberately he barred the way. Said the leader
in anger—" What does this old Kwannenbutsu Bōzu (meditating
" priest) mean, thus to obstruct us. Out of the way, grey beard!
" Women are no concern of yours. Attend to your prayers. Be
" satisfied with being allowed to live, and do not attempt a foolish
" and abortive interference." The priest frowned—" Rascals! It
" is for Sainen to aid the unhappy. You are carrying off this woman
" to divert yourselves with her. Abandon such evil intention. Let

---

* *Nattō no naka no shōga* (Momogawa). Bean paste with ginger.

Terute meets the Beggars of Ōsaka.

" the woman go free." But the scoundrels laughed at him. With
their staves they sought to drive him off. He was of extraordinary
strength and agility. They were soon forced to drop their burden
and take to their own defence. In this too they were children
and the priest an adept. His heavy cane basted their cascasses as
if pounding *mochi* (rice paste). They cried out in protest. Unable
to stand before his blows the band fled in terror. " Aiya ! Watsu !
" Moshi ! Moshi ! (I say ! I say !) Was ever such a priest met
" before ! " In disorder they scampered to the eight sides of space.

The rescuer approached Terute, weeping and cowering behind
a tree close by. Said he—" Nesan, fear not. But how comes it
" that you are without shelter in the storm at this hour ? " Terute
explained her journey, the sick husband left in the snow at the
temple gate. Said the priest—" Haste must be made. The cold
" is intense. There is danger of freezing......Ah ! Have no fear
" Nesan. The man you call husband has suffered no injury.
" What an affliction ! How pitiable ! But shelter must be sought
" somewhere." Knocking at the gate he sought entrance to the
Anneiji. On making report to the temple the priests were indignant. " These fellows at the Kogarashi wood are getting very bold.
" If the *machi-bugyō* does nothing the temples will have to act,
" although outside their precincts. Pilgrims are greatly disturbed and
" fear to come. The cash box suffers. Be sure that if the disturb-
" ance had been heard, aid would have been rendered." The
*shoke** at once issued forth. Many were the expressions of pity.
Much was the Yunomine Tōkwōji to be congratulated on securing
such a notable case. Would the sacred waters once more score a
miraculous success ? Terute and Sukeshige were brought within the
gate. Indicating a shed within which the woman and her beggar
could be lodged food and covering were sent out from the temple.
The priest Sainen established himself as nurse. As he cooked the
rice gruel the old man overflowed in kindly talk. " Don't be sad,
" nesan. Surely the healing waters of the god will prove trium-
" phant even over *gōbyō*. A terrible disease ! It is said to be a
" punishment for offence committed in an existence of which the

---

* Lowest order of Buddhist priests.

The Kwannenbutsu-bōzu rescues Terute.

"sufferer has no remembrance. But great is the efficacy of the "Buddha. Chastity and faith find their reward from the gods. "But where do you come from? Accent says the North. You "talk a little through your honourable nose. This Sainen too comes "from the Kwantō, though much has he wandered in these parts "in former years."

Said Terute—"I am from Ōta in Hitachi; my husband from "near Yūki. Deep is the reverential thanks for your kindness. "Honest reply is to be made for such unexpected aid. But we are "beggars." The priest eyed her with great attention. His eye sparkled, then dulled. He hesitated. Finally with a sigh he said— "Yes, much has Sainen wandered in these parts on hopeless search. "As beggars you see many provinces. Even from such people tid- "ings can be gleaned. Pray answer me truly. At first this "Sainen hoped that his mission had found its end. In face and "figure there is something strangely familiar. I too am from Ōta "in Hitachi. In years past my lord, Satake Atsumitsu, was mur- "dered foully by his brother Yokoyama Tarō. This was later "learned from one Dosuke, a *rōtō* who witnessed the deed and was "too cowardly to aid his lord. In bringing wife and daughter to "Hitachi her ladyship died at the hand of thieves. The Terutehime "was carried off. Since that time this Sainen has wandered from "province to province, waiting the time of vengeance, seeking his "lady. From Ōta surely you have heard of these deeds, now "freely whispered among the people. With Mito no Kosuke of "late Sainen lived at Mutsuura Ryōshimachi. News of her ladyship "was there learned. But misfortune carried her beyond reach. "Thus once more the priest set forth on his travels. What answer "is to be made? This Sainen is Gotō Makabe Genzaemon, in "younger days the *karō* of the Satake House."

Terute wept bitterly. The priest gently touched her arm as if to urge reply. Said she—"How say it in this garb? This beggar "woman is Terute, daughter of the Daimyō of Ōta in Hitachi, Satake "Atsumitsu. The eyes of Genzaemon have seen the truth. See!" She drew from her bosom the Kwannon of her charm bag, the scrolls of the Satake House, and placed them in the hand of Genzaemon.

The old man rose. Retiring to the farther wall he prostrated himself, his face on his hands. Pain and joy struggled with tears in his voice. "Ah! To meet her ladyship under such conditions. Truly Heaven "has been kind to this Genzaemon to bring him to her aid. Then "the honoured lord......?" He did not dare to finish. Said Terute simply—"Yes, this is Oguri Dono." Said Genzaemon— "But there is life! Genzaemon is here to carry him to the healing "waters of Yunomine. Assuredly the cure will be complete. The "wrongs of Satake and Oguri shall be avenged by the hand of his "lordship; the restoration of the two Houses secured." With triumph the old man rose to full height, his eyes sparkling with excitement. Then as if ashamed at this lack of control he gently made obeisance and apology to his lady. Terute smiled through her tears, and the old man raised the edge of her robe to his lips.

But 'twas no natural rôle. Sainen had carried the infant in his arms, the heir born to the House in Atsumitsu's older years. With head resting on his knee Terute told the halting tale of suffering through these years. Gently the priest with hand and voice soothed the woman, as years before he had soothed the infant; but at times his face was hard and stern; sternest when voice was most soothing. Sainen mentally was checking off the names, fit subjects for later vengeance. Then between lady and *rōtō* followed earnest consultation. Genzaemon counselled much needed rest, not too prolonged for the season was advancing, and spring in the mountains was more dangerous than the storms of winter. Perhaps much of the journey could be made by sea. Terute acquiesced. Thus for a single turn (seven days) they received the shelter of the Anneiji. Setting forth they took their way southward over the plain toward the mountains; to follow the sea route if possible, the coast if boat could not be secured. Such was the plan. Under the guidance of Genzaemon the strength of Terute was renewed. Alas! Their evil fate hung over them. On the plain of Shimoda in Izumi storm again overtook them. Shelter was distant, the falling snow so thick as to make objects almost indistinguishable. Even Genzaemon did not know where he was. They feared to move in a circle. Thus little progress was made for hours. They only walked enough to keep from freezing, in constant terror for the sick man. Toward dusk the storm ceased, the air cleared a little. Genzaemon gave an exultant shout. " Ah ! " That smoke ! Your ladyship, Koyasu sends up the notice of its " presence. Though still at some distance with earnest effort it can " be reached before night." With energy he dragged at the cart. Terute lent such aid as she could. Suddenly Genzaemon gave a sharp cry. The old man staggered, then had to seat himself in the snow. Aghast Terute hastened to him. At her alarm he said— " Nay ! It is nothing. Genzaemon is old. In his haste his foot " has run up against a root hidden by the snow. The toe nails are " turned back, the foot is torn. In younger days Genzaemon " feared neither exposure or wound. Now at seventy years he is " useless. Alas ! I can go no further. But to stay here is death " for his lordship. Deign to make every effort. The first house to " be reached is a wayside inn, the Takasagoya. The people are " kindly. They will give every aid at the name of Sainen."

Nothing else could be done. Taking the rope Terute set out for the distant village. At first at every stop the lady called out—" Genzaemon ! " The retainer answered—" Hime- " gimi ! Be confident ; seek aid for his lordship ! " Soon the answer became faint—only the " *himegimi* " reached the ears of Terute. Alas ! The distance was great for her strength. Night had long come before the shelter of the Takasagoya was reached. Here host and wife, seated before the brazier and drinking the heated *doburoku*,* were making merry over their security from the storm. With wonder they heard the call for aid. The old man exclaimed at the sight of the beautiful woman, the hideously deformed beggar. But the hearts of man and woman were kind. With his own hands *ojisan* drew the cart under the shed, carried Sukeshige to the fire. Terute disregarded his little facetiæ. As he eyed his burden curiously he asked—" What have you here, nesan ? Deign to say. He looks " like a fur seal, his face thus drawn up and black like the face of

---

* *Momorizaké—saké* with rice grains still in it ; Momogawa, here closely followed.

" a dog." The old woman rebuked him severely—" Ojisan has a
" filthy tongue. Deign not to notice him. He is only joking. All
" know his kindness of heart." And Ojisan was all repentance.
Warming *saké* he attended to the sick man's needs. Then he
turned to Terute for her story. At the name of Sainen he
wondered—" Again he has come to these parts? Ten years back
" his name was well known in Koyasu. The war of Yoshihiro
" was still fresh 'in men's minds, the country desolate. Under the
" command of Sainen the young men rid the district of its many
" thieves. All feared the fighting Kwannenbutsu. ' Truly he was
" a Buddha come among sinful men.' But how comes he in such
" company?" Doubtfully he surveyed Terute and the helpless
sick man, mere beggars shunned even by priests. Said Terute—
" The relation is that of retainer." The old man eyed her with
terror and edged away. Thought he—" Sainen in former days
" was a samurai. As retainer of this lady she must be the wife of
" some great daimyō. And this man? What sort of people is the
" Takasagoya sheltering?" It was for such as he to act with all
circumspection; not to interfere in such weighty matters, but pass
these people on as quick as possible.

A sharp gust, the howl of the renewed storm, shook the
amado. Ojisan sprang to his feet. " What is this old fool about!
" Here is Sainen Sama thus exposed. The mountains swarm with
" wolves. Helpless he will be eaten. Aid is to be summoned."
Going to the door he blew his bamboo trumpet. In a short time
lanterns carried by the young men of the village were seen hastening toward the Takasagoya. Said the Ojisan—" Sainen the Kwan-
" nenbutsu Bōzu is again in the district. Lost on the moor these
" people have come to bring notice. Rescue is to be given at once.
" All are indebted to the Kwannenbutsu." With torches and under
the guidance of Terute they set forth. The drifting snow had
almost obliterated the tracks of the *kuruma,* but she recognized a
tree standing close by the scene of the disaster. Hastening to it a
sad sight met the eye. Sainen lay doubled up, cold and stiff, frozen
to death. At least so it seemed. Delay was not permissible.
Placed on the back of one strong young man, then of another,

great haste was made back to the Takasagoya with the body of the priest. But the aid came too late. Every effort to resuscitate him was vain. Then the village gave him public burial, opportunity for the untimely courtship of one Kantarō. " He was but twenty-eight years old, with only an old father in the house, and he nearly dead. Dress, hair ornaments, food without limit " ; these were the bribes offered the beautiful beggar to desert this shapeless log she called her husband. Up spoke one Chōsokabe—" Cease this impertinent " and unseemly courtship, Kantarō San. The anger of the Kwan-" nenbutsu Bōzu, of his spirit, is not to be brought on the village. " These people are under his protection." Chōsokabe was the great man of the place. He could rebuke the rich and stingy Kantarō. All fell on the latter tooth and nail. Abashed he sought refuge in the darkest corner.

The *nembutsu* (prayer service) said, with her own hand Teru-te planted a pine over the grave of the faithful Makabe Genzaemon. Why raise dispute as to which route the *gakiyami kuruma* took to reach the Gongen Shrines? If the water soaked land with its broad streams at the head of Owari Bay, if the steep and savage hills of Ise and Iga, if the known route of mediaeval Nippon through Yamato or by the western coast, does not settle the question, let the opinion of the native scribe be followed when he says— " Has not tradition in these landmarks shown the course? The ' Terute Matsu ' (Terute's pine tree) of Koyasu still stands. Why be sceptical? " For ten days she rested at the Takasagoya, tenderly and reverently nursed by the humble couple. Prostrate the old man and old woman served her, prostrate bade her farewell. Then Ojisan resumed the rôle of *teishu*, himself headed the young men who hauled the *gakiyami kuruma* to the bounds of their district. All this was done in the name of the powerful Ajari of Kenchōji, but many a curious eye later was cast on the newly planted tree, many a hand devoted to its care. With tears Terute said farewell to the honest villagers. For days she had the gift of supply of food, such as could be carried. But what of these terrible hills lowering in the front ; for with the death of Genzaemon all thought of sea journey, the intrusting of herself and the sick man to the rough mercies of the half pirates of these waters, had to be abandoned. Besides, had not the *kuruma* been selected by divine command? Could it be abandoned? Ojisan strongly counselled the mountains, not the coast road. On the former many priests and court nobles travelled. The people were kindly in their way of mountaineers. On the coast they were a violent and evil set. "Deign lady to make your " way between Kōyasan and the mountains of Yoshino. The road " lies through Yamato, down the waters of the Totsugawa, the " ' Otonashigawa'; thus a safer, if a harder way, is found."

How did the frail woman win through the terrors of these mountains? How did she ever reach them? This rather is the question to be asked. And with such charge! The words of a poor peasant rang in the ears of Terute, comment as they passed— " Poverty is no better than the four hundred and four diseases (all " known); but poverty is vastly better than the *gakiyami*." The first month of the thirty-third year of Ōei (8th February–10 March 1426) had reached its close. In this warmer province of Kii the snows of harsher Yamato had turned into the tender buds of the surrounding forest. The river flowed merrily and easily through its lofty wooded hills, smiling under the flood of spring sunlight, and tossing back their reflection in its quiet reaches;

" Sengyokuzan (the Mountain of the Jewel Boat):
" Dai Gongen's dozen shrines;
" The jewel boat, below Dai Gongen flowing;
" The Otonashigawa."

This name the natives gave it, Peaceful River; but the great stream could be very terrible in its anger, sweeping away the work of these human bees, nay even the home of the gods themselves in its angry moods, as if they were built of straw—this Totsugawa. At its junction with the Tanigawa a bridge had been thrown across the waters here narrowed by the close proximity of the hills.* Terute approached it with confidence. Alas! The hearts of men were as hard as the rocks of these defiles. For a *chōmoku* she could pass with her burden. With the gods these farmers shared exactly the

---

* The Tanigawa is a tributary of the Totsugawa, coming in on the west side about four or five *ri* (10-12 miles) above Hongū town.

revenue of the bridge. Not a "cash" was abstracted. But too many beggars did they see, haunting the shrines of the gods to pilfer the cash of the honest peasant, to rob him if he slept carelessly by the wayside. Thus the little woman patiently remained crouched near the entrance to the bridge, waiting the propitious moment. Not hours but days passed. From time to time food was cast into their bowl. Of the needed "cash," not a sign. The pilgrims too knew and discouraged beggars. Coming, they were too near the divine aid to pay heed to the placard. Going, they were too holy to need the merit of such cheap charity. But fortune favoured. A drunken fellow, washed of his sin and lechery, came singing across the bridge. "Nesan, what pity you are of the "beggar caste. This Heihachirō would gladly take you in his "company." With contempt he cast a handful of "cash" into the bowl, and hiccoughing his song passed on in mouldy generosity. Terute rose, more than half inclined to throw the coin after him or into the river. Then in bitterness she approached the shrine erected close by the bridge. Witness of the tipsy man's extravagance the hard peasants commented on the luck of the pretty beggar girl and her hideous charge. With amazement they saw the "cash" go flying into the grated box standing before the shrine to receive the offerings of the devout. With the single necessary *mon* Terute approached the bridge and offered it for passage. For the first time the placard might have read its message to these men seared by toil and the hard hand of authority ; that these were no ordinary pilgrims on their way to Yunomine's healing waters, to the shrine of the messenger god, the Yakushi Nyōrai of Amida. But not even fear inspired a man to come forward, to haul cart and beggar a trifle on the way to Hongū town. Said Terute—" Are all men demons ? Does the beggar's guise " despoil of all sympathy ?"

     " With haste let us on to the shrines of the gods,
     " The holy ones of Kumano Hongū,
     " Healing waters of Yunomine, goal of desire ;
     " Conveyed by my wife
     " To the cure of the illness.

" Oh sound, joyful and fortunate !

" Health soon as restored,

" The head of the foe is witness to men.

" Courageous the well named noble dame.*

" Dishevelled to sight my hair.

" Iza ! Draw near and view the passage.

" Lo! The shadows of Takagiyama,

" The clouds reflected in the waters.

" Our lord shall hear truth,

" The loyalty of the honoured sire,

" The slanderers shall be destroyed.

" The Sansha Gongen of Hongū,

" The most merciful Kwannon of Nachi,

" These exact a vow

" Not vainly of Sukeshige.

" Sick, like unto a dead tree,

" Deign to make me flower again.

" Deign that for me too,

" The spring again appears.

" Prostrate in worship

" Nought more is asked.

" Quickly on to the healing Yakushi.

" The softness of spring is at hand,

" In balmy eve and shining stars.

" Draw, draw on the litter.

" The hills rise up before us.

" Thought touches me—

" To pillow of traveller, guard there is none,

" Object of pity in the ancient poems.

" Lo! The camphor tree of the forest ;

" Multitudinous its thousand buds.

" Thought goes to men of the past ;

" With my affairs none are concerned,

---

* Terute (照天) means "Shining Heaven." Routes differ, so the above
suffers some adaptation—from Matsubayashi. Terute is also written 照手 ;
and she is called Teru 照 and Terujō 照女.

" At odds with the world.
" Thus is reached this Kii no Kuni,
" The soundless village (*otonashi*) of men.
" Before lies the Oyubara
" The healing spring of ancient Yu-mune (Yunomine),
" Sacred gift to men of Rurikwō (Yakushi),
" Granted to the prayer of Kōgyō Daishi.
" The journey draws to its end.
" Many the days slipped past,
" As little by little, with tardy foot,
" The waggon is dragged along.
" The spring in the hills,
" High towering before,
" An effort ; the journey is ended."

How comes it that in the flush of effort, not unsuccessful, the spring of energy so often suddenly suffers collapse? Physical strength when tensest seems struck as by a paralysis, much as when the strongest swimmer, cramp seized, sinks helpless beneath the flood. In the moral world the same collapse is seen, this giving way of fibre is openly instanced. The man, strong of mind and intent on purpose, deadly earnest in its pursuit, turns his back on men and things which suddenly have lost to him all savour ; or struck by mental blindness misses the straight line of his purpose, blunders feebly, and loses the game which to all else is already won. At times the physical dominates the mental. The strong brain whirls, the helpless moment has come, and the watchful foe has snatched victory from defeat. Mental or physical, for the great majority of men and women exertion of power cannot be both tense and too prolonged. The crowning effort cannot be materialized, and failure all the more pronounced ensues.

With her heavy burden Terute crept into Hongū town. There was despair not triumph in her heart. The well spring of action was exhausted. Discouragement held sway. Never was aid more needed than at this stage of the journey, but she had learned how pitiless could be the men frequenting these holy places. Were the gods of equal stoniness? They were the last resource. Mankind had failed her at the crisis ; showed opposition, not encouragement. In the twilight she crossed the sacred bridge over the Otonashi-gawa, the small and sometimes turbulent stream whose name the greater river has robbed in the mouths of the peasantry. Resplendent was the home of the *kami* enshrined on its island covered by dark pines and cryptomeria. In a vast enclosure, raised on a stone-girdled dais amid the dark forest, stood the magnificent shrines of the gods looking out on the darkening waters of the river swiftly flowing round the bend, on the hills still lighted by the departing sun. Thus Terute and Sukeshige spent their night ; the lady kneeling in prayer, for she had nothing else to offer. With dawn she set out for Yunomine.

All strength had gone from her. For hours she had not tasted food ; had none to give her burden. Painfully she dragged at the little cart, surmounting these last long steep slopes, through the interminable forest. For a time she looked down on wide rice fields, soon to show a velvety emerald green, promise of food for the hundreds of monks of the priestly village. To aid not a finger was raised. Cynical smiles, blindness of vision, even roughness in pushing her aside as obstruction in the path and giving her double work to do, open-voiced complaint at the intrusion of such an unsightly vision. At dusk she had not gone one third of the distance. A great despair seized her heart; just as it had seized her with the first entrance on this holy land. The wrath of divinity over-flooded her, terrified her, weakened her. All day she and her charge had gone without food. All day she had striven against obstacles seen and felt, visible and invisible. Panic seized on Terutehime. She looked down the lofty cliff the cart was skirting. Precipitous it plunged to the valley far below. Ah ! There was the Sanzu no Kawa, the river of souls to be passed by travellers on their way to the hells of punishment. Surely she and hers were distasteful to the gods. This mad desire to make the plunge, to end the suffering, was inspiration of their wrath. In despair she looked around. Not a sign of human being ; all travel on the trail had ceased. She pulled with all the power she had. Inch by inch she edged her burden up the steep slope. Then her strength gave way. Sliding back the cart stood balanced on the cliff's edge, the task again to be performed. Ah! These angry gods! Again she tried, again failed. The cup of despair overflowed. Kwannon Sama! Kwannon Sama! The task was too severe. The injunction of the goddess could no longer be obeyed. Here it was not effort balked, but open anger of divinity displayed. With face drawn and open eyes Terute approached her husband. Together they would make the journey ; together present themselves before Emma-Ō. Not the sought for cure, but the wrath of the gods was to be appeased. With firm step she came and laid hands on the *kuruma*. A push and leap, and all would be ended on the rocks far below.

Prepared for the plunge a loud and hearty voice close by start-led her. It said—" Nesan! Nesan! Be in no such haste. Aid " is at hand." Sunk on the ground she look up in awe. Three men were standing over her. But never had Terute seen such men. Huge as Niō they stood looking down with impassive face on the woman and the unsightly object that could yet be called a man. They wore the garb of wood-cutters, and carried axes on their shoulders. They showed neither kindness nor indifference. Massive power, absolute certainty, a majesty surrounded them. Timidly Terute remained bowed to the ground. Said one—" The sick man " from the northern country is expected at the shrine of the Tōkwōji ; " hence Our Presence. Forest and land around belong to the gods " of the temple, to the Gongen of Kumano. Wood is to be obtain-" ed, trees felled, for the honourable worship of the shrine. Be of " good heart, girl. The cure will be accomplished. Aid has reach-" ed you. The cart is to be dragged to the summit of the mountain." Without further speech he laid hand to the rope. Another went before, levelling at a blow any obstruction of root or stone in the path. The third lightly lifted the worn out woman to his shoulder. Terute was as in a dream. With even rapid tread they passed up-ward and forward under the shadow of the overhanging forest. At the summit a moment's halt was made. The leader pointed to the bank close by—" The means of access to the gods' domain becomes " useless. But here is to be its resting place, end of the weary task. " Thus will it become a monument to the chastity and devotion of a

The Brink of the River of Souls.

" woman to endless generations of this land of Nippon." At a turn
in the mountain road they halted and gently put down their burden.
Said the spokesman—" Below are the lights of Yunomine, the fall
" of Rurikwō. Here the *mangwan* (vow) of a hundred days is to
" be performed. This disease is the result of sin committed in a
" previous existence. Hence the sacrilege done to the shrine of
" Kwannon at the Sasamegayatsu, the visitation of punishment on
" father and son. Recourse or expiation there is none. But the
" upright life of the faithful wife has touched the hearts of the gods.
" The sentence is revoked, the cure will be accomplished. Be of
" good heart, Terute! Be diligent Terute!"

Terute in awe full thanks prostrated herself. As she raised her
eyes the three huge men, standing with grave impassive countenances, slowly faded from sight. Only the voice—" Be of good heart,
" Terute! Be diligent, Terute!" echoed and re-echoed over the
silent hills. Long she lay on the ground in worship. Joyful was
her heart at this manifestation of the gods, this assertion of their
will. In the bright moonlight she descended the long slope toward
the little town, assured of the accomplishment of the *mangwan*, of
the successful cure. Ah! The beneficent Gongen of Kumano!
The saving grace of the Healer, the Lord of Time, Yakushi-Ruri-
kwō. It was a cry of triumph; and yet the lips were silent.

In the little village said a fellow yawning—" Ah! How sleepy
" I am! Our worthy prior is most unreasonable. The Ajari of
" Kenchōji has naught to do with Tōkwōji, far from his mind and
" thought. Thus to keep us awake to receive a beggar man of the
" North, seen in a dream, is very inconsiderate. The reverend lord abbot
" of Tōkwōji, his digestion is bad." Then some excitement was noted
among the priests strolling the roadside. They swarmed " like
boiling potatoes." Cries went up—" The *gakiyami-kuruma*! The
" *gakiyami kuruma*!" At this prompt realisation of the prior's
vision all poured forth. Terute and her charge were soon the centre
of a mass of excited clerics. The placard was read over and over.
In person the prior appeared from his disturbed slumbers to witness
this literal verification. On his orders the man was suitably lodged
with all comfort in a shed just outside the temple grounds. Terute

was established as his nurse. The next day the case was examined with due care. The doctors of divinity and medicine attached to the temple at first gravely shook their heads. Never had the temple had such a case. Surely cure would not be effected. Was it wise to undertake it, to risk injury to the reputation of the shrine and its healing waters? Who ever heard of gōbyō being affected, even palliated, in the present existence of the sufferer? But there were those to urge a different view. The prior's dream, the vision and miraculous aid afforded Terute; nay, the fact of the journey itself in this cart, dragged by a woman over these massive hills, was evidence of divine protection. Besides, the prior's word was paramount. The cure was to be undertaken. The gods were to be obeyed.

The tecnique was carefully explained to Terute. First came three days of purification. Before this it would be dangerous to expose the patient to the fury of the holy waters. If healing they were irritating to the unworthy. Then followed twice seven courses (fourteen weeks), according to the sacred and lucky formula 7-5-3 (shichi-go-san). On the hundreth day, in the fifteenth week, the mangwan would be accomplished. This course was followed. With dawn every morning Terute drew Sukeshige in the little cart to the banks of the mountain river which flows through the steep hills at Yunomine. Hot springs redolent of sulphurous fumes to-day break forth from the bank and bed of the stream. Not long since there was a rock, curiously of the shape of the divine god Yakushi Nyōrai. To preserve it from the holy enthusiasts of a late sceptical age it has been found necessary to install it in the little shrine which represents the once magnificent establishment of the Tōkwōji. But not long since it overhung the banks of the stream, and from the breast of the Buddha sprang the healing waters in twelve jets. Laid beside the pool formed in the rock for the heated waters Sukeshige was immersed in the rising vapour. Beside him knelt Terute, dipping the little towel in the hot stream and squeezing it out over the festering body of her lord. From time to time came priests and attendants. These performed the heavier task of lifting the sick men into the healing waters for immersion. Truly the bed of this little river was a sad sight, with its long line of huts for the sick on the banks, and its long line of sick men congregated in the heated waters of the stream. Taken up as she was with the dreadful fate of her lord, yet the Terutehime felt oppression and sympathy for the wretched companions in suffering. The place had a pall of misery over-hanging it.

At the upper end of the village on the Hongū road is a rock. Here Ippen Shōnin has carved on the stone the divine characters, for this remote place is scene of visitation of the wandering bishops of the Yūgyōdera. One day there was a scene of unwonted anima-tion among the sick men of Yunomine. The banks of the stream were unusually crowded. The more helpless, unless under stronger guardianship, were elbowed into remote corners. Thus Terute and Sukeshige found themselves on the extreme edge of the pool, away from the bank and temple. A priest came down to the river. As he passed up the bank he shouted—" Make ready, good Sirs, to re-" ceive with proper awe and respect the visit of the Yūgyō Shōnin. " To-day the holy man makes visitation and distributes *Jūnen*.* Be " prepared to receive the charm." With momentary hope Terute looked up. The spray from the fall of Rurikwō hardly blinded her more than the tears in her eyes. The cure was not going well. The priests already looked on them with disfavour as risking the reputa-tion of the temple. Now on the second week of the second cycle of courses there was little real improvement after the long treatment. Terute could detect glimmer of returning consciousness; but the priests paid attention only to the unsightly body, and shook their heads. Many said—" I told you so." Others regarded the beggars as frauds. But the prior held firm to his dream; Terute to the pro-mise of the Gongen. The divine messenger, the cure, would come as foretold; perhaps with suddenness, perhaps on completion of some missing link in the course of the cure. The Shōnin could aid her, at least with counsel. With despair she noted the wide distance re-moving the sick man from the coming visitation.

Then came Joa Shōnin to the bank; clad in robes of green and red, with *kesa* (stole) of green and red thrown over his shoulders

---

*A paper with the sacred characters—Na-Mu-A-Mi-Da-Bu-Tsu—written thereon.

To eager hands he distributed the *jūnen*, running over the charm.
Namu Amida Butsu! Namu Amida Butsu! Answering cries went
up to the chant of the priests. The bishop turned to leave. Then
his eye noted a man far off. A woman tended him, and evidently
he could not move to receive the holy paper. Forthwith he trod
the slender plank cast over the pool. Said he to the woman
—"Take the man's hand and receive the *jūnen*. It is as if he himself had taken it." But in reply Terute weeping seized the robe of
the holy man, prostrate at his feet. Murmurs of astonishment went
up. How strange an action! The Shōnin leaned over, gently to
disengage the robe. Said he—"What want you lady? The priest
"has but the charm to give. It is for the god to answer the prayer
"of his follower, if he will. What more can Joa do?" Said
Terute—"Reverend Sir, know you not this man?" Puzzled Joa
Shōnin shook his head. Grief had touched the woman's brain.
Great was his pity. "Nay! Lady, Joa is no longer of this world.
"Of men and its affairs he knows not. May the glorious god have
"pity on your sufferings." Terute raised her sad face to him.
With amazement he stood up to full height. "Terutehime! The
"lady of Satake! Then this log must be Sukeshige Dono himself.
"But how come you here, and in this garb? Why, most miserable
"of wretches, seek the healing waters of Kumano?" In low tones,
broken by gasping sobs, Terute told the sad tale, the delayed cure,
the growing irritation against their presence. The Shōnin's eyes
sparkled. Said he with decision—"This should not be. The will
"of the gods is not thus hastily to be judged. When the *mangwan*
"is accomplished such is made known. Deign, reverend Sirs, not
"to be hasty. Joa Shōnin will offer prayer in this matter." For
the following week the reverend bishop held unusual fast and worship. A great procession was formed and the Tetō no Gyō, or hand
lantern procession, moved through the village, worshipped at its
various shrines, returning in state to the *hondō* (main temple) of the
Tōkwōji. This curious rite, recorded by the scribe, consists in using
the palm of the hand as oil receptacle in which burns the flaming
wick of the improvised lamp. Joa Shōnin was not discouraged at
the obstinacy of the cure, though even the good prior had grown

sceptical as the last week of the last circuit was reached. Neither hot water, prayers, nor procession caused any change. But then the wonderful and long waited transformation took place. The blackened face turned white, took on the tinge of the flush of health. The whitened hair became dark. The circulation was restored in the limbs, and the fallen nails grew again. The body took on its natural rosy tint. Sukeshige was himself again.

Weeping with joy Terute led Sukeshige before the mirror. Slowly he surveyed this body thus restored to the perfection of manhood. The skin shone like satin. The firm muscles moved easily and strongly beneath their covering. A scant white hair, here and there, was the only sign of his terrible experience. Then he donned the garments of ceremony, for the visit to be paid to the holy prior of the Tōkwōji. Ready for exit he turned to the lady, and as on most formal occasion between equals made ceremonial salutation and gave thanks. In wonder Terute drew back. Then prostrate touched his hands. " Nay ! My honoured lord, between husband " and wife such ceremony is not needed or fit. Terute is at the service " of her lord ; in health or sickness, in good or evil fortune, the " humble follower of her lord. Deign not to consider these trifling " matters. The vengeance now can be accomplished." Replied Sukeshige—" Through the devotion of this Terute the vengeance " becomes possible. For only through the kindness of the gods, " effected by the chaste devotion of his wife, is Sukeshige returned " to the life of men, to carry out this holy deed. Poor and insuffi- " cient are these formal thanks for the service of such a wife." Tenderly husband and wife grasped hands and gazed in each other's eyes ; the smile of renewed happiness, more dearly cherished, on the lips of both. Then, the wife again, Terute knelt, herself to see that every fold, every line of garment and equipment were in perfect order. Thus went forth Sukeshige on his mission of joyful thanks to prelate and establishment.

Great was the joy of the Tōkwōji and its priests over this new marvel, this portentous cure. Discrete and merry were they over the " poor " service of the feast to the lord of Oguri, for no disguise was now made of his identity. Joa Shōnin mightily rejoiced. He had brought with him great news to Yunomine. On the 27th day of the 2nd month of Ōei thirty second year (17th March 1425) the Shōgun Yoshikazu had died. Yoshimochi had again resumed the office, without any direct heir. It was an open secret that the Sankwan of Kyōto looked with great disfavour on the possible succession of the Kwanryō of Kamakura or his son to the higher office. Hatakeyama Mitsuiye was openly opposed to such a course. It was known that he favoured the return to secular life of Gien, bishop of the Seirenji on Hieizan. Even before Yoshikazu had been made Shōgun he had succeeded in narrowing the breach between the two brothers, and in Ōei 29th year (1422) Yoshimochi had paid Gien a visit in full ceremonial. The reconciliation was complete. Hence there was an undercurrent in favour of the Oguri House at Kyōto. On his return to the North, Joa Shōnin was commissioned to carry the investiture of the original fief of the Oguri at Hiraoka no Kumabuse in Shinano. With an income of three thousand koku* this could be held in fief until the restoration to full favour could be effected by the vengeance on Isshiki Akihide. Joa lost no time. Leaving the husband and wife to follow slowly he set out for Miyako to make the formal petition necessary for restoration to *status*. Then proclamation was sent in all directions :

> " Oguri Kojirō Sukeshige, completely cured of
> " the illness of *gōbyō*, restored to the original fief
> " of Hiraoka no Kumabuse, summons the re-
> " tainers of the Oguri House, quickly to gather at
> " Hiraoka."

Before he left Sukeshige wished to test the fullness of his powers. Terute to be sure was well satisfied ; but how about himself ? There was a heavy stone, burden for ten men, blocking the village highway. Rolled down by a recent rain, the coolies were sweating to pull and push it out of the way. Sukeshige in company with a band of young priests chanced to pass. He laughed— " There is the test of the healing waters of Yunomine, the divine

---

* Koku=5.13 bushels *circa*. Income of daimyō was so measured.

"aid of the glorious god." Seizing the rope he
hoisted the rock on his shoulders. The priests,
panting and making merry, toiled up the hill
n his wake. With easy stride he went ahead.
Near the summit he turned. "Let this be a
"sign to later generations of the goodness and
"efficacy of the Yakushi Nyōrai. Let no man
"try to remove it, but may it stand forever."
Where he cast it down on the Hongū road
stands the relic to this very day, object of respect to every pilgrim. Then he visited the
field close by the village. Here every day
Terute had cast the *warashibe* (rice stalks)
which had bound his brow and kept a
constant damp stream percolating over his

小栗判官
照天姫車塚
湯峯

face. He clapped his hands in prayer—"May Yakushi Nyōrai
"grant the owner of this field the rice crop forever, without
"seeding ; or until such time as lack of faith renders man unworthy
"of the gift." Alas! To-day the field remains, but its virtues
have been lost to the recent generations, though well known to the
grandfathers of this latter day peasantry. Then following the
guidance of Terute the cart was taken to the summit of the mountain road and buried on the hillside close by, as the god had
directed ; and a stone was set up to indicate to passers-by the place
of the *kuruma-zuka*. Here still stands the tomb, though often
enough has the stone been renewed.

Long prayed the twain, husband and wife, at the shrine of the
Gongen of Hongū. Warm was the welcome of the lord and lady in
favour with the Shōgun's House. Sukeshige's revenue as yet was
slender, but the promise of contribution was good. Then the
mighty river, the Kumanogawa in this its lower course, was
descended in the glorious days of the fifth month (June). The air
was filled with the fragrance of wild lilies, a beautiful white tinged
into carmine in the centre of the chalice. The red azalea was
splashed in great blood-like blotches on the mountain sides ; reflected in the quiet reaches of the river the sight was magnificent.

Passing under the overhanging battlements of Shimokuzan, down the long reaches dotted with the curious tri-partite latteen sails, Shingū was reached. After due worship here they went to Nachi Mountain, to give earnest thanks to the Lady Merciful. Ah, Kwannon Sama! Kwannon Sama! The cry was no longer one of agonized petition, but of triumph finally assured, of suffering passed forever. At Katsura boat was taken to Maizaka near the Lake Hamana. Thus they landed in Tōtōmi, to take up their journey to Mount Kumabuse, to the meeting of the *rōtō* at Hiraoka.*

---

* It was while in prayer before the Shōjōden at Hongū that Ippen Shōnin had the vision of the *yamabushi* who disclosed to him the power of the *nenbutsu* (charm) of the " Namu Amida Butsu." There is a tradition that the head of Satō Tadanobu ("Go-ban " Tadanobu) the noted retainer of Yoshitsune is buried at the Chōju-in of Kamakura. The body of the infant son of Yoshitsune by his concubine Shizuka-gozen, put to death on birth by the order of Yoritomo, is also said to be buried at this hall of the Kenchōji.

PART IV

THE ACCOMPLISHMENT OF THE VENDETTA.

"Not in the sky, not in the ocean's midst,
"Not in the most secluded mountain cleft,
"Not in the whole wide world is found the spot,
"Where standing one could 'scape the snare of
"death "—(Dhammapada quoted).
       Questions and Puzzles of Milinda the King
                (Rhys—Davids).

CHAPTER XIX.

ONCHI TARŌ AND THE RŌTŌ OF OGURI.

The separation of the Oguri *rōtō* from their lord and from each other was the result of the conditions under which the battle at Yahagi had begun. The council had determined that the sally should be made at dusk, after the Imagawa had withdrawn from arrow range and were well settled for the night. At the head of his *rōtō* Sukeshige was to throw the camp in confusion by an attack on the Imagawa chiefs. The Asuke brothers were to seize the ford and thus secure a safe retreat for the castle garrison. Some hours, however, remained before the plan could be carried into effect. Meanwhile the assault of the foe was to be repulsed. As there was plain sign of its renewal the captains betook themselves to their various stations on the wall. Of these none were more efficient than the Oguri *rōtō*, none less easily spared from this important task. Sukeshige, with the Asuke brothers, rode to the main gate accompanied by Mito no Kotarō. The Kazama brothers, the Tanabe brothers, the Gotō brothers, the Kataoka brothers, in pairs went to their stations. Hardly had they reached them when the fire broke out. The confusion in the castle was immense. The enemy rushed to the attack. The sally was made in disorder, and a scattered and hopeless fight began with the hosts of the Imagawa.

To Ikeno Shōji had fallen the defence where the attack was expected to be fierce and persistent—the castle wall overlooked by the little eminence projected from the hills close by. As the enemy did in very truth expect to make their most earnest effort here a large force had been massed on this side. The worthy knight had his hands full. Bravely did he battle. But his men were cut down ruthlessly, taken in front and rear, from the interior of the castle and the walls now scaled by the foe. Plainly the fight was lost. None dared face the huge man as he raged through the battle in search of his lord, or of the Imagawa, father and son ; to rescue the first, to slay the other two. Nagatada sighed with pleasure and regret, as protected by the masses of his *rōtō* he watched the big man sweep them aside with the huge iron pole carried with deadly effect into the fight. Then he rode off to another part of the field. Shōji could not be a retainer of his; he did not care to witness the brave man's fate overcome by numbers. Himself, he would fight with the lord of Oguri, not with his *rōtō*.

Deprived of the incentive of their lord's safety, the severity of his eye, the efforts of the Imagawa *rōtō* slackened before the danger. Gradually they dropped away. The castle was being pillaged. They wanted their share. The head of Shōji did not outweigh the booty to be secured. Besides it seemed very firmly fastened on his shoulders. To the more brave who sought their lord's praise and reward, numbers lacked. They were a bare twenty to one. Soon the knight found himself alone on the hillside. In the dusk the field presented nothing but the sight of the wildly waving Imagawa banners, the masses of their *rōtō*. Evidently the Houses of Oguri and Asuke had gone down before this horde of braves. Shōji was too worn by battle for further effort. He must live as yet, to gain tidings of the fate of his lord, of his companions. The vendetta yet remained to be accomplished, if by his hand as sole survivor of the band. He strode off up the valley into the hills for some distance. Then climbing the hillside he made his way to a projecting ledge which gave a wide view over the country-side and threw himself down to rest. It was now full dark ; the moon was barely rising, the vague outlines of mountain and shadow of valley seemed as far off as the paradise of Amida. Soon he slumbered.

Voices, the cracking of the bushes, the glare of torches roused him. Shōji sat up and laid his hand on his iron staff. On all sides the Imagawa *rōtō* were beating the mountain side for wounded and fugitives. Severe had been the rebuke of their lord. When Nagatada Dono asked for the head of Shōji it was found that each *rōtō* had left the collection to someone else. " Better qualified," sneered

Nagatada savagely. Openly he jeered at them. He and his father were most dissatisfied. The heads of the Asuke brothers, of the mere boy, eldest son of Jirō Nobuyoshi, would satisfy Kyōto in one way ; but the head of Sukeshige was wanted to please Kamakura. Truly this man and his *rōtō* possessed the power of *Iddhi*, of transportation at will through the air. The earth seemed to have swallowed them. Nagatada fairly drove his lieutenants from his presence, to the mountain side to make earnest effort to show some fruit worth gleaning. With the Asuke the Imagawa had no quarrel, but much real kindly feeling. The old man Ryōshun glowered with rage, and his warlike son felt the rebuke in person. It was with a great shout of joy that the Imagawa recognized the huge form of Shōji as he rose to meet them. Eagerly they rushed forward to knock him down and seize him. As in battle, so on the mountain side the iron pole swung with savage effect. Shōji was tired and desperate. If he could not make report to his lord he would head a large company to the presence of Emma-Ō. Ribs cracked, brains flowed like water. The Imagawa *rōtō* sweated with fear and exertion. With monotonous exactitude the pole of Shōji descended, crushing bodies and limbs. The bamboo grass was spattered with gore and strewn with dead and injured. To capture this man was impossible. Withdrawing to a short distance they strung their bows. Shōji was in a great passion. He no longer had the strength to charge and break through them. "Cowards! Is this to show the courage of the "*bushi ?* Truly none but Kwantōbei (Kwantō bumpkins) have "arms to wield the sword, and guts to use it."* In rage he stamped the ground. The Imagawa gave a great shout of wonder. They rushed forward to the edge of the cliff. Shaken by the force of Shōji's foot a huge section had broken off to fall "many thousand "*jō* " (the *jō* is ten feet !) into the valley beneath. The knight disappeared with it. Plainly there was nothing more for them to do. The mangled corpse would lie buried under a mountain of rubbish.

---

* The seat of courage, to the Nipponese, is in the belly. The adventures of Shōji and Onchi Tarō are found in Momogawa.

They returned to make report to their lord of the destruction of the foe before their eyes.

Somewhat dazed Shōji woke from an unconsciousness the duration of which he could not measure. He was lying in darkness at what seemed to be the bottom of a well, for light came from above, faint and dim. Ah! He remembered. There had been the battle at the castle, his flight, the discovery by the Imagawa *rōtō*. Then there was the sensation of falling for unmeasured time through the black night. Evidently he had died. The enemy had his head. Instinctively he put his hands to his sconce. No! For some reason it was still on his shoulders. The gods were kind. He rose to his feet and shook himself. He was reasonably sound too; traces of weariness, a few contusions. The casualty list of his enemies was much greater. But where was his train with which to present himself before the king of these regions. Cowardly fellows they had fled—to Hell? Thither he had no wish to go. Perchance Paradise lay the other way. The entrance to Meido could not be difficult. He examined the well-like hole. Really it was just like a well, with stones projecting at intervals to form a rough staircase. The light was becoming stronger and brighter. He would investigate. Being dead was much like being alive. At least he was tremendously hungry and thirsty.

Prepared for the ascent he laid his hand on the blackness of the wall. He nearly fell. It was empty air, not stone he touched. Groping Shōji soon found that the well not only had a funnel, but a gallery. This Meido was a curious place. He would explore it. For the brave and upright man, he who has always aided the helpless and conscientiously put to death his enemies, served his lord without inquiry as to motive, complied with every wish of parent or elder brother no matter how base its origin, such a one has complied with and fulfilled all the Five Obligations of the sage. He has nought to fear from Emma-Ō. Gokuraku (Paradise) is his portion. If the passage led to Jigoku (Hell); so much the worse for Hell. The two jailors of the dreaded king, the ox-headed and horse-headed, he would knock their heads together first and feast on them afterward. He was quite hungry enough if he could get nothing else. So off he started, groping his way along the paved passage. For long it was fairly level; then it began gently to rise, continued for some distance. Bats flew by and grazed his head. At times the slimy wall slipped under his hand, as would the smooth cold skin of a snake. " A relative perhaps. But why should a " Jashin fear even Hebi Sensei (Snake of Snakes)." Shōji laughed uproariously, and his huge voice resounded in these depths. He laughed still more, as at an unexpected turn he stepped into the moonlight and on mother earth. He stood part way up the hillside. On a knoll of the opposite side of the valley was a ruined castle, its broken walls sharply outlined in light and shadow. Growled Shōji —" There are no castles in Hell, unless in Shuradō ; and there they " would be in better repair. So much to the good. Plainly the well " is a blind, an exit from the castle precincts. This Shōji has taken " the longer road to reach the goal." His adventure now was clear to understand. " The architect of such a place was a fool. No " wonder its walls are in ruins. A foe could play at *masu-ire* " (quoits) with stone or arrow. Evidently the garrison looked to " flight rather than to fight ; to safety on the hills." He retraced his steps, this time above ground. Toiling up the knoll, through grass and over rough stones he soon stood on the summit.

There was more to be found than he expected. Shōji grunted as he stood at the top of a flight of stone steps looking down the valley. The *torii* below indicated the shrine of the village god, a second over his head its close proximity. " At least a resting place ; " if it was not for this empty belly. Ah ! If this was but hell. " Gladly would this Shōji spear and crunch a demon. Of such he " has no fear." He approached the shrine. A shout of delight went up. The place was grass grown and neglected ; the eaves were rotten and crumbling ; but the feast laid out was fresh and appetising. *Saké* in flasks and plenty of it, bowls of red rice (*seki-han*) for the sacrifice, bowls of vegetable stew pleasant to the nostrils (*nishime*). As he gorged the food and guzzled the wine Shōji grunted with intense satisfaction. Smiling pleasantly—" Shōji ac- " cepts the offerings. The demons are ransomed. Doubtless this

"food is less peppery, this *saké* of better flavour than gore. Now
"for sleep. Surely the Imagawa *rōtō* are also wearied and need
"repose." Carefully he replaced the vessels of the offering exactly as
they had stood. Then seeking the back of the shrine he laid down
to rest, and was soon slumbering in good earnest.

Another day was declining when the sound of voices awoke
him. Shōji sat up and rubbed his eyes. Had the Imagawa again
nosed him out? Surely this old priest and his cautious son were
most obstinate. With hand on sword hilt Shōji stole forward and
peeped through the grating. But it was the sound of chanting that
met his ear. Ascending the valley came a long line of peasants, in
rain coats and straw hats, but minus their farming implements.
Negi-kannushi, Shintō priests of a low class, headed the procession.
In a litter was carried a pretty girl. As they lifted her from the
kago Shōji saw that her hands were tied behind her back, her feet
fast bound. The whole affair was easy to understand. Ravaged
by storm or thieves the village offered the girl as human sacrifice.
These were the fellows who set a white arrow on the roof ridge to
propitiate the god of storm ; or exposed the village beauty to the
teeth of the mountain wolves, or to serve the lust of some robber's
den, in order to secure a favourable harvest. The priests sent up an
exultant shout—"Rejoice villagers! The goddess is favourable.
"Sengen Daibosatsu (the divinity of Fujisan) deigns to grant a
"bumper crop for the year. The miraculous missive shot into the
"home of Josaku, its warning is accomplished. See! Food and
"wine have been consumed to the last morsel. Now it remains to
"complete the last act of the sacrifice ; to abandon the maiden to the
"will of the divinity. Rejoice! Rejoice!" As the priests and
people prostrated themselves before the shrine the divine Shōji
grumbled in fierce wrath and concealment. "Miscreants! Beasts!
"Swine! It is this Shōji who shall bear the answer to the missive.
"Would that his staff could write the answer on your backs and
"ribs." Thus with anger the knight watched them file off down the
valley, abandoning the maid to any fate by beast or brigand that
awaited her. With tears she called to them, to one hard featured
slouching man in particular. Regardless he with the others passed

from sight. Shōji clung to his hiding place, sure that more was yet to follow.

Several hours passed. No one was seen returning from the village. Then a villainous head peeped through the bushes opposite the shrine. A long, angular, active body followed. It was a hideous fellow. His face was fiery scarlet, the hair a carrotty red. Green eyes blazed in a knobby face, and a huge beard made him more beast than man.* He advanced to where the girl lay bound. With his sword he cut the rope which confined her hands. "Don't "cry my beauty. The divine favour has been shown in rescuing "you from the farmer's life; instead to live in luxury and serve the "band of this Norikiyo. Nay! To your pretty hands shall be en-"trusted the caresses of his idle hours. Take courage. This Shira-"mineyama (White Peak Mountain) is a gorgeous home." As the girl wept and struggled he became rough with her. "Come wench! "Such conduct is no passport to favour. Submit to the will of the "god." Smack! Bang! He went sprawling at full length. In fright the girl tried to escape, but her feet were bound, and trembling fingers refused their office on the hard knots. Shōji mounted the thief. From time to time he gave him a resounding thump. "Miser-"able sacriligious wretch, prepare at once for death. You personate "the god to deceive these wretched and superstitious peasants. Now "deign to receive the divine punishment from the hands of Ikeno "Shōji, *rōtō* of the lord of Oguri. Never would his lord pardon "such offence."

The prostrate brigand groaned so vigorously as to inspire pity. Said Shōji—"'Though one slays, yet does he pity the wretched "chicken whose neck is wrung.' What plea can such a fellow "make? Speak quickly." Said the man—"Deign, good Sir, to "let me strip off this disguise." As Shōji allowed him to sit up he tore off the mask and wig and cast them into the bushes. On the whole he was by no means unpresentable. With shamed face he said—"Know, honoured Sir, that matters are not so bad as they "seem. It is true that the business of thief lacks elevation; but "when the offence is committed to collect funds for war, to over-

---

* To this day the classic portraiture of the "Western barbarians."

" throw this treacherous and disloyal Ashikaga House, it finds ex-
" cuse. As for this Josaku of Inagimura, he is a hard hearted, close
" fisted, wretch. The girl, in all truth, would be better off if sold to
" Miyako to supply funds for the cause." At Shōji's sharp dissent
—" Nay! You do not know the man. Not long since he refused
" to ransom his eldest son, who had perforce to undergo the rigid
" law and meet death. His excuse was that he had others and
" could afford the loss. The first pimp from the capital or Naka-
" sendō towns will find acceptance of his offer. He has not yet
" passed this way, 'tis fair to surmise. But since it is your will let
" us return O'Haru to the village. Her safety against further moles-
" tation is agreed. At your name, honoured Sir, I rejoice. Great
" was the regret at the fall of Yahagi, the death of the Asuke
" brothers. As for the lord of Oguri, his escape is as good as certain.
" The insignificant person who now addresses you is Akamatsu Jirō
" Norikiyo, youngest son of Akamatsu Enshū, lord of Amanawa
" castle in Harima. Without doubt my word can be taken as to
" these events. Deign to join the band on Shiraminesan. At least
" seek retirement there until the Imagawa forces retire into Suruga."
With deep respect at the honoured name Shōji made obeisance; for
his news he could have fallen on Norikiyo's neck and embraced
him; but as to the girl he remained obstinate. In company they
sought the village in the dark. Then with the injunction of silence,
and the threat of pillage of house and neighbours if it was not
observed, they retired into the night. At her voice and knocking
the *amado* was opened, and she was left explaining matters to the
wide-mouthed astonished rustics by the interposition of divinity in
her favour, as had been arranged by captor and rescuer.

At Shiraminesan Shōji found matters little to his taste. If the
methods of Akamatsu Norikiyo were dubious—no more so than
scores of his compeers in the southern cause—his enthusiasm was
pure. He had all the Nipponese distortion of vision and bizarre
logic with lack of information as to what it likes or dislikes with
intensity. His company possessed kindred views without the
enthusiasm. These fellows lived in luxury on the terror of the people
and the helplessness of the Ashikaga government beset on every side

by rebellion, and with little revenue to turn from the scandalous luxury of its princes to purposes of police. The people had to look out for themselves and preferred to pay blackmail. This supplied funds for fine clothes, feasts, and wine. The village girls, freely levied on to supply the *tabo* or sold in Miyako, completed the devil's adage. After some weeks of witnessing this life Shōji determined to go forth in search of the Oguri *rōtō*. Norikiyo had loyally made every effort to gather news as to their whereabouts. When Shōji announced his intention he agreed with reluctance. Said he— "You must have funds. Disguise is easy. You should go as a "Dai Jōmyōten Rokujū Rokubu, pilgrim to Nippon's many shrines "and provinces in holy guise of priest. Whenever the flag of your "honoured lord is raised, deign to send notice to this Norikiyo." With good words and much knowledge of the movements of these bandits of the "Lost Cause," Shōji set forth on his wanderings. His first idea was to seek Ōtsu. Here his uncle Koshirō had gone in charge of the Lady Terute. Surely they knew the whereabouts of Sukeshige Dono. But the journey was in vain. Discreet inquiry soon told him that Terute and Koshirō had left the town on the North Road some days before. The beautiful woman in company with the big ugly priest could hardly escape notice. With regret Shōji hoisted his *oi* on his shoulders, and ringing his bell was already prepared to leave the town, to beat the Tokaidō villages with Yūki as his goal. As he reached the outskirts he noticed two men, like-wise in priests' robes, wearing deep straw hats, and with bell and begging bowl. Something in their gait struck his eye. He turned to follow them through the town. Seeing his persistence they held whispered consultation. Then abruptly turning into the wood at the base of Miidera's terrace they awaited his approach. Gravely they stood, grasping their *shakujō* (ringed staff) in almost threaten-ing attitude. Said one of them—"Know, good Sir, that not to "observe the etiquette of the *tengai* is bad manners.* Your obstinacy "is without excuse. Deign to pass the other way." But Shōji chuckled—"Surely that voice is not unfamiliar. It is strangely like "the voice of the honoured *karō*, Gotō Hyōsuke Dono." He raised

---

* *Tengai=komusō* or deep straw hat concealing the face.

Ikeno Shōji meets the Gotō Brothers.

his *meseki-gasa* (straw helmet). The hats of the other two went back. "Ikeno Shōji!"—"Hyōsuke Dono! Daihachirō Dono!" With tears in their eyes the brave fellows clasped hands. Shōji was filled out with his rest and feeding of weeks; but the faces of the Gotō brothers were lined and emaciated. "Ah! Our bellies are very "empty. The life of priest is not for the inexperienced. The "living is anything but fat; the fare is meagre."—"That is easily "remedied with this gold." Shōji made merry.

An inn was soon found, not over particular, for the *rōtō* knew Ōtsu well. Long was the tale of their adventures. The experience of the Gotō had been much like that of Shōji. Nothing but the banners of the Imagawa in sight they had recourse to flight. This took them into Ise. From Yamada to Kumano, to Kōyasan on the West, they had searched the country for sign of their lord. Surely he would not attempt to escape to Yūki through the Imagawa country. Shōji encouraged them with the news of his certain escape gleaned by Norikiyo. He favoured the return to Yūki through Shinano. Where else was support to be found? But the Gotō had an important hint. In Ise they learned that some at least of the Oguri *rōtō* had escaped. A boat had been seized at Hazu in Mikawa, and the fishermen compelled to set sail westward, to the protection of the Kikuchi in Kyūshū. Some part of the powerful family was in chronic rebellion. With them the lord of Oguri perhaps had taken refuge. The description was unmistakeable. One of the men was certainly Kazama Jirō. Such massive head and broad shoulders were found on few men. Another plainly was Hachirō. Doubtless they would find their lord in the southern island. The opinion of Hyōsuke carried the day. As in the days of Prince Yoshitsune, whom rumour also carried to the West when he was safe with Hidehira in Dewa, thus was the lord Sukeshige harboured in Chinzei. For Shōji no further disguise was needed. Gotō Hyōsuke took the rôle of a samurai on a long journey of business for his lord. To him Shōji with relief transferred the gold of Norikiyo. Considering its mission Hyōsuke gave it the blessing of such purification. Daihachirō got himself up as a trader in toilet articles, oils, soaps, combs, mirrors. Thus they could travel in company, and approach all classes of society.   Incongruity added to the efficiency of the disguise.

Thus they wandered from province to province toward the West.   It is at the summer's end the scribe finds them descending through the woods of Hokodakezan in Hyūga,* after visiting the *oku-in* of the shrine of Yakushi.   The sky was dark and clouded. Heavy rumbling of thunder was heard.   A flash of lightning from time to time lit up the darkness.   Gotō Hyōsuke disliked thunder storms exceedingly.   Rather would he face a line of spears.   Dai-hachirō shared the family failing.   Shōji disliked the idea of getting wet.   They looked around.   Not far off was a *wanguri* hut.   These are temporary sheds built by the men who go into the forests to cut and shape the cheap ;wooden bowls used for culinary purposes. Wood fit for their products exhausted in the particular section of the forest, they move to another and build again their temporary shelter on the new site.   This hut was an old one, but at least the wanderers could keep fairly dry during the storm.   The darkness of its interior pleased Gotō Hyōsuke.   Any place where the back could be turned on this nasty glare of the heavens.   Said he— " Some day men will bring it down from the sky, to turn night " into day "—" Why not ? " replied Shōji.   " In half the time then " our lord could be found."   Laughing he brandished in defiance his iron tipped *shakujō*.   Its rings rang merrily.   A terrific crash followed.   The Gotō brothers tumbled headlong to the floor of the hut, to all appearance lifeless.   Even the stalwart Shōji staggered and fell.   As he did so his hand touched something soft, clammy, with hair.   " A *raijū* ? " said he.   " Ah !   The filthy beast !   Doubt-" less it has found heretofore easy game among the peasant wood-" cutters.   The touch of the sacred staff has been too much for it. " Alas !   Can it have killed the noble Hyōsuke, the generous Dai-" hachirō ? "   In anger he seized and drew the mass to light.   The beast had a long snout and pig-like eyes.   A rather scant hair

---

* In the Higashi Motogatagori (district).   The *oku-in* is the particularly holy (often small and shabby) shrine found in the penetralia of the holy ground—i.e. on or near the mountain top.   The *raijū* below mentioned—" an animal suppos-ed to come down when lightning strikes ;" Brinkley's Dictionary.

covered the repulsively smooth skin. The short tail was almost hairless. Short legs and long powerful claws gave it power to cling to the rough edges of clouds—or the bark of trees. As it still retained some signs of life and viciousness Shōji plunged his dagger into its throat. He leaned over his companions. The storm still rumbled and flashed without, the fitful glare illuminating the hut with its occasional bright flashes. Was it death or funk before him? The faces still retained the colour of health. Shōji picked up a straw from the ground. Most unceremoniously he ran it up the *go-karō's* nose. Hyōsuke promptly sat up; he sneezed violently. In reproach he turned to Shōji. Said the latter—"To bring the "dead back to life there is no more powerful remedy than a "stick up their nose. Deign to accomplish the cure with Dai-"hachirō. No?" He seated himself on the prostrate form. But the younger Gotō was spared the trial. Only the massive weight of Shōji prevented his going through the roof. Daihachirō sprang up. "Ah! What a bad dream! This Daihachirō was in "Hell, and the dreaded Emma-Ō was seated on his chest. What "oppression! Truly the judge of good and evil is most hideous "—and heavy. But Shōji San; why cling thus to the rafters? "Has the glare of lightning frightened the bulky youth?" He snorted contemptuously. A bright flash, however, sent him cowering. Shōji dropped to the ground roaring with laughter at Daihachirō. Hyōsuke made fun of both, thus foils to each other. All three leaned in curiosity over the body of the *raijū*.

The storm was too fierce to last. The sun shone forth dispersing the thunder clouds. In the descent they stopped on a ledge which gave view outward. Gazing over the lines of tumbled peaks clothed in forest, the valley far below with its stream bound seaward to the wide expanse of the distant yet visible Hyūga bight, the neatly cultured fields, a thatched roof scattered here and there, a brown mass to indicate the village, the many lights and shades of the picture held them long bound by its beauty. At some distance below Shōji pointed out a bit of turf by the side of the mountain stream. "A pleasant place for a snack (*bentō*); or for the night if "lodging is too far." He lead the way down through the forest, but like most such visions it seemed to retreat before their advance. Here was a cliff to be circumvented by a long detour. Here the high waters of the brook had to be crossed after a climb to quieter passage above. But time and its course brought them to the desired spot in the late afternoon. A huge rock barred the stream. Below it was a stretch of flower dotted glade. Around was the forest. Truly it was delightful. At once they stripped and bathed in the pool close by, then lay stretched out on the pleasant turf, eyes closed or following at will the drifting clouds above. Said Hyōsuke—Under the " guidance of this Shōji Dono our success has been such as to inspire " the wish to stay. At such rate our fate will be that of Urashima (Rip " Van Winkle). It would appear safer to camp here in the open, rather " than descend the mountain in the dark." Shōji grunted at this equivocal compliment. " The words of the *go-karō* are inspired— " by age or boldness? Yet he fears not the dews of night, for he " plunges in the cold brook at risk of his joints and rheumatism." He sighed. " Why not make petition at the temple offices ; " seek appointment as care-takers (*o-rusu*) in some mountain " temple? What beauty! What peace! " The good knight lumbered to the stream and bent over to take a draught of the sparkling waters. He drew back in amazement. In his very hands the water began to flow red. At first a tiny thread, it then ran all pink with gore. Shōji sprang up, and leaning against the big rock looked up and around. The sky swayed before him ; or rather it was the rock which swayed behind him. Shōji was a man of rapid decision. At a leap he grasped a projecting root, and in a moment was on top of the boulder. A strange sight met his eyes. On the other side, one foot braced against the rock, was a tall fellow, some seven feet in height and big in proportion. His skin was tanned brown by the hot sun of Kyūshū. His hair hung in the long locks of youth down his back. There was nothing repulsive in his face which was decidedly handsome with its long oval, lofty forehead, and high peaked eyebrows. His game, in the shape of several hare and a large swollen monkey (ōzaru), lay not far off. He had a wolf held fast by the jaws, and was calmly tearing them apart. The hunting knife still remained plunged in the animal's

The Introduction of Onchi Tarō.

belly, and with his foot the youth was enlarging the wound from which the blood poured freely. The beast was at its last gasp. Throwing aside the body the boy rose and raised two sparkling jet-black eyes to the wondering face of Shōji.

Said he—" On the mountain above this Tarō saw the strangers " camped by the stream below. Your course, honoured Sirs, has " been difficult and devious. Plainly you are new-comers here. Deign " to allow me to act as guide. Wolves and bears are numerous on " the mountain. Was not this land once known as Kumaso ? " Better would it be to accept the humble shelter of my home. To- " morrow the journey can be renewed." Shōji was favourably impressed. However caution was needed. Youths who tore wolves apart and shook boulders as big as a cottage were most un- usual. His size was that of a Niō ; that is one of the smaller Niō in a country temple. He must consult his companions. With this in- timation he descended to make report. The youth gathered together his game in preparation to join him. Said Hyōsuke—" The matter " is not without suspicion. It may be some demōn in human " shape. But we are three to one ; moreover cold victuals are poor " sustenance. This Hyōsuke longs for hot meat." With ready agreement the renewed invitation was accepted. Yet it was with some misgivings they followed the youth down the almost invisible trail through the forest by the mountain stream. As they advanced a gentle hum through the trees grew into a continuous *don-don-don ;* then into an uproar. Said Tarō—" It is the *tsuzumi ga taki,* so called " from the drumlike sound. Truly it is a beautiful sight." Lead- ing them a little apart from the trail he brought them to the bank. Below in many inclined ledges plunged a water-slide. The full stream roared and leaped. It seemed to delight with all the buoy- ancy of youth at the mad plunge. Tumbling from the forest above it disappeared into the green tunnel below to leap into space and quieter waters. Long they gazed in pleasure. The voice of the youth roused them. " It is a beautiful object. This Tarō spends " many hours by its side. But honoured Sirs the way is long. " Besides, the waterfall is not yet to be dismissed." He led them by a long detour around the mountain slope, on to the end of a little spur which projected into the valley.   Here in a clearing was a small log hut.   An old woman came forth at Tarō's call.   Hyōsuke looked at her with curiosity.   " She was tall and slender, though bent at the loins by age.   The face was oval, the brow lofty, the eyebrows peaked.   She had been straight as a pine (*hiyaki no roba*), a Sotoba Komachi."*   Tarō the grandson inherited the looks of this once beauty.

With reserved courtesy and some pleasure she invited them to enter.   Warm water was brought to wash the feet.   The house and surroundings were plain but clean.   Such flowers as poverty had time to attend adorned the garden.   From the midst of a *yamabuki* sprang the bamboo pipe which gushed the spring water into a tub, whence overflowing it entered the little stone lined *ike* (pond).   The Obame San (Old Dame) followed their eyes.   As if in answer there came to her lips a poem :

> " 'Tis from midst the mountain rose,
> " The water gushes forth."

" Alas !   The rose no longer is in bloom.   Summer's close is at " hand.   The aged much regret the approach of winter.   This " Obame now reaches to the eightieth of this bitter season.   Deign " honoured Sirs to enter our humble dwelling.   Poor the repast " and entertainment, but the best the place affords is yours.   Doubt- " less you are from Miyako, unused to these parts ?   Deign to enter." She spoke as in careless-eager curiosity, for both motives sounded in her question.   Hyōsuke gravely bowed and gravely entered.   Tarō and the dame busied themselves with their guests.   Tarō put before them three rough wooden bowls, cracked and patched.   At the first sip they opened and closed their eyes with ecstasy.   The *saké* was good —and the flavour was most delicious and unusual.   Then he posted off to the hearth where he was soon busy over some mess of meat. The old dame was occupied in her kitchen.   Tarō was not long in reappearing.   He bore a rich mess of stew piled up in a wooden

---

* Sotoba="Straight as a rod." Komachi was one of the fair and frail beauties of Old Nippon of noted literary attainment. The *yamabuki* is a yellow mountain rose flowering in April. The Kuma in Kumaso means "bear." Cf. Kojiki p. 23. Note to Professor Chamberlain's translation.

dish. " Take and eat, honoured Sirs. Deign to bestow your ap-
" probation on this poor effort. In these parts this meat is much
" appreciated. The Obame would feed you on millet gruel, but as
" hunter this Tarō knows that men like a less rigid diet. Dear old
" dame ! She judges others by herself. But the *saké* jar is empty.
" Pardon temporary absence. It is very rude." He disappeared.

At the sight of the meal the peaceful log hut vanished from
their sight. The huge blood stained youth tearing the wild beast
on the mountain appeared to mind. They gazed at the contents of
the dish. Gingerly Shōji fished out a hand ; then another, and a
third ; the fractions of a skull with juicy fragments attached to it.
The dish outlined the body of a new born infant. In disgust the
Gotō drew back from the feast. Were not the giant and the aged
dame mere apparitions, to take hideous form and glut themselves on
the unwary travellers ? Other thought disappeared from mind.
Shōji turned over the mess methodically. Shōji was intensely
hungry. " Why should Shōji fear a supernatural offering ? Good
" Sirs this is to retire before the attacks of the demon. He offers
" food. Can the fight be better waged on an empty stomach ?
" If this be the corpse of a child, if these be apparitions, why not
" corpse and demon unsubstantial ? Shōji will partake.........
" Naruhodo ! What a heavenly repast ! Honoured Sirs, do not
" fail to do as this Shōji. Never has such food passed his lips." The
good knight munched and crunched. The Gotō looked on envi-
ously. The dainty smell rose to their noses. " Jakozo (monk-
" ling) ! This fellow is a true Jashin. He is making away with
" the whole meal. Why not join him ? He will make himself ill
" with over-feeding. The power of his arm will be lost to us. We
" must do likewise—out of prudence and charity." Soon the jaws
of all three were busy. They hardly looked up when the old
woman entered the room with the mess of millet. She threw up
her hands in horror. Then she laughed musically. " Ah ! This
" Obame thinks that all men tread the Buddha's Way, not only
" wear his robe." She looked expressively at the priest's robe of
Shōji, the pilgrim garments of his companions. " It is to be hoped
" that Tarō named his dish. It is the unborn monkey, of which he

" has just brought in the mother. In the district the dish is much
" esteemed." The samurai looked at each other with guilty relief as
Tarō at last entered with the *saké* which had been heating. Continued the dame—" We owe these beasts much. Doubtless you
" know the *saké*." Said Hyōsuke—" One would take it to be
" Bingo Homei-shu, the saving liquor of Tamotsu.* Nay! It is
" superior." Said she—" The making of this is much simpler.
" Hunger satisfied these cunning beasts have learned to steep peach
" and persimmon in the water filled cavities of the rocks. Here the
" juices ferment and make a sweetened liquor for them. Following
" their example the peasants add the crushed fruits to the *saké* vats
" in the brewing. Hence the unusual and pleasant flavour of the
" product, peculiar to the district. It is said to be a tonic for many
" ills, including old age "—" *Nomasshai* (Deign to drink)," and
Tarō poured, and poured again.

Excusing herself to accomplish some task the dame left Tarō
in their company. As he too went out to bring some treasures for
inspection Hyōsuke turned to his companions. " Plain it is there is
" a mystery here. Doubtless, honoured Sirs, you have noted the
" dialect in which this youth and dame speak—the pure Miyako,
" entirely different from the rough speech of this peasantry. Care
" is to be exercised not to trouble the incognito." Tarō re-entered.
He bore two long armour boxes. Opening these he laid the armour
before them. This passed from one to another, handled with reverent care. It was sewn with light green thread. The breast-
plates bore the *kikusui*, the chrysanthemum flower floating on water,
the crest of the Nankō, the princes supporting the Southern Dynasty
through all evil fortune. Hyōsuke handed the attached scrolls to his
companions. They read :

" The gift to Onchi Sakon Tarō Mitsukazu Dono."
" The gift to Onchi Sakon Jirō Mitsumoto Dono." ·

In peculiar script (*kakihan*) was the seal attached to the first.—

---

* Like vermouth, medicinal. The *kōdan* writers are ǀfull of these little
touches of popular habit and superstition. Onchi Tarō belongs to the *kōdan* of
Momogawa, and is one of the best parts of it.

" Kusunoki Masashige."*   The old woman entered behind Tarō.
In amazement and some fright she eyed armour, knights, grandson.
The Gotō brothers, with Shōji behind them, humbly made obeisance.
" Honoured lady, the armour brought by Tarō Dono but confirms
" the impression first gathered that good fortune had led us to
" no usual house."   Shōji smothered a grin at the *go karō's* circumlocution.   Continued Hyōsuke—" Deign to accept apology for our
" rudeness; to name any service required at our hands."   The dame
replied with the natural dignity of rank, the circumspection of a
woman experienced in troubled times—" To have further speech it is
" first necessary to know with whom one has to do. This careless boy
" has exposed what should have been concealed.   It is true that this
" useless dame is the wife of Onchi Sakon Mitsumoto.   This Tarō
" Nagataru is my grandson.   Mitsukazu was killed at the Minato-
" gawa in company with the prince (Masashige); son and grandson
" continued to follow the fortunes of the House, and in the years
" following the defeat of Yoshihiro fought with Prince Masakatsu
" in the mountains of Yamato.   Here died my son and last support,
" the father of this boy.   Faithful hands brought us to Kyūshū,
" where lived one Sugimoto Hyōye, serving the Kusunoki lords and
" much indebted to the *karō*.   During this man's life we wanted for
" nothing.   Now Tarō is grown into a man, and though Sugimoto
" is dead the aged dame has found support from Heaven."   She
ceased.   Then Hyōsuke told their tale; the strife with the Kamakura Kwanryō, the disastrous battle at Yahagi, the search for their
lord.

For some time the lady was silent—" In brief deign to lay
" before my ignorant self the affairs of Kamakura and Miyako.   Far
" removed but little is heard here; that little not to be trusted."
Hyōsuke exposed the state of affairs of the day.   Said she—
" Heaven's hand has guided you here.   A request is to be made."
Said Hyōsuke—" It is granted beforehand, as far as effort can
" carry it out."—" Deign then to take this Tarō with you in the
" search for your lord.   To dwell as we do, for a man of his rank is

---

    * The general and devoted adherent of Go Daigo Tennō.   He is the Japan-
ese " Bayard."

The Obame writes a Letter.

" to live the life of a demon, useless and unhappy. It is now time for
" him to put on armour, to wield the sword. Thus will the House of
" Onchi be restored to its rights and privileges as asserted. Deign good
" Sirs to hear this request." The opposition assuredly did not come
from the Oguri *rōtō*. They bowed in appreciation of the honour of
thus associating the heir of the *karō* of the Nankō in their search
and adventures. The House of Onchi should share in the prosperity
of the Houses of Oguri and Satake. Their lord would assure such
issue. But Tarō objected. At first he agreed on condition that the
Obame went also. He was " but eighteen years old and a spoiled
grandchild." The old dame laughed—" Nay ! Tarō, the grand-
" dame has no legs. Rest assured that no injury will come to her.
" Return with success, to the joy of the Obame or to burn incense
" before her tomb." The last idea was too much for Tarō. His
bawls became louder. Said Hyōsuke—" Tarō Dono will always be
" welcomed. The Oguri House restored our lord will see that Tarō
" Dono enters the world under good auspices. The House of Onchi
" shall prosper. Deign not to be alarmed." But the dame rebuked
the grief of the boy—" Tarō Dono, these honoured guests mistake
" the roar of the fall for your weeping. The sight is a beautiful one.
" Take them forth to view the water-slide, its fall. Obame will write
" directions for their journey to the sea port. It will be late on the
" return. Deign not to disturb the slumber of the aged."

Thus she dismissed them. Going forth they donned the *take-
geta*, clogs made by splitting a giant bamboo and inserting thongs.
Then Tarō led them to the edge of the jutting hill. Opposite, lit up
by the moonlight, the gleaming water tumbled and shone like a
broad stream of liquid silver. Long they gazed, until the shifting
satellite left the scene in darkness. The house was dark on their
return. Observing the injunction they laid down to rest ; the samurai in the guest room, Tarō by the hearth. Hyōsuke was first to
awake. Broad day streamed through the still closed *amado*. This
was unusual in any country house. Leaping up he roused his companions and Tarō. He felt uneasy after the scene of the night
before. In haste they entered the room to which the Obame had
retired for the night—to write and sleep. An unkind sight met

their eyes.   Her feet bound securely by the girdle, her robe neatly
arranged, she had plunged her dagger into her throat and died.   A
letter lay close to hand :

> " Age has touched the wife of Onchi Sakon Jirō
> " Mitsumoto.   Now she remains, clog on the career
> " of the Onchi House.   The affection of Tarō
> " holds him to her side.   Filial duty becomes
> " a disastrous bond.   Hence dies this Haruko,
> " for the glory of the Onchi House."

With sympathy the Oguri *rōtō* mitigated the grief of the re-
morseful Tarō.   Nothing else was to be done.   The command of
the Obame was to be obeyed.   With reverence and pity was
she laid to rest in the precincts of the village temple.   As unbefitting
the mission Tarō hid the armour, deep buried under stone and earth
in a cave near by.   To prevent its use by thieves the house was set
on fire and destroyed.   In company with the Oguri *rōtō*, Tarō Nagataru took his way to the port of Miyazaki.   The tale of their
lord's flight to Kyūshū was obviously false, so they took ship to
Shikoku.

CHAPTER XX.

The Gembuku of Onchi Tarō.

The craft, devoted to fishing or trading as its usual task, to piracy as opportunity offered, floated out of the quiet waters of the Ōyodogawa into the swell of the ocean. Camphor and wax in jars, bundles of *kasuri*, a coarse minute patterned blue dyed cloth, filled the bottom. Some of this cargo was bound to the Go-Kinai, transferring on the Tosa coast, for the Hyūga fishermen only knew of the greater Nippon in this second hand way. Among this miscellaneous mass of merchandise an equally mixed passenger list bestowed itself as best it could. There were *yamabushi* wandering home from their pilgrimage to Hikōzan by the famed shrines of Shikoku ; some genuine traders interested in the forwarding of the products of the southern province to the capital, even to the Kwantō, better assured of such transit, and fearing piracy by sea less than the piracy on land and the exactions of the *daimyō* who guarded the nameless waters enclosed by the main island and Shikoku ; a few samurai, of doubtful affairs but unlikely to interfere with these humble folk. With satisfaction the *sendō* overlooked their craft. Any interloper was more likely to suffer than themselves. The priest was a very poor specimen of his craft. He was far too well behaved. The peddler knew little of his stock, as these sharp scented peasants soon ascertained. The samurai would fight as a matter of business. The *yamabushi*, was it not their affair to slay serpents and robbers, to clear the country-side of these pests of the people ? They too, if in disrepute as clerics, were noted as brawlers. In this feature of the profession of their vows they were highly consistent.

Their prognostics of a good voyage were carried out to the letter. For a week the little ship tossed its way through the stormy waters of the late summer. Passengers and crew passed the time as best they could. Each carried his own rations of rice and radish (*daikon*) ; often cold, for an even keel was taken advantage of to prepare the mess of food which might have to last for some days. Whether our wanderers were good seamen or not history does not record. The Kwantō men notoriously disliked salt water. Was not this the base of Kajiwara Kagetoki's quarrel with the Hangwan Yoshitsune ? And was not Onchi Tarō a mountaineer, familiar with the crags of the sacred mountain, but little conversant with these unstable hills ? His three companions came to entertain a great affection for the boy. His easy willingness, unfailing good-humour, an indifference to danger and injury with a cool-headedness in meeting both, all this while suffering wretchedly on this strange element, made the pledge to the dame easy of fulfillment. On more than one occasion Tarō was most useful. Thus when mast and sail threatened to go by the board in a sudden squall, it was Tarō who threw his great height and strength against the straining pole, at imminent danger of going overboard with it, and braced himself. Shōji came to his aid, and the seamen could loose the ropes and lower the sail. Thus the danger passed. When the flurry was over *kashira* and his men came before the boy and prostrated themselves in deep obeisance of thanks—" Surely without " the aid of this wondrous youth we would have reached land—but " at the sea bottom. 'Tis the *kami* who have favoured a man with " such strength." Tarō acknowledged the obeisance as best he could, and returned to his contributions to the sea god.

Long was the consultation over him. Hyōsuke the *karō* was now a man in full middle life. The burden of the Oguri House in its desperate straits weighed heavily on the thoughtful man. Dai-hachirō, though some years younger, shared the counsel and disallusion of his brother. So much depended on the politics of the day. In their company the occasion for *harakiri* was at least as great as ultimate success. In Kamakura and Kyōto the Isshiki were fast anchored. Some great storm only could shake the powerful House and clear the sky for them. Ikeno Shōji was more optimistic. Shōji was a combination often found in the man of action.   In battle none was more terrible, none more cool-headed and quick to grasp the opportunity of a strategic position left open by the foe.   Sukeshige relied on him as captain.   Yet from this life he turned with delight to some scroll. He was but little more than thirty years of age.   With equal plea- sure he fingered the works of the Chinese tacticians, writers on the art of war, the *ki* or records of the bloody struggles of Nippon itself ; or he would turn to the writings of Mōshi (Mencius) preferred to Kōshi, or the fresh commentaries by the Nipponese of his own day. The Zen sect of the Buddhists really gave the fillip to the cast of thought of the samurai of later Ashikaga and Tokugawa times.   Purely religious meditation had little charm for such men, nor could it find much place in the strife of these days.   They abandoned Buddhism for this reason, and largely because the man of Nippon is too con- ceited at base to admit any overruling universal power to his always firm belief in the *kami* or humanized deities and deified humans of his own race.   The severe and practical teachings of the Chinese sages filled a gap for ethics.   Now knowing the condition of affairs in the political world the three men had misgivings as to bringing Onchi Tarō into the difficulties of the Ognri House. The Nankō House (Kusunoki) in its latest representative Mitsumasa was coquetting with both sides and enjoyed some credit.   Besides there was the Nitta.   With the exception of Yoshimune's son, Sadakata, its members had submitted to Kamakura and were en- rolled in its service.   The affairs of Onchi Tarō could safely be entrusted to their care.   Tarō's reply to these representations was simply—" At the command of the Obame Tarō joined the *rōtō* of " Oguri.   The person of my brother Shōji is as dear to Tarō as his " own body. If the former suffers injury it will be because Tarō is not " there to interpose and take the proffered blow.   If his companion- " ship is irksome and refused, then he will find his way to Miyako. " Breaking into the Shōgun's presence Tarō will strangle him with " his own hands; just as he strangled the *ōzaru* (big monkey). " Deign, honoured Sirs, to reconsider your determination."   What answer could be made to a reply so direct, and which they knew would certainly bear fruit.   Tarō was in less danger with them.

All embraced the youth with joy, and no more was said about separation.

At Uwajima in Iyo the *sendō* brought them to land. As pilgrims no better place could be found than this Shikoku. With its eighty-eight holy places it rivals Yamato and Kii in the number of its *omairi* and its mendicants. Here they attracted no attention, and learned nothing of their lord. Wandering up the country they approached the headwaters of the Yoshinogawa and followed its course into Tosa province. At the junction of the river with the larger Kamiyamagawa there was a village known as Kōnomura. Vaguely they had heard of it as a great resort for wandering pilgrims, a magnet for the expert among these spongers. Here was to be found a constantly shifting clientele. It was late afternoon when they reached the place. A placard stared them in the face:

" Whether the stranger be from far, or nearer,
" or of the neighbourhood ; of military caste,
" or trader ; he will find shelter."

(*Jōhenro, chūhenro, gehenro, bukehenro, akindohenro ;*
henroshū no o yado itasubeki mono nari.)

Kōnomura

Kōno Shichirō Uyemon

Ōei 12th year 1st month (March, 1405).

Tarō cut a caper of joy in the road. Hyōsuke, who was studying the placard with some care, put on a very mild frown. " Deign Tarō Dono to share your joy with the rest of us. This " notice is by no means clear." With a wave of his leg and the big toe planted on the character 宿 Tarō answered—" Deign, honoured " Sir, to note the end thereof. What ends fairly it matters little " what its beginning. The legs and belly of Tarō as well as his eyes " augur well of this ' shelter.' The former are worn out from use ; " the latter from lack of use. The more haste to refresh both, the " earlier their repair. Hence Tarō's joy, gladly shared with all." The others grunted assent, but Hyōsuke was not so easily satisfied. A farmer came along the road. His rain coat hung over his shoulders, his straw hat dangled behind. Lacking mattock or

spade he came as one returning from a journey. Hyōsuke hailed
him. "This notice good fellow : what means this *henro* 遍路* of
"so many sorts of men? And this Kōno of Kōnomura ; who is
"he?" Before priest and samurai the peasant went on his belly.
"With fear and respect : the matter is easily explained and perhaps
"much to the purpose. This Shikoku is a very holy land. It is
"here that Kōbō Daishi established on Zōzusan the greatest of its
"shrines, Kotohira. The whole circuit of the pilgrimage to the
"eighty-eight holy places is here accomplished. Many the kinds,
"many the classes, of the pilgrims. Some are mere beggars, out-
"casts, dead-beats. These are the *jōhenro*. They rarely leave the
"circuit, finding ease and a living. Then many come travelling in
"a company, or man with wife, or with a brother or with friends ;
"devout in religion yet seeking diversion from the daily round of
"toil. The pilgrimage made they return to their more distant
"homes, these good farmers and traders, to talk of it the rest of
"their lives, a marvel to their neighbours. These are seen no more.
"They are the *chūhenro* ; esteemed, for if their contributions be not
"great, yet the numbers make up for the deficiency of the indivi-
"dual giver. The *gehenro* are those travelling at ease, with mixed
"motive of religion and pleasure. The contributions are heavy,
"their reception in accordance. As for Kōno Dono, in former days
"the family was of the military caste, but the grandsire abandoned
"the privileges of the knight for the wealth of the gentleman
"farmer (*gōshi*). All the land hereabouts belongs to Kōno Dono.
"Forty-three villages obey his command. In his devotion to the
"Buddha, for years shelter and entertainment have been offered to
"the pilgrims of the religion. Both are of the best. Ah! The
"food! He who has access to the kitchen of Kōno Dono has a
"taste of the feasts of the Gokuraku of Amida. This Tarōsaku can
"speak. Deign honoured Sirs to determine on a stay." His
questioners needed little urging. That they were on pilgrimage
was certain truth. Whether it came within the definition of Kōno

---

* The characters mean—"everywhere road"; i.e. applied to people=
trampers. Cf. Momogawa 263, 264. The *jō* implies religious superiority; a
classification of Kōbō Daishi, not of the Kōno *bantō*.

Dono they gave little consideration. With their thanks the farmer went on his way. As directed the men followed the river bank, here clothed with forest to the river's edge. Emerging into an open space they found themselves before the massive gate of Kōno's rest house. With river before it, with moat and wall, it was like a fortified camp, much needed in these perilous times to every man of great possessions.

Access, however, was easy. Within the gate, opened at their call, was a sort of office. Here sat several clerks (*tedaitei*), taking names and occupations, and giving out wooden tickets which classified the recipients. The Gotō were easily placed, Hyōsuke as *bukehenro* (military pilgrim), Daihachirō as *akindohenro* (trader). Shōji gave some difficulties. "*Rokubu-henro?*" Such kind was not in their menagerie. The eighty-eight shrines of Shikoku inspired much respect; the sixty-six shrines of Nippon none whatever. Slily the *bantō* slipped him a *jōhenro* ticket, received with all respect and gratitude by the unconscious Shōji. Then came the turn of Tarō for examination. His impatience got the better of him. Before the clerk could open his mouth; "For my part I am *Nami-henro* (the average kind). The clerk countered skilfully on Tarō. Said he cooly—"The kind is well known; the "explanation is accepted. Deign good Sir to accept the slab." He passed over a *jōhenro* ticket. Tarō, as unconscious as Shōji, accepted it, though with less gratuitous thanks. As travelling in one party Hyōsuke refused better entertainment than his company. All were shown into a clean but small (four mat) room in one of the many detached buildings scattered through the enclosure. Here the Gotō waved seniority and dismissed the two younger men to the bath. Shōji went as guardian to the not too cautious Tarō. The brothers remained, carefully to go over the events of the day as bearing on their search and future movements.

The baths were beautifully arranged. In a long shed separated into compartments were ten of these receptacles. The neat cleanliness, the clear steaming water, the outlook on stream and garden in the front, everything gave promise of an enjoyable experience. But the attendant examined the tickets and politely waved them on.

Explained he—" These ten baths are reserved for *bukehenro* and
" *chūhenro*. The bath of the *jōhenro* is beyond, on the other side
" of the house. Everything is there provided for their comfort—and
" the security of their possessions." Slightly turning up his ecclesiastical nose he watched the big fellows go onward to their goal. At
least they saw something of the resources of Kōno Dono, his ability
to maintain this great charity. Store house after store house was
passed in line. Then was reached the mansion itself with its great
kitchen in the rear decorated with scores of vessels in pottery and
iron. Many cooks were busily engaged in preparing the evening meal. A savoury smell escaped into the air. Beyond was the
gate in the wall of a beautiful garden. The two men stopped and
looked. The lord of the mansion had an exquisite view from the
fine apartments facing this inclosure. All that art could do added
to the grotesque beauty of its lines ; the little pine crowned hillocks,
the artificial pebble strewn stream, the quaint trees, the grotesque
lanterns, the erratic rock work—all so unusual and so natural, backed
by the mountain Nature had thrown up close by in the rear. But Shōji
said—" A weak spot if Kōno Dono is ever attacked by enemies.
" The mountain so close at hand throws open this place." Turning
down the wall the bath for the *jōhenro* was soon reached.

The noses of Shōji and Tarō went up in the air with good
cause ; not as to the place itself, for this was kept as clean as could
be—under the conditions. The company, however, was anything
but select, or selected ; except on unsavoury principles. Four baths
provided for the swarm of beggars (*jōhenro*) seeking the charity of
Kōno Dono ; and beggars swarmed in the baths. Dirty fellows
they were. Like their countrymen of later date they detested cold
water. No mountain pool attracted them. To dip into the cascade
on the hillside was severest penance ; so regarded from ancient days,
so prescribed by all religious sects. Except Kōno, none provided
warm water for their ablutions, or tolerated them. Hence the
popularity of this bath house. These fellows swarmed with vermin,
their bodies stunk with the accretion of weeks of wandering and the
issue of filthy diseases. Tarō's eyes lit up a little. He looked back
toward the still visible roof of the bath reserved for the chosen ones.

" Is this Tarō a goat (*yagi*) ? " quoth he, assuredly unconscious of all biblical reference. But Shōji restrained him. " To quarrel with " one's host under these conditions is unseemly. It is for us to take " or leave. Perhaps there is one still in condition for use. With " backs turned away the sight of these beggars can be avoided."

Tarō went up to the fourth and most distant bath, the less sociable, better fitted for a duet than to accommodate an orchestra. A beggar was stewing himself within. So far good ; not so as to the bath itself. The water was black with filth. The excretions of their predecessors floated on the surface. Unceremoniously Tarō leaned down and seized the tub. Raising it on his shoulders he turned to leave the shed. The beggar screamed in fright. His waving legs, brought into intimate contact with the hot metal furnace, added pain to fright. The burning charcoal fell out. Fire was threatened to be added to panic. Up ran the bath attendants greatly frightened. " Heh ! You ! What are you about ! *Jōhenro,* " why make this disturbance? *Jōhenro* ! " The angry glare in Tarō's eyes, the obvious danger signal in a man able to raise bath, water, beggar, as if merely a water bucket, brought the men to their senses. The next moment tub and beggar would be cast at their own heads. Mild measures were best. Said Tarō with brief de-cision—" The water is filthy. It is to be renewed at the stream. I " shall throw the contents into the river and draw fresh water at the " fall in the garden. We will only trouble you to heat it." He made a stride as if to carry out the threat. The beggar shrieked horribly at this prospect of being cast into perdition. Cold water internally was bad enough. The Kōno *bantō* made terms—" With " fear and respect, doubtless some error is involved. Such exertion " on your part honoured Sir is needless. Leave this man to his " recreation. Another bath is already prepared. It is at your " service." Mollified Tarō carefully put beggar and tub back into their original darkness; but springing out the fellow fled in terror from his lonely isolation to the more crowded company in the large tubs. The occupants received him with jeers, and looks of black hate at these bold interlopers who thus cast insult on their kind. Under the guidance of the *bantō* Shōji and Tarō were taken to one of the coveted

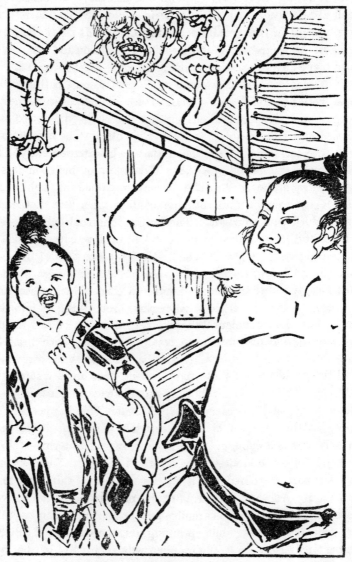

Cleanliness is neighbour to Godliness.

compartments. Here they tubbed in comfort and harmony, stewing at will in the clean water, and enjoying the outward prospect. Tarō still grumbled a little. "Ten baths for perhaps as many people ; " four tubs for a hundred of these filthy fellows ! " Said Shōji— " Deign to remember their filth—and rejoice." Replied Tarō— " Shōji Dono speaks well. One such fellow would poison the " water for all who follow. Let them poison each other."

Thus the Gotō met with no difficulty. They were conducted at once to the clean place reserved for better guests. All were united at the supper board. Said the attendant—" *Saké* is not " served. Kōbō Daishi would drink nothing but water. Those " who follow in his Way do likewise." Said Hyōsuke—" The rule is " good, especially in mixed company. Deign to receive our thanks " for the kind entertainment." But they made up for the abstinence on the food. The Kōno *genan* (men servants) looked on with amazement. Bowl after bowl of rice disappeared beneath the assault of these hungry men. Especially Onchi Tarō, already famed throughout the establishment. At the twenty-seventh bowl Tarō sighed with repletion, the *genan* with relief. A few more such pilgrims and even the great resources of the Kōno House would stagger. Nay ! Even the attendants of the House might have to draw in their belts. "And they call this *shōjin* (vegetable diet) ! " Truly one would never suspect it." The man looked at Shōji a little angry. He began—" It is the rule of Kōbō Daishi........." Hyōsuke stopped him with engaging smile. " The compliment " is to the cooks of your honoured House. The vegetable diet by " their skill has all the savour of fish and meat. Few are so strong " as not at times to repine, but none could do so here. Great and " deserved is the reputation of the House, of your master's kitchen." The man bowed flat in thanks from one to another as they repeated the praise of Hyōsuke. Tarō merely rubbed his stomach. Grinning the attendants made off with empty dishes and rice tub.

Said Hyōsuke—" What was said, was meant. The company " is very mixed. Some I do not like ; most ill-looking fellows " prowling here and there and peering into everything. Sleep " lightly this night." Tarō was poor encouragement. His jaws yawned open most frightfully from time to time. Attendants appeared with bedding. Tarō was barely stretched out than he slept like a log. The others, better trained, had one eye and ear open. At midnight Hyōsuke shook his brother Daihachirō. Shōji was on his feet. *Watsu! Watsu.* Shouts, breaking doors, screams, then the clash of weapons was heard. Shaking Tarō into semi-consciousness, and with injunction to follow, the three men opened the corner of the *amado* and sprang out. Tarō sprang to his feet. Tall, his head came into violent contact with the thin boards of the low ceiled room. When he opened his eyes all was dark as pitch. He remembered that Hyōsuke had aroused him with injunction to follow. Whither? As he had started. The timbers of the roof crashed, the tiles went flying. Thus Tarō emerged into the open. From his elevation he could see the battle going on around the mansion. Soon to ground he rooted up an ash sapling close by and flew forward to join in the battle. The band of Kuzuryū (9 headed dragon) Kurō which harboured on Meguroyama had attacked the house of Kōno. The excuse of these fellows was the same as of most of the brigand bands of these early Ashikaga days—the intent to raise funds for a rebellion against the Shōgun who had repudiated his own offer of alternate emperors chosen from the lineage of the Northern and Southern Courts. These fellows had three chiefs: this Kuzuryū, one Abukuma Jūbyōye, and Myōgi no Tarō. Under them operated as sub-chiefs Yamauba Kozō, Haguro no Tenrimbō, Nezu no Imayasha, Hayabusa Tarō, Kotengu Heisuke. In sum they commanded three hundred men. The band lived in luxury on the mountain, supplying themselves with food, drink, girls, by levying on the villages of lower Iyo and Tosa. It was the turn of Kōno to contribute. This fellow was recalcitrant. Hence this sudden attack. Despising the farmer Haguro no Tenrimbō, Nezu no Imayasha, Hayabusa Tarō led some fifty men on this raid.

This Haguro no Tenrimbō (Heaven revolving cell) was a man of no small importance. The Daishugenja, that is head of the *yamabushi* at their Dewa monastery, he wielded great influence, and was noted as a fighter among these fighting disreputable monks. His raid was assured of success before the Oguri *rōtō* appeared on the scene.

The Battle at Kōnomura.

Kōno Shichirō Uyemon faced defeat. Desperately wounded he was prepared "to fold his hands." Just at this juncture the Gotō and Ikeno Shōji came to stiffen the resistance. As the band of thieves hesitated, then rallied to fall on the demoralized Kōno men, Tarō fell on their rear. His sapling had already gained him the readier weapon of a stout staff. With this he laid right and left. Annoyed at the check in his rear Tenrimbō turned back to see what was the cause. Whirling his iron pole he rode toward this rash fellow, to punish the interruption. He directed but one blow at Tarō. The iron-wood got the best of the iron metal; or rather it got the best of the monk's hard head. The brains of Tenrimbō were spattered all over the rich saddle. As he fell backward the frightened horse planted his hoofs in the dying man and finished the work of Tarō's weapon. Shōji was already at the latter's side. As Nezu no Imayasha fled Shōji deftly stuck Tenrimbō's long pole between his legs, and smashed ribs and head as sequel. Hayabusa Tarō flew like a bird, but to escape by the river. Here Gotō Hyōsuke and Daihachirō soon laid hands on him. Wiser they trussed him for the nonce, having other use for his brains in any further necessary proceedings. Headed by Tarō and Shōji the swarming Kōno men corralled the thieves. No mercy was shown. Swords and staves did the work. Not a man was left alive to carry back the tale to the mountain fort.

With grave respect Ikeno Shōji approached Onchi Tarō. Said he—"Great have been the deeds of Onchi Dono. But deign, "honoured Sir, to favour this Sukenaga." Replied Tarō, breathing hard and leaning on his blood-stained staff—"To his brother Shōji "this Nagataru listens with fear and respect. Deign Sir to speak." Said Shōji—"Why not then, Tarō Dono make distinction between "friend and foe? See! These men of Kōno, they too nurse "bruised shins and ribs, blossoms of the staff and arm of Nagataru. "Deign, honoured Sir, this too to explain." Tarō opened wide his eyes. He was not quite sure whether Shōji was praising him, laughing at him, rebuking him. He replied in simple terms and gravely—"The men of Kōno are no better known to this Tarō than "the thieves. To speak plain truth there is little to distinguish

"them. To knock them all down, to make distinction afterward
"among the survivors, such was the plan of this Tarō." Shōji had
spoken very little in rebuke, much in laughter. At this reasoning,
simple and exact, he was all admiration. First he bowed in ceremonious respect. Then with affection he placed both hands
on the shoulders of the stalwart youth. "Tarō Dono is right.
"Shōji is a fool. Never has such a *gembuku* been seen as this of
"Nagataru. Among the *rōtō* of our lord there is none to match
"you. Deign to accept respectful thanks of this Shōji for the title
"with which he has been honoured." Thus was cemented this
formidable brotherhood in arms of Sukenaga and Nagataru.

The scene of the carnage was frightful. The men and women
servants stood aghast and pleased. It would take days to clean the
building through which the battle had raged, and which was a
fearful mess of blood and hacked and broken posts and screens.
The wounded Shichirō had been carried into a room, one of few
still habitable. Somewhat revived he asked that his unexpected
allies be introduced. As Hyōsuke made salutation, said Kōno
Shichirō—"Deign to pardon this rudeness. This Shichirō is
"an old man, and now sorely wounded. It was plain to the
"*tedaitei* that your company was no usual one. So it had been
"reported. That you should render such aid to the Kōno House
"was unexpected. This makes a request less bold." Said Hyōsuke—"If the request be within our ability it would be pleasure
"and duty to serve one so charitable and virtuous as Kōno Dono.
"Deign to express your honoured wish." Grunted the old man
with growing difficulty—"At the headwaters of the Omiyagawa
"which comes in below here, in the recesses of the ranges of Megu-
"royama, harbours this band lead by Kuzuryū Kurō. Between
"him and the Kōno House there can now be nothing but war to
"the end, with death for the defeated. Deign to lead the thousand
"men of the forty-three manors, and put to death these thieves.
"That you are worthy of the service there is no question. Reveal
"your secret to this Shichirō. It will be kept inviolable, and per-
"chance the Kōno House can give you aid of men and money."
Replied Hyōsuke—"This is not to be lightly done. Deign to dis-

"miss those present." When nurses and physician had withdrawn Hyōsuke told his tale. The wanderers were in search of their lord, hoping to secure the restoration of the Oguri House. Kōno Shichirō greatly rejoiced—" Heaven has sent you to my aid. Famed through " the land are the lord of Oguri and his *rōtō*. The resources of the " Kōno House gladly are extended to give him aid. And now, " honoured Sirs, deign to consider the request of this Shichirō." Said Hyōsuke—" That is granted forthwith. Our every effort shall be "made to defeat your enemies. The cause of the Kōno House is " that of Oguri.

Then Hayabusa Tarō was brought in for examination. This was no gentle one. Under the skilful torture of the Kōno retainers he confessed everything with more and less readiness. There were fifteen chiefs in all, three of whom were supreme. They had connections in Iyo, Awa, and Sanuki. Many men were enlisted for the future uprising and the present life of riot. He exposed the state of affairs at the mountain fort under severer treatment. When the torture could get nothing more out of him beyond an offer to guide them to the place he was removed. Said Hyōsuke grimly— " He is in little state to act as guide for many days. But he is not "needed. The information is complete. Its accuracy shall be " ascertained by Daihachirō and this Hyōsuke. These men are to " be put to death. Hayabusa's fate shall be determined by his truth-"fulness. Do you Shōji, and Tarō Dono, remain here to captain " the Kōno men and guard this Hayabusa against giving informa-" tion to the mountain fort. Be always vigilant. The news of this " night ascertained, as it will be from the peasant talk, they will " attack at once. Have guards to give prompt notice of their " advance. We will accompany them. This is best."

Prepared for the journey an interview was sought by Shichi-nosuke, eldest son of Shichirō Uemon. Said he—" To follow the " directions extorted from this rascal Hayabusa a guide will be " necessary. The man who acts as spy and go-between with the " band of Kuzuryū has returned. Through him we are kept in-' ' formed of their movements. Unfortunately my father had sent " him on a mission to the coast, from which he returned but yester-

" day to make his report. Deign, honoured Sirs, to permit his
" company. Humble as he is he possesses courage and confidence,
" and may prove useful." At the acquiescence of Hyōsuke the man
was summoned. The surprise of recognition was mutual, for the man
was none other than the farmer Tarōsaku, who had urged their stay
at the Kōno rest house ; with fortunate issue. The farmer prostrated himself in obeisance. He could hardly repress a respectful
wink at the trinket merchant, also transformed into priestly disguise
which scantily covered the samurai beneath. With mutual confidence thus the Gotō brothers and their guide set forth. Kōno
Shichinosuke knew the difficulties of the way. All day they ascended and descended confused lines of ridges, crossing the Shichikaku
ranges to the inner retreat of the thieves on Meguroyama. At last
they reached a narrow valley which pitched down steeply from the
higher range. Its sides were thickly clothed with forest in which
cedar and the camphor tree were conspicuous. This made the
climbing less difficult beneath the shade. Tarōsaku produced a
strong cord. Said he—" With fear and respect : deign Sirs to
" bind fast this Tarōsaku. Strangers in this land it is best to take
" me an unwilling guide, forced to obey your command. Thus the
" fort is entered under constraint in your company and excuse is
" found." Said Hyōsuke—" But may not the thieves take venge-
" ance on your person even for this unwilling guidance ? " Replied
the farmer—" That is as it may be. However this Tarōsaku is
" very useful to the band. More than one good raid has followed
" his advice. As long as his master is without injury Tarōsaku is
" content. Even farms of Kōno Dono have been pillaged, but fore-
" warned little harm has followed. Up to now the thieves have
" never dared attack Kōnomura. Unfortunate was the distant
" mission to the coast. In necessity and at your will, honoured
" Sirs, put in an aiding word if life is threatened."

The man spoke well. Tightly binding him the climb was
continued up the now narrow cleft of the valley. Far below the
cliffs roared the mountain stream. Well upon the shoulders
of the mountain they came out on its banks. At this place it
ran through a deep gorge, the bed of the stream a good hundred

feet below them. Opposite was a kind of shelf in the mountain side, inaccessible except through rough forest and over the towering peaks, or by access across the stream. This latter was the usual road. A guard house protected the raised bridge constructed of a floor of stout saplings bound together with wisteria creeper. A *naruko* was fastened to a pine close by. Seizing it Daihachirō proceeded to make a most hideous uproar, echoed and re-echoed among the hills. At this gentle announcement a fellow appeared yawning from the guard house. Approaching the bank he shouted—" Who goes there? Tarōsaku San, why thus in this company, trussed up like " some prisoner?" Answered the farmer—" To guide strangers to " the mountain is forbidden. Though these people bear a message " from the chief of Kongōsan in Tamba, it is only on compulsion " that this Tarō accompanies them. Deign to recommend his pardon." —" News from Hondo! That is important. Deign to wait Sirs. " Notice shall be carried to the chiefs." He disappeared. Said the farmer drily—" The credit of Tarōsaku, and the lives of all are at " stake. Deign, honoured Sirs, to exercise circumspection."

The minor thief soon returned with a guard—of honour or otherwise as the case might be. The bridge was lowered. Hyōsuke and Daihachirō, with Tarōsaku in the middle, crossed the torrent. Far below thundered the brawling river. A hand raised, with ease they would have been pitched downward, their bodies mutilated and torn on the rocks. The passage was to the Gotō brothers at least evidence of curiosity, if not safety. One thing Hyōsuke noted. No precaution was taken to blindfold them. Either they would issue in triumph, or not return at all. This sequel was evident. Gate and wall, gate and wall ; three of these were passed. Then they were ushered into a large hall. Here a banquet was spread, for night already was at hand. The chiefs occupied the upper end of the hall. Kuzu-ryū was the oldest, a man of perhaps fifty years. The others were younger men, barely thirty years of age. The assembled band ranged from mere striplings to warriors grizzled by the wars between the North and South Courts. The display of furniture was lavish. The chiefs were clad in richest damasks. Tubs of *saké*, the heads broached, supplied the merriment. The table groaned with the best sea and land afforded. As in camp these warriors used stool and table. A bevy of pretty girls swarmed to attend to the service, and each chief had his chosen beauty to look after his needs.*

Summoned from the bottom of the room Hyōsuke and Daihachirō advanced. Then they stretched out their arms. Kuzuryū was the spokesman. To his sharp question Hyōsuke answered that their names were Yamaneko [mountain (wild) cat] and Yamaitachi (mountain weasel). They were commissioned to bring a message from Oniyasha of Kongōsan. Prince Mochiuji of Kamakura and the Ashikaga Shōgun were seriously at odds. Everything was ready for the restoration of the emperor of the South Court. The fiefs were ready for distribution. None must hold back. All needed was united and earnest effort. What was the state of affairs in Tosa? Hyōsuke was full of information gleaned from Shōji, Hayabusa, and Tarōsaku. Glibly he answered the questions of the chief. The latter was glad to get this information from the main island. As to Shikoku he was well informed, but plainly the credentials of Yamaneko had been accepted elsewhere. Why should they not accept them? However he showed some anger toward the unlucky Tarōsaku. The farmer's head was in no little danger. Hyōsuke sized up his man. He agreed that the farmer had offended in acting as guide even under compulsion. It would be as well to make him a head shorter. Said he—" After all it is " but a farmer less."—" And one useful to us, honoured Sir," snapped Kuzuryū. " Tarōsaku has acted under compulsion. As farmer " he is a coward. Wisely he fears our vengeance on himself and " his farm more than the rebuke of his master. He is to be en-" couraged. His life is to be spared. Deign not to interfere." Hyōsuke bowed with indifference and spoke as to his mission. As to that consultation would be held and answer made. " Meanwhile " deign to join in the feast."

Hardly was place made at the table of the lower chiefs than disturbance was heard at the lower end of the hall. The hunting party and its leaders had returned with the product of the chase.

---

* The old prints often represent the military chiefs thus seated on stools and before tables in their curtained camps.

At the announcement of the names, Kanamono and Konomono, Daihachirō shot a glance at the impassive face of Hyōsuke. The latter went on stuffing himself as if he had fasted for a week. It was under these names that the Kazama brothers usually figured on more distant raids from Mount Tsukuba. With feigned indifference the two brothers watched the approach of the men laden with deer, boar, a bear's cub, hare by the score. The Kazama knelt before the chiefs. "With fear and respect : deign to receive " this indifferent result of the work. Perchance in the next hunt " the game will be more complacent." The chiefs rubbed their hands with glee—"Splendid indeed ! It is to be doubted if the mountains " of Tamba can furnish forth such abundance of game." Kazama Jirō, Kazama Hachirō, looked across the table. Their eyes met those of the Gotō with the indifference of strangers. Hyōsuke answered coldly—"The game in Tamba goes on two legs. The " hunters are many. Perhaps the same is to be found in Tosa." Kuzuryū coloured with anger. Truly these messengers from Kongōsan jeered at the numbers and valour of his band. Kazama Jirō said most audibly to his neighbour—" Who are these men ? They " are not from the Kwantō "—" Yamaneko and Yamaitachi, " messengers from Kongōsan Oniyasha. They bring news from " Hondo welcome to the chiefs—perhaps. Is this pleasant life to " end in the turmoil of real war ? Alas ! " Hyōsuke took the hint and greater confidence. There were no northerners in the company but the Kazama. Henceforth he was full of talk of the Go-Kinai and Kyōto ; of the North he knew but by hearsay. Their wanderings in the West and South stood him in good stead.

The banquet over they were dismissed. Consultation was to be held over the answer to the Hondo chiefs. Kuzuryū was very brusque. Offence still rankled with him. Hyōsuke was not at all sure that his mission was unsuspected. At midnight the tension was relieved. A scratching at the door, the voice of Hachirō, and the two Kazama entered. Hearty was the greeting. "Mouth to ear" their stories were exchanged, consultation held. The Kazama brought important news. The answer to Kongōsan was prepared. After the morrow's banquet it was to be delivered to the

messengers. Hyōsuke and Daihachirō were in good standing with
the chiefs. About to break up the meeting startling news was
received. The attack on Kōnomura had failed. Instead of the
triumphant return came a frightened peasant with the news, and
that two of the chiefs, Tenrinbō and Nezu no Imayasha, had been
killed. Hayabusa Tarō was a prisoner. Kuzuryū forthwith was
in a great rage. He would have vented his anger on Tarōsaku for
not reporting the calamity ; then on the messengers of Kongōsan for
preventing him. But the other chiefs derided his suspicions.
Tarōsaku had not been allowed to visit Kōnomura, he had been
forced away as guide and knew nothing of these events. The messengers were inviolable. To insult or injure them would introduce
great complications and affect the distribution of the fiefs. The
Shinnō* was in the hands of the Hondo chiefs. Kuzuryū was over-
ruled by circumstances. He admitted his error. An expedition in
force against the Kōno was to be announced on the next day.
Tarōsaku with spies was to be despatched at once, to meet the band
at his farm with full information as to the state of affairs in Kōnomura. The whole band was to issue out before these fellows could
gather to the defence. Details of the attack would be settled on the
report of the spies, informed by Tarōsaku as to condition of affairs
at Kōnomura. Strangers at the rest-house would be under grave
suspicion, not he. Never had Tarōsaku been in higher consideration.
At this news Hyōsuke rubbed his hands with glee. He thought of
Shōji and Tarō at the head of five hundred Kōno men. " Bah !
" This fellow Kuzuryū has his plan. No message need be given
" Tarōsaku. He is a spy of the Kōno." The Kazama were
amazed. The farmer was the local stand-by of the band. " As
" for us, we will go to the attack in company with the thieves, and
" announce our names and lord at fitting opportunity." Thus did
the Oguri *rōtō* arrange matters between them. In the darkness the
Kazama took their leave.

---

* The Imperial prince. The Kusunoki and Ochi near Kyōto, and the
Kikuchi in Kyūshū were always supplied with one. Kakitsu 3rd year (1443) it
was Sonshū-O. Kyōto was attacked, the palace|fired, and the Treasures carried
off to Hieisan. Yoshinori had to storm Yoshino to put to death Sonshū-Ō.
And so on.

The following morning matters turned out as expected. The chiefs early summoned the messengers of Kongōsan to deliver the answer to their message. Excuse was made. Disastrous news had been received as to a raid made by a small party on one of the villages. "Accidents will happen in this best of possible worlds "and islands," quoth Kuzuryū. He was a little shame-faced over the failure of his subordinates. Hence the offer of Hyōsuke and his brother to go in their company was gladly accepted. The messengers from Hondo should see how efficient the band was in action under his leadership. Everything was soon in readiness. The march was to be straight across the ranges to the Yoshinogawa. At Nishigakata boats could be seized. Landing at Tarōsaku's farm they would march down the river bank to the attack on the Kōno mansion. Hyōsuke with some displeasure found himself and his brother separated from the Kazama. These went in company with Kuzuryū, who was much taken with the big brothers as bodyguard. The Gotō were to accompany the van under Myōgi Tarō. Hyōsuke quickly grasped the plan of Kuzuryū. The thieves were divided into three bands of seventy men each. While Myōgi Tarō attacked and kept the Kōno busy, the second band under Abukuma Jirō would break into the rear from the mountain. In the confusion thus created Kuzuryū himself would come up and complete the defeat. Not a man was to be left alive. Hyōsuke heartily agreed with this conclusion. Fortune favoured them. The divisions were to march separately, but within easy supporting distance. Thus confusion would be avoided in their separate parts. The *karō* gave his orders to the Kazama to hold back Kuzuryū by every device. On their part the Gotō would urge forward the van. Thus taken in detail the result was sure, even if the Kōno men showed too much of the farmer in their soldiering.

At midnight Myōgi Tarō and his band reached the gate of the Kōno mansion. All was silence and darkness. As Tarōsaku had said there was no guard, no expectation of an avenging mission. These fellows should wake to die, most cruelly. Myōgi Tarō was comforted. His nag, obtained at the farm, was made to curvet. This Yamaneko and Yamaitachi had almost charged him with

Gembuku of Onchi Tarō.

cowardice, so slow was his approach.   With no intention, under the
guidance of these strangers they had shot down the swift waters of
the darkened river at most reckless speed.   Said Yamaneko, half
sneering—"All are asleep.   The glory of the deed belongs to our
"captain.   It is for the Taishō (commander) to grasp the opportunity.
"Before the other chiefs are at hand the task is complete, the ven-
"geance ripe for the harvest.   Shall this Kōno Shichirō, this Shichi-
"nosuke be roasted before slow fires?   Or shall they be sliced for
"*sashimi?*   This matter of the kind of torture to be applied should
"now be discussed.   It is forgotten that these fellows are but farmers.
"But the gate......Yamaitachi your hand."   In a trice Hyōsuke
was on the wall.   He drew up his brother.   Myōgi Tarō open-
mouthed watched the proceeding.   Then the sound of bolts being
drawn was heard.   The gates swung wide open for the band to
enter the inclosure.

Trusting to these kind and energetic men the chief rode forward
into the darkness.   Well inside did he notice that the gate had
closed behind him?   Then from a tree came the beating of a drum.
Others repeated the sound.   Before Myōgi Tarō could well gather
his wits he found himself and his band the centre of the serried
ranks of the Kōno men.   Headed by Ikeno Shōji and Onchi Tarō
these drew their arrows to the head.   From three sides came a hail of
shafts.   The thieves fell pierced by the merciless barbs.   They turned
to flee, only to find their way barred by the closed gate, the Kōno
men close at hand.   Thus trapped the mountain men turned in
desperation.   Ikeno Shōji strode forward.   " Miserable rascals!
"Stick out your heads for the well deserved blow.   Know that he
"who speaks is Ikeno Shōji, *rōtō* of the lord of Oguri, Kojirō Suke-
"shige, a daimyō of a hundred thousand *koku*.   Let the band
"surrender and suffer decapitation."   To such a gentle invitation
there could be but one answer.   Myōgi Tarō slowly rode forward.
He was noted for his skill with the spear.   He was captain enough
to know that the Kōno defence depended on these leaders.   Shōji
had but his sword against the mounted man and longer weapon.
His defence was most skilful, but so also was Myōgi's attack.
Shōji could not get within his guard.   His life was in great peril.

Then Onchi Tarō came in action. He was armed with a long iron pole ; other weapons he had discarded. At this new assailant Myōgi jeered. This naked fellow was soon to be disposed of. He would surely have cut Tarō down ; but Tarō was young. The halberd's keen edge grazed the top of his head. Before Myōgi could recover his guard the iron pole swept the legs of the horse beneath him. A moment later Shōji held up the head of the foe in the glare of the torches of the Kōno men. This ended the combat. The thieves plead for mercy. The Kōno gave them the edge of the sword. Not a man was left alive ; the barred gate prevented all escape.

On the side of the mountain the defence was equally successful. Abukuma Jūbyōye had maintained the agreed rate of speed down river and on shore. He too gathered from the obliging Tarōsaku that the Kōno were careless, Myōgi Tarō just before him. Riding up to the garden wall he peered over. The sound of cries, feeble and scattered could be heard on the river side of the mansion. Plainly Myōgi Tarō had anticipated him. The greedy fellow had sought and gained the credit. Not so with the booty ; this was not to be concealed. At his orders the band poured over the wall into the narrow inclosure. They rushed toward the silent house, intending to break in, to massacre the remaining inmates crouching in fear and darkness, awaiting the expected thieves. Their reception was that of Myōgi Tarō on the front. The *amado*, a blind or shield held in the hands of the Kōno men, fell with a crash into the garden. From the dark house came volley after volley of arrows. Instead of being attacked it was the Kōno force which poured into the garden, and interposed between wall and thieves prevented escape. Jūbyōye in rage drove all before him. Foolish man, not thinking of escape he lead the attack on the house. A shout of joy went up as he recognized Yamaneko and Yamaitachi standing on the *rōka*. The force of Myōgi Tarō was at hand. These rascals were trying to break through to escape to the mountain. He shouted this encouragement to his band. But Hyōsuke and Daihachirō with drawn swords came forward. Hyōsuke made proclamation. " This is Gotō Hyōsuke, *karō* of the lord of Oguri, Kojirō Sukeshige,

"a daimyō of a hundred thousand *koku*. His brother Daihachirō
"accompanies him. Foolish fellow, stick out your head for punish-
"ment. The time of your offences has come to an end. You and
"your wicked band have been brought here to die." He sprang
forward, followed by Daihachirō. Abukuma Jūbyōye was a big
man. His bellyguard of plates of iron sewn together with light
green (*moegi*) thread matched the colour of his frightened face in
the glare of the torches held by the jubilant Kōno men. Daihachirō
stood grimly aside. Hyōsuke warily advanced to the attack. As
the halberd made a vicious sweep he quickly leaped aside. A second
and a third blow were equally unsuccessful. Then Hyōsuke succeeded in cutting the shaft in two. "Wai!" Abukuma Jūbyōye
sprang back, to recover and to draw his sword. As he did so he
stumbled. His hands went up. Next moment severed from hip
to pap he sank to the ground. With regret Hyōsuke noted the
escape of several thieves over the wall. "After them!" said he.
"Warning will be given to the greatest rascal of all, this Kuzuryū.
"Without his head the task is incomplete."

Kuzuryū and his band had reached the edge of the clearing at
last. His course had been marked by trouble from the start. The
Kazama at the oar in the descent of the river had proved both
awkward and over-cautious. Barely mounted his horse's girth came
loose and dumped him on the ground. Sourly he rode through the
wood. Scattered cries warned him of a contest, but the buildings
and wall stood out black and silent; no sign of fire, no sign of a battle
going forward. Puzzled and suspicious he halted. Then there crept
through the wood two or three lamed figures. He recognized his own
men. At their tale his anger and fear were great. In the Oguri
rōtō he recognized a formidable foe. He was undetermined whether
to retire at once to the fort, or to seek vengeance at the house of
Kōno. On the one side he was answered by the force of the Kōno
under Ikeno Shōji and Onchi Tarō which poured out the gate.
Almost at the same time appeared the Kōno led by Shichinosuke.
In the blackness of the wood their scanty numbers could not be
detected. With the greater part of this band Hyōsuke and Daihachirō had gone on in all haste to the fort to anticipate the fugi-

tives. The chief might have escaped, had it not been for his body-
guard. He had made up his mind to flee. The cries of his men,
already falling under the arrows of the Kōno as they sought refuge
in the wood, warned him of the enemy on his flank and rear. He
would ride through them. But the Kazama interposed. With a
shout they drew their swords—" Here stand the Kazama, Jirō and
" Hachirō, *rōtō* of the lord of Oguri, Kojirō Sukeshige, a daimyō of a
" hundred thousand *koku*. Nothing remains to Kuzuryū Dono but
" to stick out his head and receive the final stroke. This is a gentler
" death than the one intended for the enemy, but fitter for one who
" served the Nitta lords." Kazama Jirō spoke truth. Kuzuryū Kurō
was Ikegami Hachirō Uyemon Tamekuni, *kerai* of Sadakata the son
of the famed Yoshimune and quite as obstinate in resistance to Kamakura. In this peculiar way for years he had served his lord's House.
The latter's death at Shichirigahama had made him in every sense a
rōnin. His life of lust and riot was appropriate to the mountain of doubtful name (*meguro*). This now was to end. Slowly, almost wearily,
he rode forward. As he warmed to the fight the halberd flashed
viciously, whirling as the arm of a windmill. But the man in
front of him, Kazama Jirō, was a most accomplished fencer. As
the sought for opportunity came the severed blade fell to the ground.
Kazama Hachirō brought horse and man to the ground by a
blow which cut through the beast's fore-legs. As Kuzuryū Kurō
rolled on the ground Jirō sprang on him, to rise with the head.
The chiefs killed the Oguri *rōtō* stood aside and watched the Kōno
men at work at these close quarters. Here the thieves were not
pent up. They took to flight in the darkness, and many escaped
toward their refuge in the mountain fort. Grimly smiling the
Oguri directed the pursuit.

The fugitives fell into their own trap. Gotō Hyōsuke and
Daihachirō had long anticipated them. In the persons of Yamaneko and Yamaitachi they sought admittance. As the fugitives of
Jūbyōye had been gathered up by Kuzuryū there was no one to
give them the lie. When they told a tale of defeat it was discredited. These strangers from Kongōsan were gifted with great
cowardice and long legs. They had taken the cries of wounded

men, the clash of swords, for defeat. Pitying and contemptuous looks greeted them as they crossed the bridge. Then Yamaneko and Yamaitachi drew their swords and drove off the guard. The Kōno forces poured from the wood, and the scanty garrison of a bare score of men was quickly put to the sword. After a time fugitives from the band of Kuzuryū began to appear. These were admitted as they came, and their throats were promptly cut. The signal for complete defeat was the arrival of Onchi Tarō and Ikeno Shōji with the Kazama brothers. These latter had met with proper introduction to the mighty youth. The big men had each put a hand on the shoulder of this fellow bigger than themselves, even bigger than Shōji, who with joy related his deeds. They gazed at him intently. Onchi Tarō looked from one to the other. Then the three clasped hands. Turning to Shōji they drew him into the circle, and a mighty shout of wonder went up from the Kōno men.

Matters at the fort were soon disposed of. Beauty and booty were packed off down the river. The girls entered Kōnomura on their legs, the goods on the shoulders of the Kōno farmers. Great was the spoil. The fort itself was destroyed by fire. Then the fighting men slowly followed, down the trail, over the hills to the Yoshinogawa. Profuse were the thanks of Shichinosuke, master of the mansion in the place of his deceased father. As the share of the Oguri *rōtō* in the booty was such as no longer to require aid from the Kōno House he acted as their banker until called on for funds for the restoration of the Houses of Oguri and Satake. The women were duly escorted to their homes. Tarōsaku, from farmer, became the chief *tedaitei* of the Kōno House with free access to its kitchen. It remained to settle the fate of Hayabusa Tarō. Here it was agreed that he should fare no worse than his companions. Brought out into the garden he was offered the choice of fighting with Onchi Tarō, or having his head struck off. He chose the latter punishment as less painful and equally certain. Then passed the days of winter and spring in this mild climate and the hospitality of the Kōno House. One day Tarōsaku in excitement brought a notice circulating through the province. It summoned the Oguri *rōtō* to meet their lord at Hiraoka no Kumabuse. Forthwith the farewells were said. With joy the *rōtō* set forth to meet their lord. With regret the Kōno saw their boat glide down the river; with pleasure at the good fortune. Said Shichinosuke—"In Kōnomura "the name of Oguri shall never be forgotten; nor the *gembuku* of "Onchi Dono," he added; nor has it.

CHAPTER XXI.

The Gathering of the Rōtō.

The tale of the *rōtō* now turns to the North. Here it is best to follow Mito no Kotarō, who forms the connecting link between them. After his adventure with the thieves of Ueno he continued his journey northward without incident to his arrival in Yūki. Here disappointment met him. Inquiry showed that it was no rendezvous of the Oguri *rōtō*. At the Yūkiya the *teishu* Denkurō could tell him that not long since the Tanabe brothers, Heirokurō and Heihachirō had been in the town. In disappointment they had gone southward, probably to Kamakura or even Kyōto; beating the Tōkaidō towns or the mountains of Shinano? With the best of will and sharpest of wits Denkurō could not advise his questioner. Mito no Kotarō decided to adopt this course. He at least was sure that his company was to be found in this direction. Surely he would fall in with some of them. At all events he would meet his lord, perhaps be of use to him, and turn him from a journey without object. Yūki with its proximity to the now Isshiki fief of Oguri he found was not the safest place for one so sought after as Sukeshige. Even the neighbourhood of Muromachi was safer ground than this within the claws of the Bakufu of Ōkuragayatsu. In the disguise of a travelling priest he returned as he came, making cautious inquiry by the way in order not to pass his lord on the road through some carelessness. As for Kamakura he had decided not to enter it. Inquiry could be made for the Tanabe after receiving the instructions of his lord. Detained by rain he halted some time at the hamlet of Ōfuna nestling at the foot of its little hill (Osaka). Time has changed matters here, and the upstart railway junction a mile away has stolen the name of the sleepy village. The rain ceasing with the late afternoon he started out again. He had reached the entrance to the valley leading down to Yamanouchi when a farmer came along the road urging his nag with all speed. Just as he reached Kotarō the girth of his saddle gave way. The worthy peasant rolled into the mud, and the beast would have made off to parts unknown if the iron hand of the priest had not seized the bridle.

The peasant was in proper position, if not shape, to offer his reverential thanks. Said Kotarō—" More care is needed when one " makes a journey in such haste. Good Sir have you met with loss " that you seek to run away from it ; or heard of good fortune that " you hasten to meet it." The peasant rubbed his bruised limbs. Grunting and groaning he hobbled toward the beast. Kotarō had removed the cloths and bags which awkwardly bound together answered for a saddle. He prepared to show the worthy man how to make a safer mount—" First the bridle should ...." ; the worthy knight got no further. The peasant was as unconscious of the approaching lecture as the priest was indifferent as to an answer to his question. But the farmer's first words in his urgent haste riveted Kotarō's attention. " Apology reverend Sir is due. With " fear and respect are the thanks of this Chōzaemon offered. But to- " day there is a great sight offered. An execution is to take place. " It is no vulgar exhibition at the Roku-Jizō* of Ōmachi. At sunset " two samurai lose their heads at the Kaihin of Yuigasato. Hence " the common people flock to the sight in greater numbers than " usual. Besides these are noted rascals. They have been stop- " ping in secret at the Suzukiya of Yuki-no-Shita. The inn is " most pleasant. But looking out on its garden their thoughts have " been most evil. Desperate over the death of their lord, killed in " battle [at Yahagi in Mikawa, these *rōnin* plotted to kill Prince " Mochiuji. But Akihide Dono is ever watchful. Informed by his " spies the *teishu* was summoned and bound. At his voice at night " joyful the *bantō* opened, to give admittance to the Isshiki *kerai*

* At the cross road—of the Hase and Yuigahama (from Ogigayatsu) machi. There is also a stone with a poem of Bashō (17th century poet) engrav- ed thereon. Near by was the execution ground for criminals.

" who filled the house. *Okamisan* and maids stood by in terror,
" not daring to whisper a warning. Thus in their sleep the two
" men were seized and bound, without *gatchi-gatchi* of breaking
" doors and opportunity to resist. Great was the joy of Isshiki
" Dono ; for great is his fear of the Oguri *rōtō*. The capture of the
" Kataoka brothers, their execution at sunset to-day is a great event
" and cause of joy in Kamakura." Alas! Alas! The mind of
man is most unstable. The lecture on horsemanship never got
farther than the first few words ; luckily for the Kataoka and the
scribe who plainly knows little about a horse. In a moment Kotarō
was on the beast's back. As the peasant in alarm sought to detain
him, with a kick Kotarō sent him back into the mire. The man
rose on hands and knees to see the flying form of the knight gallopping toward Kamakura Yuigahama.

The news was true. The Suzukiya then, the Suzukiya now, is
a pleasant little inn for quieter guests on the avenue to the Hachimangū. As the scene of the great processions, of priests visiting the
shrine, of Daimyō making *sankei*, the Kataoka, convinced of their
lord's death at Yahagi, had lodged here waiting the opportunity to
kill Isshiki Akihide, either on a *sankei* to the shrine, or a visit to the
Ōkura palace. The *teishu* welcomed his once guests with pleasure.
The fire at Kaizōji had never been connected in his mind with the
Nikaidō *rōtō* seeking better fare than temple prayers. But their
stay had not been long, the luck most unfortunate. The recalcitrant
noble seemed to prefer the Yoko-ōji or cross road lined with
yashiki, to a progress from Ōmachi along the greater avenue.
Isshiki was a man to seek the substance of power, not its show except as this gave substance. Hence his influence over his lord, who
loved the show, and disliked its exhibition in too great excess in his
greater nobles. Hence his dislike and suspicions of the great and
luxurious lords of Yamanouchi and Ōgigayatsu. With his brother
Naokane as provost of Kamakura town Akihide had eyes everywhere, and was not long in learning of the presence of the Kataoka.
After capture they were kept some days in prison. It was not
difficult to ascertain a motive of which they made boast. Plainly
they knew nothing of the hiding place of Sukeshige, if he still lived.

Akihide had recognized in the disfigured priest the *rōtō* who had attempted his life.   In very shame Yokoyama had said nothing to him about Sukeshige.   The head of Koshirō had satisfied the greater lord, and he had departed content with the statement of the beggars' punishment.   The Kataoka therefore were not tortured ; but a month in the Kamakura jail had not been a stay at the noted health resort.   With growing anger two tall priests gazed at the men as they were led forward to the head stool, trussed up like beasts, with emaciated faces and sunken eyes.   It was some satisfaction to note the still springy walk, the vigour as yet little affected.

The official cast an eye toward the temple of Hase Kwannon. The sun already approached close to the mountain's rim.   As it touched it he made a sign.   The executioner stepped forward and passed behind Kataoka Katarō.   Thus Harunori was to suffer first. The crowd swayed and pressed forward in their anxiety to see. With angry frown the officer turned, gave orders to the *yakunin* to press the people back, to give room to the swordsman to do his work.   The people cried out and shouted—" Deign not to shove! " My ear !   My nose !   My ribs !   Ideya ! "   Then the two big priests burst through the line and stood in the open.   They gave a mighty shout—" Here   stand   the   Tanabe brothers, *rōtō* "of   the   lord   of   Oguri,   Kojirō   Sukeshige,   a   daimyō   of   a "hundred thousand *koku*.   Rescue is at hand.   Deign good Sirs to " take heart."   At once great was the uproar among people and *yakunin*.   The officer made sign to the executioner to strike at once. He laid hand to his own weapon.   Neither had the chance to act. The body of a *yakunin* hurled from the strong arm of Heirokurō laid the two men flat.   In an instant Heihachirō had cut the bonds of the Kataoka.   The two swords of the prostrate magistrate were a fair start for an armoury.   The Tanabe had the swords concealed in their *shakujō*.   The *yakunin* hesitated.   The people fled.   Their curiosity led them just out of harm's way, to watch this curious battle.   The contest was less uneven than it seemed, for the Oguri *rōtō* were famed from the Bay of the Green-wood (Aomori) to the Strait of the Big Turn (Ōsumi).

Tanabe Heirokurō stood over the fallen officer.   Said he to the *yakunin*—" Your lord's head is at stake. Let no man stir." The samurai was brave. He shouted—" Your own heads are at stake " rascals. Kill or capture these men. Their heads or your own ! " Heirokurō bowed with ceremonious respect. The next moment the *bugyō's* head rolled on the ground. Then in close order the Oguri *rōtō* charged the *yakunin*. These gave way, but only to attack them in the rear. Forced to turn the battle thus swayed backward and forward without much ground being gained. Said Kataoka Katarō—" At least the ending will be more fit. These fellows will " not run. They will wear us out, and archers from Kamakura will " soon be here. Great is our regret at thus involving you, dear " Sirs, in our fate." Answered Heirokurō—" Why not share the " fate of our companions ? Besides in company we should make " report to our lord in Meido. But it is not yet the time to cut " belly. Ah ! The people are in motion. Is it the archers ? No : " they fly in disorder. Kotarō ! Kotarō ! Mito no Kotarō ! " The four men danced with glee. Driving his horse to this side and to that Kotarō scattered people and *yakunin* from before him. He used his iron tipped *shakujō* with effect. The four men rushed to his side. In company again they turned on the *yakunin*. These made no stand. They were constables, not soldiers. They were charged to handle criminals, not the *rōtō* of Oguri. Let the Ashikaga samurai look to that. Five of these desperate fellows were at their heels. Doubtless the other five, perhaps their lord himself, would appear in priestly guise to join in the fray. Incontinently police and people took to flight in all directions. The five men left alone on the Kaihin dune stared at each other as if resuscitated from death. Said Kotarō—" Our lord is in good health, on his way to Yūki. There it is " our duty to join him. What is the best means to withdraw ? " These fellows will return as soon as the news reaches Yuki-no- " Shita." Kataoka Kajirō pointed to a fisherman's boat drawn up on the beach below. Without discussion all made to it. It was soon launched, and in the growing darkness they pushed out to sea. It did the Tairō Akihide little good to learn that rescue had been effected ; that at least five of the Oguri *rōtō* had been in his grasp and had escaped, to land close by at Kotsubo. Akihide grunted—

"This stupid fellow of a *bugyō* has lost his head in battle. Un-
"fortunately his House cannot be degraded for cowardice. Of the
"*yakunin* every other man shall cast lots for death ; the rest to be-
"came *hinin* (outcasts). This is to be carried out."

In a few hours safe from pursuit the *rōtō* slowly made their
way back to Yūki. There was no news here concerning their lord,
but they found the inn of Denkurō full of country people wildly
excited over two events. Both of these were unusual and caused
wide gapes of wonder. Great was the strength of Yūki castle, great
the power of its lord ; but neither had prevented a disastrous blow
falling on Ujitomo Dono. His daughter Shiraito (White Thread)
was sixteen years old and a beauty. Great was the expectation and
the desire of the daimyō related to the Yūki to secure the daughter
of the House as wife, or for some son. Surely the maid was safe
from violence in the fief and under the protection of her father.
Riding forth one day to cross the town to the beautiful shaded
grounds of the Kōkyōji and pay a visit to its prior, Yūki Dono
noticed a new shrine just erected close by the temple gate. No
permission had been given for such building, no priest was to be
found of whom to make examination, the prior of its big neighbour
knew nothing of its builders. Somewhat disgruntled the lord returned to the castle to give his steward an overhauling. Gladly
would Yūki Dono have contributed. The official, prostrate in
apology, was greatly puzzled. The matter would be investigated.
Premature action would be punished by a heavy fine, and its revocation would be the contribution of their lord, thereby securing
great merit at a cheap rate. Shiraito, who was present, took unusual interest in the shrine. Her father had described the beauty of
its adornment, the curious carvings of birds and beasts and flowers,
the pillars in gilt and red, the lacquered ceiling panels gorgeous with
gold. A thousand handed Kwannon was installed, and Ujitomo
was particularly enthusiastic over a bronze Jizō Sama which occupied a side altar. Shiraito pleaded very prettily that the investi-
gation be left in her hands. Ujitomo laughed and yielded. He
knew—and Shiraito knew—that the steward would make an
independent and early inquiry. The girl anticipated the officer

She left the apartment ; to leave the castle at once and visit the new shrine. A boy priest ushered the lady within. With glib learning did he explain the meaning of all the many symbols, the inner thought expressed in statue and carving. The Butsuma contained a most sacred image of the goddess, floated to the waters of this part of Nippon by wave and current from Morokoshi (China). None but the eyes of the lady could see the treasure. At her order the attendants withdrew to the verandah of the temple. Time passed. The lady did not appear. Murmurs arose. Just then the *karō* arrived on a mission of inquiry. At once he rushed into the shrine. It was empty. Altar, decoration, images of goddess and gods had disappeared. In amazement the company rubbed their eyes. They were crowded into the space of an old and filthy temple, the Kōfukuji, abandoned for years as the playground of the dirty peasant children of the neighbourhood. At first the people heard the expressed wonder with ill-concealed derision. All Yūki knew this shabby shrine. Then faces grew most serious. All were agreed as to the vision. The news carried to Ujitomo he was in despair. Men he could fight; but here was something supernatural. Search high and low failed to show any signs of the vanished girl. Fortunately at this juncture the Yūgyō Shōnin reached Yūki town.

Joa had found lodging with his brethren of the sect at the Tennyōzan Kōkenji. Here daily the good priest preached the regeneration of mankind, the seeking of the true way, the entering on Bukkwa. The country people flocked to hear the holy man, to receive his blessing and the *jūnen*. In the front rank every day was a big black fellow, most devout, but never asking for the sacred writing. At last one day he seemed to consider that the proper stage of sanctity had been reached in his case. Emboldened he approached the bishop with hand outstretched for the charm. Joa Shōnin closed his eyes in blissful meditation. Expectant the man waited before him. The onlookers and those yet to follow devoutly suppressed their impatience and secured more merit for their souls and hence quicker annihilation by perhaps a few seconds in a few million years. Joa opened wide his eyes and glared at the applicant. " Ya ! Yo ! " he burst out. " Filthy beast in the shape of a man !

" Do you presume to try and impose on the patience and credulity
"of this Joa ? Get you hence to your foul iniquities. Holiness is
" not to be called to the aid of wickedness." In alarm the creature
sprang backward and fled the sacred precincts. People ran helter-
skelter to the temple gate, only to see a huge monkey leaping along
the roadside, to disappear within the neighbouring grove of the Kōkyōji. At this moment the presence of Yūki Dono was announced.
He came to seek counsel of Joa. In tears he explained the disappearance of his daughter. Joa was thoughtful. Said he—
" Perhaps this ape-man is at the bottom of the rape. Assuredly the
" Yōkai (spectre) is the ravisher. Deign to make search in the
" northern forests. If your lordship's daughter is not found, then
" seek the aid of Joa. Conditions must guide the advice of the
" priest."

Shichirō Ujitomo with a single *rōtō* at once set out for the forest
to the north-west on the slopes of Iwafuna—Teruishiyama. It was
late afternoon as their goal was being approached. Ujitomo
stood on the lower slopes of the mountain undecided what to do.
Perhaps it would be better to seek shelter and advice at the Daichiji
not far off. Yes, he would do so. As he turned to give the order to
turn back to where they had left their horses he noted a priest
standing close by under a tree. He was a big, ill looking fellow ; but
clad in a mouse coloured *kimono*, with *zukin* thrown over his head
and a rosary of crystal beads he had at least the paraphernalia of a
cleric. On being approached he began to move away. Shouted
Ujitomo—" Wait ! Wait ! Sir Priest a question only ! " The
fellow turned a scowling face—" To the priest this world no longer
" exists ; mankind no longer exists. If the men of the world seek
" shelter, it is before their eyes. Go within ; and may the Buddha
·" grant the reception you deserve. Namu Amida Butsn ! Namu
" Amida Butsu ! " Slowly he continued his course. In anger
Ujitomo could have struck him. He restrained himself. Besides,
the fellow was only churlish in manner. In the woods above appeared the tower of a pagoda. Preoccupied by his mission he had
not noticed it. Yūki Shichirō brought his eyes to earth to thank his
rough informant. He had disappeared. " What long legs ! " said

Yūki in some astonishment. "Where did the priest go?"—
"What priest!" asked the *rōtō*. Said Yūki sharply—"Arouse
"yourself. It is not time to sleep, but to watch. Sleep can be
"found above." The *rōtō* did not dare to say more to his angry
lord. Ujitomo's temper was decidedly tart since the events of the
past few days.

Followed by the *rōtō* Ujitomo pursued his route up the mountain. Their footsteps fairly dragged as if weighted, the pagoda
seemed to advance with them. It was now growing dark. When
nearly worn out by great good luck a young priest came scampering
up the slope. He would have passed without salutation, but Ujitomo
seized his robe. Thus forcibly detained he asked in some fright and
sourness what was desired. Said Ujitomo—"We seek lodging for
"the night. Deign to guide us to the temple close by, and yet
"which eludes our search."—"It is difficult to find," was the reply.
"Those who really desire entrance can find it. It requires but the
"earnest wish for accomplishment. Follow me, or your nose, at
"your will." With this acid reply he freed himself and slipped off
up the slope, to disappear as in a mist. The knight grumbled
loudly—"What an impudent set of monks! May fire and sword
"some day purify their abode! They cannot always jump on the
"right side. But most earnest is the desire to find this strange
"temple." At the words he detected the gate not far off in the
gloomy wood. He laughed—"No wonder the shaveling derided
"us. See Takeyoshi! Shelter and food at last found, and close at
"hand." The place was silent, yet its spruce and neat appearance
showed careful hands. As they entered the inner enclosure a *shoke*
came forward—"Doubtless, honoured Sir, you seek shelter for the
"night. Many come here—and remain. The place is peaceful, quiet
"as the tomb. Our prior as yet is absent, but deign to enter. With him
"explanation is to be made. It is the rule for the guests to furnish
"entertainment. There is naught here but grows from the ground."
Answered Yūki Shichirō—"The *shōjin* (vegetable food) of your
"fraternity rivals the fish and flesh of the laymen. Truly all the
"skilled cooks are to be found in the monasteries." The man
grinned—"Our cook here is skilled, the food inferior to none. Deign

" to enter." He showed them into a large inner apartment. " Here " is to be awaited the invitation of the *ōshō*. His appetite will not " allow him to wait long."

Said Yūki Dono to his *rōtō*—" What an unpleasant fellow ! " He can only sneer. I do not like his talk, or the place." Said the *rōtō*—" May the cook and the food be up to his bragging. Your " lordship needs rest and refreshment for this arduous task." For some time Ujitomo and his retainer waited. They were nodding with sleep. Suddenly Ujitomo sat up. He shook his companion— " Don't sleep in a strange place. What is that noise ? " *Gutsu, gutsu, gutsu ;* a munching crunching sound came from the neigh-. bouring apartment. Ujitomo rose and stole silently to the screen. Pushing a hole in the silk with his little finger he looked through it. Atsu ! What a sight met his eye ! The ill-favoured priest, grown to huge proportions, was before his eye. In a mortar he was grinding to a pulp freshly severed limbs and blood. This mess from time to time he sampled and munched with great satisfaction. He raised the bowl and with huge chop-sticks shovelled the last of its contents into his capacious gullet—" Now for the others," he growled. As he rose he caught the glitter of Ujitomo's eye through the screen. A roar of laughter went up. " Ha ! Ha ! The good knight comes " unbidden to the festive board. Was he not told that here guests " furnished forth the feast ? Was it not his earnest desire to enter " this holy den ? No more gluttony is practised here than else- "where. Surely this Yūki Dono shall furnish entertainment for " Yōkai Dono, in more sense than one."

Ah ! There was no question that he had the kidnapper of Shiraito before his eyes. With a shout to the *rōtō* to follow Uji- tomo dashed down the screen and faced the demon. Stringing his bow he took careful aim ; then in anger showered arrow after arrow at the foe. The Yōkai roared and stormed with merriment. The arrows he caught in his hand, in his mouth, crunching and breaking the iron points. Great was the anger and despair of Yūki Shichirō—" Come ! Hunger seizes me." Thus growled the mons- ter. " Hunger seizes me," growled Ujitomo, but his fight had to be on an empty belly. Willingly would he too tear the demon's

The Feast of the Yōkai.

flesh. "Evil communication corrupts good manners," thought Shichirō. "Too much of this fellow's company would seduce one "to his practices." Shouting horribly, grinding and gnashing his fangs the Yōkai stalked toward him. In despair Ujitomo drew his sword and slashed desperately. It was as if he hacked at granite. The edge of the weapon was blunted and broken. The claws of the demon were in his flesh. A moment more and the neck of Ujitomo would feel his teeth. "Hachiman Yumiya Marishiten!" With a final effort Ujitomo struck at the gleaming eye with his dagger. The blade met yielding substance. Ujitomo found himself on the ground. Temple, Yōkai, all sign of the filthy repast had disappeared. He was lying on the mountain side in the darkness of the forest. Close by lay his *rōtō*. By the dim light of the starry night it could be made out that he had been hacked to pieces. Ujitomo put his hand to his head. Had all this scene been vision and frenzy? Had the man died by the hand of his lord? Yūki Shichirō wept with sorrow.

At dawn he dug a grave for the remains of the unfortunate man. Then slowly he descended the slope. When well toward the bottom he came upon some girls playing before a gate. This time the genuineness of mansion and inmates could not be doubted. He approached and asked for shelter and food. The girl addressed drew back in alarm. Said she—" Deign honoured Sir, not "to enter here. How come you on this mountain? Here a most fearful "*yōkai* has his home. The country round about pays the tribute of "his horrid feasts. We girls have been carried off, or offered at the "shrines, to attend him." Then Ujitomo rejoiced. The haunt of the demon had at last been found. Said he—" Tell this Ujitomo "what is to be done. Rescue is at hand. All shall be restored to "their homes." The girl eyed him in doubt. Then she said— "Hence, brave Sir. Think better of the matter. If you will return, "bring with you rope made from hempen cloth such as is offered "to the gods. Against this he cannot struggle. Bring with you "many tubs of *saké*. He will drink and be weakened. Bring "with you plenty of dogs. In their flesh he delights. Then he will "drink the more readily. Thus can the *yōkai* perchance be slain.

"Otherwise return not. Leave us to our fate—his lust and "appetite." Said the knight. "He who speaks is lord of Yūki "castle, Shichirō Ujitomo. Without fail I shall return and subdue "the *yōkai*. Be of good heart." Rejoicing he sought his horse and rode away.

The first thing Ujitomo did was to seek out Joa and make report. The worthy bishop was in consultation with five big men clad as priests. As Yūki Dono entered he came down from his dais to meet him, and to listen to what the castle lord had to say— "The moment is most propitious. Here are fit companions for your "enterprise. Do as directed by the maid of the *yōkai's* stronghold. "Deign to take these three bags. When hard pressed and uncertain "of the issue, open the first and take out the contents. What follows "is matter of course." Joa handed to him three bags marked by their colours, and in their order. "Are these *deshi* (disciples) "reverend Sir?" said Ujitomo in envy of such stout priests in the making. He had seen these men somewhere, but could not place them. "Not mine; nor can they be of your lordship's train," was the bishop's answer. "These are *rōtō* of Oguri, in search of their "lord Sukeshige. They are men surpassed by none in strength and "skill with weapons." He turned and summoned them to consultation. With joy they accepted the dangerous mission. Preparations were few. At night all was ready—hempen rope, *saké*, dogs; great was the envy of all the local drunkards. "Surely these honoured "Sirs are already on the way to Nirvana. To none else is it permitt- "ed to consider their capacity equal to the universe of wine."

Thus equipped they set off on a leisurely progress to the mount- ain. There was no difficulty in finding the place. At the sight of the wild uncultured slopes the Oguri *rōtō* marvelled at the idea of finding human habitation, or even such that pretended to be so. Ujitomo led them up the valley, past the deceitful spur which pro- tected his find from the eyes of vulgar men gazing up from below. At the fine mansion, the gate of stone, the stretch of beautiful turf, all wondered. The women were gathered before the gate as if awaiting their approach. They prostrated themselves in fear and gratitude. Said the favoured of Ujitomo, who spoke for all—"Fear

" and reverential respect enters. Honoured lord your presence has
" long been announced by the barking of the feast brought. For-
" tunately the *yōkai* has gone to obtain human aid at the Daichiji,
" where he seeks to juggle the monks in order to restore the eye lost
" in a struggle with some demon of greater power than himself.
" Unless this can be secured some *kalpas* (innumerable years) must
" pass before it grows again. Deign to enter, and in hiding await
" the propitious moment." She and her companions looked up in
wonder at the big men in company with the lord of Yūki. " Truly
" if human kind can grapple with this beast, these are the men born
" of women. May the *kami* grant success! A favoured issue!"

Under the women's guidance the mansion was entered. Here
disguise was brought. Ujitomo and the *rōtō* donned the garments
of the women. Conducted to an apartment close to the scene of the
horrid feasts of the *yōkai* they sat down to wait the summons.
This was not for long. Soon " a gust of wind tainted with gore
swept through the apartment, a thick black cloud rolled into the
banquet hall." Gradually it was dispelled. As if summoned by
the barking and howling of his favoured feast the huge ill-favoured
priest was seen seated in the middle of the apartment. A bandage
concealed the cavity of the missing eye, punched out by the thrust
of Ujitomo's dagger. With his fist the demon struck a huge gong
close by. At once appeared the maid. She grovelled before him.
" What means this savoury riot, this barking and whining of
" canines as if ready for a feast?" He growled and glared hideously at her. " With respect and reverential terror: deign fearful
" and beloved demon to accept the apology of your hand-maid.
" Inspired by the desire to gain favour her foolish mother has been bid
" to send a gift of dogs and wine for the lord's enjoyment The peti-
" tion is that he deign to partake "—" Partake!" roared the *yōkai*.
" Aye! First of dog and then of the fair one who bestows. Both
" shall be embraced in the devil's grinders. Bring forth the dogs!"
He rolled and rumbled on his cushion in ferocious anticipation. Then
entered the other women with the many dogs, introducing the *rōtō*
and Ujitomo bending under the load of *saké* tubs. The demon
eyed the new-comers. " Women of the village who have brought

" the offering," timidly explained the maid. "And not favoured of
" Heaven," growled the *yōkai*. " Surely these are unfit for the
" harem of the mansion's lord, and equally so for his grinders.
" They look as tough as rubber." He seized a dog. Tearing it
apart he thrust his maw into its inwards, greedily to suck up the
blood. Then he crunched it, skin, flesh, and bones. A tub of *saké*
washed the repast down his huge throat. As he grasped another
dog; to the noise of the beast's cries—"And the new acquisition ;
" is she reconciled to the love of this *yōkai*? Putting aside foolish
" tears does she consent to be unbound and with graceful mien add
" to his happiness? But a true answer from such source is unlikely.
" The rule of the place is known. Sacrifice follows consent. With
" smiles or tears she follows your honoured self, lovely girl, in the
" demon's favours. This day your service ends—as dessert to this
" repast of dogs." Then he tore open another canine, tilted back
his head to guzzle another tub of *saké*. Thus was not noticed the
movement of exultant rage made by Ujitomo. His daughter as yet
was safe. Assuredly Shiraito was held prisoner by the *yōkai*.

More dogs, more *saké ;* now the demon doubled on the
saké. Two casks went to a dog—"To give appetite." Rapidly
he was approaching the stage of recklessness. This reached
and passed he began to brag. "Now for a test of strength.
" These priests are easily fooled. In pity of the *yōkai* they
" brought forth holy charms, good medicine to heal the wound
" caused by this miserable human. Nothing but the name
" of Yumiya Hachiman* guided his weapon to a vulnerable
" spot. A moment more, and the teeth of the *yōkai* would have
" crushed his spine. But these monks are sly. Perchance the dis-
" guise was penetrated, as of late by this Joa Shōnin. The medicine
" may be poison to weaken strength. Bring forth the ropes. Bind
" the *yōkai* strongly. Here, you women of the village ! Work in
" the fields hardens the muscles. Your arms shall bind me." The
maids brought out the hempen rope. The Oguri *rōtō* surrounded
the demon, strongly pulling together the cord. At a signal they
ceased. The *yōkai* yawned and stretched. The rope snapped like

---

* Hachiman of the bow and feathered shaft. Hachiman is the god of war.

thread—"Ah! What thirst! More *saké*—at once!" Again a tub of *saké*. Thus inspired another tub followed. Yūki Shichirō began to fear that the vinous capacity of the demon had been grossly underrated. And yet the topers of Yūki had sat in council, multiplying ten thousand fold the capacity of their profoundest hog in the art of guzzling. Again the *yōkai* was bound. Again he easily broke the bonds. In derision he turned to drink. Tub after tub disappeared, savoured at times with a dog. With despair Ujitomo saw the last tub go down the demon's throat. Then the *yōkai* rose. Once more he demanded to be bound. The Tanabe, the Kataoka, Mito no Kotarō, Yūki Shichirō, united their strength to make the rope secure. This time success seemed assured. The demon attempted to stretch his arms and failed. His muscles swelled, but the rope cut deep into them. "Strange!" he muttered. Again he struggled; with no better success. "Ah! My strength is gone. The "rope is too strong. Unbind me, good dames. As peasant women "you possess a charm. Great shall be the reward from the *yōkai*."

With exultant shout the lord of Yūki, the *rōtō* of Oguri, threw off their women's garments. Yūki Shichirō advanced with drawn sword. "Miserable beast! Your course of lust and crime has "reached its end. No longer shall wretched victims find an un-"honoured grave in the *yōkai's* bowels. Great has been the anguish "caused by such a neighbour to the villages round about here. Here "stands the lord of Yūki, Shichirō Ujitomo; the *rōtō* of Oguri Suke-"shige—the Tanabe brothers, the Kataoka brothers, Mito no Kotarō "Tamehisa. Prepare to go to hell, then to be reborn in some future "existence again in bestial form, to undergo many kalpas of punish-"ment." The *yōkai* groaned and struggled. "Ah! How regret-"ful! This *yōkai* has been over-reached by these wily humans. "Once free these rash men shall regret their enterprise; fearful the "torment of this treacherous maid." He made a mighty effort. Frowning hideously, his teeth grinding, and with hoarse bellows fearful to hear, he was an object fit to terrify Emma Dai-Ō the Judge of Hell. With a long cracking the bonds parted. The *rōtō* and Yūki Dono scattered to every side. Yūki Shichirō opened the first bag given by Joa. Within was an exquisite pearl.

The Struggle with the Yōkai.

The *yōkai* roared with ferocious glee. He glared from side to side. Watchful the samurai stood in readiness to aid the one attacked. "Again the *yōkai* is himself." He patted his stomach. "Within, these infamous wretches find their graves. But there is "an influence here. Perchance the *saké* was drugged; unavailing "trick with the *yōkai*. First for you, honoured lord; deign to "enter!" He sprang toward Ujitomo. As he did so Ujitomo presented the pearl. The *yōkai* stumbled as one drunk. He drew backward. The *rōtō* came to the attack. Tanabe Heirokurō threw himself on one arm. Heihachirō seized the other. The Kataoka tried to throw him down by grasping his legs. The *yōkai* jeered. "You are not the fellows for this business. The greatest of you—a "dozen of the vaunted *Shōji*—would be helpless against the demon. "Soon this faintness will pass. Then prepare to meet your fate." Ujitomo opened the second bag. At the sight the *yōkai* groaned. Within was a rope. In the strong hands of the *rōtō* again the demon stood fast bound. What was to be done? He must be put to death. On this stony flesh the weapons rebounded. These swords could penetrate steel, but not the supernatural. Again Ujitomo invoked the aid of Yumiya Hachiman. He thrust his sword into the heart of the demon. Kiyatsu! Down he fell. As he did so the head snapped off and began to roll through the apartment. The *rōtō* sought to seize it. Onward it rolled from hall to hall. At last in the open it began to soar skyward. Ujitomo opened the last bag and brought out the mirror contained within. As the sunlight flashed on its surface down fell the head into the garden. Kataoka Kajirō ran to pick it up. He brought back to Ujitomo the head of a huge ape. The many little shaveling monks, attendants of the *yōkai*, were changed into monkeys and fled to the tree tops. From these the Oguri *rōtō* brought them down with arrows. Not one escaped. Then the temple was searched. In an inner room, bound and gagged, was the hapless Shiraito. When the Tanabe brothers led the girl into her father's presence great was the joy of both at the meeting. Pretty was the confusion and repentance of the White Thread Lady as she promised never to leave the castle precincts without parental order. Then all the women were gathered together, for restoration to the parents in the villages. The few remaining dogs were set free, to range the forest and breed a strange race of half wolf, half canine, to the annoyance of future generations at the generosity of the lord of Yūki. The bodies of the great ape and of his monkey satellites were gathered on a pyre erected in the hall of hideous feasting. Fire was set thereto and the whole building consumed.

Then they set out homeward as they had come—with the recovered lady and a new recruit in the person of the maid whose courage had given success to the enterprise, and whose beauty had attracted Ujitomo. As concubine of Yūki Shichirō her issue in later years, after the unhappy siege, was to continue the line of Ujitomo. In the town due gratitude was shown for the heavenly aid. The shabby Kōfukuji received fresh paint and endowment and again deserved its name of the Temple of Brilliant Fortune. Its twin, the Kinfukuji, the Temple of Wealth and Fortune, was built to commemorate the event. At the castle a great banquet was held. In the days which followed the affairs of the Houses of Oguri and Satake were thoroughly discussed. That Yūki Dono would give his aid in re-establishment was already known. Said he—" The time is unpropitious to act. " Effort would be fatal to both Houses, arousing enemies whose " pursuit has lapsed. Alas! These Isshiki are pushing the Suze- " rain in Kamakura to his ruin. Only the earnest effort of the Shitsuji " Norizane prevents movement from Kyōto. To his lord this Uji- " tomo is loyal. But of his House he stands alone, and there are few " in his company. If Norizane prevails then the restoration of the " two Houses is assured. Be patient. On meeting with your lord thus " advise him. Time sometimes is the devil's advocate, but not in " this case. The Isshiki must fail, and Ujitomo will aid in causing " their fall. Thus make report to your lord. Here he will find aid, " counsel, and concealment, whenever he requires them. To you, " honoured Sirs, this Ujitomo is bound through all existences. Let " the Lady Shiraito appear, to add her gratitude to that of her " father." Disclaim as they would such cause for thanks, yet the thanks were given. For long the Oguri rōtō remained at Yūki

castle. Then in the early summer of the following year came a
messenger from the Yūgyōji. Joa Shōnin had been heard from ;
message was brought from the lord of Oguri in Kyōto. Yūki
Ujitomo summoned the *rōtō* to his presence. With regret he told
them that the castle could no longer shelter them. They bowed in
acquiescence, yet somewhat wondering at the cheerful manner of the
castle lord. Said he—" It is your lord's summons that you answer.
" Dear as is his allegiance to this Ujitomo no call from other source
" should demand or cajole you hence. Even now with regret is
" your departure witnessed. But Ujitomo knows the joy with
" which the summons of Oguri Dono is answered." Great was the
exultation at the news. The last feast was held. Then the men
set out in company for Hiraoka no Kumabuse. Armed with letters
from the lord of Yūki passage through the guarded towns of the
Nakasendō was easy. At the rendezvous were their lord and lady,
the Kazama, the Gotō, Ikeno Shōji. In their company was a new
recruit. The tales of his prowess were new to them. With laughter
and applause they listened to Shōji, half believing that the worthy
knight bragged in his enthusiasm. This scepticism lasted but a
short time. In fencing, wrestling, jiujutsu, Onchi Tarō soon made
good the tales of his sponsors. The men from Yūki became as
earnest in praise as the discoverers of the giant youth.

The years of Eikyō (1429-1440) were to pass in waiting. But
events showed the trend to the certain issue. In this period the
Lady Terute bore children to her lord. Sukeshige carefully watched the issues of the time ; for the sake of the Houses of Oguri and
Satake, for the restoration to its honours of the House of Onchi. To
him the youth Tarō Nagataru became as a younger brother, whose
success was as dear to him as his own. The pledge to the *obame*
was to be fulfilled to the letter.*

* Ujitomo was born in 1398. Mochitomo was his son, and twenty-two
years old when he perished at Yūki castle with his father and four brothers in
1441. Hence Ujitomo has been substituted for the Mochitomo of the *kōdan*
writers. Takarai abruptly ends his *kōdan* with the story of the *yōkai*. This
tale and that of the burning of the Kwannondō (Chap. I) are given at length in
the Oguri Gwaiden. This old book, very complete as to the adventures of
Sukeshige, is not easy to obtain.

CHAPTER XXII.

The Quarrel between Kyōto and Kamakura.

The march of events to the accomplishment of the vendetta of the Ō-Dono took its slow and inevitable course. Ever since the death of his son, the Shōgun Yoshikazu, Prince Yoshimochi had played his double game with greater zest. Himself he resumed the office of the Shōgunate, continuing his debauches, leaving affairs more than ever in the hands of the Bakufu, then directed by the great vassals, the Hatakeyama, Hosokawa, Chiba. But Yoshimochi kept up his coquetting with Kamakura. Gifts were exchanged, the civilities expressed of the kindest, and Yoshimochi had his hand all the time on the pulse of the Kwantō. Mochiuji understood this and was helpless. He inveighed fiercely against this drunkard, the disgrace and danger to the family interests. But the fruit was ripening to his hand. The marked regard shown to the Head of the Tendai Hieizan was not to be taken too seriously. Gien Sōjō, the younger brother of Yoshimochi, had left the world (*shukke*). He was not regarded as offering real ground of opposition to the now legitimate and certain succession of either Mochiuji himself or one of his sons to the Shōgunate. As Mochiuji in either case would have held the real power, the issue was to be regarded with complacency. But the obstruction to the ambition of Mochiuji lay in the double government originally established in council by Takauji and Tadayoshi his brother. The supremacy of the Kamakura House meant danger to, perhaps the breaking down of, the powerful interests surrounding the Shōgunate at Kyōto. It meant an invasion of the northern interests into the Capital. New measures in this case implied new men. The Hatakeyama, the Yamana, the Hosokawa, the Chiba, were all solidly set against the intrusion of

the Junior House into Kyōto. On the 1st month of the 1st year of
Shōchō (17 January-16 February 1428) Yoshimochi died at the age
of forty-three years. Neither of Daimyō nor of Tōzama were the
eyebrows of grief expanded. In solemn procession the Kwanryō
Hatakeyama Mitsuiye made a *sankei* to the Iwashimidzu Hachimangū. The god was to be consulted as to this knotty state of
affairs. Three times the lots were cast in the inner sanctuary before
the shrine of the god. Three times the lot fell on Gien Dai Sōjō.
Thus did he become the Lord of Heaven's Terrace.

On the 12th day of the 3rd month (27th March 1428) Gien
made his formal return to the secular life. By the Imperial order
he was given the rank of Sama no Kami with lower fifth grade,
as Yoshinobu Ason. On the 20th day of the 7th month (30th
August) the Emperor died, childless. The succession to the throne
lay wholly in the hands of Yoshinori and his advisers ; particularly so in this case. To put aside the absurd official chronology
which follows the effete Southern Court exiled to Yoshino,* the
succession of the ruling Northern Dynasty in the Capital had been
complicated by the kidnapping of Sukō Tennō in the 3rd year of
Kwan-ō (1352 A.D.). It was not until Embun 2nd year (1357)
that Sukō with his son Yoshihito re-entered the capital. Meanwhile
Go Kōgon, his younger brother, had been made emperor, and
the councillors of the Shōgun relegated Sukō and Yoshihito to private life. Go Enyu, Go Komatsu, Shōkō followed Go Kōgon in
regular order ; the northern line being recognized by the Southern
Court in the person of Go Komatsu Tennō. This emperor had
shown favour to the exiled princes, and had honoured them with
wealth and titles. Shōkō felt differently, perhaps on personal

---

* Based on the possession of the Three Treasures. These are decidedly
apocryphal. The sword was known to be lost at Dannoura finally and forever.
The other two are the jewel and mirror. All, before and since, have passed
through repeated accidents of fire and theft, and have been *miraculously* restored.
Their authenticity as originals is more than doubtful. According to this theory
the imperial line establishes its legitimacy by the possession of " The Treasures," not in its own right. This has been very recently and officially laid
down—in this twentieth century ! Unless the King of England be crowned on
the Stone of Scone, he is no legitimate king—to transfer the doctrine westward.

grounds, for in him the agreement to choose alternately a Tennō from the North and South branches of the Imperial family was violated, and the Northern Dynasty exclusively recognized. Though a child when he became Tennō (at twelve years) he was a grown man (twenty-eight years) at his death in 1428. Sadanari, the son of Yoshihito, had inherited a large fortune from his father, but he spent it all in truly sovereign dissipation. Shōkō forced the blue-blooded youth into the priesthood and poverty under the name of Dōkin. Shōkō neglected his wives for the more congenial practice of magic. When he died childless all his wealth was confiscated from his heirs. Then a message was sent to Dōkin at Fushimi, notifying him to send his son Hikohito to Miyako, to be inducted as successor to the deceased emperor. Great was the joy of the poverty stricken household, when on the following day the Kwan-ryō Hatakeyama Mitsuiye and Nyūdō Dōtan at the head of five hundred men came to make good the invitation and furnish proper escort. Thus this Tennō, to be known as Go Hanazono, took the position of the gilded figure-head of State ; and the thickness of the gilt could be very nicely adjusted at the will of his sponsors. Such pretence of a party or faction as he possessed had its headquarters in the Muromachi palace, or rather would have, for one of the Shōgun's first acts was to rebuild this creation of Yoshimitsu. On Eikyō 1st year 3rd month 9th day (7th October 1429) the *gembuku* of the Shōgun was performed. At last he had grown enough hair to admit of the ceremony. On the 15th day (13th October) his appointment as Sangi and Sei-i-tai-Shōgun was issued by the im-perial court. Thereupon he changed his name to Yoshinori, to become known in history as one of the ablest, coldest, and most cruel of the long line of Shōgun furnished by this Seiwa Genji. A real governor of men he was thirty-four years old when he took power and began to re-establish the position of the Bakufu as under Yoshimitsu.

Mochiuji was an able impetuous man. His anger at these events was great, his faith in the loaded dice of Hatakeyama very small. Probably he was right in his wish to make war at once on the Muromachi Bakufu. But the Uesugi in the person of the

Shitsuji Norizane blocked his way.   Norizane supported the will of Takauji in the bluntest fashion.   The affairs of Kyōto were not in the province of the Kamakura House.   Harmony between the two capitals was to be the ruling principle ; the ambitions of either did not figure.   Mochiuji was forced to restrain his impetuosity.   Evidently he could do nothing without the support of the Uesugi.   It was true that his House in every way was qualified to grasp the succession, that the return of a priest to secular life, to rule under any other form than as the power behind the throne, was unheard of.   But he was able to see the obstacles in his path ; sharp-sighted enough to fear and grasp the design of the astute cleric who now governed the land from Kyōto.   Mochiuji, however, made the great error of underestimating these obstacles in the light of ambition. The object of his policy was now directed to the removal of the Uesugi opposition, the degradation of the great House.   In alliance with them he was safe.   The House, of Fujiwara origin, was thoroughly loyal to the Kwantō interests.   Thus did it interpret the will of the founder Takauji.   Supported by Kyōto it was impregnable, but it only sought that support when the cardinal principle of harmony between the Ashikaga branches was threatened, and its own existence attacked.   A monopoly of either branch was fatal to the government of the country, as subsequent decades proved. The feudal Government of Kyōto could not dictate to the Kwantō imbued with the desire for home rule.   The Imperial Government had fallen into innocuous desuetude.   None but an antiquated writer and statesman of the Southern Court could be so out of touch with his own times, could dream of such as an active issue.   Taira Kiyomori had tried to direct a *buke* (military caste) government on *kuge* (court noble) principles from the old capital, and had failed. Minamoto Yoritomo, with headquarters in the Kwantō and an office in Kyōto had better success.   Takauji had been compelled to establish two governments, under penalty of failure in both.   On the whole the first Ashikaga Shōgun has been underrated as a statesman.   He was so busy with war that the iron necessity of his plan of statesmanship, confronting a warring military caste, at first escapes observation.

Mochiuji waited for the effect of time. The difficulty was he did not wait long enough ; in fact just missed his object. To all appearance at first Yoshinori was taken up with the lighter side of his office as Shōgun. Eikyō 1st year 8th month (September 1429) he made a religious visitation to the Iwashimizu shrine ; the 9th month (October) to the shrines of Hiyoshi and Kasuga. Eikyō 2nd year (1430) he is exchanging visits and making pleasure excursions in company with the Tennō. The 3rd year (1430) he made a pilgrimage to Ise and Kōyasan ; and the rebuilding of the Muro-machi palace was completed. Be it added that these progresses of the Shōgun were a terrific burden on the country. When therefore Yoshinori announced his desire to make a progress to view Fuji-yama, the council of Shiba, Hatakeyama, Hosokawa advised against it. Yoshinori was obstinate. It had always been his wish to visit the holy mountain—and to get in closer touch with the spirit mov-ing the Kwantō and his cousin Mochiuji.[*] Against such deep desire remonstrance was feeble and the precedent of the visit of Yoshi-mitsu powerful. Eikyō 4th year 9th month (end of September) he set forth. The Kwanryō saw to it that the Shōgun was well escorted, had other support than the long train of priests and poets he always carried with him. Hatakeyama Owari no Kami Mitsu-iye, the two Hosokawa, Shimotsuke no Kami Mochiharu and Uma no Kami Mochikata, Isshiki Sakyū no Tayū Mochinobu, with six thousand men formed the escort. Silks and damasks covered the nakedness of horse and man, to dazzle with the brilliant display. The end of the journey was to be at the site of the Udaishō Yori-tomo's old hunting lodge at Gotemba. Warned beforehand Imagawa Norimasa had a new palace erected. Here all was in readiness for the suzerain's reception. On the 17th day (11th October) he arrived at Fujieda. The lords west of the Hakone barrier swarmed to make obeisance. Then a great feast was held. Food of sea and mountain for " the dinner table " was of the most delicate kind. " At night a banquet with dancing and music was

---

[*] Hayashi—" Ō-Dai-Ichiran " mentions this motive. Takegoshi (Ni-Sen-Go-Hyaku Nenshi 467) of modern writers culls from his authorities the same impression.

held. In the daytime a high pass was climbed whence Fujiyama could be viewed. This mountain surpasses the five lofty peaks of Karatomo (China). The fine view first displays the wonderful white peak with its everlasting snows. In part clouds encircle the flanks of the mountain. Half way it is girdled by mists. Ancient trees enclose and closely conceal the foothills. The red of autumn is reflected on the ground. The damask of Shōkuzan is no deeper. Green and mossy cliffs present slippery surfaces. Forests of pine and oak throw their shadow. The peaks, eight leaved, are heaped up ; and amid the masses of the eight piles, from the concave centres overflow the waters of ponds. Their water is the colour of indigo ; their taste pleasantly bitter, curing diseases. The mountain of the gods extends into three provinces. Its peak sends forth snow. In the cool of early morn the birds sing amid the luxuriantly blooming trees. Smoke rises from the lofty peak, and more and more covers the sky over the mountain. The pine moor of Miho, the wind roughening the waves of Tago's shore and reflecting the colours of Fuji's snow, the far extending surface of the sea, are wholly visible. There is no limit to its boundaries."

Surely here was work for the famous artists in the Shōgun's train ; for Chinese precedent required the presence of these men, and Yoshinori, as priest, aped the Chinese style. Then at his summons Imagawa Suruga no Kami Norimasa came close to tell more of this wondrous hill. In Kōan's 92nd year (286 B.C. ?) * it had gushed forth from the ground. In its recesses rich treasures were concealed, invisible to the eyes of man, and all the more assured their presence. In the 17th year of Chōkwan, the 5th day of the 11th month (11th December 869 A.D.) a divine female had descended on the mountain. Here she sang and danced ; and as yet at times song and music were heard by mortal ears. This was the Sengen Daimyōjin, the Honchi Dainichi Nyōrai, the original glorious deity of the holy mount. The very name, by length

---

* Kōan died at 137 years. Kōrei his successor reigned 76 years. His " 75th year " would be 216 B.C. Like Jimmu these early Japanese sovereigns are apocryphal ; most especially those in the list following him to cover six hundred years. They are mere names with elaborate genealogies.

and sanctity, was enough to make one's hair stand on end. But a yet more easily verified tale was told of the mountain. In the 72nd year of Kōrei* the then emperor of Kara (China) was Shikōjō (Shi Huang Ti-246 to 210 B.C.). With regret he viewed the passing years, the beautiful women, his failing powers ; for he was much enamoured of all three. Now in Mount Hōrai was to be had the Elixir of Life. This obtained the emperor could continue his round of pleasure. But where was Hōrai-San ? The monarch was getting no younger with the years. Then one Jofuku (Shin no Ch'in Hsū Fu) appeared. This worthy Chinaman knew the way to the wondrous pile—or said he did. Forthwith he was clapped into a boat. A number of young men and young women to represent vigour were put in with him. They pushed out "into the vacant sea, over the smoky waves." Thus was the land of Nippon, its Fujiyama reached. With prayer, fasting, and offering, Jofuku besought the aid of the mountain god. Alas ! Without result. There either was no elixir, or it was for home consumption only. Jofuku argued wisely and soberly. " If for home consumption only, why " should not Jofuku profit thereby ? Besides, Shikō-tei is a most " cruel prince. Surely there will be no immortality, but short will be " the days and painful of Jofuku, if he returns to make report of " failure." Convinced by his able argument the Chinaman settled in the land, on the flanks of the holy mount. Here he lived to an unconscionable age. His companions male and female did likewise, performed well their mission in life, and taking the name of Shin left many offspring to continue the tradition of the founder. Partly they lived by farming, partly by their flocks of pilgrims. These once corralled were allowed to go hence, happy and deluded. Thus had it always been ; thus would it always be throughout the generations of men. The first day of the sixth month (July) was set for the shearing, for the beginning of the Senjō Mairi (the pilgrimage to the mountain). If anyone blabbed of his or her experience on the mountain life was the forfeit. On this point the divine goddess allowed no trifling.†

---

* See note of 413 p.

† Shingū (in Kumano) people would strongly object to ¡the transfer of Jofuku's exploits elsewhere. His grave is close by their railway station,

The curiosity of Yoshinori was aroused. A pilgrim was to be produced, to tell his tale of the wondrous mysteries involved. To the suzerain's command demur could not be made. With bustling activity the honoured individual, the cleanest and best qualified that could be selected at such short notice, wriggled forward. Prostrate on hands and knees he made obeisance. Then squatting he began his tale—" Fuji Sengen.........." He could get no further. His eyes bolted from his head ; his face was the colour of boiled shrimp ; his tongue, swelled to enormous size, forced apart the unwilling jaws. Not a word could he utter. He was hustled from the Presence, to settle matters with outraged divinity as best he could. Then stepped forward a big *yamabushi* to fill the rôle. A rough awkward fellow he slouched his way with small respect for the suzerain's presence, for the notable assembly. None dared chide or interfere. Yoshinori was merely curious. Then he began with the tale of Nitta Tadatsuna. In the time of Udaishō Yoritomo this bold knight had forced his way from the cave of Benten-Enoshima into the bowels of the earth, emerging in the depths of the mountain. As for this latter, it was said to reach to the dragon hall (Ryūgūkai) in the depths of the sea ; to extend from Heaven (Tenninkai) to the depths of Hell (Konrinzai). " But he who is the slave of passion, " or of this world of passion, cannot understand these matters. The " divine beings of the mountain have cause for anger with men. " Silence is enjoined under penalty of the displeasure of the Dai " Gongen, the great divinity. But at the suzerain's command men " have no regret. They sport with life itself." The *yamabushi* took on huge proportions. He became a Niō of ten feet in height. He roared forth—" This Shōgun is not of the temper of one who " reasons. At the bottom of his heart he does not regard the Buddha " as preacher of the Truth. Put aside this loose life led during " these past years." With threatening gesture he melted into thin air. Great was the fright of Shōgun and *kuge*, of *daimyō* and attendants. Their " livers were cooled." Bows were strung, swords

---

together with those of some followers. Shi Huang Ti reigned 246-210 B.C.
Ō-tei = great emperor : Shin = China.

partly drawn. Surely this *yamabushi* was a *tengu* of the mountain, sent by the goddess.*

The fright of Yoshinori was of short duration. His cool demeanour restored the assembly to its wits. The uneasiness lasted but for the hours, to be forgotten the next day. Other matters occupied attention. Prince Yoshinori ascended the dais. Unfortunately space does not permit the full report of the outburst of song which followed. Between Fuji and Kyōto the old chronicle gives thirty-six of these gems; some of them very smoky quartz, others bright diamond :

" Sunrise : Fuji's lofty peak its shadow casts ;
" And hence the sun becomes more dazzling ! " **

Yoshinori.

" The snow tinged pink seen on the lofty peak.†
" Shadow of the coming dawn on Fuji."

Minamoto Norimasa.

" To brilliance of moon and snow add Fuji's peak unmoveable, ‡
" A kind of world it seems."

Minamoto Norimasa.

When Yoshinori unexpectedly received his wadded floss-silk head covering (*wataboshi*) appropriate was his comment; ditto the answer—to a Shōgun :

" We had it not ; this morn the peak Fuji Suruga, §
" Its headgear, lo ! 'tis snow ! "

---

* The *Yamabushi* were of an order of priests of loose discipline and lives. Their centre was at Haguro in Dewa; but they were strongly entrenched in Echigo and at Hikōsan in Kyūshū. A *tengu* was a goblin with very long nose and wings like a huge bird. There were many varieties—*karasu-tengu* (crow tengu) etc.

** *Asai kage sasu yori Fuji no takamine naru*
Yuki mo hitoshi wo iro masaru kana.

† *Kurenai no yuki wo takamine ni arawashite*
Fuji yori izuru asai kage kana.

‡ *Tsuki yuki no hikari wo soete Fuji no mine no*
Ugoki naki yo no hodo wo mise tsutsu.

§ *Ware narazu kesa wa Suruga no Fuji no mine no*
Wataboshi tomo nareru yuki kana.

And chanted Yamana Ranshin :

 " The clouds! These with the snow on Fuji's peak,°
 " Together age-old *watabōshi*."

Enough of these effusions, trying to the patience of the reader, to
the doubtful efforts of the scribe. Prince Yoshinori returned ;
satisfied as to the loyalty of the Uesugi, the bad intentions of
Mochiuji, his own power to cope with the situation in pursuit of the
plans of the Kyōto House. Left to himself Mochiuji would start
the conflagration. Yoshinori had his own immediate position to
strengthen. His difficulties with the Kitabatake in Kii and the
Ochi family in Yamato, were chronic and uncomfortably close to
Kyōto. In the 8th year of Eikyō (1436) the slowly evolving crisis
was at hand. Murakami Yorikiyo was in rebellion in Shinano.
Ogasawara Shinano-no-Kami Masayasu was ordered to suppress
him. Defeated Yorikiyo sought refuge and aid in Kamakura. In
full council Mochiuji declared his intention to support him with an
army. Norizane the Shitsuji at once protested, and somewhat
roughly—" The affairs of Shinano belong to the Government of the
" Kyōto House. Aid should not be given to the Murakami."
Prince Mochiuji left the council, the cup of bitterness overflowing.
He turned at once to Uesugi Norinao and Isshiki Naokane. These
were to rid him of this insolent tutor.

 Mochiuji's earliest effort to break his bonds was not successful.
The Ōgigayatsu* Uesugi were too close to Yamanouchi for this
movement not to leak out. Norizane had merely to raise his hand
and the samurai began to flock in from Musashi. But it was not
to join the army supposed to go to the aid of Yorikiyo. The gathering of the levies was held at Yamanouchi, that key to Kamakura
on the North. In fright Mochiuji learned that the stronghold of

---

 ° *Kumo ya kore yuki itadaku Fuji no mine ni*
  Tomo ni oisenu watabōshi kana.

 * Split off from the Yamanouchi branch. With the establishment of the
Uesugi as Kwanryō of the Kwantō began the determined battle for supremacy
between the two branches, the Ōgigayatsu gradually drawing ahead. Yamanouchi (Kosaka) holds Kamakura on the North, with easy access to either Kanazawa or Fujisawa. Noriaki undoubtedly had an eye to its military advantages.

the Shitsuji was swarming with his own cohorts. But one course was open to him, and he took it. Mounting his horse he rode off with a meagre train into the tiger's mouth ; the lord to interview and apologize to his vassal. Norizane himself was almost ashamed of the business. Prince Mochiuji was received with all due obeisance. But one stipulation was made, and that had already been foreseen by its object. Uesugi Norinao, the active offender, had hastened to the Yūgyōji at Fujisawa. Here he hid himself until the storm of the 9th year of Eikyō (1437) had passed. Mochiuji returned to the palace at Ōkuragayatsu ; to figure as the Kubōsama, and to chafe at this drastic exhibition to all of the little real power he exercised. The samurai returned to their fiefs, near and far, all somewhat disgruntled at this contest between lord and vassal. There was much uncertainty of mind.

Mochiuji profited by his experience. The 10th year of Eikyō (1438) opened. His eldest son Takao was then sixteen years old. To the astonishment of all Prince Mochiuji announced that the *gembuku* was to take place—at Kamakura. Here was a direct insult to the Kyōto Shōgun. Since the office of the Kwantō Kwan-ryō had been established the eldest son and successor of Kamakura Dono had gone up to the capital to go through the ceremony and receive the name from the Shōgun of the allied House. Norizane in the council made energetic protest. He demanded that the rule of the House ancestor, Prince Takauji, be followed. Mochiuji made indignant reply. What claim had the Shōgun's House of right to the ceremony? The ancestral hall had been the place of the *gembuku* of Mutsu-no-Kami Yoshiiye. Was not the example of Hachiman Tarō himself to be followed? Here at Kamakura was the ancestral shrine of Tsurugaoka. Here should the *gembuku* be performed. With this uncivil excuse and answer the messenger was sent back to the capital. Mochiuji made every preparation for the ceremony, which included the assassination of Norizane as a particular incident. The first part of the programme was carried out without a hitch. Mochiuji himself as sponsor cut the boy's hair and gave him the name of Yoshihisa, the Yoshi (義) borrowed from the name of Hachiman Tarō. The second feature did not

The Protest of Norizane to Mochiuji Kō.

materialize; neither did Norizane. Suspecting a trap he pleaded illness and sent his brother Kiyokata to represent him. When Norizane met the Kwanryō in council he acted as if the whole affair had been a rehearsal of some farce. " Deign to give com-" mand that precedent be followed. The separation of a fraction of " a foot can grow to that of a thousand *ri*. It is much easier to " destroy than to construct. A great calamity can ensue under " one's eyes. Let a message be sent to Kyōto revoking the action, " and precedent be followed."

With rage Mochiuji watched his great vassal leave the palace. Isshiki Naokane counselled immediate action. The ceremony had brought many partisans to Kamakura. Norizane had held aloof from the whole affair. It was decided to strike at once, to arrest the Shitsuji. The news was quick to reach Yamanouchi. Norizane would not take hasty action. Family and *rōtō* were to be consult-ed. Said he with tears—" For the good one exerts oneself; but " there is no restraint to wickedness, and one secures but tribulation, " so 'tis said. In former years it was deigned to dislike the reproof " administered by the Nyūdō of Inukake. The Kwantō was thrown " into great confusion, and eyes of grief it was deigned to witness. " Matters are no different. Disregarding former offences now again " is it deigned to treat Norizane as an enemy. Casting away the " destiny reserved by Heaven, it is plain that the prosperity of the " House must be exhausted. There is naught to be gained by " remaining in Kamakura." On this very 8th month 5th day (25th August 1438) he left Yamanouchi for Hirai castle in Kōtsuke. Isshiki Naokane and Tokinaga, commissioned to bring back the head of the Shitsuji, found the palace empty. When they made report to Mochiuji, the Prince at once saw the importance of im-mediate action. At the news the Kwantō was in a blaze. A peril was felt " as when one treads on the tiger's tail or on the edge of a sword." Kamakura was in the greatest turmoil. All was uncer-tainty and fright. In this struggle between Kwanryō and Shitsuji now brought into the open field which side was to be taken ? On the 13th day (1st September) Mochiuji was at Kōanji in Musashi with three thousand men. From here he issued his summons.

Kyōto had not spoken.   Yūki Ujitomo, the Chiba father and son, the Satake father and son, the Kawagoe, Hasunuma, Koyama, answered with more or less reluctance and twenty thousand men.

With the Isshiki, Hyōbu no Taisuke Naokane and Sama no Kami Sadatoki, in command this force surrounded Hiraijō and the siege was begun.   Just before reaching Takasaki, near Iwahana, the railroad crosses the broad stream of the: Karasugawa near its junction with the Kaburagawa flowing into it from the South.   It is on a third and smaller stream, the Ayugawa or Trout River, tributary to this latter, that this strong place was situated.*   Great was the number of the besieging army.   " By night the fires sent up many thousand clouds.   The starry field of Heaven glittered on Earth, making a galaxy (balustrade) not to be numbered."   What was to be done ?   On one point Norizane was firm.   Not an arrow was to be discharged against the assailants.   On the walls attack could be met and repulsed, but no initiative was to be taken.   Even the shadow of armed rebellion was repulsive to this loyal soldier.   Now and hereafter his conduct was inspired first and last with the single idea of what was best for the Ashikaga House.   In this issue the rebuke of the loyal vassal was the important feature.   " Even if life " be lost, and one be exposed as a criminal, yet one's name will live " savoury to the minds of men.   The Inukake Nyudō was a rebel, " in arms against his lord.   Norizane goes no farther.   Is it not " proper at this time to cut belly ? "   A howl of dissent went up from the assembled family and rōtō.   They were in for it, to suffer with their lord.   They wanted at least to stuff themselves with fighting, before incurring such a belly-ache as was proposed.   Nagao Inaba no Kami acted as spokesman—" The time is inopportune.   This is " a matter on which the suzerain at Kyōto has the right to be heard. " His command is to be obeyed.   If he condemns the action of the " Shitsuji, then all are to cut belly.   To neglect to make report is to " incur censure."   Norizane was impressed with the fineness of the point.   Nagao Hōden himself should be the messenger.   Family

* Often writlen 白井 (white well).   The maps write it 平井 (level).   Thus also the Jitsuyō Teikoku Chimmei Jiten.   There is East and West Hirai on the opposite banks of the river in Tagogōri, Shimotsuke.

and *rōtō* gasped with relief. Of Kyōto's action they had greater hopes
than of that of Norizane. All patted their stomachs with renewed
confidence in their digestion. They sat down to the good things
with which the castle was replete. Meanwhile Nagao Dono spurred
in haste through Kai and Shinano toward Kyōto. If ever mission
depended on the messenger none had more earnest advocate than in
this case. The Daijū (Great Tree) deigned to be amazed. This
fellow Mochiuji lacked all virtue and manners. Besides he was
thoughtless. Was there not at the council board Uesugi Chumu no
Taisuke Mochifusa, son of the prematurely deceased Ujinori? Had
not the younger son Noritomo been standing on hot coals for these
long years? Had they not long been eager to try for Mochiuji's
head? These should be the Taishō (commanders) of the army of
punishment. All the men west of the Kwantō were to form the
host. The Kwantō could take its choice, but it had the written
command of the Muromachi Shōgun to join his army in enforce-
ment of the Imperial rescript, under penalty of being declared rebels
to the damask flag (Nishiki Hata). Letters to Norizane, from
Tennō and Shōgun, commanded him to put Mochiuji Kō to death.

CHAPTER XXIII.

THE SPIRIT OF THE Ō-DONO TRANQUILLIZED.

With head, or rather belly, at stake there were few to outstrip Nagao Hōden as he gallopped up the Nakasendō to the capital, there to seek aid and comfort from the Shōgun and his advisers. He left all in his wake, high and low, in great excitement. Close behind him rode the Oguri, lord and retainers thirteen in number. The province of Kai was already mustering under the orders of Takeda Shigenobu. Shinano, under its lord Ogasawara Masayasu, was not slow in following the example. All felt sure that action would be taken in Kyōto. Now there were several reasons why the lord of Oguri should not ride in either contingent. The most important of these was that as vassal of Prince Mochiuji he could not thus appear without taint of rebellion. Against such rôle Sukeshige was wholly prejudiced. With the first news of Hōden's message he announced his intention of making petition to the Taishō of the Kyōto army ; thus to ride down to the Kwantō under the direct command of the suzerain. At last the time of vengeance had come. The uneasy spirit of the Ō-Dono was to be gratified with the head of Isshiki Akihide, his slanderer and murderer. The vendetta would be accomplished.

Then the Terutehime came forward and knelt before her lord to make petition. Said Sukeshige—" What lies in the hand of this " Sukeshige shall surely be granted. Deign to make known the " request." Answered Terute—" The time of vengeance has come. " The House of Oguri is to be restored to all its honours with the " offering of the head of Akihide. But this Terute has to pacify the " Spirit of her father, Satake Atsumitsu. Deign to allow her pre- " sence, to give the death blow to the base Yokoyama Yasuhide, to

" avenge Atsumitsu. Great is the regret and shame at this peti-
" tion, thus embarassing the sacred mission with the impediment of
" a woman. With fear and respect : deign my lord to grant the
" prayer of this Terute." The *rōtō* clapped their hands in approval.
In one movement they made petition to their lord that the Lady
Terute be allowed to accompany them. Sukeshige smiled ; then
became thoughtful—" What Terute claims is but a right, to give
" the death cut to the slayer of Atsumitsu Dono. There are grave
" difficulties in the way. Since the days of the Heike women have
" not gone to war in Nippon. These filled their camp at Fujikawa
" with prostitutes and feasting, and ran away before a flock of geese.
" Again, at Dannoura their time was spent in dalliance to the sound
" of lute and *koto*. With women hanging at their neck they found
" a grave at the sea-bottom. It is to be feared the Taishō at Kyōto,
" whoever he be, will make objection to the presence of a woman.
" However, deign to allow postponement of decision, until his will
" be known. This Sukeshige will be earnest in request. The case
" is exceptional." Then he looked over the earnest faces of the *rōtō*.
Choice was difficult and invidious among these brave men. Finally
he said—" To Onchi Dono is entrusted the vengeance of the Terute-
" hime. Deign, honoured Sir, to accept the mission." Onchi
Tarō Nagataru bowed low before her ladyship.

Prince Mochifusa was busy in this 9th month of Eikyō 10th
year (20 Sept.-19 Oct. 1438). The Kyōto army was almost ready
to move. Uesugi Harube no Taisuke Noritomo, his brother, had
already set out by the Hokurikudō from Echigo with an army of
seven thousand men, which rapidly grew as it advanced. In these
intervening summer and fall months the siege of Hirai was conducted most idly. Great dissension reigned in the army of the
Isshiki. The defence made no sally ; the assailants were as ready
to attack one another as to attack the castle. This was good news.
Mochifusa rubbed his hands and went over in mind the latest styles
for a head-box. Meanwhile a great uproar arose at the gate of the
yashiki. Two men wearing deep straw hats sought to pass the
guard. This interposed—" Sirs, there is no passage here. Deign to
" remove your honourable hats. Admission to the prince is only

"granted by name and petition. Stop! Stop!" The samurai grew nettled at this interference. The bigger of the two big men was obstinate—"Such uncivil treatment is not to be endured. As " these scurvy fellows demand the removal of the hats, on our heads "they remain. Interview is sought with Mochifusa Kō. The "mission requires secrecy. Be satisfied with this explanation. "Announce the visit."—"Whose visit?" bellowed the now enraged *monban.* "Are two filthy fellows (*yatsu*) thus to force their way "into the presence of his Highness, without appointment and due "observance of all rule! Kill them! Cast them forth into the "ditch! Deign to take your leave!" With such discordant cries and counsel the guard armed with their staves came to drive forth the intruders. The leader of the two men seemed inclined to compromise. "Assuredly a test of strength, a visible witness to his "lordship of your muscles and confidence, is that the meaning of "this obstinate stand? Well! Look out for yourself. An umpire "is needed. Consider the office filled "—"Deign my lord to judge "the issue. Time and feeding have diminished neither." The bigger man stepped forward. Soon the air was full of flying staves and *yakunin.* He played with them as a juggler with his balls. Seeing the guard so roughly handled three or four samurai decided to come to their aid. Decidedly these fellows were not of the kind to have audience. With drawn swords they advanced. Their treatment was hardly better. The judge of the issue now joined his companion. The *yakunin* were used to knock down the samurai, then the samurai followed the aerial trail of the *yakunin.* As Prince Mochifusa came to the entrance to learn the cause of the uproar, one of the latter landed sprawling on all fours at his lord's feet, in due form to make obeisance and report.

On the prince's appearance the deep straw hats were removed and the two samurai knelt. Mochifusa threw up his hands in surprise. "Surely this is the lord of Oguri, Sukeshige Dono. Deign honour-"ed Sir to enter. And this big fellow who plays cup and ball with "my retainers can be none other than Ikeno Shōji. It was on your "honoured and fortunate return from Kii province that this Mochi-"fusa saw Sukeshige Dono at the Hana-gosho (Flower palace).

" Strong was the recommendation to Mitsuiye Kō.   The time is yet
" more favourable for the restoration of the Oguri House."   Sukeshige
gave reverential thanks to the Prince.   Then turning to Shōji he
said—" Shōji, apology is to be made for such rough treatment and
" rude entrance.   For his share this Sukeshige feels much shame.
·· Deign to follow his example in ample proportion, in accordance
" with the display of vigour."   Solemnly Shōji made obeisance and
apology—" Alas !   The muscles are not always well controlled.
" Deign to assess any punishment.   At his lord's command this
" Shōji will cut belly.   Although too much trouble has already been
" given."   Prince and lord smiled at the earnestness with which the
worthy knight took the situation.   Court and capital were new to
Shōji.   He had the tinge of contempt of the Kwantō *bushi* for those
of Kyōto, considered somewhat as carpet-knights.   Yet as being on
unfamiliar ground there were misgivings as to the propriety of the
late display of vigour.   Mochifusa tapped his shoulder.   " See how
" these fellows stand in wonder.   The name of Ikeno Shōji is a
" password to each and all.   Being tossed at your hands, good Sir,
" is an honour for them.   May they profit by the experience.
" Surely they have little to brag of in this encounter."   As they
entered and sat at a sign from the prince—" Mochifusa too is from
" the Kwantō.   A display of the superior strength of the men of the
" Hasshū (Eight Strands) is as water to a thirsty man."   He had a
twinkle in his eyes.

Then on the order of the Prince the petition was offered—that
Sukeshige be allowed to join the Kyōto force on its march to Kamakura, thus to accomplish the vendetta of Mitsushige.   Mochifusa
was joyful—" The earnestness and filial piety shown by Sukeshige
" Dono is known to all Nippon.   In the face of difficulties, hard-
" ship, and desperate sickness, never has the duty of the son to the
" father been forgotten.   Your example, honoured Sir, is a beacon
" to such as have idled the years in the luxury of Kyōto.   This
" Mochifusa has a grudge to satisfy.   The long years have passed,
" the end is at hand.   Prince Yoshinori never will remit the death
" punishment of Mochiuji Kō.   This is the culmination of a policy
" extending through the years from the dissension with Ujimitsu and

" Mitsukane. However, as direct vassal of Kamakura the matter
" is complicated. The petition of the Lady Terute offers exit. Why
"not go in company to witness the war? Thus opportunity is
" offered to accomplish your lordship's holy duty and to serve the
" suzerain without attacking Prince Mochiuji. He can well be left
" to those interested in his fall. Their strength is ample." Sukeshige was overcome at the kind foresight of the Prince. With tears
in his eyes he replied—" Your lordship reads the thoughts of this
" Sukeshige. With fear and reverence deign, honoured lord, to
" receive insufficient thanks. Sukeshige would not raise his hand
"against his master "—" The affair then is decided," replied
Mochifusa. " The army starts within a week. It would be well to
" summon the retainers to the standard."—" They are at hand.
" We are lodged close by at Fushimi ; " thus Sukeshige—" Deign
" to honour this Mochifusa with the presence of the lord of Oguri.
" The *yashiki* is befitting quarters." Urged by the prince the
transfer was made to the headquarters of the war. Sukeshige, as
trained soldier familiar with the Kwantō, could give substantial aid.
During this short stay summons was received to appear at the
Muromachi palace. Yoshinori Kō had heard much of the horsemanship of the Kwantō knight. The desire was easier to satisfy
and less expensive than the trip to Fuji. In the presence of the
suzerain and his court Sukeshige made exhibition of his skill. Great
was the amazement and delight of Yoshinori. Then the knight
stood forward and made petition that it be deigned to command
archers arrayed in two parallel lines. Through this he would ride
without injury ; or failing skill accept death without complaint.
Yoshinori Kō clapped his hands with joy. Here was a game to his
liking. With grave faces the Gotō brothers inspected every line of
harness and equipment. The archers, picked men, ten on each side,
were ranged in line to shoot down this human game—if they could.
Without armour, without belly-guard, arrayed in *hakama* and a
daimon (court robe) of dark blue ground on which were figured the
white *kikyō* (platycidon grandiflorum), with braided *eboshi* (head-
gear), his sleeves folded back at the side to allow free movement of
the arms, the knight mounted. After forcing his horse to curvet

and gallop a little, slowly Sukeshige rode forward and into the lines of archers. The arrows came like hail, the archers strained eye and arm to bring down the laughing *bushi*. With whirling sword he rode by, the severed shafts falling beside him. Then in the centre he halted for a moment, sword and hand busy intercepting the flying shafts. As he rode out of the deadly line the assembly rose with a mighty shout. Yoshinori Kō fairly trembled with pleasure. The Oguri *rōtō* with stolid faces went forward to the aid of their lord, but Gotō Hyōsuke dug his nails into his wrists to repress the shout of triumph on his lips. Then the *saké* cup was handed down at the order of the Prince. Summoned to the presence of Yoshinori, the Shōgun signed to Sukeshige to come close. At the suzerain's command he told the tale of his life, or of the vendetta which was the object of life. Yoshinori marvelled. " Such deeds deserve " reward. Long is the memory of the Shōgun ; long is his arm. " Be diligent Sukeshige." The audience was ended. Mochifusa gave to Sukeshige under the Shōgun's seal the command to put to death Isshiki Akihide and Yokoyama Yasuhide. The stigma of beggary was removed. No taint remained on the name of Oguri.

On the 10th month 3rd day (21st October 1438) the army of Mochifusa left Kyōto. The presence of a lady's litter caused comment, but the reason was soon whispered through the camp. A mere *kembutsu* (sight-seeing) of the miserable scenes of war would have aroused disgust. Such as had the thought soon learned the truth. The rare glimpses of the dame aroused curiosity, How could such a frail creature hope to accomplish a vendetta, no matter how just ? The sight of the mighty proportions of Onchi Tarō inspired different ideas. " The *sukedachi* (second) is a fearful fellow. " The gods are good. The vendetta rests not against humble me." At the East end of Biwako was approached a body of men standing in battle order by the road side. Silence and military precision reigned. Plainly they were Kwantō men. The Kyōto army at first thought the strangers were hostile, perhaps the van guard of an army of the Kamakura prince. Their banner marked with the white *kikyō* was soon recognized as that of the lord of Oguri. These were the retainers from Hiraoka recruited by many from Hitachi·

They had responded to the summons of war, but it was to march South to join their chief, not to join the contingent of the Isshiki. With this added strength of three hundred men the Oguri *rōtō* entered Aohakamachi.

The *yakunin* came to Manchō's place with the *bugyō's* order. With fear and respect at the official summons, and some impatience, Manchō answered his call. The army of Kyōto was at hand. Quarters were to be found in temple and home of lord and plebeian. Three hundred men with their chief were to be quartered on Manchō. Outwardly the innkeeper grumbled, inwardly he was pleased. These fellows would leave ample reward, in one way or another at such a place as his. "The order is received and reverentially "understood : *kashikomarimashita.*" The *yakunin* sneered. "Man- "chō does not ask the name of his guest ; though he knows it well. "It is a daimyō much sought after in Kamakura, the lord of Oguri." In a moment Manchō was grovelling at the official's feet—"Deign "to consider. Lodge these people elsewhere. Take half the wealth "of Manchō. His life is at stake"—"Bah !" said the *yakunin.* "A head shorter would do the world no harm and travellers much "good. Your fate is deserved. This is the man reported to Jinroku "the Daikwan by this very Manchō. The Daikwan lost his life. "Why should not Manchō ? Besides, by special order the lord of "Oguri has requisitioned the house of Manchō. Plainly he was "pleased with his entertainment." Laughing he departed, to make respectful obeisance at the entrance as the Oguri *rōtō* poured into it. In terror Manchō fled to a little room in the rear. Then a litter was brought into the inclosure. Women and attendants watched the care exercised with the lady who occupied it. The heavy conveyance was lifted on the shoulders of strong men and conveyed into the inner apartments fronting on the garden. With curiosity Terute looked again on this scene of her trials. How different were the conditions. Mighty was the hand of the goddess.

The house was busy providing entertainment for these guests. The *rōtō* of Oguri showed no unkindness or roughness to these people, yet there was an ominous air overhanging their pre-

sence. There seemed business to be done. The meal provided
and removed Ikeno Shōji appeared in the little room where was
crouched the happily neglected *teishu*. Said he—" The lord of
" Oguri wishes to give thanks to Manchō for his entertainment. Sir,
" it is your place to come before him, and be honoured at the sum-
" mons." Manchō grovelled and stammered. He was very ill.
How gladly would he have welcomed this honoured guest, but he
could not rise. Pains in the stomach made him an unseemly object,
his affliction unfitted him to come in person before the lord of Oguri.
Shōji put aside all ceremony and disguise—" This Manchō is a liar.
" He looks as well as Shōji. He suffers from fright. This makes
" him a trifle pale ; otherwise his weakness is in his heart, not in his
" legs or bowels. Come along ! For pain in the belly there is the
" sovereign cure of pain in the head. The flux in one direction
" shall be stopped by flux in another. Death is the cure for all
" diseases." He made sign to two soldiers. In a moment Manchō
was stood up. Thus was he dragged into the garden of the
haginoma.

Sukeshige was seated at the *rōka* to judge the case. The Gotō
and Tanabe stood behind him. The Kataoka and Kazama were lounging in the garden. They glared at the *teishu*, this wicked beast who
had so ill-treated their lady, who had betrayed their lord. Mito no
Kotarō as witness stood before Sukeshige. Onchi Tarō was engaged in grinding into powder a huge and curious boulder figuring
as ornament to the garden. His implement was a long iron pole.
He looked up as Manchō passed. The man nearly fainted with
fright. With gravity Sukeshige received him at the *rōka*.—" Man-
" chō, the justice of Heaven is witnessed in this meeting. Your case
" is now to be judged. Unless full and satisfactory answer be made
" your present existence has come to an end." In reply Manchō
fell on the ground—" This wretched fellow has no answer to make
" to the injured lord of Oguri, no apology to meet his crime. Deign
" revered lord to consider that benevolence and pity have always
" been counselled by the sages. Show mercy to such an humble
" creature as this Manchō. His crime was according to his nature,
" and unwitting." Said Sukeshige—" You lie Manchō. A man of

" intelligence, in business and brought into contact with many kinds
" of men, you have known how to amass wealth. To be sure this
" has been gained by the foulest of means. Let this pass. Are
" you to be treated with benevolence and pity? You, who thus
" maltreated an unhappy woman, delivered into your hands not by
" her consent nor circumstances, but by the hand of a kidnapper?
" This wretched fellow, turned thief, has perished on the com-
" mon execution ground. But you; nay, your offence is still
" greater. You add craft to robbery and kidnapping. Ransomed
" by this Sukeshige, a second time ransom is demanded and obtained.
" To this you have no ready answer. That you should betray this
" Sukeshige to the Daikwan, this offence is pardoned. For the
" other crimes you are condemned. Summon this man's people ! "

At their lord's order the Oguri *rōtō* drove the frightened men
and women, the wife of Manchō, into the inclosure. A solid back-
ground, silent and tearful, they stood to witness the punishment.
Said Sukeshige—" Shōji, this man is intrusted to your hands."
" Shōji stepped forward and made obeisance—" Will my lord deign
" to receive a petition? Ikeno Shōji is a *bushi*, of small reputation
" but clean hands. His sword is pure. The blood of this scoundrel
" would contaminate it. Condescend to hear the prayer of Shōji.
" Let me twist off the villain's head." Sukeshige slapped his knee.
" Be it so. The suggestion is good in every way. Such is the
" punishment." As Shōji approached and put his hands on Manchō's shoulders the wretched man screamed in fright. Growled
the knight—" Stick out your head rascal ! Why not die comfort-
" ably, since die you must. The more you shrivel up the longer
" will the trial of strength last. Assuredly this Shōji will sever
" completely head from body, simply by the strength of his hands."
He thrust a knee between the shoulders of Manchō and took firm
hold of the head below the jaws. A frightful groan from the very
depths of Manchō's body, the shrill screams of the wife, the hysteri-
cal tears of the women present, ushered in the strange scene.

Then the *shōji* of the apartment in the rear opened. The
Terutehime appeared. Advancing she prostrated herself before her
lord, with a hand extended in protest toward the unhappy Manchō.

Manchō brought to Judgment.

Sukeshige made sign to Shōji to wait—" What is it Terute ?   Surely
" it is not to ask the life of this fellow !   Do you not see that this is
" Manchō ?   He who for long weeks sought in every way the life of
" Terute by his oppression ; who dared to lay hands upon her
" person ?   Such petition this Sukeshige could not grant.   The
" punishment of Manchō is far milder than his wickedness demands.
" For years this wretch has prospered on iniquity.   Now let him
" die a fitting death."   Terute raised eyes to her lord, in which
pain as well as loving affection found expression.—" Nay, my lord !
" This man has appealed to the benevolence and pity of the lord of
" Oguri.   Consider that all has not been said.   While this Terute
" was inmate of his house this man gave her nourishment and
" shelter for her body.   If this Terute had not been lodged with
" Manchō then the meeting with her lord would not have oc-
" curred.   These two deeds, the act of Kwannon Sama, plead
" in mitigation.   Deign to receive the petition of Terute   Spare this
" man's life."   For long Sukeshige remained, his hands shading his
eyes.   Then smiling he seized the hands of Terute with pleased admiration and affection.   " Let him go Shōji."   Grumbling the *bushi*
released his grasp on the victim.   Said Sukeshige severely—" The
" reprieve of Manchō is allowed only on the fulfillment of these
" conditions.   Man and wife are to leave the world, he as mendi-
" cant priest, she as nun.   These women are to be dismissed to their
" homes with ample presents.   The ill gotten wealth is to be distri-
" buted in alms to the temples.   On such terms Manchō possesses
" life.   Such is the decision of Sukeshige."   Rising the lord of
Oguri took Terute by the hand to lead her within.   Under the
direction of Gotō Hyōsuke the *karō*, in consultation with the rector
(*jūshoku*) of the Kokuzō Bosatsu shrine, the decree was carried out.
Next day the Oguri *rotō* marched northward with their lord and
lady.   At the same time the begging friar knelt by the roadside
with his bowl.   His novitiate was shortened by the wealth contributed, his state of *nyūdō*, and the urgency of the lord of Oguri.

In Suruga were added the contingents of the lord of the province, Imagawa Suruga no Kami Norimasa, of those of the province
of Shinano under the command of Ogasawara Masayasu, of those

of Kai under Takeda Shigenobu. The army of fifty thousand men
rolled into the passes across Hakone and the base of Fuji. Uesugi
Norinao had much at stake. Also he had three thousand men.
The great army overwhelmed the opposition, not too easily in these
rough passes. The last effort was made at Kawajiri. Norinao was
left, pondering the probable result, his head in his hands, an occupation only too sure to be turned over to others. As the army
slowly passed the Banyūgawa the news of its accomplished mission
came to hand. When the banners of Noritomo's army—the forces
of the Hokurikudō—came in sight, the finishing touch was put to
the idle siege which the Kwantō army of Prince Mochiuji was conducting before Hirai-jō. The contingents of Yūki, of Chiba, of
Satake, promptly furled the flag and disappeared over the horizon
of the Musashi plain. The relieving army set out in chase. The
Shōgun's order in his hands Norizane emerged, to take command
and summon the Kwantō to its duty. The Isshiki appeared at
Kōanji with none in attendance but their own retainers. This place
was too near the advancing foe. Mochiuji removed to Ebina.*
While news was awaited from Kamakura the scanty force dwindled
day by day. The desertions to Norizane's army followed in rapid
succession. Then came the finishing touch. A courier arrived from
the northern capital. Miura Tokitaka, left in military command of
Kamakura had been ciphering vigourously. As the army of Mochifusa flowed through the passes of Hakone, with the news of the
army of Norizane forcing back the Isshiki on lower Musashi, this
simple sum of 2 + 2 was solved. The next day at dawn the shops
and houses of the plebeians in flames were the signal of his rebellion.
Screams " as of fire scorched demons in the hell of Shōnetsu (flames)
arose. Pity was put aside." Three thousand men were hammering at the gates of the Ōkura palace. There were but a hundred
men on the night-guard. These died to a man. The prince
Yoshihisa escaped by the hills to Ōgigayatsu. Here the pursuit

---

* In Sa ami province Kōzagōri—two miles from the Banyūgawa and ten
miles in air line from the sea. It is on the highway leaving the Ashigara road
at Matsuda and crossing the plain direct to the head of Edo bay, passing through
Atsugimachi, Kawabaraguchi, Ebina, Nagatsuda. It enters Tōkyō at Shibuya.

caught up with him. Surrounded, his two devoted attendants Yanadabō and Nazukabō died in the defence. Yoshihisa was made prisoner. The Kyōto army was pouring into the city, and on this side all was lost.

Mochiuji would have cut belly forthwith. Isshiki Naokane objected—" It is the practice of soldiers to deceive. When the time " of irretrievable misfortune is reached suicide is easy. For the " present deign to wait. His lordship should finesse. First deign " to learn the intentions of the Shitsuji." It was a fair and straight-forward speech by the best and bravest of these brothers. His own fate was sealed. With Norizane his feud was implacable. He made the attempt to save his prince. Then, while Isshiki went forth to his last desperate battle, Prince Mochiuji entered the Shōmyōji of Kanazawa. Here he shaved his head and made humble apology to the Shitsuji. Norizane could do little, but he took the responsi-bility of asking for further orders, and a change of sentence from Kyōto. Meanwhile Mochiuji was escorted to Kamakura. Here under the guard of Nagao Inaba no Kami Hōden he entered the Eianji of Momijigayatsu, to pass the days and months before the final decision could be reached.

It was here that he granted audience to such vassals as dared to present themselves. Of those present many were ladies who thus vicariously represented their lords. Mochiuji spoke severely— " What an example of filial conduct has been this last uprising ! " If the prince, the father of his people, is thus to be neglected and " betrayed, cast aside by those who owe him the service of child to " parent, what can you, the mothers of such sons, wives of such " husbands, expect in this existence or the next ? Most dastardly " has been the conduct of these lords. To this Mochiuji the result " is indifferent ; but the blow to all loyalty of child and vassal has " been deadly." Yūki Ujitomo rose to make answer—" Iza ! With " fear and reverence, august prince : the difficulty lies not with all " the vassals, but only with a few. Our lord's ear has been stopped " by slander. Evil men have stood between him and his vassals, to " prevent or distort all communication. Matters are not at such " desperate pass. Cast away these Isshiki root and branch, these

" evil speaking Yamana.   Throw open the prince's court to his lords
" of the Kwantō.   Who then would dare to face the Eight Pro-
" vinces united in defence of their suzerain ?   Never has this Uji-
" tomo swerved in loyalty to his prince, but men have been found
" to have no access to their lord except through Isshiki or Yamana.
" Deign my lord thus to act."   The prince eyed him kindly—" It
" is true.   Ujitomo has stood almost alone.   Mochiuji gives thanks.
" You have a request to make ; speak."   Then Ujitomo offered petition from Oguri Sukeshige, that Kamakura Dono issue command
to put to death Isshiki Akihide and Yokoyama Tarō.   Thus the
Houses of Oguri and Satake could make formal petition for restoration to honours and fiefs.   Mochiuji readily granted the request.
Naokane, defeated in battle, had cut belly, and with him his principal retainers.   Why should not Akihide be given the same opportunity ! Then he called Ujitomo close to him.   They spoke in
whispers.   Vigorous was Ujitomo's sign of dissent.   Mochiuji smiled
sadly.   He knew the course of coming events better than the good-
hearted and somewhat heavy-witted knight.   Speaking aloud finally
he said—" This is to be remembered ; this the charge given by his
" prince to Ujitomo.   When the time comes, act.   The faith of this
" man in Kyōto is bad.   To the charge of Ujitomo his prince
" commits the heritage of what he holds most dear."   Weeping
Ujitomo prostrated himself, his face on his hands before his lord.
" The life of Ujitomo is the pledge, and himself he will make report
" to his lord in Meido."

Prince Mochifusa was first to learn of the mission of vendetta.
His action was kind and prompt.   The task was no light one.
Yokoyama Shōgen and Isshiki Akihide, anticipating the fall of the
Kwanryō, had determined to make a stand in the mountain fort
some time before established by Shōgen at Gokenmura.   Their
position was sure to improve with time, and an obstinate resistance
of some months would give opportunity to effect a reconciliation
with the prevailing interests at Kamakura, the more so as Akihide
relied on support near the Shōgun.   In the district behind
Fujisawa, parallel with the Banyūgawa, the hills run back in
long ridges badly cut and distorted by erosion.   Rarely more than

a hundred feet in height they offer facilities for defence in a very difficult cut-up country. This Gokenmura was established on Kuriyama, its formidable name being much shortened by the application of the *ri* of six *chō* (less than half a mile) used in this district.* The hill is almost equally well known among the peasantry as Yokoyama's mountain, from the tradition still preserved of the robber's den here established. Akihide and Yokoyama had gathered some fifteen hundred men, mainly *rōnin* and thieves. The position, moreover, was a strong one. When therefore Imagawa Noritada presented himself with the order of Prince Mochifusa and the offer of two thousand men great was the joy of Sukeshige. The Imagawa too were pleased. This fellow Yokoyama had often enough carried his raids into Suruga. The opportunity to put an end to him was golden.

The Suruga forces had not advanced beyond the Banyūgawa. Oguri Sukeshige had kept aloof from the active movements which were crushing Prince Mochiuji from South to North as in a vise. The two contingents against Isshiki and Yokoyama were camped in and close by Ōiso town. The Banyūgawa therefore had to be crossed. It was planned to make the march by night, and to raise the battle-shout at dawn before the stronghold of the thieves. However, when the three thousand men reached the river not a sign of a boat was to be seen. In this predicament Ikeno Shōji stepped forward. " Probably the enemy suspect an attack and " have corralled the craft on the other side of the river. To ensure " escape they would hardly destroy them. Deign my lord to com- " mand this Shōji to cross the river and returning make report. " No other companion is needed than Onchi Dono. Thus the " matter will be certified. Many of these men do not swim. The " crossing without boats in the night will be dangerous." The counsel was adopted. Shōji stripped off armour and clothes. Carrying nothing but his sword he pushed boldly across the river bearing the end of a stout rope. Fastening this to a tree, Onchi Tarō did the same on his side. No monkey could give lessons to

* The official maps, however, give this locality the character 栗; as in Kurihara. It is near Ebina.

Tarō as to climbing trees and springing over rocks ; and Tarō could drown as readily as the ape. Shōji was the true Kwantō-bei of the provinces bordering the sea. He swam like a fish. Tarō crossed the stream, swallowing no small part of it in his progress. As half blinded he was dragged up on the other bank—" A bridge, but a " poor one. If three thousand men have to use one of such " fashion Akihide Dono ·and this Yokoyama will have died of old " age before an attack can be made." Said Shōji—" Be sure the "boats are not far off. With the aid of Tarō Dono this Shōji will " include them in his report to his lord."

His surmise was correct. They had tramped up stream but the part of an hour when they came upon a patrol sitting around a fire gambling and drinking. It was cold in this 12th month (end of December) and the fire looked grateful to the shivering Shōji and Tarō. They burst into its warmth and circle. At the apparition of two naked men with swords the thieves sprang in confusion to every side. Shōji straddled the leader and held him down, his sword at his throat. Tarō stationed himself on the narrow footway of the dyke which even then protected the lowlands from flood. He shouted—" Scoundrels, rascals, let no man attempt to escape ! " We are naked and without fear or shame. Moreover here stand " Ikeno Shōji and Onchi Tarō, well known as *rōtō* of Oguri Suke- " shige. Stick out your heads, furnish the needed boats for the " army of his lordship, covering for the twain. Thus shall your lives " be spared, ourselves warmed, and his lordship find recruits in your " persons. From thieves you shall become *sendō* (boatmen). Both " are robbers." A roar of laughter from the thieves, a chuckle from the prostrate member, astonished Shōji. Kizukuri Oniyasha advanced from the band—" Deign honoured Sirs to receive a warm " welcome. The name of Oguri is well known to Oniyasha. He " stands here ready to redeem his pledge. For a second time has " Akamatsu Dono been worsted in contest with Shōji Dono." A little discomfited Shōji recognized the prostrate thief as the quondam lord of Amanawa. Hence the chuckle. To laugh with a sword at his gizzard took a stronger mind than that of Norikiyo. Shōji stood aside to allow him to rise. A kind of covering was made up by contribution from the band. Oniyasha explained matters. It was all well enough to practice with the band of Yokoyama. Contributions for war were boldly levied on the countryside, and great preparations against attack had been made. The news of the command given to Oguri had reached Shōgen as soon as it had reached Sukeshige. Hence he was expected. The boats had been corralled to impede his movements and furnish escape if necessary. Oniyasha and Akamatsu had been put in charge of them. The two bandits had no idea but of joining the force of the lord of Oguri. But where would he cross the river? Spies had been sent out, but as yet no report had been made. With fear and reverence service was offered ; and accepted with joy. Manned by these new recruits the boats were soon on their way down the stream. At first Sukeshige could not understand this force descending the river. No one could get through the guard at the lower ferry. As they came closer they were seen to be accompanied by Shōji and Onchi Tarō. Brought to land Oniyasha and Akamatsu made obeisance and petition to join the attacking army. This granted the crossing of the river was begun and soon accomplished. Then the march to the hills was started.

Yokoyama Shōgen had too much at stake to run away on mere rumour. Gokenmura was stuffed with the plunder of years. He determined on more than mere resistance. The attacking force was to be ambushed as it crossed the river. But " the council of thieves is timid and disorderly." This undisciplined force much preferred to guzzle and not to march in the cold night of early winter. It was the dark before dawn in which the assailants reached the thieves' den. As arranged the Imagawa men passed to the hill in the rear, here to make their assault as the Oguri burst into the front gate. But how was Sukeshige to effect his object? A deep moat surrounded the place. The walls rose straight from the water. A bridge of bamboo crossed the gap, but this was hauled up on the other side. Deep silence prevailed. The thieves slept in security. Not even a guard was placed. Shōji advanced and looked into the moat. A fly or beetle could, a man might climb the slippery wall beyond. His eye fell on two huge trees. Springing up on the two

sides of the moat their branches approached far above. He grinned
—"Tarō Dono, this is your task. Deign to lower the bridge
" yonder, give free passage to this Shōji. Before our efforts this
" gate will give way." Onchi Tarō in a moment was on his way
up the tree. With all the caution of mountaineer and monkey he
crept out on the extending branches. They began to bend and
sway under him. Swinging his body he made the leap. With
suppressed joy the onlookers saw him grasp the opposing branch.
It bent but did not break under the weight. Tarō remained thus
suspended over the water for but a short time. He was soon to
ground again. The bridge was lowered. The Oguri *rōtō* poured
across it. Soon the gate was bending and breaking under their
blows. With shouts they poured into the inclosure.

Great was the confusion which ensued. The thieves were
roused from drunken slumber to meet the attack. Hardly had they
advanced to oppose the Oguri *rōtō*, slashing and driving the garrison
before them, when uproar was heard in the rear. Warned by the
noise the Imagawa men were breaking into the postern gate. Men
leaped on horseback and spurred forward, only to find the animal
still tied to his rack. Helmets were thrown on back side front.
Armour was buckled on at any angle that agitation would permit.
In such guise it was only sought to escape. By the orders of Sukeshige and Noritada fire was not set to the place. The object was to
capture Akihide and Shōgen. Their heads overtopped all else. To
the soldiery the booty of this den of thieves was a great object.
Yokoyama Tarō for years had levied tribute on all who passed, on
all who lived, within reach of his long claws. The first to ride forward were the two sons of Yokoyama—Tarō Yasukuni and Jirō
Yasutsugu. In disorderly mass and with shouts the robber band
sought to cut its way out at the postern gate. The Imagawa
were already looting. Only the Oguri were there to oppose them.
Yasukuni and his brother never left the inclosure. The eldest
brother whirling his halberd rode forward. Onchi Tarō sprang to
meet him. The iron pole swept the horse's legs from under it. As
Yasukuni lay struggling on the ground down the pole descended
on his head. " Helmet, head, brains, body, were beaten into

flour. Immersed in smoking blood he died." Kataoka Kataro
thrust his spear into the belly of Yasutsugu. In a trice his head
was off. In fright the thieves had scattered, to be cut down for the
most part by the Oguri *rōtō*.

Then rode forth a man on a tall black horse. He wore black
armour, a belly-guard of black lacquer sewn with black thread. It
was Yokoyama Tarō. He shouted in challenge—" Where is this
" Oguri Sukeshige ; this cowardly Taishō ? It is with him that
" Shōgen would fight, with him settle the rivalry of long years.
" Lord of Oguri, deign to do battle " Laughing Sukeshige rode
forward.—" That Sukeshige should fight with Tarō Dono is no
" great honour. The gift of his head lies in other hands. Deign
" to receive a sword cut." Contemptuous he came to the attack.
Fiercely did the halberd of Shōgen whirl as a windmill in a strong
gale. Then as if by clumsiness Sukeshige fell directly under the
feet of Shōgen's horse. The robber gave a shout of triumph and
raised his halberd to strike. Next moment man and weapon rolled
in different directions as the horse pitched forward to the ground.
Sukeshige had thrust his spear into its belly and disembowelled it.
He stood aside and watched Shōgen rise. Said he—" Call the
" Lady Terute."

Then Terute, accompanied by Mito no Kotarō and Onchi Tarō,
came forward. All stood apart. She wore trousers of white *neri*
(a floss silk), *hachimaki* (head towel), an outer cloak of white *aya*
(damask) over all. In her hand she brandished a long halberd.
Yokoyama Tarō eyed her laughing in his wrath. Sword and dagger
deftly removed by Mito no Kotarō he was weaponless—"By this hand
" died Satake Atsumitsu. By this hand and brain many other men
" have met their end. Now this Tarō dies at the hand of a woman !
" It is Heaven's punishment, such shameful end. But the task
" will not be found easy." Nor was it. Try as she could Terute
had neither the skill nor the strength. She could not succeed in
giving a fatal stroke. Yokoyama retreated and retreated ; gradually
he was edging his way toward wall and gate, his trail marked by
blood sprinkled from the trifling cuts incurred in parrying the thrusts
of Terute. Then two strong arms seized and held him as in a vise.

Terute at Go-ken Mura—the Battle.

Yokoyama tried to wriggle away, but in vain. The halberd of
Terute thrust him through the buttocks and brought him to the
ground—"A regular woman's trick!" he growled. "Let this
"affair be ended." He turned full toward the foe, exposing chest and
belly. The weapon pierced his heart. Mito no Kotarō struck off
his head. Thus died Yokoyama Tarō. With flushed face and
frightened shining eyes Terute presented herself before Sukeshige.
Mito no Kotarō performed a dance.

His wife greeted with cheerful countenance, again the knight
stood in gloomy meditation. Noritada tried to comfort him.
The thieves' den had been ransacked from end to end. The
heads of Shirō Yasutaka and of Gorō Yasunaga, found crouching in the stables, had been secured. But not a sign of Akihide could be found. Yet Oniyasha and Akamatsu could answer
for his presence. Then the search was turned to the moat;
but the nets brought up nothing but fish and frogs, not Isshiki.
Had all the bloodshed and effort ended in nothing? Then
a shout was raised down the hillside. Oguri and Imagawa went
forward to meet the newcomer. With some surprise they found
it to be Yūki Ujitomo. Said he—"Much has the Satake House
"suffered from this rascal Yokoyama. Ujitomo also desired to take
"part in the vengeance. Ah! The head of Tarō is secured—and
"by the Lady Terute herself! The mission of Ujitomo has then
"been successful. In the hills below, on the Fujisawa road, we
"came upon these fellows encamped. Evidently fugitives from some
"battle they were surrounded and made prisoners. Deign to look.
"Here is none other than Isshiki Dono himself. Honoured Sir
"accept this gift from Ujitomo. Akihide becomes the prisoner of
"Oguri Dono."

Bound hard and fast Akihide, garbed as an *ashigaru* (common
soldier), was brought into the presence of the captains. Said Sukeshige—"Thus ends the contest! Thus is accomplished the vendetta
"of the Ō-Dono." Slowly he raised his sword. The severed bonds
of Isshiki fell to the ground. Then Sukeshige cast down his weapon
before Akihide. He turned to Ujitomo—"Deign, Yūki Dono, to
"grant the service of your sword to this Sukeshige." Facing Akihide

he continued—" Sukeshige does not attack an unarmed man, a
" prisoner. Deign Sir to take the weapon and fight with him. Thus
" is Heaven's will accomplished." Akihide remained crouched,
without raising his head. Finally a voice came as from the ground
—" The affair is ended. Akihide has lost in the fight. With his
" lord's fall his own hopes perish. The fruit of years is bitter.
" Akihide will not fight with Oguri Dono. He makes surrender.
" At once let death be meted out."

Then Sukeshige turned to Ujitomo—" As your prisoner,
" honoured Sir, to you belongs the sword-cut, the prize of this
" cowardly villain's head. Great should be your joy. All the
" troubles of the Satake House, all the woes of Mochiuji Kō centre
" in this fellow." But Ujitomo in his turned refused—" The
" vendetta of Oguri Mitsushige is to be accomplished. To Kojirō
" Dono belongs the prize." Thus they strove with each other. Imagawa proposed a settlement—" Turn and turn about. Let Oguri
" Dono deign to give the first cut ; then Ujitomo Dono a second."
This advice was followed. With his sword Sukeshige made a cut
into the right side of Akihide's neck. Ujitomo followed with one
on the left. Then Sukeshige struck the head from the body. At
this final cut a shout of joy went up from the *rōtō* of the Oguri and
Satake Houses.

The booty was divided, the stronghold of the thieves set on fire.
Then they rode back ; the Imagawa to their camp at Ōiso ; the
Oguri to Kamakura, to make report to the suzerain Prince Mochiuji through the Shitsuji, to secure the re-establishment of the Houses
of Oguri and Satake. On the way, lord and retainers, they rode
into the inclosure of the Yūgyōji of Fujisawa. The aged Joa
Shōnin tottered out to meet them. He was now nearly ninety
years of age. The closed wooden lotus of the temple gave timely
notice of the approaching end. The aged priest had returned to
meet it. Great was his joy at this culminating success of a long
life. On the hillside Sukeshige selected a site for future rest. From
the bosom of her robe Terute produced a little lacquer box. Advancing she knelt and gave it into the hands of her lord. It was
the gift of Mitsushige, sent to his beloved son Kojirō ; a lock of hair.

Then with solemn mass and chant of priests the hair was buried within the chosen site. Sukeshige and his Ten Valiants cut locks from their hair. Thus severed these were to rest here, until in turn their bodies came to take their place together. With the head of Akihide all turned their faces northward to ride to Oguri ; to place the trophy before the monument erected by the monk Unzen faithful to the memory of his old lord.

Thus does the lord of Oguri, the Terutehime his wife, take leave of this tale, the favoured romance of story-teller and puppet show for many long decades of the history of this strange people so given to hero worship. But more is heard of Sukeshige in sober history. The House of Oguri was restored to its honours and wealth. For long he figures as direct vassal of the Shōgun, receiving at the New Year his gift of *ayaginu* or *neriginu* (damask or floss silk). When in the ripeness of years Sukeshige saw the rising generation come to maturity, then he laid down his burden and left the world (*shukke*). Entering the Sōkokuji of Kyōto he put himself under the tuition of Shūbun, that great artist and forerunner of the Chinese school of painting. " In mind Shūbun had swallowed the precious rules. With his eyes he observed carefully *chiaroscuro*. In the three secrets of painting he made Jōsetsu the model. The result of this style was cause of wonder. In later times Sesshū, Oguri, Kanō, all followed in the steps of Shūbun. In the school of Sōtan the style was further advanced."

Thus did Oguri Kojirō resume his name of Sōtan under the true priest's robe, taking up his favourite art under the influence of this foremost artist of his times. The Sung and Ming schools of drawing or painting have given great results in the development of light and shade, foreign to the earlier Chinese artists with the brush. The Japanese adepts fell not a whit behind them. Landscapes were a favoured subject of Sōtan, but " great was his study and diligence in securing the inner purpose. Hence Kikei Ōshō named him Jimaki. The subjects of his sketches were landscapes, living beings, grass, flowers, birds, and beasts. His pictures were drawn with great attention to detail and shading. His brush was rich in power and vigour, deeply impregnated with the taste of the Sō period.

Chōshō-In Butsu (Terute) at Fujisawa.

On account of his reputation Kanō Masanobu came to learn drawing of Sōtan, and so became attached to the school of Shūbun."
In later years Sukeshige, under the name of Jōza, entered the
Daikokuji. And here he figures as the teacher and inspiration of
his son Oguri Sōritsu. In Kwanshō 5th year 1st month 9th day
(16th February 1464) he died.

It was as the nun Chōshō Shūbutsu that Terute too left the
world. Her mission in life was accomplished. In the persons of her
sons the Houses of Oguri and Satake flourished. Close by the place
of the graves of the Oguri, lord and retainers, stands the little temple
established by her piety. " In the morning, while dew was yet
heavy, she gathered flowers. At evening, when rain dashed the
window, her light was hung." Thus years passed, to witness
one by one the graves filled beneath her eyes. She has left a poem :

" The sadness of this world besets me :
" At last this road of the Hotoke brings deliverance."

Whether the bones of the monk Sōtan ever took their place with the
buried hair of Mitsushige and Sukeshige is unrecorded. But in
due time came the call to Terute. " Facing the West, and seated
with clasped hands, she died." Close by the other graves, under
the shadow of a pine stands the gravestone of the Terutehime.
Close by is the tiny pond on which shone the light of lantern suspended. For the eyes of the curious there yet remains the little
metal image of the Lady Kwannon, carried by the wife faithful and
brave. Thus ends the vendetta of Kojirō Sukeshige, the epic of
Terutehime, in the shadow of the pine and cedar of the Chōshō-In.

EPILOGUE.

Something remains to be said as to the fate of the characters so prominent in this tale. The foresight of Prince Mochiuji was good. When he "stuck out his head" it was with but little hope that life would be spared. However the advice of Isshiki was to the point; and moreover the intentions of the Shōgun toward the issue of his House was as yet undefined. It was with a bilious eye that the Prince looked out as he was carried in his *norimon* up the Momiji-gayatsu (Maple Valley), past the darkly gaping cave where the unfortunate Ōtōnomiya, son of Go Daigo Tennō, had met his end through the intrigues of his forebears. The journey ended in the secluded temple of Eianji. It was the end of the 10th month of this 10th year of Eikyō (19th October—18th November 1438). The maples of the hills close shutting in the sister temples of the Zuisenji, Eianji, Eifukuji, still retained some trace of colour in the shrivelled leaves. He had left them in their glory; now he was never again to see this bloom in death.

The Shitsuji Norizane did his best for his unfortunate lord. The messenger despatched to Kyōto bore urgent petition that the prince's fate be banishment to some distant island. Then, as some argument came to mind, another messenger was despatched; then another before the second had reached the Hakone hills. Thus ten express riders bore the earnest prayers of Norizane to the deaf ears of Yoshinori. Yoshinori must have smiled at the message announcing that Mochiuji had "cut his hair," become a priest. He too had "cut his hair." A second case of resurrection was quite possible.

Prince Mochiuji dwelt quietly at the Eianji. This was the foundation of his ancestor Ujimitsu, whose tomb was close by the temple. Mochiuji was under the guard of Uesugi Mochitomo.

Chiba no Suke Tanenao, Oichi Noriyoshi. Nagao Hōden in hot
pursuit had compelled Isshiki Naokane to cut belly. All his
train followed the example. Uesugi Norinao, likewise guilty of
slandering Norizane, was put to death. The 2nd month of the
11th year of Eikyō (15 March—14 April 1439) came. The delay
in the decision of Kyōto was sinister. Devoted vassals of Mochiuji
began to gather in Kamakura. The excitement was great when
the command came that Mochiuji Kō be directed to cut belly in the
presence of Mochitomo and Tanenao. The accounts differ. In
the Uesugi Norizane Ki it says—" On the 10th day of the 2nd month
(24th March 1439) at the hour of the hare (5—7 A.M.) Mochiuji
killed himself at the Eianji. Thirty of his followers accompanied
him in death. A fierce wind raging at the time, the Buddhist
temples and shrines in Kamakura, the dwellings of the common
people of the Seven Valleys, without exception were reduced to
ashes and charred timbers. Within all was grief. In the temple buildings of Eianji, the august divine dwelling, lived the
wives of many tens of men. Not knowing what was going on
these perished in the flames. Pitiable ! Haruō Dono, Yasuō Dono,
and their nurse, escaped and fled to Nikkō-san in Shimotsuke no
Kuni." The soldiers of Norizane had surrounded the temple.
The order for the *harakiri* was delivered. Some futile resistance was
offered. Mochiuji Kō gave orders to set fire to the temple. Then
entering the Butsuma he cut his belly open. The Nihon Gwaishi
says that his wife accompanied him in death. In the Hōkokuji,
which faces the Sugimoto temple to Kwannon, Yoshihisa followed
the example of his father. " With the flowers of spring it was
deigned for him to fall and die. Evanescent is the course of the
fleeting world. Mankind is like the flowers of a dream. In pity
for self this escapes notice." Mitsusada his uncle also killed himself.
Many of their followers died with their lord. Haruō, Yasuō, Eijuō
were the three younger sons of Mochiuji. They had been placed in
the charge of the Nagao clan. Certainly no strenuous effort was
made to secure them. They were carried off in haste to Nikkō. On
the road the brothers were separated ; by great good fortune as
subsequent events proved. The youngest child Eijuōmaru was

taken to Shinano and hidden away in the charge of his uncle Oi Michimitsu.

In the 6th month of this year Norizane went in state to the Chōjuji.* Seating himself before the image of Mochiuji there installed he recited prayer after prayer. As he bent forward the keen eyes of his watching *rōtō* detected the flash of steel. Springing forward they seized the arm of the Shitsuji. Then he was carried into the apartments of the prior. Examination showed that the attempt to cut belly had failed. Norizane accepted the rebuke of Heaven. From Kyōto had come the appointment of the Uesugi House, in the person of Norizane, to the office of Kwanryō of the Tōkoku or East Provinces. Norizane refused the honour. His brother Kiyokata, aided by Uesugi Noritomo, took the position. In the 11th month (7th December—5th January 1440) Norizane left Kamakura, to hide his grief in the Kokuseiji of Izu Province. There was still bitter work for him to do ; more unavailing effort to stem the hatred of the unrelenting man at Muromachi Kyōto.

Prince Yoshinori was tolerably well occupied. Fighting was always to be had. That with the Ochi clan in Yamato was chronic. This time he hoped to suppress them. With the 12th year of Eikyō (1440) came hot news from the North. The first idea had been that Haruōmaru and Yasuōmaru should remove themselves from pursuit by cutting their hair, becoming priests. Order was sent that they be brought to Kyōto. The partisans of the two children knew what the message implied. Urgent notice was sent to Yūki Ujitomo. Ogasawara Masayasu was commissioned with the arrest and delivery. Ujitomo lost no time. The 12th year 1st month (January) at the head of seven hundred men he rode into Nikkō. There were tears in the eyes of the honest knight when he saw the two boys tricked out in priest's garb—" Off with it ! " he shouted. " Shukke ! It is death which awaits them in Kyōto. If safety is " not to be found in Yūki castle, all shall perish together." With

---

* So says that old plodder Hayashi in the Ō-Dai-Ichiran. Most writers say the Eianji, which implies that buildings of the temple escaped destruction. The Chōjuji is close by the site of the Yamanouchi Kwanryō *yashiki*, N.W. corner of the Kamegayatsu-zaka road and the main road to Ōfuna.

the children in the midst Ujitomo and Mochitomo, guarding front and rear, rode home to Yūki. Then a circular letter was sent out to the old vassals of Mochiuji in the Kwantō. The Isshiki, Noda, Oi, Yoshimi, gathered at the call. Ten thousand men garrisoned the two neighbouring castles of Yūki and Kōga.

The importance of this news was realized at Kyōto. The Kwantō was trembling in the balance. On instructions from the capital the Uesugi began slowly to gather an army. In the 7th month (August) this appeared before Yūki and the siege began. But it was conducted most idly. A few assaults were made, but eight hundred picked archers of Yūki caused severe havoc. Then began " a distant siege." The castle was well provided and watered. Fuel for many days had been stored. Half the besieging army were in sympathy. The other half were willing to support the Kwanryō, but pitied the two children Haruō and Yasuō. Men pleaded sickness, pressing home affairs. They appeared and disappeared with their retainers. The state of affairs was made known by letter to the Shōgun. Besides, Norizane from the Kokuseiji was continually urging and pleading for a pardon to the surviving family of Mochiuji.

Near by to Kyōto Yoshinori had his difficulties. With news of the death of Mochiuji, the slaughter in the Isshiki clan, followed the revolt of Isshiki Keibu Naonobu. He seized Shikiryōmorisan in Yamato Province. The place was impregnable, and he quickly gathered six thousand men, mostly *rōnin* and yamabushi, all more or less affiliated to the lost cause of the South Court. In a night attack he soundly thrashed the army of thirty thousand men sent against him, headed by the Hosokawa, Akamatsu, and his clansman Isshiki Mochinobu. Great was the agitation when the news of the battle, fought Eikyō 12th year 5th month 7th day (6 June 1440) reached Kyōto. They seemed to hear the exultant shouts of the soldiers of Naonobu marching into the city. " The Daijū deigned to be greatly frightened ; " although scare was not much in Yoshinori's line. His council was perturbed, had no advice to give. Then came forward one Takeda Taizen no Tayǔ Shingen. He was lord of Aki province, noted as a boaster and coward. At his offer to suppress the rebellion all present "rolled their tongues." They were ready to burst with laughter. "What a shameless action; this coward and braggart to ask for "the office of Taishō!" Yoshinori thought differently. He called Shingen to him and questioned him. At the order of Yoshinori the braggart left Kyōto with three thousand men. Isshiki Naonobu was as amazed and discomfited as the council of Yoshinori. He who had hurled back five times his number in flight; to be so insulted! In rage he burst forth from his stronghold. Both sides rushed eagerly to the attack. Shingen was a huge fellow. He had but one plan of battle. Personal encounter was sought with Isshiki himself. As Shingen rose from the ground with the severed head of the rebel he listened to the victorious shouts of his men driving the leaderless foe in every direction. From the field of battle to the capital city the bragging tongue of Takeda Shingen never stopped. Yoshinori knew his man. He gave him much praise and little profit. Shingen was satisfied, and Nippon has made him a popular hero, brave beyond compeer, ever since. The Shōgun was the wiser of the two—prince and people.

Then Prince Yoshinori announced that this siege of Yūki must come to an end. All else could wait on the Kwantō affair. The gods were enraged. The Shōgun's visit to the Hachiman shrine of Iwashimidzu gave most disastrous omens. A large army was sent from Kyōto. To allow Kyōto to play a single hand would never do. Norizane left his retirement in Izu and camped at Oyama. The siege was to be pressed vigorously. It was the 16th day of the 4th month of Kakitsu 1st year (6th May 1441) that the huge investing army of eighty thousand men advanced to the attack. A column of smoke rising from the castle was the signal. An arrow letter had been shot into the inclosure. The hopelessness of resistance was emphasized; the fears of some traitor within touched. Now in *gyorin* (fish scales) and *kwaku-yoku* (crane's wings) the host was marshalled. "The Heavens rocked at the thunderclap. The *konjichō* (earthquake causing-bird) flew abroad, the earth trembled." As the conflagration spread the Yūki, father and son, realized that the position was hopeless. It only remained to die in battle. Intrusting the princes to a selected band of retainers who were to break through the host and take the road to Mutsu, Ujitomo and his sons rode out the gate into the masses of the enemy. The struggle would have been short had it not been for the space too confined for such great numbers of men. The river swollen by rains had turned this flat country into a marsh. The blinding smoke hid friend from foe. The Uesugi cut down, trampled down, their own men. The loss of life was hideous. But the result was fore-ordained. Ujitomo and Mochitomo lay dead on the battle field; their bodies, trampled beyond recognition into the mire under the horses' hoofs. Of ten thousand men, women, and children confined within the castle all perished. It was with pity, however, that the victors watched the litters of the two princes go forward to Kamakura under the guard of Norizane's soldiers. The little band of fugitives was detected making off in the hills. Ogasawara, Satake, and Chiba went in hot pursuit. With a few attendants Haruō and Yasuō fled north, to fall into the hands of the men of Norizane awaiting them. Their defenders died under the swords of the westerners. Naritomo, the youngest son of Ujitomo, was saved by the coolness of the country maid once honoured by her lord. Thus ended the famous Yūki Zeishō.*

---

* The site of Yūki castle is about three quarters of a mile from the railway station, to the north-east of the town, and a bare hundred and fifty yards from the large Yūki Grammar School (Jinjō Kotō Gakkō). It is a slight but extensive elevation above the almost level⸗ plain of Shimōsa-Musashi, more marked at the eastern edge. There is a bluff on this side, as if the Kokaigawa, now at some distance, once had its course close by. The western face could well be artificial. A small stream here bounds it, fifteen or twenty feet in width, four feet in depth. The castle keep occupied the south-east corner of the plateau, and the deep moat is plainly marked, forming a little valley now turned into *hatake* (dry farming). A shrine has been erected on the site of the keep. The long railway bridge and the sandy desert of the Kokaigawa are hints as to how terrible this river can be in flood. It is quite possible for melting snows and spring rains to cause a disastrous overflow on the flat plain. The last structure on the site was built by Mizuno Katsunaga in Genroku 16th year (1703). In the Meiji campaign the castle was the base of supplies for the Imperial army. When this was withdrawn the castle was destroyed. (The fall of

Under escort the prisoners set out for Kyōto. Behind came a long procession of head-boxes, thirty in number. Most important were those supposed to belong to Ujitomo and his five sons, recognized by their torn and battered armour. Says the scribe—"The rough roads of Hakone seemed as mountain paths in Shide (Hell)." Noted to travellers is the post town at the Kikugawa. Here in Genkō (1331-1333), when Kurando Ushōben Toshimoto came down to Kamakura an exile, he wrote on a pillar of the inn :

"As in ancient days, so now ;
"The Kikugawa flows in tranquil stream."

Condemned to die at this place Mitsuchika Kyō had written :

"The ancient time : I too in sorrow read,
"And deign a song."

Haruō-maru asked for the *fudé* (brush pen) :

"Now again, yet more evanescent Kikugawa's stream ;
"Thoughts of the tranquil tomb."

The sunset bell of Tōyamadera was sounding as they entered the town of Tarui. A crowd was gathered. People were groaning and in tears. In wonder the escort advanced to find itself in the midst of the serried ranks of a large force sent from Kyōto. With indignation the Kwantō officers read the order under the Shōgun's seal. At this place the two princes, Haruō and Yasuō, were to suffer death. Great was the rage at this violation of the tacit agreement. These were mere children. They were to be permitted to become priests ; thus to pray for father and brother ushered into Meido. The order was peremptory, resistance impossible. Grimly the children were handed over to the tender care of the *kenshi*—Hagino Misaka Nyūdō and Kobayagawa Ukon Shōgen Harukira. The final scene took place at once in the Kinrenji of Tarui. The request of the princes was that no common blade should touch them, so Harukira had to act. They seated themselves facing west toward the paradise of Amida Buddha. Clasping hands they recited a prayer. The signal given the sword flashed and the head of

Kōga castle on the 17th day supplemented the deaths of Ujitomo and his five sons and the capture of the princes, at Yūki on the day before. Cf.: Nihon Gwaishi p. 420 seq. and the writer of the Dai Nihon Jimmei Jishō—"Yūki Ujitomo.")

Haruō rolled on the ground. The lapse of a few seconds and that of Yasuō was severed from the body ; their ages, thirteen and eleven years.*

Norizane's mission was ended. His loyalty to the will of the founder prince, to the Ashikaga House, had cost dear in the person of this cold hearted suzerain who played on his loyalty. No grace had been granted. The sons, mere children, had followed the father in death. Norizane had sinned. He shaved his head and entered the Zen sect of priests. Taking his beggar's bowl he left the shelter of the Kokuseiji in Izu. The three worlds were abandoned. " As a palmer he passed from province to province. His dwelling was beneath trees, on the broad surface of rocks. The emptiness of his bowl he did not grudge. At last at Tanabe in Suwō province he deigned to die."

The Shōgun had a younger brother, a priest named Gishō. With the son of the Hō-ō, Go Kameyama, he entered into a plot to secure the Shōgunate for the one, the throne for the other. East and West were in turmoil, Yūki was holding out bravely. The Kikuchi and Ōmura in Kyūshū whispered soft words. Gishō let his hair grow. Yoshinori learned of this and sent to seize him. He was too late.

In the 3rd month of Kakitsu 1st year (23rd March-21st April, 1441) it was learned that the Kitabatake were harbouring Gishō. In the 4th month (21st April to 21st May) Yūki and Kōga fell. The Kitabatake sought light and found it. In the 5th month (to 19th June) Gishō's head reached Kyōto, It was horribly out of repair, unrecognizable. Dog will not eat dog ; brother ought to recognize brother. But Yoshinori was non-plussed. A familiar of Gishō, a young playmate was summoned. Said he—" If it be the head of the bishop two teeth are missing." This was found to be the case. Yoshinori greatly rejoiced.

The head of Gishō was hardly removed when the long train of boxes from Yūki town was introduced. Those of the vassals were easily dismissed. To identify the heads of Haruō and Yasuō to the

---

* Another account says they were put to death on the common execution ground.

satisfaction of the suspicious Shōgun their nurse͵ was brought in. To every question she was silent. Stolid, without word or movement, she sat before the stands on which were placed the heads. Finally in anger Yoshinori ordered that her tongue be torn out. This was done forthwith ; and she died.

To this miserable end came the line of the Ashikaga Kwanryō of Kamakura. The observation of the acute statesman who wrote the " Nihon Gwaishi " illuminates this struggle between the rival Houses of the same blood. Takauji and Tadayoshi in consultation had planned union between Kamakura and Kyōto. Motouji aided Yoshiakira. But the Shōgun who followed—Yoshimitsu and Yoshimochi—sought the destruction of Kamakura. Yoshinori merely carried out their plan. The House of Motouji was destroyed. The House of Yoshiakira was thrown into disorder. The single surviving issue of Mochiuji, Eijuōmaru or Nariuji, became the underlying cause of troubles which later overthrew the Uesugi Kwanryō and split the Kwantō into factions of warring nobles and a strife which lasted for a century.

In the 6th month of this year (19th June to 18th July 1441) Prince Yoshinori turned his attention to the powerful and greedy House of the Akamatsu. He did not deprive Nyūdō Mitsusuke of his fiefs of Bizen, Harima, Mimasaka ; but he made him divide them with Akamatsu Sadamura. The Nyūdō was very angry. Naturally the son Noriyasu was still more angry. Besides, Yoshinori in derision had called Mitsusuke the " three foot Nyūdō." Then the Shōgun made the only mistake of his career, and a fatal one. On the 24th day (12th July) of the same month he deigned to accept an invitation to a musical banquet at the mansion of Mitsusuke. The feast was at its height. The *saké* cup had circulated freely. The Shōgun was more or less drunk. Suddenly an uproar arose without. The horses had been let out into the inclosure and were biting and fighting with each other. Attendants and guests rushed to separate them. The doors were at once shut. Noriyasu and Uesuke Sama no Suke approached Yoshinori and seized his hands. The prince, greatly frightened, called for an aid which could not reach him. A *rōtō* of the Akamatsu, one Asumi by

name, cut off his head at a blow. Thus died this cruel man—
perhaps the ablest of his line; certainly the superior of any who
followed him.

Kamakura,
    6th May to 30th June, 1914.

FINIS.

APPENDICES.

OGURI RYAKU ENGI (ABRIDGED TRADITION OF THE OGURI.)

SŌSHŪ (SAGAMI) FUJISAWA SANNAI
CHŌSHŌ-IN.

" One hundred and one generations from Jimmu, in the reign of Go Komatsu-In, the lord of Oguri castle in Jōshū (Hitachi) was Oguri Mago Gorō Taira Mitsushige, doubly furnished with the wisdom and courage of a *bushi*. At the beginning of Ōei (1394—1427) a slander was started in his own party that he was plotting rebellion. The Kamakura Kwanryō, Prince Mochiuji, deigned to be in a great rage. Isshiki Sakon Chūgen and Kido Takumi no Suke were sent to punish him. Oguri Mitsushige vigorously defended himself, and there was no sign of the fall of the castle. So Yoshimi Iyo no Kami and Uesugi Shirō came to aid with reinforcements. Thus shut up in the castle (Mitsushige) could do nothing more. According to the tradition, Mitsushige, lord and retainers eleven men in all, slipped out of the castle in the guise of tradesmen, with the intention of escaping to Mikawa no Kuni. But in the vicinity of Sōshū (Sagami) Fujisawa, overtaken by night they entered the house of Yokoyama Tarō, a den of thieves masquerading as an inn, and stopped here. Yokoyama Tarō secretly rejoiced at such a prize. Entertainment of varied kind (was offered). Fastened to an ancient cherry tree in the garden was a swift horse. (It was) a fearful and wicked horse, killing and eating men ; its name, Onikage. No one went near it. Oguri Mitsushige had always been noted as an expert horseman. Seeing this fine horse he drew it near him and having mounted without difficulty, at ease and will rode up and down the garden front. The robber Yokoyama seeing this was greatly frightened. To kill people of such strength was out of his power.

He had this plan ; to gather his many dancing girls, and put poison in the *saké* which the lord and retainers were to drink.

At the time referred to among the dancing girls was one called Terute. Her father was a *hokumen no rōshi* (a *rōnin* from the emperor's body-guard). Sorrowing because he had no child he made petition to Kwanze-on (Kwannon). A daughter was the issue. The parents died early and she was established here in Yokoyama's house. Deeply did she regret that Mitsushige should be killed by poison. Thus thinking she secretly warned him. Mitsushige, pretending sickness, did not drink. Yokoyama's band, plying the *saké* still more, did not notice his manner, that he barely touched his lips to the *saké* cup. As quick as a " ya ! " every sense writhed in unendurable pain. Thus he died with every symptom of poison. So was it with the ten *rōtō* (retainers). Their bodies like mud, and vomiting blood, they died on the spot. Yokoyama greatly rejoiced, and stealing their property and clothes cast away the bodies on Ueno moor. At that time Yūgyō, 14th generation, Taiku was Shōnin. That night he dreamed that a messenger from Emma-Ō (god of hell) delivered a letter to the Shōnin. Opening this and deigning to look he learned that in Hitachi of Nippon, on Ueno moor, Oguri Mitsushige and ten *shisotsu* (common soldiers) were suffering from poison. The fate of the *shisotsu* was determined. Mitsushige alone as yet had not accomplished his destiny. To restore him to health quickly bathe him in the Kumano *onsen* (hot spring), and at once he would be restored to health. Then the Shōnin woke up from his dream, and without thinking it strange went to the place and deigned to look. The barking dogs and the crows, assembled to eat the dead bodies, showed the way to Mitsushige who was yet alive. With him he returned. But at the Emmadō (temple to Emma) life seemed extinct. It could not be helped, and there seemed to be nothing to do but to go on with the burial. To the amazement of the Shōnin the Hangwan returned to life. At once a *kuruma* was made ready. Drawn by two priests he deigned to send him in this to Kishū. After an interval of some days they reached the Kumano Hongū Yunomine. Putting him in the hot pool he was fully restored to health.

And now as to Teru-hime. Seeing Mitsushige killed by poison she was greatly distressed. Secretly she stole away from Yokoyama's house, and made her way to Kanazawa in Musashi. The guards (monban) came in search of her, and having caught her put her to the torture. Then they took her clothes and threw her in the Jijūgawa. Then they went back. Teru-hime prayed earnestly to Kwanze-on. Wonderful, ya! The Mutsuura Senkyō Kwannon of that place immediately was illuminated and deigned to (aid her). At that time at Nojimazaki there was a fisherman. Seeing her predicament he took Teru-hime along with him when he returned home. His wife was a very jealous person, and hating the presence of the lady (hime) piled up great branches of the pine trees, intending to smoke her to death. But although she did this, immediately the fresh breeze blew the smoke to one side, and the person of the lady was not injured. All this was due to the efficacy of the prayer to Kwannon. That wife did not further try to burn her, but transferred her to the hands of a kidnapper. Later she was the inmate of a house at Noshū (Mino) no Aohaka. Here unfriended she passed months and days in pitiful condition.

Meanwhile Mitsushige, wholly restored to health, returned to Sanshū (Mikawa). Through his relations he made petition to Kyōto; saying that from the first he had never harboured rebellious thoughts, and sought an order to make clear the right and wrong. His original fief being restored he returned to Hitachi-no-Kuni. Then on the orders of Kyōto he seized and bound the bandit Yokoyama, and put him to death. Going to Fujisawa he gave thanks to the Shōnin for his kind action. He carved an image of himself restored to health, and placed it in the Emma-dō for the favour (received). Remembrance was kept of this restoration to life. Then he returned to his native country. Getting Teru-hime, who was in Noshū (Mino), the years and months accumulated. Ōei 33rd year 3rd month 16th day (23rd April, 1426) Mitsushige died an old man. His *hōmyō* (posthumous name) is Jugen-in Mitsu Amida Butsu. His filial son Kojirō Sukeshige received his father's fiefs at Kamakura. His father's body was interred at Fujisawa-san, beside the graves of the ten retainers at the edge of

The Chōshō Shūbutsu of Fujisawa.

the Yatoku Ike (Eight Virtues Pond). The offerings to the dead required by filial piety accomplished he (Sukeshige) returned to his native country. From the start Terute was deeply inspired to follow the path of *bodai* (salvation). So that year she shaved her head and took the vows as Chōshō Bikuni. In the Emma-dō she contemplated the image of Jizō, and took care of the image of Mitsushige. In the morning while the dew was yet heavy she gathered flowers. At evening when rain dashed the window her light was hung. Devoting herself wholly to prayer, on Eikyō 12th year 10th month 14th day (9th November 1440) facing the west and seated with clasped hands she died. She was called Chōshō-In Shūbutsu. Later the still existing Chōshō-In was erected, the Fujisawa Saishin no Ippō (derivative temple). Thus it happens that this temple possesses the relics of Oguri and his retainers, as can be seen.

The Chōshō-In treasures :

Oguri Reigenki (image) ; Teruhime Sugata Mikōkyō (mirror) ; Onikage's bridle ; Claws of a Tengu ; Sonei Tsūhō Kōsei (Money of Sonei) ; Oguri Mitsushige, a poem by his own brush ; Aioi Gōkan Saku (growing old together) ; Terute Bodai Itanzaku (poem by Terute) ; Hōraku-waka (poem for the sacred dance).

Taira Mitsushige :

" Within the heart reflected, clouds conceal ;
" Truly the gods of Kumano will protect."

And also Chōshō Hōni (Terute) :

" The sadness of this world besets me ;
" At last this road of the *hotoke* brings deliverance."

The names of the ten *kerai* of Oguri :

Ikeno Shōji Sukenaga, Kazama Jirō Masaoki, Kazama Hachirō Masakuni, Gotō Hyōsuke Suketaka, Tanabe Heihachirō Nagatame, Kataoka Katarō Harunori, Kataoka Kojirō Harutake, Tanabe Heirokurō Nagahide, Gotō Daihachirō Takatsugu, Mito Kotarō Tamehisa.

Complete list of the ten men.

Again—Shō-Kwannon—height 1 *sun* 8 *bu* (2 inches). It was the charm carried by Teruhime on her person.

II.*

DAI NIHON JIMMEI JISHŌ.

Oguri Mitsushige—commonly called Mago Gorō ; a native of Hitachi. He was descended from the Chinjufu Shōgun Taira Shigemori, and was the fourth son of Shigemiki. Shigemori's grandchild Shigeyoshi held Makabe-gun Oguri. Therefore he was called Oguri. His son Shigenari served the Shōgun Yoritomo. His children and grandchildren, and descendants, were lords of Oguri. Mitsushige's grandfather served in Kamakura. In the intercalary tenth month of Ōei 29th year (16th October-15th November, 1422) Mitsushige enlisted soldiers and refused obedience to Kamakura. He attacked Ashikaga Mochiuji and Uesugi Shigekata. Koyama Mitsuyasu was ordered to aid Shigekata. Therefore he came to his assistance, and in the 11th month (14th December-13th January 1423) with Shigekata he attacked Oguri castle. Mitsushige fought and defeated them. Ōei 30th year (1423) Mochiuji took men and came to Yūki, and attacked Oguri castle. Mitsushige's defence on this occasion was unsuccessful. He hid his son Sukeshige, and together with Masahide and Shigetoyo killed himself. The castle was taken. The Kamakura Daisōshi and Nanhōki says that Oguri fled with Utsunomiya Mochitsuna. Enya Suruga no Kami attacked them. When Mitsushige went to Mikawa, on the road he stopped for the night at the house of Yokoyama Tarō at Fujisawa. But Tarō was a thief. Therefore he wanted to rob Mitsushige and his company of their property. So he gave poisoned *sakè* to Mitsushige. There was a dancing girl named Terute. Secretly she informed Mitsushige. Therefore he did not get much of the *sakè*. The thieves

---

* For the translation I am indebted to my wife.

had stolen a fierce horse from somewhere. Mitsushige mounted the
horse and fled. On the road he fell down from the effects of the
poison. Fujisawa-san aided him, and sent him to Kumano Hongū
Yunomine where he was treated. Terute was closely questioned by
the Yokoyama people as to Mitsushige's flight. Therefore she could
not remain. She fled to Būshū (Musashi) Kanazawa. Here a
fisherman helped her, and took her to his house. His wife became
jealous, tied her to a pine tree, and tried to burn her to death. On
account of this ill-treatment she went to Mino Aohaka no Sato and
became a *joro*. After Mitsushige reached Mikawa he made petition
at the capital as innocent and was absolved. On his return he killed
Yokoyama and ransomed Terute, making her his wife. (Terute's
story is in the Sukeshige Den, in which tradition has fearfully inter-
mingled matters (*ato*) concerning Mitsushige). Ōei 33rd year 3rd
month 16th day (23 April 1426) he died in Hitachi. The son
Kojirō Sukeshige succeeded his father. Terute entered Fujisawa
San and became a nun under the name of Chōshō. The 12th year
10th month 14th day of Eikyō (9th November 1440) she died at
this place. She lived at the temple known as Chōshō-In (Authority—
Chōshō-In Engi).

    Oguri Sōtan—His name was Sukeshige, and he was called
Kojirō. His father Mitsushige revolted against Ashikaga Mochiuji
at Oguri castle in Hitachi. Sukeshige was staying there. Isshiki
Akihide had lied. He was to restore tranquillity and try to take the
castle. Yūki Mochitomo, known to Sukeshige, told of the plot of
Akihide. Therefore, to remove Sukeshige from peril, when the
castle was taken his father sent away Sukeshige in company with
his attendants Ikeno Sukenaga and Gotō Suketaka. Ōei 32nd
year (1425) Sukeshige and his attendants secretly journeyed to
Kamakura with the wish to kill Akihide. They lived at an inn in
the Gongendō. A man, Yokoyama Yasuhide by name, wished to
kill Sukeshige and get his property. He talked with the landlord
of the Gongendō inn. A large number of thieves were assembled
and a great feast prepared. Dancing girls were summoned, and
poisoned wine was given to Sukeshige. But during the meeting a
dancing girl named Terute secretly by a song told him not to drink

this wine. Sukeshige caught the meaning of the song at once and did not drink. Excusing himself he went out, and at once fled from the house. Entering a wood a horse was found. He was a very spirited horse and ate human flesh. All the thieves feared him, and he was tied to a tree. Sukeshige mounted the horse and soon reached the exercise hall of Fujisawa. The priests greatly pitied him and sent him to Mikawa with attendants. Sukeshige built a grave for the attendants who had died by poison. He desired to kill Isshiki Akihide and satisfy his resentment. At last in Eikyō 6th year (1434) he sent a petition to the Bakufu. In the 5th month (7th June—7th July) at Kamakura the death punishment was allotted to Akihide. Sukeshige received the order, and the 9th month (3rd October —1st November) reached Daijūfu and put to death Yokoyama and Akihide. Then he made inquiries after and met with Terujō. Later he cut his hair (turned priest) and was known as Sōtan (according to one authority, Sōkan). Also he was called Jimaki. Going to the Sōkokuji at Kyōto, entering as priest he was called Jōza. His last years he passed at the Daitokuji. He painted pictures, his teacher being Shūbun. He had a great preference for valleys, rolling billows, the beauties of summer, and horses in motion. These interested him. At such things he was very clever—landscapes, persons, flowers, birds. He was especially skilful at landscapes. One day he asked the priest Kikei Ōshō for another name. Said the priest—" this fine picture is a reproduction of the valley." So he signed it with the name Jimaki. Kanō Motonobu was the first to be taught by Sōtan. Sōtan introduced him to the method of Shūbun. From that time his art developed. The world highly extols him. He died 5th year 1st month 9th day of Kwanshō (16 February 1464) at the age of sixty seven years. (Authorities— Honchōgashi, Fusōgajinten, Gajoryaku, Enjō Buiran, Meijin Kishinroku).

Oguri Sōritsu—A famous painter, son of Sōtan and pupil of his father. A most skilful artist his specialty was the horse in motion, and horses in general............His art displayed great fidelity in execution...............Then he moved to the Daitokuji at Kyōto, at that time a centre for painters.

Oguri Sōkyū—Painter, son of Sōritsu and a follower of the school of Sōtan.

III.

KOKUSHI DAI JITEN.

Oguri Uji—Clan name, Taira. Shigemune, called Oguri Gorō and fourth son of Taien Shigemiki, constructed and took charge of Oguri in Hitachi Niibarugōri. Hence the name of the clan. The third generation Shigenari served Yoritomo and showed ability. In Kemmu (1334—1335) Shigetada served the founder of the Ashikaga (Takauji). In Ōei (1394—1427) Mitsushige sided with Uesugi Zenshū. Mochiuji was defeated in battle. Many fiefs had been confiscated, and in resentment this rebellion against Kamakura was planned. This made manifest (men) maintained themselves in their castles and Mochiuji did not punish them. In the 28th year (1421) Mitsushige, Iwamatsu, and others gathered together soldiers. As result Shimōsa and Hitachi were in great disorder. The 29th year (1422) Mochiuji and Uesugi collected soldiers and came against these. The castle levies were not successful in the defence. At last the castle fell. Mitsushige and his son Sukeshige fled to Mikawa and sought shelter with Tadashige their relative. Mitsushige thus lost his fief. Later Sukeshige went to Mutsu and found refuge with Shinogawa Mitsutada. Then the Shōgun Yoshinori quarrelled with Mochiuji. Sukeshige thereupon sent a letter to Uesugi Nagayoshi petitioning that his former fief be restored. Nagayoshi presented it to the Bakufu (feudal Government). Bestowing the headship of the fief the appointment was issued, together with an order to display the utmost energy. Then Sukeshige returned to Oguri to raise soldiers. However Mochiuji killed himself, and the two orphan children of Mochiuji, aged twelve years, Haruō and Yasuō were besieged and captured at Yūki castle. Then the Bakufu restored the former fiefs. Kōshō 1st year (1455) Uesugi Mochitomo fought a battle against Ashikaga Nariuji (sole surviving son of Mochiuji) at Kotesashibara. Defeated (Mochitomo) took refuge in Oguri castle. Nariuji besieged and captured it. At last the Oguri clan was destroyed. (Shinken Hitachi Kokushi, Keien Sanyō).

Shigemune – Shigeyoshi – Shigenari – Shigenobu – Asashige-Shigemi-Mitsushige-Sukeshige-Sukemasa-Tadamiki.

Oguri Sōtan—called Sukeshige, personal name Kojirō. Sōtan also signs Sōkan and Jimaki. The father Mitsushige at Hitachi Oguri castle plotted against Ashikaga Mochiuji, and rebelled. Ōei 30th year (1423) Mochiuji Kō raised an army and came to besiege him. Isshiki Akihide was to put the castle garrison to the sword. Mitsushige, lacking power, sent away his son Sukeshige with retainers. Then he killed himself. Sukeshige lodged at the Kamakura Gongendō. There was a robber who plotted to kill Sukeshige and to seize the travellers' possessions. A singing girl (*asobime*) Terujo privately betrayed the hidden plot. Sukeshige fled and entered the Fujisawa *dōjō* (reading or assembly hall). Eikyō 6th year (1434) he petitioned the Bakufu for permission to kill Akihide. He put the robber to death and rewarded Terujo. Later he entered the Kyōto Sōkokuji and became a priest. His last years were passed at the Daitokuji. He executed beautiful paintings—landscapes, seascapes, the beauties of summer, pictures of gallopping horses—in these he was especially skilled. His subjects for portrayal were landscapes, men, objects, plants and flowers, birds, animals, presented in Nature's colours, together with beautiful and rich light effects. To a great extent the style was that of the men of the Sō epoch (now called Kananshō). But there was not merely land, mountains, water. Mist, cloud, the changing and unchanging, forest, spring, shadow, tints, the sky, these were subjects of composition. Men and objects were painted with a brush used without display ; flowers and birds, painted mostly in colour. The remains of his brush are scanty. He is preferred to Shūbun. Kanō Masanobu who followed is said to have learned his style. Kwanshō 5th year 1st month (8th February to 8th March 1464) he died aged sixty-seven years. (Authority—Fusōgajinten).

Oguri Sōritsu—Son of Sōtan. A painter and disciple of his father he followed the rules of Shūbun. He was noted for his skill.

He painted barbarians mounted on horseback, and made many pictures of horses. His inspiration was Rianchū. At first he lived at Wakasa Shōhama ; later at Kyōto Daitokuji. A man of Bummei (1469—1486).

Oguri Jō (castle)—In Hitachi province, Makabegōri, Oguri-mura. The greater part is mound, and its area in round numbers 4000 *tsubo* (3¼ acres). The Kokaigawa borders it. On the North-East it was three storied ; on the South five storied. The base line of the castle measured 50-60 *tsubo* (300-360 feet). Taien Shigeyoshi first received the Oguri district and built there. Mitsu-shige, by supporting Uesugi Zenshū, lost the fief. His son Suke-shige, by the good fortune of war in which he displayed ability, again received the fief. Kōshō 1st year (1455) Uesugi Mochitomo and Oda Kagenaka fought a battle with Nariuji. Being defeated they took refuge in the castle. Nariuji, himself in command, besieged and captured it. Vassals of Utsunomiya Tsunaiye held it. Tembun 21st year (1552) Yūki Masakatsu besieged and took it. Taga Awauji had it in charge. Eiroku 3rd year (1560) it was returned to Utsunomiya Hirotsuna, and Kotaku Naotoki was its warden. It descended to his son Takaharu. The Utsunomiya lost the province and the castle was destroyed. It was then Keichō 2nd year (1597).

Authority—Shinken Hitachi Kokushi.

IV.

FUSŌGAJINTEN.

Shūbun—Lived at the Kyōto Sōkokuji—name Shūbun. Appellation commonly used Tokei Ekkei or ʻGakuhō, or Shūniku. All can be seen written. In the " Shunseki " the name is often mentioned, and can be regarded as verified. Likewise in Kennin (1201-1203) there was a Shuniku. Gōshū (Ōmi) Ekkei was a disciple and learned painting of Jōsetsu.*   In the " Fusōgakōfu " it says—

---

* Jōsetsu came from Kyūshū to the Shōkokuji temple at Kyōto—Vol. III. No. 3. The Shūbun here treated is the native Japanese of the Sōkokuji ; not the naturalized Chinaman Shūbun of the Daitokuji.

" Ōei 21st year 1st month 8th day (29th January 1414), from Jōsetsu he learnt the traditional methods of the great masters, especially as to the secrets of the painter's art." In the Honchō-gashi it says—" He adopted the school as to landscapes, men, things, flowers, birds, horses, summer, portraits. In charcoal drawings, displaying the beauties of pasture land he carried technique to the extreme." The Yōgenryū says—" In mind he absorbed the precious rules ; with his eyes he looked sharply to the light and heavy. In the three secrets of painting he made Jōsetsu the model. The result of the style was admirable. Later times (found) Sesshū, Oguri, Kanō, all these following in the steps of Shūbun. In the school of Sōtan it was more advanced." Thus resulted an able school. In execution the colours were minutely laid on. Especially did the brush ably execute mountains and water. The technique in treating wind effects is very wonderful and highly commended by people. Reaching maturity in the middle of the Ōei period (1394-1427) he died in Ōei. Up to Meiji 16th year approximately 457 years have passed. (Vol. III. No. 4).

Oguri Uji—name Sōtan ; Jimaki the nom-de-plume. A *kerai* of the Ashikaga House. Later he cut his hair and entered the Kyōto Sōkokuji, becoming a priest. In the latter part of his life he lived at the Daitokuji under the name of Jōza. Having a liking for painting animals he became a pupil of Shūbun, learning the rules of drawing. Later he practised the Sō style, turning to landscapes. Great was his study and diligence in securing the inner purport. In consequence Kikei Ōshō named him Jimaki. The subjects of his sketches were landscapes, living beings, grass, flowers, birds, and beasts. Wholly in shades selected his pictures were drawn in great detail. That brush was rich in power and vigour, deeply impregnated with the taste of the Sō period. On account of the praise bestowed Kanō Motonobu first came to learn drawing from Sōtan. On Motonobu* doing so Sōtan attached him to the school

---

* The Fusōgajinten gives in great detail the life and work of Motonobu (and Masanobu) cf. Vol. II. pp. 1—4. Motonobu is here connected with Sōtan. The Kanō of Izu have already been mentioned in connection with the rebellion of Uesugi Zenshū.

of Shūbun, and thus the Kanō no Gigei (polite art) took its rise. Again, the remaining (examples) are very scarce. Thus as to the predecessors of Shūbun, their productions are highly prized. To Meiji 16th year (1883) about 430 years have passed. (Note to the text). The statements that Motonobu was a pupil of Sōtan, and that Sōtan was connected with Shūbun, are of early date. (Vol. 3 No. 5).

Sōritsu (No. 6).—Oguri Uji son of Sōtan. Affiliated with the school of Shūbun. Taught by his father Sōtan he was still more expert in execution. He executed many pictures of barbarians on horseback, and many equine sketches. The execution of Rianchū being very beautiful, in his own pictures he imitated the brush of Rianchū.† He first lived at Wakasa Kohama. Later he entered the Daitokuji of Kyōto. To Meiji 16th year (1883) 400 years have elapsed.

V.

HONCHŌ-GASHI.

This adds but little to the above. Condensed—Probably the family name of Oguri Sōtan is unknown. Having a liking for drawing and painting he became wonderfully successful with the brush. He was a pupil of Shūbun, and formed a school of his own. He served the Ashikaga House (Muromachi-Kyōto). At the New Year he always paid his respects with delivery of a specimen of his handiwork. He received an *ayaginu* (damask silk) and *nerikinu* (floss-silk) garment. In middle life he entered the Sōkoku-Zenji (i.e. of the Zen sect), shaved his head, and as priest was called Sōtan and Jōza. Kanō or Yūsei was his pupil. Hence it is thought that Sōtan in the latter part of his life lived at the Daitokuji. The origin

---

† A famous Chinese painter of the first half of the twelfth century, Li-An-Chung. On the defeat of the Sung emperor Kisō he moved to the South, and figures under both Northern and Southern Sung. Cf. Fenollosa II. 29, 37. " Epochs of Chinese and Japanese Art."

of the nickname Jimaki and the nature and quality of his painting and drawing is then described. (Vol. II. pp. 6 and 7. The Kanō mentioned is Masanobu).

VI.

KII KUMANO YUNOMINE YAKU-Ō-SAN TŌKWŌJI RIAKU ENGI.

That destruction should ensue to the doctrine of the unfailing pure region and its establishment there is no sign; but followed in faithful obedience the vicissitudes of bloom and decay are lacking.

Within the small shrine which holds the idol of this establishment is revered as principal image Tōhō Yakushi Nyōrai. Strange to say the spontaneous issue of hot water in depositing (solid)* takes the shape of a stone *hotoke* (Buddha). Rising more than twenty feet from the ground the august image deigns to give issue to a gush of hot water. If inquiry be made into history, in the august reign of Keikō Tennō (71-130 A.D. ?), 12th generation from Jimmu, there came a priest from India named Rakyō Shōnin. Among the men of that day at the Kumano Kami-no-Kura of the present Shingū, he accumulated merit by hard study. Attaining the period of Nintoku Tennō (313-399 ? A.D.) at 700 years of age at Nachi-san he deigned to die. In this country he received the name of Takinomoto Kūgyō Shichi Gentoku. [Successors of Rakyō Shōnin were Dengyō Daishi, Kōbō Daishi, Chishō Daishi, Eigō Shōnin, Hanshun Sōshō]. The then Shōnin leaving the Kumano Otonashi (soundless), [now Hongū] village climbed up to Oyubara (hot water moor) [in ancient times Yumine, now Yunomine]. There, at the Fudō water fall, for a thousand days of prayer and meditation, in the morning he immersed himself to secure purification. At evening, seating himself on the moss of the damp rocky slope he was plunged in abstract contemplation. Thus meditating he became oblivious to his surroundings. Dawn came in regular course. At

---

* ( ) are inserted by the translator. [ ] appear in the original.

once in the East a purple haze suffused the sky and the brilliant light of Ruri gleamed brightly. There was manifested a very deep and very small sounding voice, himself deigning to bring the tidings to the Shōnin. " I am Yakushi Nyōrai, from the immeasureable distance. In pity for the suffering caused by the diseases of mankind in this world of illusion I have made the vow that on request this very curative (bitter) mineral spring is given in charity. By once calling on my name, and conforming to my vow, all kinds of sickness will be removed by the guardian of the happiness of the two worlds."

These tidings he deigned. The Shōnin, at heart admiring, was moved to tears; a true heart openly showing feeling. With bowed head and clasped hands he worshipped the august person. Springing from the breast of the Nyōrai, from twelve apertures issued medicinal hot water. Greatly rejoicing the Shōnin had thatched huts at once erected at the place where the vision of Yakushi Nyōrai was experienced. In the passage of time came Kimmei Tennō (540-571 A.D.). " Henceforth the Law of the Buddha at my court shall be widespread, and proclamation made over wide extent." And it went very deep. Long years elapsed. Kōbō Daishi, in the course of his peregrinations, was struck with admiration at the efficiency of prayer to Yakushi Nyōrai. He put up a fresh inscription—" *Nikkō kekkō oyobi ju ni jinshō wa uyauyashiku mo ittō san rei ni bukkyō wo anchi mashimashi* (Sun Brightness, Moon Brightness, the twelve divine shrines; reverentially with one cut and three bows* the Buddha's image finds being)." Jikaku Daishi restored this; and later Kakun Shōnin and Kōgyō Daishi [the founder of the Konraiji of this district]. A fine structure of large timber was built, and Fudō Myō-Ō, Kongara and Seitaka the Nidōji, were established. And so inquiry shows that the generality of those outside the married state know this conquest of the present world (Shaba) through connection with the Buddhas.

---

* Bowing three times for each stroke of the chisel in carving a Buddhist idol—Brinkley's Dictionary. The Sun goddess and Moon goddess (Kwannon and Seshidō Amida) accompany Yakushi; perhaps better " Glorious Sun," " Glorious Moon."

So is it as to the efficacy of prayer to Yakushi Nyōrai. Moreover there is the hot spring as plain evidence. The august generations of the Tennō, one after another, making imperial progresses to the Kumano Sansha Gongen, entered and augustly dwelt in the land. Particularly when Toba Tennō turned to Buddhism the management of the chief temples had to provide for the august lodging, besides making provision for the imperial petition to the Buddha. More particularly the imperial household expenses were distributed according to the custom of provision. In the time of Toyotomi Ason, when Katō Kiyomasa was Katsumoto Bugyō, great repairs were made in turn to the *hondō* and *tahōtō* (main temples and treasuries). Very beautiful structures were erected, and more than ever before or after were *tahōtō* erected. Shaka (Sakyamuni), Monju (Buddhist god of wisdom), Fugen (pictured as riding a white elephant), Bishamon-ten (God of war—and luck : Vaisramana)—these revered images of divinities and Buddhas (*hotoke*) were the work of Shōtoku Taishi ; all were examined and judged in Toba Tenno's reign. In establishing divinities the said shrines were erected as two storied Buddhist temples ; generally speaking three jō (thirty feet) in height, three ken (eighteen feet) wide, and square. The carving was splendid and skilfully executed. The restoration was the work of Hida no Kami Fujiwara Takumi (commonly known as Sajin Gorō). At the time of the restoration (1868) there was a collapse. It is known that now only three *hondō* (main temples) are maintained with sufficient revenue.

However, as to paintings on the inner panels [Nikkō Kekkō one brush, and Matsu-Take-Ume (pine, bamboo, plum)]—there is a splendid Buddha from the brush of Chō-Densu. In the former temple was kept a genuine autograph of Ippen Shōnin the founder of Sōshū Fujisawa Yūgyō (temple). The noted name Kiyozuka of the Kōkoku *nengō* [South Court Year name (1340-1345)] follows. Others are the Kurumazuka of Oguri Hangwan, the *chikara-ishi* (strength testing stone), and the *makazu ine no kyūzeki* (perennial sprouting young rice). Besides, among notable treasures are—the brush work of Hei-sokoku Kiyomori Kō, gold and silver characters on dark blue ground [Bosatsu or Ketsumakyō] ; a Hokkekyō made by Komatsu Naifu Shigemori as vow to the Kumano Gongen [clearly referred to in the Dai Nihonshi], copied in five colours*. Also there are useful articles of the Ashikaga, Tokugawa, and Kii Dainagon, (household implements), but these cannot be described in detail. All belong to the ancient past—from the steps of the throne and from the military commanders below it. Up to the present time the founder has been followed by a succession of noted priests. Capital and country, from far and near, nobles and plebeians, old and young, have made the pilgrimage. Upright practice gives rise to zealous hope. Within this universe many are the places known where (stands) the image of the Buddha, but the virtue of the Nyōrai is the greatest. From the great vow of grief to Meiji's deeply enlightened era two thousand years have passed to this present day. Always has this Nyōrai been revered ; wholly through the honoured virtue of Ragyō Shōnin handed down. There is shown a faithful spreading abroad of the Buddha's Law. The Imperial Empire is a rare image without equal. The visit to the shrine once made quickly the rebellious mind shows heartfelt repentance. Created from all eternity crime and obstruction (sins excluding from Paradise) are annihilated. Then the gain of the two worlds, present and future, is secured. The happiness of release from human existence is experienced. Let every man come to worship. Prayer is still of effect. With respect,

Seal. Wakayama Ken Kumano Yunomine
Tōkwōji Jūshoku (rector),
KŌNO CHIKYŌ.

Kishū Kumano Tōkwōji.

---

* Anyone who sees these beautiful pieces of work can hardly regard these warriors as rough and uncultured. Of the two that by Kiyomori is the more striking. The Hokkekyō is the Saddharma Pundarika. Chō-Densu, painter of the time of Ashikaga Yoshimitsu.

VII.

HISTORY OF THE KURUMA-ZUKA.

17CHŌ FROM HONGŪ; 8 CHŌ FROM YUNOMINE.*

It is in this manner that the history of the Kuruma-zuka has been handed down. In olden time there was an Oguri Hangwan Kaneuji, born in Hitachi, but who lived at Kamakura. He was an official of Sagami province. In the 6th year of Eikyō (1434) he was given poisoned wine. All his body was drawn together and falling in pieces. Therefore people spoke of the disease as gakiyami. The name of his concubine was Terute. She was distressed at his incurable disease. Forthwith she prayed at all the temples and to the Hotoke (Buddhas). She made petition to the Yūgyō Shōnin of Fujisawa as to her desire (to go) to the Kumano Gongen. A waggon was made and (Oguri) was put in it. She left the district with the placard—"if this waggon be pulled once it is in behalf of one's ancestors; if pulled twice-10000 times." She feared neither mountain nor river. She was three days and three nights in reaching Kii. Here there was a hot spring and (Oguri) recovered after one week. Then the waggon was left there, and a mound raised over it to show the divine aid of the Kumano Gongen and the efficacy of the hot spring. Truly the hot spring is famous. Even if crippled in both limbs at this present day the means of conveyance are discarded on going home. Moreover the hot spring is efficacious in any disease. Two or three chō ($\frac{1}{7}$–$\frac{3}{14}$ of a mile) from Yunomine-mura there is a stone called the chikara-ishi, and there is a rice field called the "Tane-makazu-ine." When Oguri recovered he tested his strength by the stone; and his strength was unchanged from its condition in health. Therefore people named that stone the "Kongyoku-seki." As to the rice: during his stay at the spring his hair was tied with *warashibe* (stalks to which the grains are still attached). The *warashibe* were thrown into this

---

* For this translation I am indebted to my wife. The distances mentioned above are $1\frac{2}{14}$ and $\frac{2}{7}$ of a mile respectively.

The Kuruma-zuka near Yunomine.

field. Every year the rice sprang up though no one sowed seed. This tale does not hold good now, but it is not the only place of such endless wonder. Generally speaking the record is correct.

Nanki Kumano Yunomine Kuruma-tōge.

Tōkwōji, Yunomine Kumano, Kishū.

(Wiped out by fire and flood but one small shrine, facing the square, remains of the once great establishment of the Tōkwōji. The sulphur coated image of the Yakushi Nyōrai is installed as the *honzon*. In the rear passage are gathered promiscuously a number of statues saved when the *hondō* and subsidiary shrines were destroyed by fire. Among them are a Fudō noted for its miraculous powers, a Kwannon, Shaka, and Bishamon, together with others of less art and power in bronze and wood. Not the least curious object is a pillar of the bridge which has been completely petrified, the firm and worm eaten parts well marked in Nature's preservation. Acknowledgment is to be made here of the kind interest shown by the reverend incumbent of the Tōkwōji, Mr. Kōno Chikyō, who for a good part of an afternoon brought forth and explained the many remains of the one time glory of the temple; an attention and guidance not confined to the precincts of the shrine—The Author).

VIII.

(What follows from Takarai not only has interest as anecdote, but is a good example of his style, and gives an idea of the *kōdan* writers in general. The reader is to supply the lively and expressive gestures and fan work, and the skilful modulation of voice as practised by these lecturers (*kōdanshi*).

Mito no Kotarō expresses his thanks to the guardian of the Ueno temple. "Rejoicing he entered. Miyoshino-no-Hara, as it was called, is the present Tōkyō Kanda-Fu (ward). At this period as yet there was not a single house. Of course Gongen Sama (Tokugawa Iyeyasu) was the founder. For

long there was no Hamachō or Kakigarachō. These streets
were then mere swamps, though now so busy as to cause
wonder. Nor was there any Asakusa Kwannon to whom
so many sutras (Buddhist scriptures) have been recited. Here
colts (ran loose). Trees were planted in rows in this manner,
a row of pine trees and within were placed the cherry trees.
These cherry trees were planted at Mukōjima. As the tale goes,
in the neighbourhood of the Kwannon Sama there were booths
for the sale of tea of a poor astringent kind. In the middle of
the sixth month (July) came Tokugawa Iyeyasu with his Shi-
Tennō.* At this period governing the country, before the Revolution (1868) the Tokugawa were called Shōgun Sama. To
get them down there had to be some little smoke and disturbance. This was then their fief ; whereas now they are only
nobles.

Iyeyasu—' Ah, Jii †! Allow me.'

Old Man—' Hai! Please come in.'

Iyeyasu—' A cup of tea please, yo ! '

Old Man—' Hai! Hai ! '

Now beside him there was something like grass. Its use
was unfamiliar. It was like paper put out to dry.

Iyeyasu—' I say, Oyaji! Oyaji! Oyaji ! '

Old Man—' Hai ! '

Iyeyasu—' That stuff there, what is it ? '

Old Man—' Eh ? '

Iyeyasu—' What is it ? '

Old Man—' Don't you know what it is ? ' **

Iyeyasu—' As I don't know I asked.'

Old Man—' You must be a countryman not to know that.'

Iyeyasu—' Iya ! I differ in no respect from a countryman.
What is it ?'

---

* The four captains in immediate attendance, ready for anything and
everything ; so called from the Four Guardians of Heaven.

† Jii and oyaji are common and familiar terms of addressing one much
inferior and an oldish man. The language of the Ojisan is couched in the most
familiar terms in addressing the prince.

** " Omae-Sama ! "

Old Man—' That is obtained here. It is Asakusa *nori* (laver or sloke ; dried the sea weed is edible).'

Now it is obtained at Shinagawa or at Ōmori. In these days gone by it was obtained at the Kwannon Sama. The name of Asakusa *nori* is no longer used as it is not obtained there.

Iyeyasu—' Is such stuff eaten ?'

Old Man—' Ma ! Take a mouthful and see.'

Prince Iyeyasu was obstinate. He had the old man cook a little of this dirty stuff. Lo ! It was delicious.

Iyeyasu—' Heigh-ho ! It has a delicious taste. Ah, remarkable ! And you who have prepared this mess, where were you born ? '

Old Man—' Nakajima is the name of my birth place.'

Iyeyasu—' You were born at Nakajima. And what is your name ? '

Old Man—' I am called Heishirō.'

Iyeyasu—' It is the best tasting thing I have eaten. You shall be raised in grade. Irai Nakajima Heishirō shall be your name, and you shall receive fifty *koku* (of rice income).

And as every one knows there were Asakusa Nakajima Heishirō up to the Revolution (1868), and they still exist.

From this place (Iyeyasu) went to Hamachō, now a fine district. At that time it was most desolate. As it was very hot, when he reached here his throat was fairly on fire. With but one thought he spoke of his thirst to Sakakibara, Honda, Ise, and Sakai, who accompanied him. ' Ah ! Ah ! for some water to drink.' Looking round about a well was seen close by. It had a cover over it. Prince Iyeyasu wanted to drink from it. On seeing it :

Iyeyasu—' Ah ! I'll drink here.'

But to his annoyance the cover was locked. ' Iya ! Twist it off and get a drink,' said Gongen Sama. So Lord Sakai—*pishari*—twisted off the lock to the gratification of his lord. Gongen Sama drank, dipping up the water in his hands. His Shi-Tenno, thirsty as their master, followed his example and drank from their hands. Then from behind—don, don,

don,—came a *Yamabushi* (wandering priest) to strike Gongen Sama crossways with his staff. As he reached Gongen Sama said Sakakibara Koheita :

Koheita—' You wicked scoundrel ! Wai ! '

About to drive him away, said Prince Iyeyasu :

Iyeyasu—' Hey ! Wait ! There is no reason to get angry. We broke open the fellow's well to get a drink. I am in the wrong. As it is Iyeyasu have patience.'

On hearing this the Yamabushi was greatly frightened.

Yamabushi—'And is it the Shōgun Sama? Really—Domo !' And he became very pale.

Iyeyasu—' Iya ! Iya ! I am the one in the wrong. Put aside any misgivings on account of this matter. But tell me, who are you ? '

Yamabushi—' I am a worthless kind of person. My name is Ryūben.'

Iyeyasu—' And what is your business ? '

Ryuben—' Eh ! I gather reeds and make matting for the *nori*.'

Iyeyasu—' And were you so occupied to-day ? '

Ryūben—' At your highness will : I am now a *yamabushi*.'

Iyeyasu—' Um ! However, I give you fifty *koku* (rice income) and your name shall be Yoshino Iori.

Thus he received fifty *koku* (income) and a name. The well was called the Yamabushi's Well. This being its condition at that time, in these still more ancient days the Miyoshinobara was even more lonely and desolate. Not a child dared to approach it. Said the guardian of the temple "—etc. etc. (pp. 228-232 ; or 253-258 old edition—Ogawa).

SOURCES OF THE OGURI HANGWAN ICHIDAIKI.

(BIOGRAPHY OF THE COUNCILLOR OGURI.)

1. Oguri Hangwan Jitsuroku—*Kōdan* by Takarai Kinryō.
2. Oguri Hangwan—*Kōdan* by Momogawa Joen.
3. Jitsu-Setsu Oguri Hangwan—*Kōdan* by Matsubayashi Hakuen.
4. Oguri Gwaiden ; published Bunkwa 10th year—1813. The preface is signed Hōzan............
5. Go Taiheiki—Shinnen Sōan.

HISTORICAL BACKGROUND FOR THE PERIOD.

6. Dai Nihon Rekishi—Ariga Nagao.
7. Ni-Sen-Go-Hyaku Nenshi—Takegoshi Yosaburo.
8. Nihon Gwaishi—Rai Sanyō (mentions the rebellion of Oguri Mitsushige).
9. O-Dai-Ichi-Ran—Hayashi.
10. Dai Nihonshi.

DICTIONARY REFERENCES AS TO OGURI.

11. Dai Nihon Jimmei Jishō.
12. Kokushi Dai Jiten.
13. Fūsōgajinten.
14. Honchōgashi.

LOCAL HISTORIES AND GUIDE BOOKS.

15. Kamakura—Ōmori Kingorō.
16. Kamakura Taikwan—Satō Zenjirō.
17. Enoshima Monogatari—Okazaki Hōkichi.
18. Kamakura Annai—Tōmura Yōroku.

---

* Much assistance from Government maps, in English and Japanese, on geographical and topographical points.

19. Kamakura, Enoshima, Kanazawa Meisho no Saisetsu—Kawa-kami Anjirō.
20. Hakone Taikwan—Okabe Seiichi.
21. Hakone Annai—Satō Hokusei.
22. Hakone Yūki—Reizan Senshi.

TEMPLE PAMPHLETS AND LEAFLETS.

23. Oguri Ryaku-Engi—Chōsō-In.
24. Fujisawa Ryaku-Engi—Temple authorities.
25. Kii Kumano Yunomine Yakuōzan Tōkwōji Ryaku Engi—Kōno Chikyō (incumbent).
26. Kuruma-zuka Yurai—Kōno Chikyō.

IN ENGLISH AND FRENCH.

Dictionnaire d'Histoire et de Geographie du Japon—E. Papinot.
Handbook for Japan (Murray)—Chamberlain and Mason.
History of Japan Vol. I.—J. Murdoch.
The Mikado's Empire—W. Griffis.
Feudal and Modern Japan—A. Knapp.
Japanese Feudal Law—J. C. Hall (Papers in the Transactions of the Asiatic Society of Japan).
The Nightless City—J. E. de Becker.
Feudal Kamakura—J. E. de Becker.

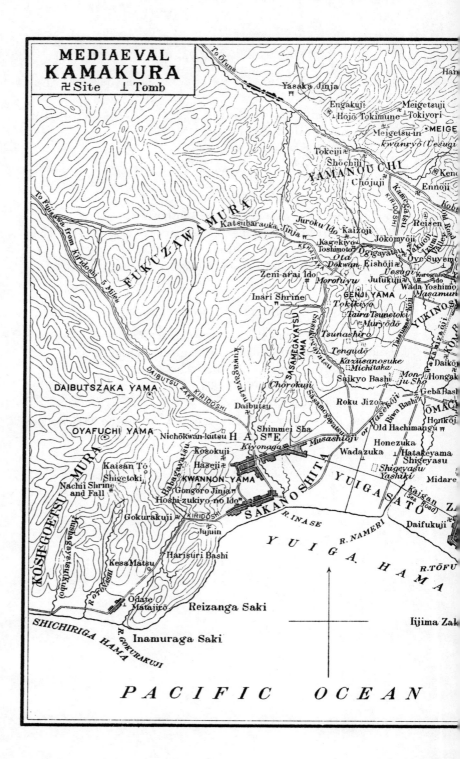

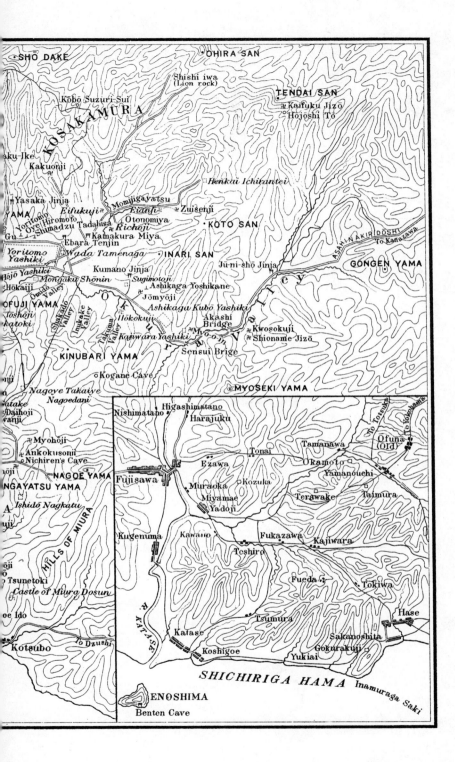

SHŌ DAKE

·OHIRA SAN

Shishi iwa
(Lion rock)

Kōbō Suzuri-Sui

TENDAI SAN
₮ Kaifuku Jizō
° Hōjōshi Tō

KOSAKAMURA

Henkai Ichirantei

...aku Ike

Kakuonji

·Yasaka Jinja

Eifukuji ₮ Eianji ₮ Zuisenji

·KOTO SAN

...YAMA
Yoritomo
Ōye Hiromoto
Shimadzu Tadahisa ·Richōji
Ōtonomiya

Gu...

₮ Kamakura Miya

Ebara Tenjin
Wada Tamènaga ·INARI SAN

Yoritomo
Yashiki

Ju-ni-shō Jinja

GONGEN YAMA

ASAHINA KIRIDŌSHI
To Kanazawa

Hōjō Yashiki

Kumano Jinja

Hōkaiji Mongaku Shōnin ₮Sugimotoji ·Ashikaga Yoshikane

...OFUJI YAMA Ōmido Valley ₮ Jōmyōji

Toshōji ...katoki

Shakado Valley Inukake Valley Takuma Valley Ashikaga Kubo Yashiki

Hōkokuji Akashi Bridge

Kajiwara Yashiki ₮ Kwosokuji ₮ Shioname Jizō

KINUBARI YAMA

Sensui Brige

·Kogane Cave

·MYOSEKI YAMA

...uji ·Nagoye Takaiye
Nagoedani

...atake Daihōji
...anji

·Myōhōji
₮ Ankokusonji
·Nichiren's Cave

...oji NAGOE YAMA

NGAYATSU YAMA

·Ishidō Nagkatu
A...

...oji ·Tsunetoki
Castle of Miura Dōsun

HILLS OF MIURA

...oe Ido

Kotsubo

To Dzushi

Nishimatano ·Higashimatano
·Harajuku

To Totsuka
To Yokobama

Tonai ·Tamanawa

Ofuna
(Old)

·Ezawa

Okamoto

Yamanouchi

Fujisawa Muraoka ·Kozuka

Miyamae
Yadoji Terawake Taimura

Kugenuma Kawano Fukazawa Kajiwara

Teshiro

Fueda ₮ ₮ Tokiwa

Tsumura

Hase

Katase Koshigoe Sakanoshita
Gokurakuji

Yukiai

ENOSHIMA
Benten Cave

SHICHIRIGA HAMA Inamuraga Saki

MORE ABOUT KPI BOOKS

If you would like further information about books available from KPI please write to

The Marketing Department
KPI Limited
Routledge & Kegan Paul plc
11 New Fetter Lane
London EC4P 4EE

In the USA write to

The Marketing Department
KPI Limited
Methuen Inc.,
Routledge & Kegan Paul
29 West 35th Street,
New York
N.Y. 10001, USA

KPI